NEWCOMERS
IN THE
WORKPLACE

In the series Labor and Social Change,
edited by Paula Rayman and Carmen Sirianni

NEWCOMERS IN THE WORKPLACE

Immigrants and the Restructuring of the U.S. Economy

Edited by Louise Lamphere,
Alex Stepick, and Guillermo Grenier

TEMPLE UNIVERSITY PRESS
PHILADELPHIA

Temple University Press, Philadelphia 19122
Copyright © 1994 by Temple University. All rights reserved
Published 1994
Printed in the United States of America

Library of Congress Cataloging-in-Publication Data
Newcomers in the workplace : immigrants and the
    restructuring of the U.S. economy / edited by Louise
    Lamphere, Alex Stepick, and Guillermo Grenier.
        p.   cm. — (Labor and social change)
    Includes bibliographical references and index.
    ISBN 1-56639-124-5 cloth
    ISBN 1-56639-131-8 paper
        1. Alien labor—Kansas—Garden City. 2. Alien labor—
Florida—Miami. 3. Alien labor—Pennsylvania—
Philadelphia. 4. Immigrants—Kansas—Garden
City. 5. Immigrants—Florida—Miami.
6. Immigrants—Pennsylvania—Philadelphia. 7. United
States—Emigration and immigration—Economic
aspects. 8. United States—Economic conditions—
1981–   . I. Lamphere, Louise. II. Stepick,
Alex. III. Grenier, Guillermo J. IV. Series.
HD8085.G373N49   1994
331.6′2′0973—dc20   93-15205

Contents

Acknowledgments

1 Introduction   *Louise Lamphere, Guillermo Grenier, and Alex Stepick*   1

GARDEN CITY

2 Beef Stew: Cattle, Immigrants, and Established Residents in a Kansas Beefpacking Town *Michael Broadway*   25

3 Knock 'Em Dead: Work on the Killfloor of a Modern Beefpacking Plant   *Donald D. Stull*   44

4 Guys in White Hats: Short-Term Participant Observation among Beef-Processing Workers and Managers   *Ken C. Erickson*   78

5 The Effects of Packinghouse Work on Southeast Asian Refugee Families   *Janet E. Benson*   99

MIAMI

6 Miami: Capital of Latin America   *Alex Stepick*   129

7 Brothers in Wood   *Alex Stepick and Guillermo Grenier, with Steve Morris and Debbie Draznin*   145

8   Grounding the Saturn Plant: Failed Restructuring in a Miami Apparel Plant   *Guillermo Grenier and Alex Stepick, with Aline LaBorwit*   164

9   The View from the Back of the House: Restaurants and Hotels in Miami   *Alex Stepick and Guillermo Grenier, with Hafidh A. Hafidh, Sue Chaffee, and Debbie Draznin*   181

PHILADELPHIA

10 Polishing the Rustbelt: Immigrants Enter a Restructuring Philadelphia   *Judith Goode*   199

11 Facing Job Loss: Changing Relationships in a Multicultural Urban Factory   *Carole Cohen*   231

12 Encounters Over the Counter: Bosses, Workers, and Customers on a Changing Shopping Strip   *Judith Goode*   251

13 Poverty and Politics: Practice and Ideology among Small Business Owners in an Urban Enterprise Zone   *Cynthia Carter Ninivaggi*   281

Contributors' Notes   303
Index   305

Tables and Figures

TABLES

2.1 Location, Date of Construction, Capacity, and
Ownership of Meatpacking Plants Employing More
Than 1,000 Workers, 1987   31

7.1 Miami's Construction Industry: Employment, Earnings,
and Firms, 1973–1989   147

8.1 Miami's Apparel Industry: Employment, Earnings, and
Firms, 1973–1989   166

9.1 Miami's Hotel and Restaurant Industries: Employment,
Earnings, and Firms,
1973–1989   183

11.1 Numbers and Percentages of Summit Lighting
Employees, March 25, 1988   235

12.1 Stores on the Olney Strip   255

FIGURES

2.1 The Location of Garden City, Kansas   26

2.2 Distribution of Newcomers to Garden City, by Ethnic
Group   35

3.1 Killfloor of IBP's Finney County Plant, Summer
1989   54

6.1 Percentage of Foreign-born Population in Major U.S.
Cities   130

6.2 Population and Ethnicity in Dade County,
1950–1990   131

6.3 Ethnicity and Occupation in Miami: Professionals,
Executives, and Laborers, 1970 and 1980   137

7.1   Ethnic Employment Percentages in Miami's
        Construction Industry, 1960 and 1980   149
8.1   Ethnic Employment Percentages in Miami's Apparel
        Industry, 1960 and 1980   167
9.1   Ethnic Employment Percentages in Miami's Hotel and
        Restaurant Industries, 1960 and 1980   184
10.1 Proportion of Blacks in Philadelphia Neighborhoods,
        1940, 1960, and 1980   212
10.2 Philadelphia Median Housing Value, 1980   214

Acknowledgments

Since this collection emerged from a larger project on "Changing Relations: Newcomers and Established Residents in U.S. Communities," funded by the Ford Foundation, a number of people were instrumental in helping to bring about the research on which this book is based. We would like to thank Shepard Forman, Diana Morris, and William Diaz, as well as Mary McClymont and Andrea Taylor, all of the Ford Foundation, for their support. We would also like to thank members of the board of the Changing Relations Project: Karen Ito, chair; Robert Bach, codirector; Niara Sudarkasa and Rudolfo de la Garza, as well as Roger Sanjek, who served as codirector during 1988 and was an important source of guidance and support for the Garden City, Philadelphia, and Miami teams. Louise Lamphere would also like to thank Jocelyn DeHaas for her help in preparing the manuscript. Many of the team members who assisted in the research on work in each of the three projects are acknowledged in particular chapters, but we would especially like to thank Jo Anne Schneider, who was instrumental in organizing two sessions at the American Anthropological Association meetings at which some of this material was presented. We have also enjoyed an excellent working relationship with the staff of Temple University Press. We would like to thank our editor, Michael Ames, as well as Richard Gilbertie and Irene Glynn, for the attention and care they gave to the manuscript. We are, of course, also indebted to the newcomers in the workplace, as well as established residents, who shared their daily experiences with team members and who gave us a sense of how work in America is being transformed in the late twentieth century.

1 Introduction

Louise Lamphere, Guillermo Grenier, and
Alex Stepick

On the plains of western Kansas, Nguyen, like hundreds of other Vietnamese and Laotian immigrants, wields his knife in a modern slaughterhouse, on the "disassembly" line of a major beef-processing plant. This is dangerous work, the most dangerous in the country according to official figures, and he does not plan to continue working at the plant for more than a few years. He knows the chances of injury are high and a worker can be fired for many reasons, making his future uncertain. But where else can a non-English-speaking refugee make $7 an hour? Nguyen's goal is to work hard, accumulate as much capital as possible, and, together with relatives, finance a fishing boat on the Gulf. Many Vietnamese and Laotians work on his shift, twenty or so on his line, so he does not lack companionship. Nguyen is a chuckboner; he is quick and precise at his job. He keeps his knife sharp on the steel hanging from his waist so that he can slice the meat away from the bone with strong, smooth strokes after he pulls the 130-pound chuck from the conveyor belt.

Nguyen was a Buddhist monk for a time in his own country. How does he reconcile religious beliefs and slaughterhouse work where thousands of animals are killed daily? He says that some people feel it is not sinful if they do not actually kill the animals. In his heart, he feels that all the work in the plant is sinful, but he has no alternative at present.

In Miami, Bernadette, a recent immigrant from Haiti, sews collars on designer men's suit coats in one of the city's largest garment factories. Although a good number of Haitians work in the press-

1

ing department, she was the first one to be hired in over a year, and she suspects that is because the plant is dominated by Cuban women. From the front offices to the machines, Cuban women are everywhere—and this in a plant owned by Americans from Chicago.

To Bernadette, all the varieties of Latin Americans that work by her side fit the mold of the dominant Cuban woman: loud arrogant, and bigoted. The hiring process is designed for them and by them. All the forms and tests not in English are in Spanish, and no one speaks Creole. Despite the difficulties in communication evident when she was being hired, no one called Fritz, the lone Haitian supervisor, to help. If it had not been for the fact that Alex Stepick (the Creole-speaking anthropologist who was beginning research in the plant) happened by during her interview, it is hard to imagine how she would have made it past the first step.

But since being hired, she finds that it is not as bad as she imagined it would be. Some Cuban women help her and encourage her to stick with her work, even on the roughest days. A few are friendly, and even if they speak mostly Spanish, they do not ignore her. They still exclude her from many of the little fiestas they sometimes have in the cafeteria, but there is nothing she can do about that. Her hope is that she will be transferred to pressing, where most of her compatriots work. They tell her that she can make more money there. If this does not happen soon, she could go work at a hotel in Miami Beach. There the work is not as grueling, and she would be with other Haitians, since many work in the hotels and restaurants in and around Miami.

In Philadelphia, Gilberto, who works for Summit Lighting, has watched the plant's labor force decline as each month an additional assembly line becomes idle and production is sent to the new plant in Mexico. That is why he is doing everything he can to get his daughter through college. "There is no future in factory work here," he tells her. He should know. Gilberto is Puerto Rican, from the island and proud of it. He has been working at Summit Lighting in Philadelphia since he came to the States in the mid-1980s. He got his job because another *Borinqueño* friend, the first Puerto Rican to work at the plant, told him about the opening. Asked whether he likes his work, he laughs, as if to say, "What does liking have to do with it?" He is proud of his effort. He is proud of the money he makes doing the "hardest and most dangerous" work on the shopfloor, polishing the various bulbs and fixtures produced in small batches at the plant. He makes the top piece rate, no matter what kind of fixture is coming down the line. Sometimes that is not easy to do. Yesterday, for example, they were doing small fixtures. That meant that if a worker polished 189 pieces an hour, he received the base rate of $8.07. To make the top rate of $12.40, like Gilberto does, a worker has to polish 400 small pieces an hour—and this is at a rotating polishing wheel that spins waist high and can cut a path through a stomach if given a chance. He is proud that he has not had his belly gashed, like some new workers, even if his wife warns him that he had better cut back on the meats and sweets that are dangerously increasing his waistline.

He could do easier work, but he needs the money. Besides, when they put him in assembly, he felt strange doing "woman's" work, work with no danger or heavy lifting. There are no women in polishing. Most women work in assembly, where their small hands enable them to work faster than the clumsy men; or they are scattered throughout the plant, assigned to other, less demanding jobs. Gilberto gets to see some of the women during the breaks, but since there are three break rooms, he does not know how many women there are.

But he knows how many other Puerto Ricans there are: not many. He has seen the numbers decline as the plant shrinks. Between 1987 and 1988, 35 percent of the Puerto Ricans have lost their jobs. Now there are twenty-seven workers in polishing, sixteen of whom are Puerto Rican. There are even fewer Poles, and they used to dominate the department a few years back. He does not see any future in factory work, especially for Puerto Ricans, now that the plant is shrinking. The one Puerto Rican success story he can mention is full of irony. The lone Puerto Rican that made it to the level of supervisor has now been transferred to the newly opened Mexican plant—the same plant that is taking the work from Summit Lighting in Philadelphia.

These workers are pulling shift in the great American workplace, a workplace that is rapidly changing as the United States undergoes the deep and irreversible process of economic restructuring. The work experiences of these employees, as individuals and as members of ethnic and gender groups, are like haiku of the process of globalization that is rapidly transforming the economies of the world. A Vietnamese in Kansas makes meat for McDonald's, maybe for the one that opened in 1990 in Moscow's Red Square; a Haitian woman in Miami works shoulder to shoulder with earlier immigrants, like her, products of failed American foreign policy maneuvers and plundered economies; and a Puerto Rican in Philadelphia does work that Poles used to do. All these workers are joining the world economy that bypassed their countries of origin during key years of development by working, as the famed Cuban poet José Marti would say, "en las entranas del monstro," in the bowels of the monster.

The essays in this collection explore the American workplace at a critical juncture in American history when two trends (the new immigration and the restructuring of the U.S. economy) have brought about a new level of transformation. Beginning with changes in the U.S. immigration law in 1965, large numbers of immigrants from Asia and Latin America have entered the United States. By 1992, many key manufacturing jobs were occupied by new immigrants, and they were increasingly present in retail and service employment. At the same time the economy has changed dramatically. Many jobs have migrated to rural areas in the South and West, while others have been transferred to the Third World. The U.S. manufacturing base (particularly in the Northeast and Midwest) has declined, and most expansion has taken place primarily in low-level retail and service employment.

As U.S. cities expand or decline with the movement of industry, they are also becoming multiethnic, nonwhite communities. The workplace is a crucial arena where new immigrants and established residents (whites, African Americans, and Mexican Americans) meet. What kind of work do immigrants perform in these changing local economies? How do these workers fit into their communities, and how do the established residents respond to their presence? How do their experiences vary across regions and industries? Are they as pliable as much of managerial literature leads us to believe, easily threatened and intimidated, or do they resent and resist managerial controls? Are male and female work roles changing as a result of the new immigration, or is the gender division of labor being solidified so that women continue in low-paying, dead-end jobs? Are immigrants trapped in low-wage positions in dying industries, or has their presence revitalized large segments of the American economy?

We examine these questions through the ethnographic description and micro-level analysis of the shopfloor, the retail store, and the restaurant encounter—a perspective that gives particular emphasis to the experience of immigrant workers themselves. Yet we also pay attention to the larger economic forces that have shaped both immigration to the United States and the restructuring of our national economy. We focus on workers in three local economies, each representing a concrete instance of the conjunction between new immigrant streams and industrial realignment. Garden City, in southwest Kansas, is the site of two large beefpacking plants. It has attracted a labor force of new immigrants composed largely of Vietnamese, Laotians, Mexicans, and other Hispanics. Miami is a growing coastal city that has been transformed both by a large new immigrant population (primarily of Cubans but also of Haitians, Jamaicans, Nicaraguans, and others from the Caribbean and Central America) and the reorientation of its economy toward Latin America. Philadelphia, in contrast, is an example of industrial decline, as industries have moved abroad or to the suburbs. New immigrants, including Puerto Ricans, Poles, and others, have been laid off from jobs in declining firms or excluded altogether. Yet, finding work in retail employment has not been easy, since small shops, low wages, and part-time work prevail in this sector.

Our data come from research on "Changing Relations: Newcomers and Established Residents in Six U.S. Communities," a project funded by the Ford Foundation through the Research Foundation of the State University of New York. The project, which began in January 1988 and was completed in February 1990, focused on the ways in which new immigrants and established residents adjusted to each other in five urban areas (Miami, Los Angeles, Chicago, Philadelphia, and Houston) and one small community (Garden City, Kansas). The purpose of the project was to "uncover a more representative portrait of the full range of relationships between immigrants and established residents, including interactions that may produce conflict, accord, and other modes of accommodation" (Ford Foundation 1987:1). In each community, a team of researchers focused on the ethnography of interrelations. Through participant observation and intensive interviewing, team members examined interrelations in particular "arenas," such as workplaces, schools, and community organizations. Researchers also gathered information about the local economy, demographic change, and power relations in order to understand the broader context in which face-to-face relations were taking place. Three teams—in Philadelphia, Miami, and Garden City—studied workplaces as one of their arenas, collecting the data that are the basis for the essays in this collection.

This volume goes beyond the current literature in providing a multilayered, integrated, comparative approach to the workplace, emphasizing the dynamics of restructuring as it takes place in local political economies. We break new ground by focusing on the importance and tremendous variability of the work experience of new immigrants in our society. As in the best of the current literature, we combine macro- and micro-level data, to focus on issues of gender, ethnicity, and immigration as they relate to interrelations in the age of restructuring.

Industrial Restructuring in America

Manufacturing propelled the U.S. economy to wealth and power, emerging in the late nineteenth century and peaking in the mid-twentieth century. In the immediate post–World War II era, public and scholarly attention fixed on the distribution of affluence among various segments of the population, rather than on production itself. More recently, we have turned our attention to problems utterly unforeseen twenty years ago—the decline of the American economy and, most shockingly, the loss of its manufacturing base.

Gordon, Edwards, and Reich, in *Segmented Work, Divided Workers* (1982), show us that America has been characterized by three previous periods of industrial structure, each followed by a time of industrial transformation ushering in a new era of labor–management relations and control over the workforce.

During the first period of proletarianization (1820–1870), a large supply of wage workers was created from a nonproletarian population, many of them immigrants from England, Ireland, and French Canada. Wage labor became the dominant manner of organizing production, yet employer control over the workforce remained minimal. The labor market was still rudimentary, and in many workplaces the direction of the labor process was left to workers who were relatively skilled and were able to pass these skills on to younger employees (Gordon, Edwards, and Reich 1982:3).

In the second period of homogenization (1870–1940), managers began to control the labor force through mechanization, and workers were deskilled. Immigrants continued to be a source of cheap labor, but employers also began to divide workers from each other, often by using language and ethnic differences as a means of segregation (Gordon, Edwards, and Reich 1982:142). With the entrance of the United States into World War II, a third period of labor control began (1940–1970). Rather than divide immigrants from native workers in the same workplace (so that they held different jobs) or mix workers of different ethnicities in the same department so it would be difficult to create a unified labor force, separation and control were created through segmented labor markets. Minorities and women became segregated into semiskilled and unskilled clerical and blue-collar jobs in peripheral labor markets, while white males or second- and third-generation ethnic males dominated a core, skilled labor market (Gordon, Edwards, and Reich 1982:211). In addition, workers in the peripheral economy received lower wages and benefits and fewer long-term rewards than those in the core economy (Averitt 1968; O'Connor 1973; Piore 1974).

In the 1970s and 1980s, the United States entered a fourth period, characterized by the movement of plants to the South and West and to the Third World. New types of labor control exemplified by participative management policies, quality circles, teams, and other forms of "debureaucratized control" (Grenier 1988) emerged along with "flexible specialization"—a new industrial structure that emphasized cutting-edge technological production, small firms producing small batches, and specialized (as well as fluctuating) labor forces (Piore and Sable 1984; Reich 1983). At the same time, the secondary labor market and older forms of labor control persisted.

Bluestone and Harrison, in *The Deindustrialization of America* (1982), documented the magnitude of this latest round of economic restructuring. During the late 1970s,

> between 450,000 and 650,000 jobs in the private sector, in both manufacturing and non-manufacturing, were wiped out somewhere in the United States by the movement of both large and small runaway shops. But it turns out that such physical relations are only the tip of a huge iceberg. When the employment lost as a direct result of plant, store, and office shutdowns during the 1970s is added to the job loss associated with runaway shops, it appears that more than 32 million jobs were destroyed. Together, runaways, shutdowns, and permanent physical cutbacks of complete closure may have cost the country as many as 38 million jobs. (Bluestone and Harrison 1982:25-26)

The victims of restructuring were regions and cities. The rustbelt suffered a decline in such heavy industries as auto, steel, and rubber. Shutdowns of textile plants devastated southern towns, and the off-shore shift of a significant portion of the garment industry displaced workers in Los Angeles and Chicago. Rustbelt cities such as Philadelphia lost 36 percent of their manufacturing base between 1970 and 1980, but industrial decline was not confined to the Northeast or Midwest. In Los Angeles, the twelve largest non-aerospace plant closings displaced 75,000 blue-collar workers, while 321 other local warehouses and factories moved to new industrial parks outside the city limits (Davis 1990:304). The free-trade agreement with Mexico and Canada promises to bring a new round of restructuring and job loss during the 1990s.

The three local economies we examine in this collection reflect the range of transformations that are currently shaping U.S. workplaces with immigrant labor forces. Garden City and Miami are contrasting examples of growing local economies, while Philadelphia represents a city with industrial decline and restructuring. We have taken a deliberately comparative approach in order to gain an understanding of how immigrants from different national backgrounds have been pulled into the local economy and how recent industrial restructuring has affected their position in the labor force. This comparative approach using macro-level data constitutes the first layer of our analysis.

Each of the three sections of this book begins with an introduction to the history and structure of a local economy. These introductory essays examine labor, capital, and community: how local economies have been shaped and transformed over the twentieth century; how industries were created, structured, and managed; how various populations have been recruited to a local labor force; and how community social and political institutions are related to both the industrial base and the local population.

Michael Broadway's description of Garden City, Kansas, a small city of twenty-four thousand in mid-America, demonstrates that industrial restructuring has had an impact on America's heartland and on communities in more rural areas. Miami, as Alex Stepick's introduction tells us, is a large, urban metropolis—a growing sunbelt economy on the southern tip of the country, one that has retained industry partly through its orientation to Latin America. Its location has also meant that it could expand as a tourist center, creating jobs in construction, the hotel and restaurant industry, and related occupations. Our last case, Philadelphia, described by Judith Goode, is an excellent example of a "rustbelt city" that has lost industry to other parts of the United States or abroad and corporate headquarters to the suburbs. Like so many other cities in the East and Midwest (New York, Chicago, Detroit, Cleveland), industrial decline has coincided with urban decay, a loss of a tax base and social services, often stranding minority and immigrant populations in city centers as white middle- and working-class families moved to the suburbs. Philadelphia illustrates the effect of a decade of urban neglect by the Reagan and Bush administrations; it will feel the impact of policies worked out in the aftermath of the 1992 Los Angeles unrest—policies that focus on enterprise zones, welfare reform, and privatization of public housing. These three cases represent the range of political economies that have undergone economic transformation in the 1980s: the industrializing rural hinterland, the coastal growth cities, and the rustbelt areas of decline.

Micro-Level Analysis of the Workplace

Our second layer of analysis is that of particular workplaces in each of the three local economies. Our ethnographic approach owes much to Harry Braverman's *Labor and Monopoly Capital* (1974) and those who used Braverman's analysis of the deskilling of the American workplace to examine further management's control over labor. We have been particularly influenced by Richard Edwards's *Contested Terrain*, which outlines three different managerial systems: simple control (where owners and foremen exercise power personally through direct intervention in the labor process and in the hiring and firing of workers), technical control (where the physical structure of the labor process, for example, an assembly line, controls the pace of work), and bureaucratic control (where the social structure of the workplace, rules, and "company policy" control output and discipline workers) (Edwards 1979:18–21).

Although in some parts of the United States, notably in Los Angeles and the Silicon Valley, immigrants have been incorporated into new high-tech industries that are part of the new "flexible specialization" and participative management structures (see Fernández-Kelly and Sassen 1991; Hossfeld 1993), most immigrants work in traditional firms that use simple, technological, and bureaucratic control. Many are in the secondary labor market, either in marginal industrial firms or, increasingly, in service occupations in retail trade, restaurants, and hotels. The places described in this collection represent this trend.

We examine relations in the workplace itself, particularly focusing on techniques of management control, the nature of the work process, and the impact these two factors have on relations between workers. In this way, we focus on three kinds of interrelations—between managers and workers, between workers and customers, and among workers themselves. By analyzing these interactions we discover the dynamics of bureaucratic and technical control, of worker cooperation and resistance, of class and gender struggles that make up the daily work experiences of immigrants in our restructured economy.

In Garden City, we focus on beefpacking, an industry that has relied primarily on hierarchical management practices and "disassembly" lines, a form of technological control. Beefpacking is constrained in its mobility by the availability of cattle and water (which is needed in processing). Beginning in the 1960s, a number of large-capacity plants using nonunion labor opened in rural Iowa, Kansas, and Nebraska. In response, the old packing companies using unionized labor in urban centers either cut workers' pay (epitomized by Barbara Koppel's 1990 film of the strike at the Hormel plant in Austin, Minnesota) or shut the plants down. Southwestern Kansas has been one of the principal regions to benefit from this restructuring process. Since the early 1970s, beef-packing plants have opened in Liberal, Dodge City, and Garden City. Garden City is the center of the industry with two large plants employing a total of four thousand workers. During the 1980s, Garden City's population increased from eighteen thousand to twenty-four thousand, largely as a result of migration. Workers and their families were drawn to the town by the prospect of employment in the plants. Approximately, two-thirds of the newcomers were from Southeast Asia, Mexico, or other Latin American countries.

The Garden City plants are typical examples of old-style management dressed up in the latest assembly-line technology. Both IBP and Monfort have large departments, a hierarchical relationship between managers and workers, and a philosophy of "getting it out the door" by speeding up the chain or disassembly line. In terms of technological control they resemble many all-male industries, such as automobile plants (Garson 1972; Pfeffer 1979), steel mills (Kornblum 1974), and machine shops (Burawoy 1979). Whether such plants operate with assembly lines, piece rates, or continuous process or whether they make piston rings, steel ingots, or machine tools, these workplaces have a male work culture. As described in ethnographies written during the 1970s, this work culture was characterized by shopfloor banter and joking (often to take the edge off difficult interethnic relations) (Burawoy 1979; Kornblum 1974), after-work socializing at local pubs and bars (which were often ethnically segregated) (Kornblum 1974; LeMasters 1975), and union activities (which included both militant shopfloor tactics and moribund entrenched unionism) (Fantasia 1988; Pfeffer 1979).

The Garden City plants, however, are a product of restructuring and the search for cheap labor. As such, they introduce two elements not present in the traditional male worksites studied in the 1970s: new immigrants and an increasing female labor force (both immigrant and native). Like the Bumble Bee tuna factory described by Garson (1972) and the meatpacking plant studied by Remy and Sawers (1984), women (both Vietnamese and white in Garden City) are being incorporated in the processing lines, while minority males dominate the killfloor. Don Stull's chapter vividly describes work on the killfloor, while Ken Erickson's experiences in a meatpacking plant in Nebraska give us a sense of what it is like to be a plate boner and "pull count" while dressed in cumbersome garb and wielding a dull knife. Their accounts tell us that, on the line, Vietnamese, Mexican, and Anglo workers are not so much separated by intentional management policies as by differences in language; the noise of the plant, which makes communication difficult; and informal recruitment practices that concentrate Vietnamese and Hispanics on different shifts and at different plant locations. In a small town such as Garden City, off-hours socializing still takes place in local bars; Tom's Tavern is as lively as the midwestern blue-collar tavern described by LeMasters (1975). But the Vietnamese are more likely to socialize in their own apartments or trailers, gambling, planning for a funeral, or keeping their Buddhist traditions.

Both plants have increasingly incorporated women into their labor forces, hiring them in processing jobs. Janet Benson's chapter describes the impact of women's employment on Vietnamese families. Vietnamese wives take jobs in meatpacking in order to support their families, send funds to relatives still abroad, and accumulate capital to purchase their own businesses, educate their children, or make a new start elsewhere. They often work two shifts—one at the plant from 3:00 P.M. to midnight and another at home during the day cooking, cleaning, and caring for their children. Families may take in boarders so that they can pay for their newly acquired trailers or their utility bills. Women may hire babysitters or unemployed relatives to take care of their children while they work at the meatpacking plant, though some couples work different shifts in order to share child care; other children are left to fend for themselves. Although women and their spouses have forged a number of different strategies to deal with their dual-worker family structure, Benson argues that there have been negative impacts as well—unsupervised children, less than adequate prenatal care, and divorce or separation as the stress and instability of meatpacking jobs take their toll.

Taken together, the Garden City section demonstrates that the flow of new capital into a small community has brought new industry, an increased population, and a growing community. Nevertheless, this has not been without its costs in terms of the increased needs for housing, education, police, welfare, and other social services. The city has adapted to these costs, but low profit margins and authoritarian company policies that squeeze the workforce have created high turnover, job instability, and work-related injuries. Janet Benson's story of the Vietnamese family forced to leave Garden City after the wife lost her job when she was not able to work overtime and Don Stull's accounts of workers' testimony at the monthly workers' compensation hearings make it clear that "workers are still cheap and expendable." As Stull reminds us: "Until we are willing to pay more for our meat—and until we demand fair wages and decent working conditions for meatpacking workers—the jungle will remain in our midst."

In Miami, our research focused on workplaces in three sectors: construction, apparel, and the hotel and restaurant business. The construction site studied represents one of the last bastions of exclusive male occupation, where unionized skilled male workers dominate. Minorities (African Americans, Cubans, and Haitians) have been reluctantly incorporated into the unions, but only after nonunion Cuban construction firms made serious inroads into the industry. Alex Stepick and Steve Morris describe one of Miami's largest construction projects, a half-million-square-foot addition to the Miami Beach Convention Center. As in the construction industry elsewhere (Applebaum 1981; LeMasters 1975), craft autonomy and individual skill are highly valued aspects of this work setting, where the simple control exercised by a supervisor, rather than the technical control of an assembly line, predominates. Yet workers are also defiant and resistant. They are critical of supervisors and take their own stand on safety issues, refusing to work in dangerous situations. The presence of new immigrants (Cubans and Haitians) has had an important impact on worker–management and worker–worker relations as well. Anglo carpenters are the most confrontational, while Cubans are likely to express their dissatisfaction "out of earshot" of supervisors, and Haitians and African Americans are the most careful and respectful.

Trade segregation has also created hierarchy and distance with Anglos dominating the high-paying trades, Cubans present among the mid-level Carpenters, and most Haitians and African Americans concentrated among Laborers. Steve Morris reports instances of cross-ethnic solidarity as well as difficulties in communication, but interaction is eased by a set of informal work rules surrounding access to tools and work reciprocity. Of all the workplaces we studied, these construction workers exhibit the greatest control over their labor, the most class consciousness, and the clearest strategies of resistance. There is also distance and separation, however, and "workers seemingly inhabit a world permeated by contradictions between profound solidarity and the cruel contrasts associated with an ideology of individual autonomy."

Guillermo Grenier's chapter on a Miami apparel plant adds to a number of well-known studies of women in light industries. In many of these settings women work under piece-rate systems with batch processing and a management structure that often combines elements of simple control (exercised by floor ladies in garment shops and supervisors in jewelry plants), bureaucratic control (embodied in elaborate instructions for sewing a particular operation in a garment factory), and technological control (stuffing boards on an assembly line in an electronics plant). Some researchers have outlined the strategies of resistance pursued by both European ethnic women and new immigrants in these plants (Bookman 1988; Lamphere 1987; Safa 1986, 1987), while others have cautioned that values learned in the wider American culture and the precariousness of many industrial jobs have produced consent on the shopfloor (Shapiro-Perl 1979). New immigrants, particularly in the Northeast, have been integrated into these workforces and cross-ethnic ties have been forged through the celebration of such shopfloor rituals as birthdays, wedding and baby showers, and retirements (Lamphere 1984).

In Miami, Grenier and his fellow researchers found workers to be less class conscious and more conservative, despite the fact that the plant was unionized. Grenier emphasizes the role of a previous paternalistic management (utilizing simple control) and the dominance of Cuban women workers over more recent Haitian and Central American immigrants in shaping this atmosphere. In 1985 the apparel plant was purchased by a large men's clothing firm, and the new management introduced a new production method and a new regime of bureaucratic control. The women workers, particularly the Cubans, resisted the innovations that worked so well in other regions. But this resistance was less a brand of class-conscious militance than a reaction against the newer, more bureaucratic order that replaced an older paternalism.

Grenier argues that in this apparel plant, at least, the placement of Haitians in the pressing department, the pace of the work, and the piece-rate system kept Haitian and Cuban workers apart. Unlike the plant studied by Lamphere, shopfloor rituals rarely forged relations across ethnic boundaries. Cuban women dominated the informal use of space and were only beginning to include Haitian women in their socializing.

Minority workers have been a component of Miami's hotel and

restaurant industry for decades, but with the new immigration, Cubans, Nicaraguans, and Haitians have entered this sector as well. Latinos have displaced Anglos, but the proportion of Blacks has remained the same (although probably including growing numbers of Haitians). The nonunion nature of the industry and management's violation of labor law are but two of the factors that have kept wages low. In the restaurants described by Alex Stepick, beneath a facade of a bureaucratic structure with rules and regulations, simple control is exercised by managers in a much more personalistic way than by construction-site bosses or floor ladies in an apparel plant. Restaurant managers seem to make decisions in a capricious manner and hire and fire on the whim of the moment. The different requirements of their work, the role of customers in demanding good service, and competition over tips often sets chefs and kitchen help against servers, and servers against busboys. Management attempts at deskilling (firing a well-trained chef and hiring a less experienced replacement), as well as the part-time nature of the work, only exacerbate the situation. Furthermore, management preference for hiring compliant workers (including Haitians, who are seen as hard workers who do not complain) has undercut the nature of resistance in the workplace. Worker tactics seem limited to breaking management rules (such as eating extra meals) and "taking it easy" during slack times. Contrasted with the solidary work culture of department store workers described by Susan Benson (1986) and the tough independent New Jersey waitresses studied by Greta Paules (1991), the highly unpredictable atmosphere described by Stepick has created a weak work culture, reinforced individualism, and alienated workers from one another and from the work itself.

In Miami, a metropolis with an economic base that includes industry, commerce, and tourism, we find much more variability in new immigrants' experience in the workplace than we described for Garden City's one-industry economy. Immigrant labor was critical to the creation and growth of the apparel industry in Miami in the 1970s and 1980s. In contrast, older patterns have been intensified as new immigrants move into the long-established and locally based construction and hotel–restaurant sectors. In the three workplaces we studied, we can see how the structure of work itself and the management strategies used to control labor interact to create very different responses. These range from relatively autonomous and class-conscious construction workers (where management exercises little control) to the personalistic and traditional apparel workers (who resist the new bureaucratic forms of management) to the individualistic restaurant workers (who are dominated by management).

In Philadelphia we begin with Carole Cohen's analysis of the effect of decline on workers at a light manufacturing plant. Summit Lighting represents just the kind of light industry that had been most drastically affected by buyouts and the phenomenon of the runaway shop. A profitable, locally owned firm, Summit was first bought out by a conglomerate, and by 1988 seemed to be the target of a potential shutdown, where production would be sent to other facilities in the South and in Mexico. Decline shut out many Polish immigrants, and the remaining Puerto Rican immigrant workers were those who had years of seniority. Like other blue-collar workers who are laid off or facing unemployment, Summit Lighting workers felt angry, resentful, and betrayed (Rosen 1987: 124–125). As one woman commented, "Summit was one of the places you could always count on for work." Those facing layoffs felt the average worker was getting lost as the plant kept sending production to other branches of the company.

Unlike the Singer Company workers in Elizabeth, New Jersey, Summit Lighting employees did not blame new immigrants and minorities within the plant for the company's plight. Nevertheless, as at Singer, workers did develop a critique about the loss of pride in quality work (Newman 1988:183–187, 194–196). Summit employees scorned the management's "business as usual" approach, exemplified by the renovation of the cafeteria and continued emphasis on educational and health programs. Some workers started a reform movement within the union to elect officials that would push the union to stand up to arbitrary supervisors, discrimination in promotion, and management's rigid absence policy, which resulted in more dismissals so that workers would not receive unemployment benefits when the inevitable layoffs came.

Summit, like many light industrial firms that specialize in assembly, has a traditional hierarchical management with a variety of different wage and production systems, depending on production processes used in particular departments. Plating is a male-dominated department where workers have high hourly wages, whereas polishing (another male department) is organized around a piece-rate system and skilled males with high seniority often earn as much as $12.40 an hour. Batch processing is the norm in both of these departments, but assembly-line belts organize work in the much larger assembly department, which is also characterized by relatively low hourly rates of $8.07 an hour.

Many workers had difficulty adjusting to jobs and lower pay in new departments as they were "bumped down," especially men who found themselves in the assembly department, which was traditionally seen as "women's work." Some workers supported each other in break groups, while others complained at times and were somewhat difficult to work with. Interethnic relations within the plant (between whites, Blacks, Puerto Ricans, and newcomer Poles) remained cordial as workers developed a "discourse of blame" that pointed to welfare recipients encountered outside the workplace.

Cohen's account reminds us of the great variety of relations that spring up in the workplace. At Summit, the Puerto Rican men were most likely to socialize with each other, but even some of these preferred to eat by themselves. Cohen also found "loners" among the new immigrant Polish workers in the polishing department, among other new immigrants, but also among the majority white workers of European ancestry.

Judith Goode's chapter contrasts small businesses on a Philadelphia shopping strip and a chain-owned supermarket, two components of the retail sector where new immigrants may be owners, workers, and customers. As retail trade has been restructured in many urban areas (with new shopping malls and large supermarket centers in the suburbs), struggling small businesses and unrenovated supermarkets are left in the inner cities. Although they provide some jobs for new immigrants, they are not an expanding employment sector and cannot make up for jobs lost in industry. Owners of small shops have slim profit margins and can often make ends meet only by hiring family members or taking on a few part-time workers from the neighborhood. Supermarkets, faced with a declining customer base, are converting to a part-time labor force and are giving priority to workers (including minorities and women) who have high seniority and come from the local area.

In Olney, there have been tensions around the Korean-owned stores. Community members have protested all-Korean signs, have felt unwelcome in Korean-owned stores, and feel that Korean wholesalers have no stake in the community, selling out and moving as soon as a better opportunity arises. Yet some Korean owners have hired minority residents and have become members of the local businessmen's association. This mirrors a similar split between non-Korean owners committed to the local community versus chain stores along the shopping strip and some local supermarkets that have little interests in local issues or building ties with the community.

Judith Goode's accounts add to the growing literature on work in the service sector by exploring the relations between owners, workers, and customers in multiethnic settings where power differences and workplace-control issues shape workers' strategies and often produce tensions. Some of these racial–ethnic and class issues have been spelled out in the literature on domestic workers (Glenn 1986; Rollins 1985; Romero 1992) as minority and immigrant women deal with the "maternalism" and personalistic stance of their female employers in private homes. Public as opposed to private service work always involves a triangle, however. As Goode points out, the customer is a third party and a major actor who adds a source of control to the typical dyadic employer–worker relationship (see Benson 1986). But the literature on service encounters has rarely explored issues of race and class in a local setting. Since customers in Olney are part of a local multiethnic community, they have particularly important leverage on owners and managers.

Stores as workplaces are fraught with difficulties whether they are "mom and pop" operations or supermarkets. In small businesses along the Olney strip, personalistic ties to owners are expected, and cultural and language differences (between non-immigrant minority workers and Korean owners, for example) are great. Minority workers have been hired as "buffers" between owners and clientele, a strategy that has reduced tensions. In chain stores and supermarkets, staffing has become increasingly part-time, turnover continues to climb, and after-work safety is a matter of concern. Many pit workers against customers and give contradictory messages concerning the store's commitment to the local community and "good service." Contrasted with the tension between African American and Korean store owners in Los Angeles in 1992, however, residents of Olney and Korean store owners have accommodated to each other, and African Americans have a solid place in the supermarket workforce.

Finally, in Philadelphia, we examine governmental efforts to create "enterprise zones" and revitalize industry. Although such zones were touted as an important solution to urban decline in the wake of the 1992 Los Angeles riots, Cynthia Ninivaggi's chapter shows that enterprise zones as funded by city and state governments have been little more than "booster associations" and create very few jobs. The Philadelphia Enterprise Zone described in this collection did not include the small-business retail sector (where many new immigrants and minorities were already located). In addition, the program assumed that local residents were passive benefactors of new industry, yet there was little articulation between the zone program and the local community. There were no incentives for hiring local workers (jobs were created "on paper" only), and the program was not evaluated by outside professionals. Clearly, much more needs to be done to bring jobs to inner-city areas like Philadelphia.

Conclusions

When we examine the role of immigrants in conjunction with the restructuring of the U.S. economy, we see that immigrants have often played a very positive and crucial role and at other times a much more limited one. Immigrants are often attracted to areas that provide labor for relocated plants (as in the Garden City example) or revitalize industries that are hard pressed by foreign competition (as in the apparel industry in Miami). But they may be excluded from industries on the downturn (as at Summit Lighting in Philadelphia) or hired part-time in retail establishments.

This collection also emphasizes the variety of workplaces in which new immigrants are hired and the varying experiences of men and women as they work in situations with a gendered division of labor and different patterns of hiring new immigrants and minorities. As we examined this variation, we became alert to ways in which new immigrants, whether they are Cubans, Haitians, Koreans, Puerto Ricans, Laotians, or Vietnamese, are active participants in the workplaces where they are employed. As they respond to very different work structures and management tactics, they join established residents (Anglo Americans, Hispanics, and African Americans) in strategies of resistance, in establishing ties that build bridges across ethnic boundaries, in conflictual relationships with other workers or with management, in acts that foster individualism, and in decisions that ensure economic survival. In making sense out of the variability we found, we argue that the labor process—whether around assembling or disassembling a product, constructing a building, or serving people—and the structure of management control were central in shaping workers' experiences and responses.

Immigrants are "between a rock and a hard place." Both immigrant men and women are employed in workplaces where, along with co-workers from minority backgrounds, they often face difficult work conditions, health hazards, low pay, and gender and ethnic segregation. For example, Mexican workers are on the killfloor in the Garden City IBP plant, and Vietnamese and Laotian men and women are employed in the processing lines at IBP and in Dupaco in Nebraska. Management policies that focus on "getting it out the door" and write-ups or firings lead to high turnover and exact a heavy toll on immigrant families, particularly when both the husband and wife work on the disassembly line.

Others, like the workers at Summit Lighting in Philadelphia, face job loss as their employers shift production to the sunbelt or abroad. Even those who have gained a foothold in good jobs in construction or apparel may be handicapped by the vulnerability of these industries to economic recession or imports. Jobs in the service sector, in inner-city supermarkets, small stores, restaurants, and hotels, are low paid and often have irregular hours or shifts. Ethnic owners of small shops may simply hire family members, while chain stores are increasing the number of part-timers and are overstaffed with those who have lived in the city longer. The major exceptions to these trends are the middle- and upper-class Cubans in Miami and the Korean entrepreneurs in Philadelphia. These immigrants came to the United States with capital and professional or business skills that have allowed them to play a key role in developing enclave economies. Koreans in Philadelphia, for example, are often owner–operators of small shops who work long hours alongside their employees but who are able to accumulate capital for their children's education or to buy homes in the suburbs.

In the three political economies we studied, we became painfully aware that immigrants were often in difficult jobs with low pay, poor conditions, and few benefits—at the bottom of the labor force regardless of whether the local economy was growing or declining. That immigrants, as well as many minority group members, are not yet part of the American Dream is perhaps an indication of the overall decline of our industrial economy and the need for a radical rebuilding of our infrastructure.

Bibliography

Applebaum, Herbert A. 1981. *Royal Blue: The Culture of Construction Workers.* New York: Holt, Rinehart and Winston.

Averitt, Robert. 1968. *The Dual Economy.* New York: Norton.

Benson, Susan Porter. 1986. *Counter Cultures: Saleswomen, Managers, and Customers in American Department Stores, 1890–1940.* Urbana: University of Illinois Press.

Bluestone, Barry, and Bennett Harrison. 1982. *The Deindustrialization of America.* New York: Basic Books.

Bookman, Ann. 1988. "Unionization in an Electronics Factory: The Interplay of Gender, Ethnicity, and Class." In *Women and the Politics of Empowerment,* edited by A. Bookman and Sandra Morgen, pp. 159–179. Philadelphia: Temple University Press.

Braverman, Harry. 1974. *Labor and Monopoly Capital: The Degradation of Work in the Twentieth Century.* New York: Monthly Review Press.

Burawoy, Michael. 1979. *Manufacturing Consent: Changes in the Labor Process under Monopoly Capitalism.* Chicago: University of Chicago Press.

Davis, Mike. 1990. *City of Quartz: Excavating the Future in Los Angeles.* London: Verso.

Edwards, Richard. 1979. *Contested Terrain.* New York: Basic Books.

Fantasia, Rick. 1988. *Cultures of Solidarity: Consciousness, Action, and Contemporary American Workers.* Berkeley: University of California Press.

Fernández-Kelly, Maria Patricia, and Saskia Sassen. 1991. *A Collaborative Study of Hispanic Women in the Garment and Electronics Industries.* Final Report to the Ford, Revson, and Tinker Foundations. New York University, Center for Latin American and Caribbean Studies.

Ford Foundation. 1987. "Project Statement." Manuscript authored by Changing Relations Project Board, New York. Typescript.

Garson, Barbara. 1972. *All the Livelong Day.* Harmondsworth, England: Penguin.

Glenn, Evelyn Nakano. 1986. *Issei, Nissei, War Bride.* Philadelphia: Temple University Press.

Gordon, David, Richard Edwards, and Michael Reich. 1982. *Segmented Work, Divided Workers.* Cambridge, England: Cambridge University Press.

Grenier, Guillermo. 1988. *Inhuman Relations: Quality Circles and Anti-Unionism in American Industry.* Philadelphia: Temple University Press.

Hossfeld, Karen. 1993. "Divisions of Labor, Divisions of Lives: Immigrant Women Workers and the High-Tech Division of Labor." Manuscript.

Kornblum, William. 1974. *Blue Collar Community.* Chicago: University of Chicago Press.

Lamphere, Louise. 1984. "On the Shop Floor: Multi-Ethnic Unity against the Conglomerate." In *My Troubles Are Going to Have Trouble with Me*, edited by K. B. Sacks and D. Remy, pp. 247–263. New Brunswick, N.J.: Rutgers University Press.

———. 1987. *From Working Daughters to Working Mothers: Immigrant Women in a New England Industrial Community.* Ithaca: Cornell University Press.

LeMasters, E. E. 1975. *Blue Collar Aristocrats: Life-styles at a Working-Class Tavern.* Madison: University of Wisconsin Press.

Newman, Katherine. 1988. *Falling from Grace: The Experience of Downward Mobility in the American Middle Class.* New York: Free Press.

O'Connor, James. 1973. *The Fiscal Crisis of the State.* New York: St. Martin's.

Paules, Greta Foss. 1991. *Dishing It Out: Power and Resistance among Waitresses in a New Jersey Restaurant.* Philadelphia: Temple University Press.

Pfeffer, Richard M. 1979. *Working for Capitalism.* New York: Columbia University Press.

Piore, M. J. 1974. "Notes for a Theory of Labor Market Stratification." In *Labor Market Segmentation*, edited by R. C. Edwards, M. Reich, and D. U. Gordon, pp. 135–150. Lexington, Mass.: D. C. Heath.

Piore, M. J., and Charles Sable. 1984. *The Second Industrial Divide.* New York: Basic Books.

Portes, Alejandro, and Ruben G. Rumbaud. 1990. *Immigrant America: A Portrait.* Berkeley: University of California Press.

Reich, Robert R. 1983. *The Next American Frontier.* New York: Times Books.

Remy, Dorothy, and Larry Sawers. 1984. "Economic Stagnation and Discrimination." In *My Troubles Are Going to Have Trouble with Me,* edited by K. B. Sacks and D. Remy, pp. 95–112. New Brunswick, N.J.: Rutgers University Press.

Rollins, Judith. 1985. *Between Women: Domestics and Their Employers.* Philadelphia: Temple University Press.

Romero, Mary. 1992. *Maid in America.* New York: Routledge.

Rosen, Ellen Israel. 1987. *Bitter Choices: Blue-Collar Women in and out of Work.* Chicago: University of Chicago Press.

Safa, Helen. 1986. "Runaway Shops and Female Employment: The Search for Cheap Labor." In *Women's Work: Development and the Division of Labor by Gender,* edited by E. Leacock and H. Safa. South Hadley, Mass.: Bergin and Garvey.

———. 1987. "Work and Women's Liberation: A Case Study of Garment Workers." In *Cities of the United States: Studies in Urban Anthropology,* edited by L. Mullings, pp. 243–268. New York: Columbia University Press.

Shapiro-Perl, Nina. 1979. "The Piece Rate: Class Struggle on the Shop Floor. Evidence in the Costume Jewelry Industry in Providence, Rhode Island." In *Case Studies on the Labor Process,* edited by A. Zimbalist, pp. 277–298. New York: Monthly Review Press.

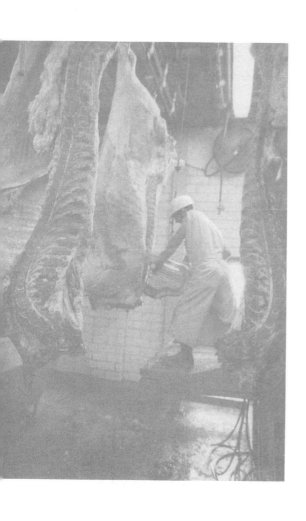

GARDEN CITY

2   Beef Stew: Cattle, Immigrants and Established Residents in a Kansas Beefpacking Town

Michael Broadway

Over the past thirty years, the meatpacking industry has been transformed from an urban to a rural-based industry. This restructuring has been made possible by technological innovations that have enabled new packing companies to site their plants in rural areas close to feedlots in right-to-work states (Skaggs 1986:180–211). One of the areas most affected by this restructing process is southwestern Kansas. Since 1969, the region has witnessed the construction of four major beefpacking plants, employing more than seven thousand persons, including the world's largest plant, in Holcomb, seven miles west of Garden City (Figure 2.1). The new packing companies emphasize cost reduction, and unlike the old packing companies, they have avoided negotiating industrywide agreements with unions. Instead, technology has enabled the new companies to simplify the meatpacking process, thereby reducing the need for highly skilled and highly paid butchers and allowing for their replacement by lower-paid and less-skilled labor. The success of this strategy is evident: In 1960, meatpacking wages were 121 percent of the average manufacturing wage; by 1988, the figure was 84 percent (U.S. Department of Labor 1985, 1989).

A decline in relative wage levels coupled with the worst safety record of any industry in the United States over the past decade (U.S. Department of Labor 1988) has served to make meatpacking an unattractive employment option for many Americans. Moreover, as labor has been in short supply in rural areas, the packers have been forced to recruit increasing numbers of minority-group members. IBP, for example, has attempted to recruit Southeast

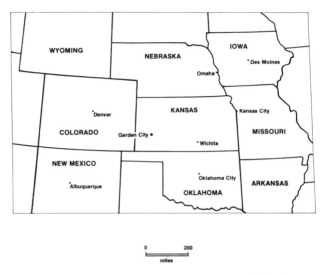

Figure 2.1. The location of Garden City, Kansas. *From* Michael J. Broadway, "Settlement and Mobility among Newcomers to Garden City, Kansas," *Journal of Cultural Geography* 10, no. 1 (1990): 2. Reprinted by permission.

Asian refugees for its Dakota City plant from California's Central Valley and Orange County areas (Risen 1987). It now recruits Hispanics from the Rio Grande Valley to work in the plant (Brennan 1990). A similar pattern is evident among the company's hog-processing plants in Perry and Columbus Junction in Iowa and in Madison, Nebraska (Broadway 1992). The influx of these and other minority groups is radically altering the character of rural meatpacking communities, just as urban America is being reshaped by the new immigrants. This chapter examines how the restructuring of the beefpacking industry has affected the small southwestern Kansas community of Garden City.

Industrial Restructuring

The restructuring of the American economy can be summarized by noting that changes have occurred in terms of *what* is produced and *how* and *where* it is produced (Knox 1988). Manufacturing and agriculture have declined in terms of their overall contribution to the economy, while improvements in productivity have resulted in a decrease in the proportion of persons employed in both sectors. Corporate mergers have resulted in individual sectors of the economy becoming dominated by just a few companies.

Finally, there has been a redeployment of capital away from the old industrial core of the country to states in the South and West. States attracting new manufacturing jobs are characterized by having relatively low wage levels, few unions, and right-to-work laws. Within this overall pattern, nonmetropolitan areas in the South and West enjoyed the highest growth rates in manufacturing employment during the 1970s and early 1980s (Bluestone and Long 1989:10; Haren and Halling 1979:29).

The movement of capital has been made possible by recent changes in technology and institutions. Improvements in transport and communication technologies have reduced the necessity for market locations. The construction of the interstate highway system, for example, has reduced the locational advantages of railroad centers. Changes in design have also enabled complex production processes previously carried out by highly skilled labor to be reduced to simple tasks by less-skilled workers, thereby lowering costs. Finally, an international market for capital has developed, enabling money to be transferred from one area of the world to another. The net effect of these institutional and technological innovations has been to allow corporations to transfer many of their routine production activities away from the industrial heartland to peripheral regions in the United States and overseas.

Structural Changes in the Meatpacking Industry

Meatpacking has undergone the same structural changes as the rest of U.S. manufacturing. Employment in the industry fell by a third from 1967 to 1987. Production of beef and hogs is now dominated by three companies: IBP, ConAgra, and Cargill. This concentration of production has been made possible by internal expansion and a series of acquisitions. ConAgra, for example, was not in the beefpacking business at the beginning of the 1980s; however, during the decade it acquired several major beefpacking companies, including Monfort and SIPCO (Swift Independent Packing Company). The increasing concentration of production is a particular concern for cattle feeders, who have fewer buyers bidding for their animals (National Cattlemen's Association 1989). Indeed, the current level of concentration in the industry is unprecedented. During the 1920s, the federal government used antitrust legislation to break up the packing industry when the top five companies slaughtered just half of the beef cattle (Center for Rural Affairs 1990).

The biggest declines in meatpacking employment have occurred in the Manufacturing Belt, in states with high levels of unionization; increases in employment have occurred in right-to-work states (Broadway and Ward 1990). In Kansas, meatpacking employment increased by over 80 percent during the 1967–1987 period; by contrast, states such as Pennsylvania, Ohio, Illinois, Wisconsin, Missouri, and Minnesota all experienced reductions of over 25 percent (U.S. Bureau of the Census 1967, 1987). Within this overall pattern, the biggest reductions in employment have occurred in major urban centers such as Chicago, St. Louis, and Philadelphia, with black workers being disproportionately affected by plant closures (Remy and Sawers 1984:97). The new meatpacking plants have generally been constructed in small towns in nonmetropolitan areas. This transformation from an urban to a rural-based industry is part of an overall cost-cutting strategy by the new packing companies. IBP is the recognized leader in this movement, and since the company's founding in 1960 it has acquired approximately one-third of the U.S. market for boxed beef and has annual sales of over $8 billion. The majority of the company's meatpacking plants are located in communities with fewer than twenty-five thousand persons (Broadway and Ward 1990).

Meatpacking is a marginally profitable industry. For every $100 in sales in 1986, over $93 were accounted for in direct production costs, while profits averaged about $.81 (Austin 1988a). This fundamental characteristic of the industry has forced companies to reduce production costs and increase productivity. The new packers have been extremely successful in raising productivity. Between 1967 and 1982, productivity within the industry, as measured by output per hour, increased at an average annual rate of 2.8 percent; and from 1976, the rate increased to 3.2 percent. In contrast, the comparable figures for all manufacturing industries were 2.4 and 1.6 percent respectively (Carnes 1984).

Improvements in productivity have been made possible by increasing mechanization. Mechanization has been most pronounced among departments with the highest concentrations of African American and female workers. Sausage manufacturing, for example, was considered a "woman's job" and was replaced by a machine that fed sausage into artificial casings. African Americans concentrated in ham-curing departments, and their job of injecting the curing solution into the animal's main arteries was replaced by a machine (Remy and Sawers 1984:98). Plants have also been completely redesigned to provide an uninterrupted flow of products from one stage of processing to another. This dissassembly use has eliminated the need for highly skilled butchers; in their place, less-skilled labor is now utilized to perform repetitive tasks that frequently lead to hand, arm, and wrist disorders, the most common being carpal tunnel syndrome. Union leaders contend that many of these work-related injuries are associated with increases in the chain speed. At IBP's Dakota City plant, workers and union officials estimate that the chain speed on the slaughter floor increased more than 22 percent, from 225 head of cattle an hour to 275 head per hour between 1981 and 1986, while employment on the line remained stable (Risen 1987).

The result of this process has been to make meatpacking the most hazardous industry in America with an injury rate that is more than four times greater than the national average for all industries (U.S. Department of Labor 1988). Every year, on average, more than one in three workers in a meatpacking plant suffers a work-related injury or illness. This appalling record shows little signs of improvement; in fact, the number of lost workdays increased steadily throughout the 1980s. The federal government's Occupational Safety and Health Administration (OSHA) has cited IBP for failing to report work-related injuries and willfully ignoring hazards that hurt workers; however, this has yet to have an impact on the industry's overall safety record (Austin 1988b).

As part of their cost-cutting strategy, the new packers have refused to agree to the terms of the master contracts between the Meat Cutters Union and other packers. They argue that the work is less skilled and should therefore be remunerated at a lower rate. At one plant organized by the Meat Cutters Union, in Dakota City, labor–management relations have been marred by several long, violent strikes. In 1982, the union called a strike when IBP asked for a four-year wage freeze. The strike resulted in the use of company strikebreakers and in violent confrontations between the strikers and Nebraska State Police and National Guard members (Robbins 1982). A year later, the union signed a contract that reduced workers' pay by $1.05 an hour. In the face of this competition, the old companies have either declared bankruptcy or slashed wages. During the early 1980s, Wilson Foods Corporation filed for Chapter 11 bankruptcy protection and abrogated its labor contracts, while Hormel reduced wages at its Austin, Minnesota, plant by 23 percent (*Business Week*, 1984). In Columbus Junction, Iowa, workers took voluntary pay cuts in an attempt to save the Rath plant from closure, but despite these efforts, the plant was closed in 1984 (Broadway 1992).

Other cost-cutting strategies utilized by the packers include locating large-capacity plants close to feedlots. This strategy eliminates the need for middlemen and shortens transporation distances, which minimizes the shrinkage and bruising of cattle. Large-capacity plants are much more economical to operate than smaller plants. For example, in 1986 the estimated slaughter cost for a plant that operated at 25 head an hour was $41 a head; the corresponding figure for a plant operating at 325 head an hour was $22 a head (Miller 1986:19). The expansion of these large-capacity plants is reflected by the fact that in 1973 only 2 of 795 federally inspected plants slaughtered more than half a million animals a year, and they handled only 7.5 percent of the slaughter. By 1988, there were nineteen such plants, and they slaughtered nearly two-thirds of the cattle (Center for Rural Affairs 1990:5).

The movement of packing plants to rural areas has also been facilitated by the innovation of boxed beef. Boxed beef was developed and marketed by IBP in 1967. Under this process, fat and bone are eliminated at the plant, thereby reducing transportation costs. It also reduces the need for retailers to employ highly skilled butchers. The rural industrialization strategy of the new packers is exemplified by IBP's recent decision to locate a 4,000-head-a-day plant in Lexington, Nebraska. Lexington has a population of approximately seventy-one hundred persons (1987 est.) and is situated in Dawson County, 220 miles west of Omaha on Interstate 80. Dawson County has one of the largest feedlot capacities in Nebraska and lies atop the Ogallala Aquifer, which has provided a plentiful supply of water to the plant since it opened in November 1990. And the local Council for Economic Development (1990) proudly boasts of "no strikes, work stoppages or labor disputes ever!"

Meatpacking is clearly representative of the overall structural changes that have occurred in the wider U.S. economy. Technical innovations and capital mobility have enabled the new packing companies to locate their plants in rural areas close to feedlots in right-to-work states and away from unionized urban areas. Kansas has been one of the few states to experience an increase in meatpacking employment as a result of this overall process. The next section provides a brief overview of the industry within the state, before discussing the impact of the industry on the community of Garden City.

Structural Changes in the Kansas Beefpacking Industry

Within Kansas, meatpacking is dominated by beefpacking, and it has undergone the same structural changes noted at the national level. Plant closures have occurred in urban areas, and new plants have been constructed in rural areas. In 1959 Wyandotte County, which is part of the Kansas City Metropolitan Area, reported eleven plants; by 1987, no plants were operating in the county (U.S. Bureau of the Census 1959, 1988). Beginning in late 1969, two large-capacity plants were built in Emporia and Liberal. Subsequently, three other large-capacity plants have been constructed in the southwest portion of the state, at Dodge City, Holcomb, and Garden City (Table 2.1).

The packers have been attracted to southwestern Kansas by several factors. The introduction of center-pivot irrigation in the mid-1960s enabled local farmers to utilize water from the Ogallala Aquifer and cultivate a variety of feed grains. The widespread availability of both water and feed led in turn to the introduction of feedyards. In 1964, there were 197,000 cattle fattened on grain in southwest Kansas; ten years later, the number was 935,000; and by 1987, the figure had reached 2.4 million (U.S. Bureau of the Census 1969, 1987). The widespread availability of cattle served to attract the packers. Modern plants also require an abundant water supply; indeed, the availability of water from the Ogallala Aquifer was critical in IBP's decision to build the world's largest beefpacking plant (1990 capacity of 6,000 head a day) at Holcomb in Finney County, rather than in Lamar, Colorado.

At the local level, incentives were used to attract packers to specific sites. In the case of IBP's plant at Holcomb, the Finney County commissioners provided the company with $3.5 million in property tax relief for a ten-year period and helped finance the construction of the plant with an issue of $100 million in industrial revenue

Table 2.1. Location, Date of Construction, Capacity, and Ownership of Meatpacking Plants Employing More Than 1,000 Workers, 1987

Town	Date	Ownership	Employees	Maximum Daily Slaughter Capacity
Emporia	1969	IBP	1,800	3,255
Liberal	1969	National Beef	2,400	4,000
Dodge City	1980	Excel	1,600	4,800
Holcomb	1980	IBP	2,600	5,200
Garden City	1983	ConAgra	1,100	3,500

Source: "Our Beef Boom: What's at Stake," *Wichita Eagle Beacon,* September 11, 1988; and IBP common stock prospectus.

bonds. IBP began slaughtering cattle at its plant in December 1980, and by 1982 a second shift was added. In 1983 Val-Agri, Inc. purchased Garden City's idle Kansas Beef Processors plant and more than doubled its capacity (Skaggs 1986:217–218). This plant was later sold to Swift Independent Packing Company and is now owned by Monfort, a division of ConAgra, the nation's second-largest beefpacker. Currently these two plants employ approximately four thousand workers, and they slaughter and process up to 8,700 head a day, six days a week.

Although southwestern Kansas contains excellent physical resources to support the meatpacking industry, the region lacks a traditional attraction for a manufacturing plant, namely, an available labor force. Unemployment, for example, in Finney County averaged 432 persons, or 3.3 percent, in the year before IBP's Holcomb plant began operating (Kansas Department of Human Resources 1988). Packinghouse recruiters ranged far and wide—Birmingham, Alabama; San Antonio, Texas; Las Vegas; New Mexico—in search of unemployed labor. Packinghouses pay well by regional standards, starting between $6 and $6.40 an hour for production workers and climbing as high as $9.58 an hour. Few previous skills—not even a command of English—are required. The "push" of sustained recession and the "pull" of an expanding industry soon made Garden City the fastest-growing community in Kansas. From 1980 to 1985, the city grew by an estimated six thousand people, or 33 percent. The majority of newcomers were Southeast Asian refugees and Hispanics, many from Mexico. The other two packinghouse towns, Dodge City and Liberal, received similar influxes.

Garden City

Garden City is located in southwest Kansas, 215 miles west of Wichita and 309 miles southeast of Denver, Colorado (Figure 2.1). At an elevation of approximately 2,900 feet it rests amid a semiarid region of short grass and sandsage prairie. With an estimated population of twenty-five thousand, it is a regional center for the surrounding five-state area, as well as the Finney County seat of government (Garden City Planning Department 1989). Early settlers to Garden City in the 1880s were drawn there by the prospect of cheap land. But an average rainfall of eighteen inches coupled with droughts served as a major constraint on the region's agricultural development until irrigation technology allowed water to be drawn from the Arkansas River. The water was used to establish a sugar-beet industry that lasted until the mid-1950s when technological and market forces forced its decline. The introduction of center-pivot irrigation systems in the mid-1960s allowed farmers to exploit the vast underground reserves of water in the Ogallala Aquifer and enabled the cultivation of feed grains. This in turn led to the growth of the cattle feeder industry. By the late 1980s, Kansas ranked third (behind Nebraska and Texas) in terms of the number of cattle on feed, with more than half of the state's feeder cattle being located in the counties surrounding Garden City (Stull 1990).

In 1980 Garden City had a population of 18,256 and in many ways typified the "heartland." The town was predominantly Anglo (82 percent). The largest minority was Hispanics (16 percent), who first came in the 1900s to work on the Sante Fe railroad and in the sugar-beet fields. One percent was African American and .5 percent each was American Indian and Asian (Garden City Planning Department 1989:16). The 1980s brought rapid growth to the community with the opening of the two beefpacking plants and the subsequent inmigration of Anglos, Southeast Asians, and Hispanics.

Newcomer Origin and Settlement Patterns

A 1984 survey of approximately 930 Southeast Asian refugees residing in Finney County found that more than half of those surveyed had previously resided in Wichita. The majority of the refugees came to Garden City in 1982, soon after IBP added a second shift at its Holcomb plant (Broadway 1985:17). Wichita provided the majority of refugees because it was the principal area of refugee resettlement in the state by virtue of its being the largest city in the state and the presence of McConnell Air Force Base, which attracted a large number of refugee sponsors. In the early 1980s Wichita's principal employer, the aircraft industry, began widespread layoffs as a result of the 1981–1982 recession. This factor, coupled with the federal government's policy of encouraging refugees to get off assistance as quickly as possible, served to "push" some of the refugees out of Wichita. Conversely, the availability of employment that could be performed with a minimal understanding of English served to "pull" the refugees to southwestern Kansas. By 1984, an estimated four thousand Southeast Asian refugees resided in the three communities of Dodge City, Liberal, and Garden City. The Hispanic newcomers to Garden City consist primarily of documented and undocumented nationals from Mexico. Small numbers of immigrants from El Salvador, Cuba, and other Central and South American countries are also present in the community. They have moved there primarily to work (Wood 1988:45). Indeed, Hispanics provided approximately 64 percent of the employees at the ConAgra plant in 1988 (then owned by Monfort), while they constituted only about 25 percent of the population (Stull 1990).

Conventional assimilation theory would predict that the newcomers to Garden City would seek the support and assistance of other members of the same ethnic group in adjusting to life in the new community and would, therefore, cluster together in the same residential areas (Marston and Van Valey 1979). Among Southeast Asians and Hispanic migrants, an additional factor in fostering the development of residential enclaves is the central role of the extended family in facilitating economic adaptation and emotional adjustment to the host society. The importance of these constraints in affecting settlement is also likely to vary with the refugees' socioeconomic status. Southeast Asian refugees who arrived prior to 1978 could either speak English or had been exposed to American or French cultural practices. By contrast, later arrivals have fewer marketable job skills and less education than the first group. Indeed, many of the later arrivals "are illiterate in their own language and have never held a job" (Strand 1984:51). In Garden City, these two groups were found to have different settlement patterns. The majority of Southeast Asians from the first group live in newly constructed suburban areas in single-family homes, whereas the majority of refugees from the second group reside in trailer parks (Broadway 1987). The Hispanic newcomers are generally of low socioeconomic status with little knowledge of English, which should result in their clustering in the same residential area; however, an examination of newcomer settlement patterns found little evidence that ethnicity influenced where newcomers settled (Broadway 1990a). Anglos, Hispanics, and Southeast Asian newcomers were found throughout the city. The principal newcomer concentration is the East Garden Village mobile home park on the eastern edge of town (Figure 2.2). All three groups are found in this mobile home park, with Southeast Asian newcomers having the highest proportion of their migrants residing in the park. Further evidence of residential intermixing among the newcomer groups is provided by the neighborhood surrounding Finnup Park in the southern portion of the town. This areas was once known as "Little Mexico" and served as the center for Hispanic settlement in Garden City (Hope 1988). Nevertheless, Anglo, Southeast Asian, and Hispanic newcomers are all found in this neighborhood and in some instances reside in houses adjacent to each other. The absence of distinctive ethnic

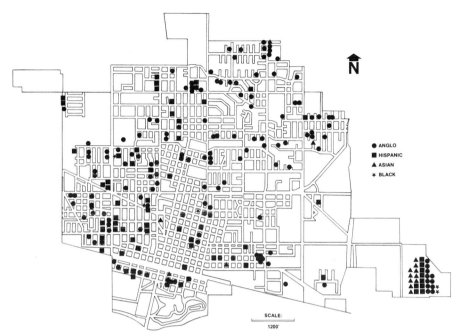

Figure 2.2. Distribution of newcomers to Garden City, by ethnic group. *From* Michael J. Broadway, "Settlement and Mobility among Newcomers to Garden City, Kansas," *Journal of Cultural Geography* 10, no. 1 (1990): 60. Reprinted by permission.

neighborhoods is attributable, in part, to a tight housing market, which characterized Garden City's sudden growth during the 1980s. This market meant that there was no clearly defined area within the town with lost-cost housing, which could serve to attract newcomer groups.

Effects of Rapid Growth on Local Services

The addition of more than six thousand persons to Garden City's population from 1980 to 1985 created an immediate housing shortage within the community. IBP successfully dramatized the seriousness of this situation in the fall of 1981 when they surveyed the housing conditions of more than six hundred of their employees. According to the survey, 5 percent of the workforce were living in motels or cars, while 33 percent felt they were paying excessive rent (Fisher 1981). These results were used to delay the start-up of a second shift and pressure local officials into allowing the construction of the East Garden Village mobile home park.

Additional evidence of a housing shortage can be seen in housing sale prices and rents. Between 1981 and 1982, the mean selling price of homes in Garden City increased by over $7,000, or 15 percent, during the time of a nationwide recession! Since 1982, housing sale prices have declined, indicating a weakening in the demand for housing. Rental prices also peaked in 1982 for mobile home and three-bedroom accommodations, while rents for one- and two-bedroom accommodations peaked a year later. Rents for all these properties have subsequently declined (Broadway 1990b: 328). The housing shortage was relatively short-lived with the addition of mobile homes. This type of housing is controversial, since mobile home owners add nothing to the property tax base yet require community services such as schools and fire and police protection.

The sudden influx of migrants dramatically increased enrollment in local schools. From 1980 to 1986, the number of children enrolled in Finney County schools increased by nearly a thousand, or 37 percent. By comparison, statewide enrollment remained stable during the same period. In response to this dramatic growth, voters in Garden City approved three separate bond issues for the construction of three elementary schools. Accompanying the increase in students has been an increase in the demand for bilingual and English as a Second Language (ESL) instruction. Although the total number of students enrolled in these programs remained relatively stable during the 1980s, some shifts in origin groups occurred. The number of Southeast Asian students increased rapidly during the early 1980s, but by 1988–1989 Hispanic students were increasing more rapidly. In responding to this situation, the school district was confronted with the difficult task of attracting primarily Vietnamese and Spanish-speaking bilingual/ESL instructors to an isolated rural area of the country. In recognition of this problem, the Garden City school district in 1988 established a scholarship program for graduating bilingual high school students. Three scholarships are provided each year for students who wish to become bilingual instructors and return to Garden City on graduation. In addition to alleviating a critical shortage, this program is intended to provide minority students with role models of students who successfully graduate from high school and college.

The influx of minority students has created other problems for the Garden City school district. In the spring of 1988 the school district proposed to deal with an overcrowding problem in a neighborhood elementary school and maintain "racial balance" by busing children from a predominantly affluent Anglo middle-class subdi-

vision (Indian Hills) to the principal immigrant school (Victor Ornelas). Parents in Indian Hills vigorously protested the proposal
and forced its withdrawal by the administration. Since then, the
proportion of minority students at Victor Ornelas has continued to
increase (Broadway and Stull 1991).

Although there is no exact demographic profile of all the newcomer groups, it is clear that among the Southeast Asian adult population, young adult single males dominated the influx of migrants
into Garden City in 1982, 1983, and 1984 (Broadway 1985). This
pattern also reflects the predominance of this group among the
refugee population. Moreover, migration theory would predict that
young adult males between the ages of twenty and thirty-four
would have the highest mobility rates and would be drawn to Garden City (Clark 1986). This group also has a higher incidence of
crime than most other demographic groups and would therefore
be expected to increase the crime rate. A longitudinal analysis of
crime in Garden City and the surrounding area of Finney County
found an increase in violent crime throughout the decade, while
property crimes fluctuated (Broadway 1990b). An examination of
crimes reported to the Finney County Sheriff's Department and
the Garden City Police Department in 1980 and 1988 found that
domestic violence cases were most responsible for the increase in
violent crimes. The majority of such cases consisted of husbands or
boy friends returning home after drinking heavily and becoming
involved in a dispute with a spouse or girl friend. It should also be
noted that few victims ever formally pressed charges in these cases.
The reasons for the long-term upward trend in Garden City's
crime rate are beyond the bounds of this chapter; nevertheless, the
influx of young males to work in the plants and other local industry must be considered a major contributory factor.

Economic Effects of Rapid Population Growth

From 1980 to 1988, the numbers of persons employed in local
industry increased by 55 percent, with manufacturing employment
increasing by over 200 percent, largely as a result of the opening of
the IBP and Val-Agri beefpacking plants. Indeed, of the forty-two
hundred additional jobs created between 1980 and 1988, over 70
percent were created within the manufacturing sector. The next-
largest sector of the economy to experience an increase in employment was the retail sector, with a 17 percent increase (U.S. Bureau
of Census 1980, 1988). A new shopping center was established on
the town's east side, with Penney and Wal Mart serving as anchor
stores.

The growth of the meatpacking industry has also led to the creation of other jobs within the manufacturing and service sectors. The demand for boxes and trucking services by the packers has resulted in the addition of several hundred jobs within these two industries. The effect of the increase in the local payroll is noticeable wihtin the retail sector, where, for example, the number of eating and drinking establishments increased from thirty-one to forty-eight, and employment increased from 395 to 642 between 1980 and 1988 (U.S. Bureau of the Census 1988). The town has attracted primarily fast-food franchises and is proud of the fact that it now possesses two McDonald's restaurants! The presence of Hispanic and Southeast Asian groups also led to the establishment of several Mexican and Vietnamese restaurants by local entrepreneurs. These data clearly indicate the positive effect that the beef-packing industry has had on the creation of jobs in the local economy.

A more detailed analysis of the effects of job growth on personal income within the county suggests that many of the jobs that have been created are relatively low paying. Indeed, by 1990 the beginning hourly wage for production workers at IBP was $6.60; it was $6 at Monfort. Gross annual income for processing line workers at IBP ranges from about $15,500 to $22,000, depending on grade level and length of employment. Many workers, especially new arrivals and those with large families, are forced to rely on social service agencies for supplemental food, medical care, and other basic needs (Broadway and Stull 1991).

The Social Impact of Rapid Population Growth

Rapid population growth in small communities has frequently been associated with increases in social dislocation and disorder as newcomers are confronted with the stress of adjusting to a new community (Gilmore and Duff 1975; McKeown and Lantz 1977). As noted earlier, there is some evidence to link the influx of young adult single males with increases in crime. An analysis of divorces and annulments granted within Finney County found a slight increase in divorces in 1982; however, the overall divorce rate has declined since 1980. This decline may be attributable to the changing population structure of the community, rather than a decline in family stress, since many of the newcomers consist of young single males. Clearly, if fewer married couples reside in a community, the divorce rate will decline. In short, without identifying individual married couples and their length of residence within Finney County, there is little evidence to link the influx of migrants with an increase in the divorce rate.

Admissions from Finney County to the Area Mental Health Center peaked in the early 1980s with the rapid influx of population, indicating that some of the newcomers may have experienced difficulty in adjusting to life in southwestern Kansas. The rate of admissions has since declined, which may reflect the ethnic composition of the subsequent newcomers. Counselors at the center note a general reluctance among members of the different minority communities in Garden City to utilize their services, and they attribute this pattern to cultural and linguistic barriers. An analysis of confirmed cases of child abuse and neglect found a dramatic increase in the rate of child abuse from 1981 to 1982. Indeed, the rate tripled between 1980 and 1985. By comparison with the state, Finney County began the decade with a child-abuse or neglect rate below the state average, but by 1982 it had surpassed the state figure. Further evidence of social dislocation is provided by an analysis of admissions from Finney County to Larned State Psychiatric Hospital. While such admissions are representative of only the most extreme cases, such as detoxification for an alcoholic, the admissions from Finney County nevertheless show a sustained increase for both alcoholic and psychiatric care throughout the 1980–1986 period (Broadway 1990b).

Anglo Attitudes toward the Newcomers

Most Anglo "old-timers" feel that the quality of life in Garden City has deteriorated with the arrival of IBP. They complain of the increase in crime and traffic, while admitting that IBP has brought "progress" to their community along with "urban problems." The Anglo community is divided in its attitudes toward the new immigrants. Educators, clergy, and service providers generally applaud Garden City's growing cosmopolitan flavor. They take pride in their response to the influx of Southeast Asian refugees and the attention it has brought the community. Working-class Anglos provide a different perspective. These men and women often work side by side with the newcomers in packinghouses and feedyards and therefore have more daily contact with other ethnic groups. While they may appear overtly hostile in their use of racial slurs and complain about growing numbers of "wetbacks," in their everyday dealings with individuals they manifest a pattern of accommodation and accord (Stull 1990).

The absence of conflict between the groups is explained, in

part, by the fact that the new immigrants came to Garden City to find work. Jobs in the packinghouses were readily available, and therefore the newcomers did not take jobs away from established residents. The nature of work in the packinghouses has also prevented the establishment of a permanent ethnic core group, which could serve as a vehicle for securing a group's "fair share" of community resources. High levels of personal mobility characterize the community, regardless of ethnic background or type of employment. A longitudinal analysis of newcomer families who enrolled their children in the Garden City school district found that, within a year, 40 percent of them had left; a year later, a further 20 percent left. There was no difference between the children of meatpacking employees and nonmeatpacking employees, nor was there any difference between Anglos, Hispanics, and Southeast Asians in their length of stay in the community (Broadway 1990a).

Summary and Conclusions

Since the 1950s, the U.S. beefpacking industry has been transformed from an urban, railroad-terminal-based industry to a rural, feedlot-based industry. In the late 1970s, southwest Kansas feedlots produced a surplus of cattle. This factor and Kansas's status as a right-to-work state served to attract IBP and Val-Agri to the region. The construction of the plants, and their subsequent operation and expansion, resulted in Finney County's population increasing by 33 percent from 1980 to 1988. Many of the newcomers to Garden City consisted of Southeast Asians and Hispanics drawn to the region by the prospect of employment within the plants. Most of the four thousand jobs created both directly and indirectly as a result of the beefpacking industry are low paying. This reflects the broad structural change that has occurred in U.S. manufacturing over the past thirty years, as companies have sought to lower operating costs through the use of cheaper sources of labor. The social impact of this sudden growth was effectively dealt with by the construction of new schools and increases in the town's housing stock. More complex problems have yet to be resolved; these include the provision of special services to minority-group members, a rising crime rate, and a general increase in various social disorders. The absence of conflict between newcomers and established residents is explained by the fact that the newcomers come to Garden City to work and then they move on, normally within two years of their arrival.

Garden City's rapid growth also brought the community tangible benefits in the form of new businesses and a more cosmopolitan character, which is now celebrated by such public rituals as the International Festival, Tet, Cinco de Mayo, and Mexican Fiesta. The benefits of economic development consisted of an increase in employment and purchasing power. The increase in employment is of particular significance because it occurred in a region that had lost population over the past sixty years. But the reversal of this long-term trend did not occur without substantial social costs for the community.

Bibliography

Austin, L. 1988a. "Packers Put Everything but the Moo up for Sale." *Wichita Eagle-Beacon*, September 12.

———. 1988b. "Union Push Started Wave." *Wichita Eagle-Beacon*, December 18.

Bluestone, H., and C. Long. 1989. "Growth Falters in Most Rural Counties: Manufacturing Both Hero and Goat." *Rural Development Perspectives* 5(2): 8–10.

Brennan, J. 1990. "Hispanics, IBP Work to Coexist." *Omaha World-Herald*, March 4.

Broadway, M. J. 1985. "The Characteristics of Southeast Asian Refugees Residing in Garden City, Kansas." *Kansas Geographer* 19:5–18.

———. 1987. "Indochinese Refugee Settlement Patterns in Garden City, Kansas." *Transactions of the Kansas Academy of Science* 90(3–4):127–137.

———. 1990a. "Settlement and Mobility among Newcomers to Garden City, Kansas." *Journal of Cultural Geography* 9(3):51–63.

———. 1990b. "Meatpacking and Its Social and Economic Consequences for Garden City, Kansas, in the 1980s." *Urban Anthropology* 19(4):321–344.

———. 1992. "Hog Wild: Recent Changes in Meatpacking Towns in Iowa and Nebraska." Paper presented at the annual meeting of the Association of American Geographers, San Diego, April.

Broadway, M. J., and D. Stull. 1991. "Rural Industrialization: The Example of Garden City, Kansas." *Kansas Business Review* 14(4):1–9.

Broadway, M. J., and T. Ward. 1990. "Recent Changes in the Structure and Location of the U.S. Meatpacking Industry." *Geography* 75(1):76–79.

Business Week. 1984. "Two More Meatpackers Take a Cleaver to Wages," October 29.

Carnes, R. B. 1984. "Meatpacking and Prepared Meats Industry: Above Average Productivity Crisis." *Monthly Labor Review*, April, pp. 37–42.

Center for Rural Affairs. 1990. *Competition and the Livestock Market.* Walthill, Nebraska.

Clark, W.A.V. 1986. *Human Migration.* Beverly Hills, Calif.: Sage.

Council for Economic Development—Greater Lexington Corporation. 1990. *Industrial and Business Facts, Lexington, Nebraska.*

Fisher, R. 1981. "Garden City Plant Seeks Housing but Town Rejects Mobile Homes." *Wichita Eagle-Beacon*, October 23.

Garden City Planning Department. 1989. *Garden City Community Information Profile.*

Gilmore, T. S., and M. K. Duff. 1975. *Boomtown Growth Mangement: A Case Study of Rock Springs—Green River, Wyoming.* Boulder, Colo.: Westview.

Haren, C. C., and R. W. Halling. 1979. "Industrial Development in Nonmetropolitan America: A Locational Perspective." In *Nonmetropolitan Industrialization,* edited by R. E. Lonsdale and H. L. Seyler. New York: Wiley.

Hope, H. 1988. *Garden City: Dreams in a Kansas Town.* Norman: University of Oklahoma Press.

Kansas Department of Human Resources, Research and Analysis Section. 1988. *Finney County, Kansas, Labor Force History.* Topeka.

Knox, P. L. 1988. "The Economic Organization of U.S. Space." In *The United States: A Contemporary Human Geography,* edited by P. L. Knox et al. New York: Wiley.

McKeown, R. L., and A. Lantz. 1977. *Rapid Growth and the Impact on Quality of Life in Rural Communities: A Case Study.* Glenwood Springs: Colorado Mental Health Center.

Marston, W. G., and T. L. Van Valey. 1979. "The Role of Residential Segregation in the Assimilation Process." *Annals of the American Academy of Political and Social Sciences* 441:13–23.

Miller, B. 1986. "Why the Packer Crunch Will Continue." *Farm Journal Beef Extra,* June/July 1986, p. 19.

National Cattlemen's Association. 1989. *Beef in a Competitive World.* Englewood, Colo.: National Cattlemen's Association.

Remy, D., and L. Sawers. 1984. "Economic Stagnation and Discrimination." In *My Troubles Are Going to Have Trouble with Me,* edited by K. B. Sacks and D. Remy. New Brunswick, N.J.: Rutgers University Press.

Risen, J. 1987. "Injury Rate Soaring, Workers at Meatpacking Plant Say." *Los Angeles Times,* March 2.

Robbins, W. 1982. "Police Use Tear Gas to Rout Meat Plant Marchers." *New York Times,* July 27.

Skaggs, J. M. 1986. *Prime Cut: Livestock Raising and Meatpacking in the United States, 1607–1983.* College Station: Texas A&M University Press.

Strand, P. J. 1984. "Employment Predictors among Indochinese Refugees." *International Migration Review* 18:50–64.

Stull, D. 1990. "I Come to the Garden: Changing Ethnic Relations in Garden City, Kansas." *Urban Anthropology* 19:4:303–320.

U.S. Bureau of the Census. 1959, 1980, 1988. *Kansas County Business Patterns.* Washington, D.C.: Government Printing Office.

———. 1967, 1987. *U.S. Census of Manufacturers.* Washington, D.C.: Government Printing Office.

———. 1969, 1987. *Census of Agriculture.* Vol. 1. Area Reports Part 21, Kansas. Washington, D.C.: Government Printing Office.

U.S. Department of Labor, Bureau of Labor Statistics, 1985. *Employment Hours and Earnings, United States, 1909–84.* Vol. 1. Washington, D.C.: Government Printing Office.

————. 1988. *Occupational Injuries and Illnesses in the United States by Industry.* Washington, D.C.: Government Printing Office.

————. 1989. *Supplement to Employment and Earnings.* Washington, D.C.: Government Printing Office.

Wood, A. 1988. *The Beefpacking Industry: A Study of Three Communities in Southwestern Kansas: Dodge City, Liberal and Garden City, Kansas.* Final Report to the Department of Migrant Education. Flagstaff, Ariz.: Wood and Wood Associates.

3   Knock 'em Dead: Work on the Killfloor of a Modern Beefpacking Plant

Donald D. Stull

> Entering one of the Durham buildings, they found a number of other visitors waiting; and before long there came a guide to escort them through the place. They make a great feature of showing strangers through the packing plants, for it is a good advertisement. But ponas Jokubas whispered maliciously that the visitors did not see any more than the packers wanted them to.
>
> —Upton Sinclair, *The Jungle*

The Tour

The doors to the guard station were marked in Spanish and Vietnamese—but not in English. The uniformed guard behind the glass window said to sign in, mentioning who we represented and the time. After we all finished, he let us inside the high chain-link fence, where we were met by someone who led us down a long walkway and into the plant. From there we were ushered through the cafeteria and into a training room, given brand new white hardhats and smocks along with yellow foam-rubber earplugs. As we clumsily adjusted the plastic headbands inside the hardhats, buttoned up our smocks, and removed the earplugs from their plastic envelopes, a middle-aged Anglo man dressed in a golf shirt, polyester western dress jeans held up by a trophy buckle, and snakeskin boots began to speak.

"Welcome to IBP. IBP is the largest beefpacking company, and this is the largest and most sophisticated plant in the world. Please

44

do not talk to the employees, for their safety and yours, since they are operating machinery and using knives. And please stay together for your safety. Because of the high noise level, and since you'll be wearing earplugs, we won't be able to answer your questions in the plant, but we will return here after the tour and you can ask questions then."

Our guide was a Vietnamese man in his early thirties. We followed him through two heavy swinging metal doors and out onto the "killfloor," where we were met by a moving row of dead cows, suspended upside down on meathooks, their tongues hanging out, their limbs jerking. As they passed by, like monstrous red and black quivering shirts being called up at the dry cleaners, an Anglo man clipped off their hooves with a tool resembling large pruning shears, while above us, on a catwalk, a Latina slapped plastic sheets onto their skinned rumps.

Forty-five minutes later, back in the training room, we removed our earplugs and took off our smocks and hardhats, still dazed by what we had experienced. The man in the snakeskin boots (who turned out to be the personnel manager) asked if we had any questions. For almost an hour, he cheerfully answered our questions, taking great pleasure in his statistics and in our wonder at "the Cadillac of all packing plants."

"Here at the Finney County plant, we kill between 30,000 and 32,000 head of cattle a week. Since many feedyards in this area have a capacity of about 40,000 head, we empty the equivalent of about one feedyard per week. Every day we receive 101 trucks of live cattle and load out one truck of boxed beef every twenty-two minutes of every day, seven days a week. From hoof to box, the longest a cow will stay in this plant is six days; the prime time is two to three days.

"There is little demand for hanging beef anymore. About 95 percent of what we send out is boxed beef—the only carcasses we sell are those that do not grade out to our specifications. IBP boxes only the best—quality grades Prime, Choice, and Select, and yield grades 1, 2, and 3.[1] Those that don't meet our specifications are sold as hanging beef to other packers in the area.

"This plant can slaughter about 350 head of cattle an hour. The number of head we can process depends on whether we're doing 'bone-in' or 'bone-out.' Bone-out is largely for institutional buyers, such as hospitals and restaurants, and requires more cuts, since most of the bones are removed. It's heavy work—and hard—we can do about 350 head an hour on bone-out. Bone-in is mainly what the housewife will buy at the local grocery store, and it moves

View of a modern killfloor. The "blood pit," necessary for the blood drainage required by the Humane Slaughter Act, is at left. Behind the blood pit, severed, skinned heads, suspended on hooks, move toward their own line, while a "whitehat"—an hourly worker—takes time to sharpen his knife on his "steel." (Photograph courtesy of MEAT&POULTRY Magazine)

a lot faster—400 head an hour or more. They do 240 cuts of meat here; 9 of ground beef alone!

"Right now, this plant has 2,650 employees and an annual payroll of $42 million. Each job is ranked, and paid, according to importance and difficulty. There are seven levels. Starting pay for someone just off the street with no experience on a level-1 job is $6.40 an hour in Processing, $6.70 in Slaughter. The base for level-7 employees is $9.40 in Processing, $9.58 in Slaughter. After six months you get an automatic 50-cent raise and another 72 cents at the end of one year. We have profit sharing and yearly bonuses. IBP is self-insured. We offer an excellent insurance package— health, dental, vision, retirement, disability, alcohol and drug abuse coverage. Line workers are eligible for coverage after six months.

"Absenteeism normally averages 1.7 percent. We compensate

for absenteeism by having more workers on a shift than we absolutely need. If too many show up, we assign the extra workers to different tasks, which helps them qualify for more than one job, or we experiment with new techniques."

In spite of the ease with which he threw out statistics in response to our questions, the man in the snakeskin boots neatly side-stepped a query about the rate of worker turnover. Instead, he informed us that "more than a thousand of our workers have been in this plant for two or more years. As plants get older, their work-force becomes more stable. Most workers stay on the same job for about a year. By then they are getting bored and usually bid to another job.

"We have an internal job posting system here at IBP. Current employees are given the opportunity to apply for and fill jobs before we hire from outside. New hires are placed wherever the need is greatest. After the initial ninety-day probationary period, you can bid on other jobs and move around the floor. The more jobs you are qualified for, the more competitive you are for supervisory jobs. Each supervisor oversees forty-five employees and has a trainer working under him. Although it helps, supervisors don't have to be qualified on the jobs they oversee. We look around the plant for workers who show real promise—leadership, potential, interpersonal communications skills. The supervisor runs his own business out there; he is responsible for his crew's production and is given daily reports on its output.

"We stress safety here. We spend $1 million a year on training and employ twenty-eight hourly trainers. Each new hire receives three days of orientation, then comes back each day for thirty minutes of stretching exercises until he gets into shape to do his job. Depending on their job, each worker may wear as much as $600 worth of safety equipment—hardhat, earplugs, cloth and steel-mesh gloves, mail aprons and leggings, weight-lifting belts, or shin guards. They don't have to buy any of this equipment. Knife users normally carry three knives. Each one is owned by IBP and has its own identification number. The workers use the same knives as long as they work here. They grow very attached to their knives, they know their feel, and this helps them do a better job. Knives are turned in at the end of the day for sharpening and are picked up at the beginning of the next shift. They also carry sharpening steels with them and sharpen their knives while they work."

"With all those knives, they must cut themselves a lot?" one of us asked. "The most common injuries are punctures, not lacerations," he replied. "These wounds usually occur when a knife slips and pokes the other hand. Such injuries are usually caused by workers not wearing their safety equipment. But we've had very few such injuries so far this year. In fact, we won the President's Award for the best safety record of any IBP plant."

As I listened to him speak, I recalled the signs admonishing safety scattered along the corridors, interspersed with printouts of crew performance records highlighted in yellow. In their margins were handwritten calls for the team to pull together. On the stark walls of the training room three charts showed stretching and flex-ibility exercises for wrists and fingers. Next to the door was a large poster entitled "5 Reasons to Stay Non-Union." Underneath was a picture of cops in riot gear and newspaper headlines about the lengthy plant closure and the number of people injured at a strike at the Dakota City plant.

"The list of products we produce at this plant is almost never-ending. We separate the white and red blood cells right here in the plant and each is used for different things. Blood is used to make perfume. Bone meal is used as a feed additive. Kodak is the biggest buyer of our bone gelatin, which is used in making film paper. Intestines are used to string tennis rackets. The hairs from inside the cow's ears are used for paintbrushes. Spleens are used in phar-maceuticals.

"Processing begins at 6:05 A.M. Slaughter starts an hour later. Workers get a fifteen-minute break after about two and a half hours and a thirty-minute lunch break after about five-and-a-half hours. The day shift, we call it 'A' shift, ends at 2:35. 'B' shift be-gins at 3:05. In between shifts we do a quick, dry cleanup. From midnight to 6:00 A.M. we contract out for a wet cleanup, which holds down bacteria."

Our heads were swimming. There was so much more we wanted to know, but we were exhausted from trying to absorb it all and remember even a fraction of the facts and figures he glibly tossed back in response to our questions. The man in the snakeskin boots made no attempt to hurry us, and he seemed a little disappointed when we could no longer think of anything more to ask. As we uneasily shuffled in tacit recognition that this adventure was about to end, someone asked, "Do you get any flak from the animal rights people?" "Not really," he quipped; "most people enjoy a good steak."[2]

So began my research on beefpacking and beefpacking workers. Even as I write this, three years later, my fieldnotes still evoke the awe and excitement I felt that day as I followed our guide through a confusing maze of men, machines, and meat. Only now am I beginning to comprehend the place and the process. Try as I might, I can never convey the sights, sounds, smells of this massive factory where almost three thousand men and women toil on "disassembly" lines killing, bleeding, skinning, gutting, sawing, boning, cutting, trimming, shrink-wrapping, boxing, and loading hundreds of cattle an hour, sixteen hours a day, six days a week. I can only try to give a sense of what the killfloor of one modern plant is like, what the workers do, how they feel about their work, and the strategies adopted by their supervisors to maximize their productivity, often at the cost of their safety.

Methodology

There are learned people who can tell you out of the statistics that beef-boners make forty cents an hour, but, perhaps, these people have never looked into a beef-boner's hands.

—Sinclair, *The Jungle*

While finagling a tour of a beef plant is not so hard, doing ethnographic research on beefpacking and beefpacking workers certainly is. Politely but firmly, IBP and Monfort declined my request to participate directly in a study of ethnic relations in Garden City that I was directing, forcing me to rely primarily on indirect methods of data collection concerning work and worker relations on the plant floor.

I conducted formal, audiotaped interviews with packinghouse line workers and supervisors, with feedyard managers, and with others familiar with cattle feeding and beefpacking. And I was able to draw on interview materials collected by other team members. I subscribed to *Beef Today* and went on every plant tour I could. I attended monthly workers' compensation hearings, which offered detailed job descriptions and graphically demonstrated why meatpacking is America's most dangerous industry. I enrolled in Meat and Carcass Evaluation at Garden City Community College to learn more about the industry, make contacts, and gain regular entry into "the cooler," where carcasses are graded for quality and cutabilty. Perhaps the only person ever to pursue postdoctoral training at a community college, I received an "A" in the course and am learning to speak, though haltingly, an arcane jargon of "cutters" and "canners"; of "bloom" and "KPH"; of "bullers," "black baldies," and "heiferettes." I helped tag carcasses for Beef Empire Days as they snaked along the chain at IBP, being skinned and gutted before entering the cooler. One afternoon, I helped my instructor tag the carcasses of one hundred cattle for the Certified Angus Board (CAB). A couple of times I rode on the work train out to IBP to pick up tallow and hides, taking pictures and even managing to get onto the Hides floor.

But it was in Tom's Tavern that I did much of my research on work in the packing plants. There I could meet a cross-section of Garden City—beefpacking line workers and supervisors, farmers and feedyard cowboys, dentists and accountants—the well-to-do and the unemployed; Anglo Americans, African Americans, and Mexican Americans; Latino immigrants up from Mexico or perhaps Central America, even an occasional Vietnamese; old-timers and newcomers alike. Without ready access to the packinghouse floors, Tom's offered the best opportunity to talk candidly with workers. In its relaxed atmosphere, people spoke often and openly about their work. I soon became a "regular," playing Trivial Pursuit or hearts with a circle of devotees, shuffleboard and pool with friends and acquaintances. On Thursdays—payday at the packinghouses—I helped tend bar from midnight till closing at 2:00 A.M., waiting on, listening to, and talking with thirsty line workers coming off "B" shift. On "zoo day"—Sunday—the only day off for packers and many others, I worked from 10:00 P.M. till 2:00 A.M.

Tending bar allowed me to meet and sound out potential interviewees, and productive interviews came from these contacts. I could listen to and participate in conversations with a wide range of people, many of whom I would never have talked with otherwise. My research was well known, if somewhat mysterious, and a cause for suspicion among some. Bartending gave me "real" work in the eyes of those who found it odd that a college professor spent most of his time sitting around talking to people.

The description of jobs and plant layout that follows is based on five formal interviews and several informal conversations with a long-time Slaughter worker with extensive experience in several jobs. The information "Enrique" provided has been supplemented by my own observations, as well as formal interviews and informal conversations with other current and former workers. This description is based on research during 1988 and 1989, although the job descriptions and plant layout refer to the summer of 1989—changes in personnel and specific jobs have taken place since then. The lack of cooperation from plant management and my inability to spend more than short, sporadic periods in the plant may at times lead to gaps in my knowledge.

Background

> The *Appeal* was a "propaganda" paper. It had a manner all its own—it was full of ginger and spice, of Western slang and hustle. . . . The people of Packingtown had lost their strike, if ever a people had, and so they read these papers gladly, and twenty thousand were hardly enough to go round.
>
> —Sinclair, *The Jungle*

The literature on today's meatpacking industry presents an interesting paradox. Talk of consumer trends, and of new developments in procurement, processing, and marketing, fill the trade journals. Newspapers carry articles on meat safety, cattle ranching's environmental impact, the dangers of red meat for health-conscious consumers; stories on the changing workforce and hazardous working conditions even appear from time to time. But scholarly treatises are spotty at best, and more often than not are found in obscure reports. Skaggs (1986) presents the most comprehensive history of meatpacking in America, but he stops in 1983 and pays scant attention to the nature of work in the plants. Wood's (1980) history of the Kansas beef industry focuses on beef production and devotes only eighteen pages to the period after 1940. Economists look at the impact of restructuring on productivity (Carnes 1984) and occupational hazards (Personick and Taylor-Shirley 1989); geographers describe the industry's recent restructuring (Broadway 1990) and its impact on local communities (Broadway, Chapter 2 in this volume).

As policy analysts and cattle producers debate the consequences of packer concentration and vertical integration (Center for Rural Affairs 1990; National Cattlemen's Association 1989), activists decry the suffering of animals during slaughter (Birchall 1990) and even suggest "ecotage" (Mooney 1989). Reporters from the *Kansas City Star* win a Pulitzer Prize with their exposé of the U.S. Department of Agriculture (USDA), which included revelations of tainted meat, inadequate inspection procedures, and serious conflicts of interest (McGraw 1991; McGraw and Taylor 1991). Hidden cameras reveal the contamination that can result from high-speed, streamlined inspection procedures in beef plants on ABC's "Prime Time Live." k. d. lang tells her fans that "meat stinks," and Linda McCartney says she couldn't kiss a man who was a meat eater. Jeremy Rifkin launches "Beyond Beef," an eight-year campaign intended to cut American beef consumption in half.

Amid all this hullabaloo, surprisingly little is said about meatpacking workers and the nature of their work. Slayton (1986) and Barrett (1990) tell of life in Back of the Yards and work on the floors of Chicago's packinghouses at the turn of the century. Hardy Green (1990) gives an insider's view of the protracted strike against the Hormel plant in Austin, Minnesota, in 1985–1986. But descriptions of work on the chains and lines of modern meatpacking plants are few and far between. Remy and Sawers (1984) offer a glimpse of the floor at the "Square Deal Packing Company" in their analysis of the consequences of retrenchment for women and Blacks. Until recently, only Thompson (1983) has described in detail what it is like to work in a modern packing plant.

This chapter and those accompanying it seek to turn attention to meatpacking workers, to their work and how it influences their lives and the communities in which they make their homes. While the story that follows is set in Garden City, Kansas, it could just as easily have been told about beef and pork workers in any number of towns in Kansas, Nebraska, or Iowa. (For complementary descriptions of work in modern beef plants and the consequences for local communities, see Broadway and Stull 1991; Stull and Broadway 1990; Stull, Broadway, and Erickson 1992.)

Power and Authority on the Floor

Jurgis was like a boy, a boy from the country. He was the sort of man the bosses like to get hold of, the sort they make a grievance they cannot get hold of. When he was told to go to a certain place, he would go there on the run. . . . If he were working in a line of men, the line always moved too slowly for him, and you could pick him out by his impatience and restlessness. That was why he had been picked.

—Sinclair, *The Jungle*

On the packinghouse floor authority is circumscribed, the hierarchy rigid. Job type—and status—are marked by the color of the hardhat everyone must wear. The floor supervisor is a greenhat; the general foreman a yellowhat, as are the three line supervisors or foremen. Each is assisted by a leadman, or bluehat. Below them are the whitehats—the hourly line workers.

Bluehats are "utility people" or "leadmen." They should know how to perform most, if not all, the jobs on their line; to fill in as needed and assist the yellowhat in other ways. Whitehats jokingly call them "back scratchers" and "peter shakers," and they often say the way to become a bluehat is to "suck up" to your supervisor—

take him hunting, buy him beer. The bluehat's job includes keeping tabs on whitehats and "writing them up" for infractions.

"Jim" says supervisors should practice the "Three Fs": "Be firm, be fair, and be friendly." Beginning supervisors may be told to practice the Three Fs in training sessions, but on the line it's a different matter.

> "Dave" has worked at the plant for three years. They made him a bluehat, but there was "too much bullshit" and he asked to go back to being a whitehat. He found keeping tabs on those workers who were on the yellowhat's "shitlist" especially distasteful. There are plenty of ways a supervisor can find to fire you if he gets it in for you. Dave knows them all because when he first came to work his yellowhat took a liking to him and taught him the ropes. For example, you are allowed 6 minutes for a "piss break." But there is no way you can get to the bathroom, take off all your gear, take care of business, wash up, put your gear back on, and get back on the line in 6 minutes—especially for women who are having their period. But the supervisor can enforce that (as well as deny or simply ignore the worker's request altogether) by having his bluehat keep time on the person and hound that person out or easily build a case for firing him. (Stull fieldnotes 1/27–2/20/89:5)

Write-ups may be issued for many reasons—failure to show up for work or call in sick, safety infractions, horseplay, taunting or arguing with another worker, or simply not being able to do the job. If you are written up, you have to sign the form. If you refuse to sign, you are sent home.

> If you can't do your job the supervisors will tell you, "Either do your job or go home." Enrique has been used as a translator in several instances, and apparently language difficulties contribute to some Hispanics being fired. He spoke of Hispanics who were told by the supervisor to "go home." When they returned to work the next day, they were told they had abandoned their post and were terminated. However, Enrique says yellowhats are now being held more accountable, that you can appeal a write-up, and in some cases supervisors have been reprimanded for bad write-ups. (Stull fieldnotes 6/14–19/89:11–12)

The company does not control worker behavior with the threat of write-ups alone. When the plant found punitive measures were not significantly reducing accidents, it adopted incentives. If a line goes fifteen days without an accident, its members get a free lunch; thirty days gets five pounds of hamburger; sixty days a cap; still

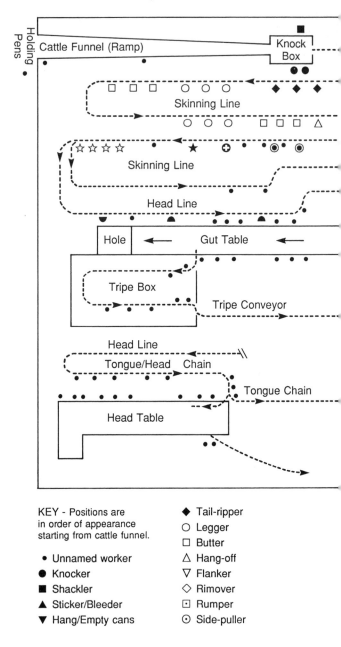

KEY - Positions are
in order of appearance
starting from cattle funnel.

- Unnamed worker   ◆ Tail-ripper
- ● Knocker   ○ Legger
- ■ Shackler   □ Butter
- ▲ Sticker/Bleeder   △ Hang-off
- ▼ Hang/Empty cans   ▽ Flanker
                      ◇ Rimover
                      ⊡ Rumper
                      ⊙ Side-puller

Figure 3.1. Killfloor of IBP's Finney County plant, Summer 1989. Stations on the lines and locations on the floor are keyed to the text. Not all jobs and operations are depicted. *Drawing by* Laura Kriegstrom Poracsky.

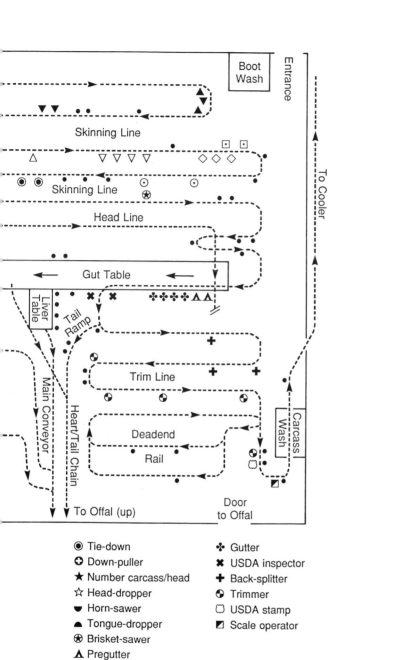

Boot Wash

Entrance

Skinning Line

Skinning Line

Head Line

To Cooler

Gut Table

Liver Table

Tail Ramp

Main Conveyor

Heart/Tail Chain

Trim Line

Deadend

Rail

Carcass Wash

To Offal (up)

Door to Offal

◉	Tie-down	✢	Gutter
✚	Down-puller	✖	USDA inspector
★	Number carcass/head	✚	Back-splitter
☆	Head-dropper	◓	Trimmer
▼	Horn-sawer	◡	USDA stamp
▲	Tongue-dropper	◪	Scale operator
✳	Brisket-sawer		
▲	Pregutter		

longer brings a jacket. This system has proved successful, although yellowhats still carry green cards to write workers up for infractions (Stull fieldnotes 7/12–16/89:12).

Supervisors and bluehats are not the only ones who exert power on the floor. Whitehats may contest for power among themselves, crossing over and back across the thin line between horseplay and open conflict.

> A couple of times that same week I got hit by the heads. See, I was working on my head, I grabbed it like this, and with my steel, like that, pulling on the meat, and the other guy, when the other head came, instead of throwing it in the front of me so after I finish with mine I can grab it myself, he threw it straight and hit me with the head. . . . And he hit me a couple of times and they just laughed. The second time I get mad and I threw him a head. He, of course, got mad, but he stopped it, too. . . . The person that is going to do something like that, he won't do it when the foreman is there, he will wait until he's not in sight. . . .
>
> I was threatened a couple of times with knives . . . on the floor. You know, there is somebody joking, throwing you pieces of fat or something. . . . So one time I was washing my boots, I wash them with a pressure hose, and he threatened me with a knife. And I just told him . . . "Just drop it." . . . I talk to a lot of people, and sometimes joke, not heavy, though. I know when to stop. And I tell them, too, when they are getting out of hand. I never had any trouble in the floor. . . . The only problem that I had that got threatened that time was with a Vietnamese guy. . . .
>
> Q: With the knife?
>
> A: [Yes.] It was an air knife, those round ones. [We were in the boot wash] washing up. That time I got smart, so I wash him off with a pressure hose when he turn around. I said, "If you can't take any jokes then don't joke." He said, "Forget about it." And he did. So that's how far it got. (Stull interview 8/13/89:32–35, 37–38)

From the Knocker to the Cooler: Work on the Killfloor

Then the party went across the street to where they did the killing of beef—where every hour they turned four or five hundred cattle into meat. . . . [T]here were fifteen or twenty lines, and the men moved from one to another of these. . . . [I]t was only a couple of minutes to knock fifteen or twenty cattle and roll them out. . . . The manner in which they did this was something to be seen and never forgotten. They worked with furious intensity, literally upon the run. . . . It was all highly specialized labor, each man having his task to do; generally this would consist of only two or three specific cuts, and he would pass down the line of fifteen or twenty carcasses, making these cuts upon each. . . . There were men to cut it, and men to split it, and men to gut it and scrape it clean inside. There were some with hoses which threw jets of boiling water upon it, and others who removed the feet and added the final touches. In the end . . . the finished beef was run into the chilling room, to hang its appointed time.

—Sinclair, *The Jungle*

The Skinning Line

Cattle arrive in trucks a few hours before slaughter. They are unloaded into holding pens, weighed, given a lot number, and when their time comes, driven onto a ramp, or *funnel*. The funnel gradually narrows as it winds upward to the *knock box* high above the killfloor. There each animal is immobilized, as two *knockers* take turns applying cylindrical stun guns to each animal's forehead. On impact, the gun discharges a .25-caliber cap that propels a short steel piston into the skull, causing a displaced skull fracture and unconsciousness. Underneath the knockers stands the *shackler*, who wraps a hook and chain around the animal's left hind hoof—easier said than done, since its legs may be jerking from the stun. As each animal (referred to in both the singular and plural as "cattle") is knocked and shackled, it falls forward and down onto a mechanized overhead trolley and swings out onto the floor, hanging upside down from its left hind hoof.

After traveling the full width of the floor, the suspended animal makes a 90-degree turn to meet the *sticker*. Holding a knife with a four-inch blade, he deftly makes an incision in the hide at the base of the throat, careful not to pierce the throat itself. The *can-hanger*[3] then hooks a stainless-steel cylinder under the animal's open throat. The *bleeder* quickly severs an artery and blood gushes into the cans, spilling over to drench the workers and run through the grated floor beneath their feet. The three stand shoulder to shoulder like gladiators, wearing hockey helmets and face masks for protection from flailing hoofs and their own knives, which are sometimes knocked into their faces. The bleeder deals the fatal blow, but dying is a process. Signs of life such as muscle twitches and jerking limbs may continue well down the line.

After the bleeder, the chain makes another 90-degree turn. Ten feet or so down the chain, the cans, now full of blood, are emptied into a vat and placed on a hook, for their ride on the chain back to the can-hanger by way of a "box," where they are washed with high-pressure water spray. Farther down the line, severed heads and carcasses are washed in similar "boxes."[4]

Because the hide is hard to cut, the sticker exerts more effort than the bleeder, who reaches up inside the cattle's throat to slice an artery. The can-emptiers do not face the same risk of being kicked by the cattle as the can-hangers, but they must lift and empty the heavy cans. So at break, stickers and bleeders, can-hangers and can-emptiers, switch positions. They switch again after lunch. Since there is no break after lunch, they switch again the following morning to maintain equity.

The skinning line is the hardest of all the lines on the killfloor because

> the hide is the hardest part, the toughest thing to cut. Those knives have to be pretty sharp in order to do a good job. . . . So if you're working with the butt knife, man, your hands swell, get blisters and everything, and finally [workers] have to either move out or they have to tell the foreman they want to move out, [take] some other job that you don't need to use a knife. It's up to them. A lot of people quit. (Stull interview 6/19/89:6)

As the cattle pass by the can-emptier on the second leg of the snaking journey through the killfloor, most of the work stations are on raised grated platforms. The knockers stand high above the floor; the sticker and the bleeder, the can-hanger and can-emptier, stand on the floor. Most of the rest of the workers stand on grated steel platforms at varying heights off the floor, depending on what part of the carcass they work on.

The skinning begins with the *tail rippers*, who "cut out the ass" (rectum), slice the hide all the way to the cod, and remove the pizzle (penis) if it is a bull—a dangerous job because the cattle are often still kicking. The *first legger* removes the hoof from the loose hind leg and slits the hide down the full length of the rear flank. Then three *first butters* skin down the loose leg, "peeling" the whole round (hindquarter). At this point, the carcass is still on the chain. The *first hang-off* inserts a hook attached to a roller (the "trolley") in a tendon between two bones in the gam (in the hock of the loose leg) and places it on the "rail" above the workers.

The carcass was initially suspended from its left hind leg. Now it hangs on the trolley from its right hind leg. Three *second leggers* take the chain off the left hind leg, then cut the hoof off and slice the hide the length of the leg up to the first joint. Three *second butters* peel the round on the loose leg, and the *second hang-off* puts a trolley in the loose leg and places it on the rail. The carcass now travels down the rail suspended by both hind legs; both rounds are now peeled.

The cattle are now traversing the floor for the third time, while *flankers*, *rimovers*, and *rumpers* skin more and more of the carcass. Interspersed among them, others remove ears, horns, and hooves. Doing a good job, and doing it right, is vital—if you don't, it will soon take a toll on your body.

> Those guys know what they're doing, because if they don't do it right, boy, that gets hard. Any job that you do, if you don't do it right, you get tired in a flash, because that chain is going too fast to keep up with it if you're not doing it right. (Stull interview 6/19/89:5)

If something goes wrong, *redhats*—maintenance workers— weighed down by sagging implement belts, are summoned by pre- arranged blasts on sirens. Maintenance crews are on duty around the clock in rotating shifts—six weeks on graveyard, six weeks on swings, six weeks on days.

> There's a lot of breakdown. . . . You replace what you can, but you're just barely keeping ahead of the game, keeping things running. . . . At this point they're more interested in keeping it running than they are in maintenance. They're more interested in keeping it running as a basis of putting the product out than, you know, the fights with equip- ment. I foresee that is going to be the downfall here sooner or later. (Maintenance worker 5/9/89:4–5)

When the flank and the rump have been peeled, the *side-puller* attaches a machine by the same name to the hide on both sides of the carcass, which hangs limply upside down. The push of a button sends an electrical shock coursing through the carcass—it con- tracts, arches its back, and the hide is stripped cleanly away from the ribs. (Carcasses are shocked at several stages in the slaughter process: initially to stimulate blood loss before the cans are emp- tied, later to hasten rigor mortis and to keep them from being torn apart by the massive skinning machines.)

The scissor-like *tie-down* machine grasps the head as the *ban- nana bar* skins the loin and hindquarters; the *down-puller* then strips the hide from the back and shoulders down over the foreshanks and the head. Another electrical charge is needed at this point, otherwise the head and forequarters would be pulled off by the massive down-puller. Even so, carcasses with backs broken in skinning are a common sight. Hides travel beneath the floor on a conveyor belt out of Slaughter and over to the Hides building, where they are first bathed in a brine solution, then bailed and shipped out to tanneries by rail.

After the hide is removed, the carcass and the head are numbered; the head is then "dropped" (severed) and placed on a hook.

The Head Line

Skinned heads, resting on hooks inserted at the base of the skull, proceed down the "head line," then make a turn at a right angle onto the "head table"—a grisly sight as they round the U at one end of the building, naked with eyes and tongues still intact.

Workers with air-powered saws cut the horns flush with the skull, then wash the head by inserting a long metal tube into the back of the skull, which shoots water out the nose and mouth to clean the inside of the skull. Tongues are "dropped," then "hung" on a hook. Heads and tongues travel, side by side, down the line on hooks into a "box," where they are sprayed with a fine mist of water.

USDA inspectors check the glands of the tongue for disease by making incisions both inside and outside the head. On down the line, workers take the tongue apart, trim fat from its side, remove the windpipe, and put it on the conveyor headed to Rendering. Tongues go on the chain to Offal, there to be packed for shipping.

Meanwhile, whitehats on the head table use straight knives, hydraulic machines with tigerlike claws, and Whizard knives—circular blades, operated by a lever, with teeth like a hacksaw—to remove the lower jaw, then loosen, separate, and save meat from the jaw, cheek, and head. Once every bit of flesh has been removed, skulls are split open with a hydraulic machine, then pushed into a hole, later to be ground up for bone meal or gelatin. Brains are saved, washed, and bagged. "And that's the end of the line for the heads," says Enrique.

The Gut Table

While heads make their way down their own line, carcasses move toward the gut table. The *brisket-sawer* splits the sternum. Two *pregutters* then slice the length of the belly, remove the bladder, and open the skin from the cod to where the brisket saw stopped. The stomach sags. Five *gutters*, sometimes six, pull the paunch and viscera out and "drop" them on a conveyor belt. This

Gutters "drop" the paunch and viscera onto a conveyor; farther down the gut table, USDA inspectors check for contamination. (Photograph courtesy of MEAT&POULTRY Magazine)

is very hard because the steam rising from the still-warm insides and chest cavity makes it difficult to see. If the viscera do not come loose from their own weight, they are cut loose and proceed in a pile down the gut table.

> You watch these guys who gut cattle, the gutters themselves, they're removing the viscera with as much skill as a surgeon. They're standing there, they're soaking wet a lot of time from the heat, you know the moisture coming up off the table, and they're working inside this hot carcass all day, and their skill level is a helluva lot more than just a common laborer. (Respondent with wide industry experience 3/30/89:22)

The guts come down the conveyor belt in two lines as five *USDA inspectors* stand on both sides of the table, looking them over. One inspector checks carcasses as they move on down the line, another the livers, the other three check stomachs and hearts. Any diseased or contaminated organs are condemned with blue dye and discarded down "the hole." Once the viscera pass USDA, they are sorted and processed. Hearts are separated from lungs then hung on hooks headed for Offal; livers are stamped with "USDA" and then boxed, sealed, and placed on a conveyor belt; lungs and windpipes are separated; "rounds" (intestines) are saved. A worker hangs tripe on a chain that carries it into the "tripe box," there to be washed and bleached, then weighed, boxed, and placed on a conveyor belt that moves past the head table, rising steadily till it exits the killfloor on the second floor.

The Trim Line

After the gut table, carcasses move onto the "trim line," where tails are removed, washed, then hung, interspersed between hearts on a chain, which travels to Offal where they are sealed in plastic, boxed, labeled, and frozen.

Next come the *back-splitters*, arguably the most important job in Slaughter. Using a Jarvis Buster IV saw—a large band saw suspended from the rail above—the back-splitter cuts the carcass in half from bottom to top, since the carcass hangs upside down. He must do his job with great precision, splitting the backbone exactly in half. A bad cut costs the company money.

The carcass, now split in two, passes by a series of *trimmers* who remove pieces of hide, dirt, internal organs—anything missed earlier. USDA inspectors watch for pieces of liver, pus, bad kidneys—anything that should not be there. Carcasses failing inspection are railed off to the "deadrail" or "deadend rail," where a yellowhat from the trim line, and maybe one or two whitehats, fix the problem. The USDA inspector then rechecks these carcasses, and they are pushed back onto the main rail.

The carcass is given a USDA stamp, weighed, and labeled, after which it exits the killfloor behind a plastic "wall" or "fence." It cools in the hotbox for twenty-two to twenty-four hours, then enters the cooler, where it is given a yield and quality grade. From the cooler the carcass goes to Processing, where it is broken down into subprimal cuts, shrink-wrapped, then boxed for shipment to wholesale and retail outlets (see Erickson, Chapter 4 in this volume, for a discussion of work on the Processing floor). In all, the trip from knock box to cooler takes a mere forty-two minutes, in which time a steer or a heifer is transformed from an animal to a carcass (Stull fieldnotes 2/21/89:6). In two or three days, it will be shipped out in boxes as meat.

A back-splitter deftly sawing a carcass into "sides" of beef. (Photograph courtesy of MEAT&POULTRY Magazine)

Discussion

Jurgis would find out these things for himself if he stayed there long enough; it was the men who had to do all the dirty jobs, and so there was no deceiving them; and they caught the spirit of the place, and did like all the rest.

—Sinclair, *The Jungle*

In spite of a "century of progress" since Upton Sinclair wrote *The Jungle*, I am struck by how little the industry—its work or its workers—has really changed. Knockers still start the killing, but now they use a stun gun instead of a sledgehammer. Splitters are still the most expert and highly paid workers on the killfloor, deftly cutting carcasses in half with Jarvis Buster IV band saws on moving platforms, where once they used massive cleavers. Today's luggers carry 200-pound beef quarters into refrigerated semis, rather than boxcars. Still, stickers and gutters, trimmers and droppers wield razor-sharp knives as they turn 400 cattle an hour into meat.

Beefpacking plants remain massive factories, in so many ways reminiscent of the turn of the century. They continue employing hundreds or even thousands of workers to toil on their disassembly lines. And immigrants are still attracted to packinghouse jobs because command of English is not required, and wages are relatively high. But instead of the German, Irish, Lithuanian, and Polish workers of Sinclair's day, today's packinghouses are crowded with Southeast Asian refugees, Mexican migrants, African Americans, Latinos, and Anglos from our farms and cities.

Yes, the "chain" connecting meatpacking's past and present runs strong. Companies still "make a great feature of showing strangers through the packing plants, for it is a good advertisement" (Sinclair 1985:43). And somewhere in between pointing out the "wonderful efficiency" of the plant, the unbelievable speed with which they kill and disassemble cattle, and the "many strange and unlikely products (that come from) such things as feet, knuckles, hide clippings, and sinews" (Sinclair 1985:50), the guide will chuckle and say: "They don't waste anything here. IBP markets every part of the cow but the moo. My father used to work at IBP before me, and he used to tell me that the little toy boxes that moo were made by IBP" (Stull fieldnotes 7/22/88:1). The group laughs, and he is pleased that we should take this ancient witticism as his own.

Training
As in Jurgis's time, new hires are placed in jobs according to vacancies and prior experience.

> When they start . . . they have to be in the job the foreman assigns them, or in other words where they need them, and if that person doesn't make it there, he can ask to be changed or has the choice to quit. And it's easier to make a person quit when they start because they are hurting all over and they want a change, and they won't change them because they need them there. And they are all with bandages. (Slaughter worker 7/16/89:10)

Training new employees should be vitally important in an industry where workers with no previous experience, often with limited English skills, are expected to perform precise tasks rapidly. The company claims to provide each worker with extensive orientation and training. Workers say training consists of little more than watching and imitating the person you are to replace for a day or two—then you are on your own. The company, after all, does not want to pay two people to do the job of one.

Q: What did [your] training consist of?

A: I just started that job. They should have trained me for two weeks, and they only trained me for four days, and they wanted to leave me after two days. . . . Initially they had me just watching and doing one or two [pieces] while the other ones were working the place. Nobody told me how to grab the steel to do the job or how to handle it—just by look. I had to stay there and look and try to just imitate what the other ones were doing. (Enrique 6/4/89)

Such training practices at first seem counterproductive to the packers' avowed goal of high productivity, but Enrique goes on to explain.

Q: Doesn't that mess up the line speed and stuff?

A: No, because what it does is it puts a burden a little more to somebody else down the line, that other person that has already been there for quite a while and they are used to it. . . . It's a little bit more to the one next in the line, coming down in the line, because the person they put there is not going to do it right, so it just puts a little bit more work to the next one. But when they see it's a new [worker], they take it. They try kind of helping out. There are some people, they don't, but they complain, but they still do it. (6/4/89:2–3)

In part, new workers receive inadequate training because the leadmen, who serve as trainers, spend much of their time filling in for absentees on the line. The man in the snakeskin boots says they compensate for absenteeism by having more workers on a shift than are absolutely needed. But workers complain of "short crews," which they attribute to attempts to cut costs. A former supervisor put it this way:

We're shorthanded out there, just continuously. Seems like we never have enough people, and when we do get crewed somebody quits or gets fired or bids off. And normally the bluehat is just like anybody else, just out there filling a position, a position that needs filling. He doesn't get a chance to train very often, which isn't right. And that's not how it's designed to work, but that's how it works most generally. (Stull interview 5/29/89:18)

Probation

Hourly workers are assigned to their initial job and are on probation ninety days. After successfully completing the probationary period, the worker is given seniority and may "bid" on any "posted" job within the same department (Slaughter, Processing, Hides, Offal, etc.). Workers may not bid out of their own department. The qualified bidder with the highest seniority "wins" a job. A worker who wins a new job and "can't stay with it" is "frozen" in his prior job for six months before again becoming a "qualified bidder."

Whether a worker is on probation or has won seniority, he is subject to strict rules and rigid sanctions. Probationary employees may be discharged without notice or recourse. All employees are "written up" for being late or absent without an excuse, excessive excused absences, failure to report on-the-job injuries, overstaying lunch or relief breaks, deliberate discourtesy, horseplay, substandard job performance. Workers with four such infractions within a calendar year are discharged. More serious offenses bring even quicker termination—malicious mischief that results in property damage or injury, gambling, alcohol or drug use, theft, abusive or threatening language. Fighting, even in the parking lot, results in immediate discharge—with so many knives so close at hand, it cannot be otherwise (National Beef Packing Company n.d.:14).

For whitehats, and their supervisors, the work is hard. One Mexican immigrant called it *esclavitud*—slavery. "They make you hump for your seven or eight dollars. The first ninety days it's tough till you get in shape. I'm a supervisor, and I'm not supposed to work hard, but I bet I run ten miles a day in my job. It's no place to be if you don't like to work" (Stull fieldnotes 8/7/88:7).

Communication and Interaction

Communication must be quick and to the point; workers have little time for idle conversation, or even work-related discussion, as carcasses whiz by at 400 or more an hour. When communication does take place, it is restricted to workers at the same or nearby stations, or with yellowhats or their bluehats.

Interaction with co-workers is a function of proximity. It is also a function of the job itself—how demanding it is and how many people do it. Once a job is mastered, especially if several workers share the same task, there may be time for a bit of conversation and rest. Still, interaction is largely confined to those at the same or nearby work station. Workers are allowed two scheduled breaks a day—fifteen minutes approximately two and a half hours into their shift and thirty minutes for lunch after about five and a half hours.

Breaks, as well as starting and quitting times, are staggered down the line.

To the outsider, IBP's Slaughter lunchroom appears segregated by ethnicity and gender. Mexican immigrants occupy the northeast and southwest corners; Southeast Asians sit at a couple of tables in the middle of the room; an Anglo couple sits across from one another near the south wall. There are exceptions—an Anglo sitting with Hispanics here and there, an Asian and a Hispanic woman sitting at a center table. When only a few workers are on break, they quietly watch the color television that runs continuously from atop its perch at the southeast corner. When the lunchroom is crowded, most pay little attention to it. Instead, they visit among themselves, often sharpening their knives or rubbing down their steels.

This clustering is only partly explained by workers' preferences to socialize with others of the same sex or ethnic group. Those from the same station also congregate together. For example, workers from the cooler always sit at a table in the northeast corner—the part of the lunchroom closest to their station. In Slaughter, fifteen or twenty workers at a time go on break. Who one sits by is thus a *combination* of ethnic, gender, personal bonds *and* work station proximity. While those of the same ethnic group will sit with one another if they have the opportunity, ties developed on the line may take precedence.

In spite of tension between supervisors and line workers, between members of different ethnic groups, common workplace experiences help build shared concerns and identity that transcend ethnic boundaries. The community's general antipathy toward packinghouse workers serves to reinforce their common identity. All are subjected to the power and authority of large and indifferent corporations, who appear to value machinery and daily quotas over the welfare of their workers.

The Price of Work: Tales from Workers' Compensation Hearings

There is another interesting set of statistics that a person might have gathered in Packingtown—those of the various afflictions of the workers.

—Sinclair, *The Jungle*

On the killfloor—indeed throughout the plant—production quotas, driven by daily fluctuations in the fat-cattle and boxed-beef markets, take precedence over other considerations, including safety and equipment maintenance. And chain speed takes a heavy toll on the workers, not only in the high job turnover that plagues the industry, but on the very bodies and lives of line workers. Investigations by the Occupational Safety and Health Administration (OSHA) reveal that the packers go to great lengths to camouflage the incidence and prevalence of injuries. They say they are trying to reduce risk by ergonomics and better training, not to mention extensive safety equipment, but they are quick to point out that by its very nature meatpacking has always been—and always will be—dangerous. This may be, and it certainly will be as long as chains run fast, as long as cheap meat is prized above human welfare. But let us hear from the workers themselves. What follows are a few cases from monthly workers' compensation hearings I attended in Garden City in 1988 and 1989. They tell not only of the work and the risks that attend it but of the true price of our meat—the price in human suffering, in broken bodies and lives.

His wife drove him over from Dodge. He was in his mid-30s, did not finish high school in Vietnam, could not speak English, and had worked only in meatpacking since coming to the U.S. He wore sandals in spite of the morning chill, but kept on his heavy coat throughout his testimony.

His attorney and the company both brought their own interpreter: his was a young man, the company's was a woman in her mid-30s who someone said was a restaurateur. The lawyers argued over whose interpreter should be used during the hearing—the judge decided in Solomonic fashion that the claimant's interpreter be used in examination and the company's in cross-examination. When it came time to cross-examine, the company attorney chose to stick with the young man.

"Huong" was fired for allegedly failing to call in sick, though he says he did. He was a cow-sticker, and he got down off the stand to graphically demonstrate his job. He earned $256 a week. On November 18, 1987—some 26 months ago—he was knocked unconscious when a carcass fell on him. He was carried to the plant office by co-workers, then taken to Dr. X by his Hispanic supervisor—no interpreter accompanied them.

After examining him, the doctor—the one the company always uses—signed a card giving him two days off. When Huong asked for a week off (how I'm not sure), Dr. X got mad, tore up the slip, and sent him back to work immediately, prescribing "light duty" and one hour of physical therapy a day for five or six days. When he got back to work his light duty turned out to require lifting 60-pound meat trays. The next day he called in sick and was then "terminated" (fired). He has not worked since and still has problems with his ears, head, and chest.

Since the accident, Huong has seen several doctors, including a Vietnamese physician in town, all of whom have told him he cannot work. He has borrowed $5,000–6,000 from friends, but he still owes on doctor bills and has been refused treatment for failure to pay. He moves back and forth between Wichita and Dodge City, living with friends and borrowing money from them.

The judge concluded from testimony that Dr. X could not understand Huong, didn't want to be bothered, failed to note the extent and severity of his injuries, and just sent him back to work. He ordered 70 days of vocational rehabilitation. (Stull fieldnotes 1/16–1/20/89:6–8)

What was left unsaid, but understood by all, was that Dr. X is the "company doctor" for both the packing plants—his diagnoses have more to do with the company's welfare than those of the workers he sees.

John was 32 years old, an Anglo from the next county to the north. He graduated from high school in 1974 and received an associate of arts degree in auto mechanics in 1986. He had been a manual laborer before he began working for IBP in September 1987. He started as a knocker on "B" shift. His first injury came in January 1988.

"I was knocking—killing—cows. They run cattle through like a revolving chute, a restrainer, and the animals weren't being cleaned and the (stun) gun kept misfiring, so it bounced off most of the time. Instead of knocking them once, you had to knock them two or three times. It kicked my right arm back into the cow's head. ("As that occurred, did you have physical problems?") My back hurt real bad, on my shoulder blade, the top part of my back.

Attorney: Did you report that to anyone?

John: Yes, the foreman and then the nurse.

Attorney: As a result of notifying the foreman and the nurse was your job changed in any way?

John: Yes, ma'am. I went home the night my back was hurting and I saw the nurse, and then I came (in the next night) and then I had to cut ears and tails.

Attorney: What happened on January 12, 1988?

John: The trolley that lowered the cows, that the cows were hanging from, came loose at the back. It's like a roller, it's got a hook in it. The hook goes through the cow's leg. It weighs about 5 or 6 pounds, and it came down and hit me in the shoulder blades.

Attorney: Did you report the incident to anyone?

John: There was a foreman standing right beside me when it happened.

Attorney: Did you receive medical treatment as a result of that injury?

John: No.

Attorney: Did you request medical treatment?

John: No.

Attorney: Why didn't you request treatment?

John: I was scared.

Attorney: What do you mean you were scared?

John: When I went in the first time, and they sent me into the nurse, they just kept telling me that if I couldn't tell them what it was that happened to hurt my back I couldn't see the doctor. And I kept saying, "The guns aren't going off right." And they said that I had to be more specific, and I didn't know how to be more specific.

On February 2, John slipped and fell in a pool of frozen blood, landing on his buttocks and then his back. The next day he could not get out of bed. IBP did not at first provide medical treatment, so John went on his own. His doctor prescribed painkillers and nothing more. IBP subsequently sent him to the company doctor. He referred him to another physician for examination, who diagnosed a soft tissue problem and told John to go back to work. John did not feel able to go back to work and when he asked to see another doctor he was terminated. The date was February 15.

Attorney: Currently do you feel capable of employment?

John: No.

Attorney: Why not?

John: I can't do anything. My back hurts, right above the belt line. I have to change positions, lay down for a while, sit for a while. Sitting, laying, I change positions about 20–30 times per night, walking. I don't pick up anything, and just sometimes, heck, one time that I wanted to get up and I just, everything didn't work, and I just fell flat on my face. (Stull fieldnotes and audiotape transcriptions 8/14/88)

"Rock 'n Roll Ron" is Anglo, in his mid-20s, an on-again, off-again regular at Tom's. He has worked at Monfort for five months; before that he worked at National Beef in Liberal for two years. He was hitchhiking from Florida to California and stopped off in Liberal because he heard there were jobs. He applied at National and was hired the next day. He told them he would only work in Loadout, "I've never used a knife and don't know how." He's worked in Loadout ever since. He figured he'd work a couple of months, earn some money, then continue on to California—he hasn't made it yet.

Loadout works three eight-hour shifts, seven days a week—other crews work two shifts, five days a week. He likes Loadout, in part because it is safe, but he says that many guys bid out of Loadout to get "knife jobs" because the pay is better. It's the most dangerous and dirty jobs that pay the best; he says that people aren't that concerned about injuries, they want the money. He makes $6.75 an hour. When the Teamster's contract goes into effect in September, his pay will go to $7, but it really won't make any difference to him since it'll be eaten up in union dues.

The last time I'd seen him he was on crutches with a full leg brace. I asked him about it, and he said that in early June he was picking up a 100-pound box of chuck and the handles on the box gave way and fell on his knee, tearing ligaments and cartilage. It's his first injury in two and a half years in meatpacking. He expected to be put on workers' comp, but that's not what happened. "The company doctor wanted no part of it" and sent him instead to a bone specialist here in town, who recommended light duty. He said his light duty consisted mainly of sitting around drinking coffee from 8 to 4 every day. Lately, he's been nailing cardboard onto wooden slats that the boxes sit on in the trucks.

He goes off light duty on Monday and is anxious to get back to his old job, even though his leg is still not completely healed. But he is afraid of being fired. One reason he thinks he didn't get workers' comp and may get fired is because after his accident he "failed the piss test." The accident took place on a Friday on the "B" shift. Normally drug testing is done immediately after accidents, but because it happened on a weekend he was not tested till Monday—he tested positive for alcohol and drugs. The implication was that he would have tested clean had he been tested immediately, but I have my doubts.

He said there is a lot of drug use at the plant, much of it sold by supervisors: "If you want some coke, go to a supervisor." Many workers also use speed, in part to keep up with the line. Boxes weighing from 40 to 120 pounds come down the line every 10 seconds or so, sometimes even faster. You can't stop just because they are heavy and you're tired. "It gets you in great shape and makes an old man of ya real quick—both at the same time." (Stull fieldnotes 8/5/88:17–21)

Case 5 was a 40-year-old Anglo with severe pains from her shoulders to her fingertips. She must cross her arms and clench her fists to fight the pain. She found it hard, if not impossible, to work, to do housework, even to turn pages while reading. ["Do you read?" "Sometimes." "Do you turn pages?" "It hurts, that's why I said sometimes."]

She'd been a housewife till 1986 when she went to work at the packinghouse. She worked there till September 1987. At the time she was terminated she was making $359 a week. This was the first paying job she ever held. She was forced to go to work when a divorce left her with two boys, now 19 and 17, to support.

She started out in Slaughter on the "head table" cutting sinew off skulls. The heads go around the chain at about 6 per minute and she had to make 5–7 cuts per head. After she cut the sinew off, she put it in a bucket.

She began developing problems in her fingers and shoulders and as a result she was moved to "brains," where she took brains out of skulls, put them in a bucket, and when the bucket weighed about 30 pounds, she carried it to a different station and emptied it. Much of her job was to wash, weigh, and put the brains in a box. She also massaged the membrane that covers the brain, removing it—this involved the constant motion of her fingers.

The sinew cutting and the brain cleaning were part of the same process. There were two cutters—one Black, one Vietnamese. Also working with her were several women and a supervisor named "Rudolfo." At times she was the only person doing the brains, other times not.

The new job did little to alleviate the pain in her arms and shoulders, and she was often helped to lift her load by one of the men on the line. She calculated that when working on the brains, she lifted a 30-pound bucket every 5 minutes and performed approximately 1,800 squishing movements per hour with her hands in removing the membrane.

She complained of her pain to her supervisor. First she was sent to the company doctor, then to a local specialist, then back to the company doctor, then to a specialist in Wichita. This specialist had her taken off work, but the company then canceled her subsequent appointments with him, which meant she had to go back to work. They later sent her to a specialist in Denver. Ultimately she was terminated.

She still has the pain; she can't use her fingers at all now and keeps her hands clenched because it hurts to open them. She stays at home, where she does only minimal housework. Her new husband, whom she met at work, still works for the company. He and her boys do most of the cooking and cleaning.

The company position is that her pain is not related to work but is caused by an underlying emotional problem. Their attorney questioned her emotional state, attacked her personality, and tried to suggest that divorce was the cause of her problem. The judge intervened and stopped this line of questioning. (Stull fieldnotes 8/14/88:13–15)

The pathos in this case and many others like it shows in the testimony of a Hispanic man against another employer later the same day: "Only thing I know is labor. I can't go back to being a lugger. I lugged beef for 9 years. That's the only thing I really know" (Stull fieldnotes 8/14/88:19).

Conclusion

Upton Sinclair provided a voice to the great masses of immigrants who had come to America yearning to be free and comfortable and who had found instead the wage slavery and misery of mill, factory, sweatshop, and slum. Jacob Riis had shown *How the Other Half Lives* in 1890; Sinclair showed how more than the other half worked in 1905—in conditions of physical danger, insecurity, fear, exploitation, corruption, and filth.

—Ronald Gottesman, Introduction to *The Jungle*

Sadly, Gottesman's words ring no less true for meatpacking workers of his own day than for those of Sinclair's—the killfloor is still a jungle. After all, the Beef Trust has merely been replaced by the "Big Three." Concentration and vertical integration are worse now than in 1890, when the packers' excesses contributed to the passage of the Sherman Antitrust Act.

The public has not changed all that much either. It is still much easier to hit them in the stomach than in the heart. Thanks in large measure to *The Jungle*, the Pure Food and Drug Act and the Meat Inspection Act, both passed in 1906, soon after the book's publication, have (until the recent revelations on "Prime Time Live") dispelled serious doubts about what might be lurking in our burgers. Today we are more likely to worry about global emissions of methane, animal rights, and cholesterol, while the packers and producers keep an uneasy eye on the steady decline in Americans' consumption of red meat as they try to come up with ever leaner cuts of meat "to fit into today's balanced diet."

We wince and, perhaps for a moment or two, our hearts go out to packing-plant line workers and their families when we read of the deaths of three maintenance workers overcome by toxic fumes in a blood-collection tank at the National Beef Packing plant in Liberal, Kansas (*Garden City Telegram* 1991), or the twenty-five who died in the fire at the Imperial Food Products chicken plant in Hamlet, North Carolina, later the same year (Tabor 1991). But all too soon, our hearts once again give way to our stomachs, and if we think of meat processing at all, it is to worry about hormone-laced steaks or salmonella-infected chicken.

But meat-processing workers are the miner's canary for us all. Their unions have been busted, their wages slashed. And their work is the most dangerous—in 1988 the probability of injury was .39 in meatpacking, compared to .13 in manufacturing overall (U.S. Department of Labor 1989). We now know "butcher's wrist" as carpal tunnel syndrome, one of the more common and debilitating forms of cumulative trauma disorder (CTD). CTDs make up a quarter of the injuries in meatpacking (Austin 1988). In 1988, they accounted for 48 percent of *all* occupational illnesses—up 30 percent since 1981—with an estimated cost of $27 billion a year in medical bills and lost time on the job. But record OSHA fines have not slowed the chains in packing plants (*U.S. News & World Report* 1990): The price of cattle has been up, the demand for beef down. So are the profit margins. Workers are still cheap—and expendable. Despite health and environmental concerns, price remains the major reason consumers buy less beef. Until we are willing to pay more for our meat—and until we demand fair wages and decent working conditions for meatpacking workers—the jungle will remain in our midst.

> The peculiar bitterness of all this was that Jurgis saw so plainly the meaning of it. In the beginning he had been fresh and strong . . . but now he was second-hand, a damaged article, so to speak, and they did not want him. They had got the best out of him—they had worn him out, with their speeding-up and their carelessness, and now they had thrown him away! And Jurgis would make the acquaintance of others of these unemployed men and find that they had all had the same experience. (Sinclair 1985:149)

Acknowledgments

What I have learned about beefpacking—its work and its workers—is conditioned by how I learned it, by who has collaborated with me, and who has not. In this description of work and its consequences, the voices are at times mine, at others those of my native teachers and collaborators. I am indebted to Gale Seibert, my instructor in Meat and Carcass Evaluation at Garden City Community College, my classmates, and the many beefpacking workers who patiently tried to instruct me in the ways of cattle, meat, and men. I have tried to render faithfully what I saw, heard, and was told, but these many teachers bear no responsibility for my errors or interpretations. I also wish to acknowledge the Ford Foundation's Changing Relations Project, the General Research Fund of the University of Kansas, and a sabbatical leave in providing the necessary funding and time to conduct my fieldwork. Michael Broadway, Janet Benson, and Carol Warren read drafts of this chapter and provided me with helpful comments. Finally, I am grateful to MEAT&POULTRY Magazine for kindly providing pictures of Slaughter workers and to Laura Kriegstrom Poracsky for transforming my arcane sketching into a real map.

Notes

1. Beef carcass quality grade (QG) is determined by degree of marbling (intramuscular fat) and maturity. Color, texture, and firmness of lean meat in the ribeye at the twelfth rib are considered in assigning one of eight USDA quality grades. Yield grade (YG) measures cutability—the percentage of boneless, closely trimmed retail cuts from the round, rib, loin, and chuck. Yield grades range from 1.0 (54.6 percent) to 5.9 (43.3 percent) (Boggs and Merkel 1984). USDA graders assign both quality and yield grades to each carcass by sight. Quality grade determines the value of the carcass—a Choice carcass brings about $8 more per hundredweight than one graded Select. Graders have about seven seconds to assign both a QG and YG to each carcass (Seibert 1989).

2. The information presented in the question-and-answer period after the tour is from several sessions over more than a year (Stull fieldnotes 6/17/88, 7/10/88, 7/22/88, 5/6/89). Although it did not come in a single session, or in such a flowing narrative, most is from the man in the snakeskin boots. Supervisors, line workers, and industry observers at times dispute some of these facts, and the conclusions drawn from them.

3. The job titles used in this description combine IBP line worker terminology and my own. Whenever I know the proper IBP term, I use it; when I don't, I make one up, using various sources as guides. The general rule of thumb appears to be to name the job after the activity (e.g., dropping heads). Terminology varies somewhat from plant to plant. In the journey from knocker to cooler, not all jobs are presented—space and reader interest prohibit a complete description. Photographs of work on the killfloor presented in this chapter were *not* taken at an IBP plant. The photos are, in fact, several years old and do not necessarily represent the present state of technology in modern beefpacking plants. But given the general ban on photographs of their installations imposed by IBP and other major packers, these prints do convey a good sense of what the work looks like.

4. I was never able to get officials to say how much water is actually used at the Finney County plant, but Fund and Clement (1982:53) claim IBP uses 400 gallons of rinse water per animal per day. If this figure is correct it means that with a daily slaughter capacity of 6,000 head, IBP uses as much as 2.4 million gallons of water a day, six days a week! This estimate is probably conservative, since company officials say they use 600–650 gallons per head at their Lexington, Nebraska, plant, which opened in November 1990.

Bibliography

Austin, Lisa. 1988. "Riskiest Job in Kansas Escapes Close Scrutiny." *Wichita Eagle-Beacon*, December 4.

Barrett, James R. 1990. *Work and Community in the Jungle: Chicago's Packinghouse Workers, 1894–1922*. Urbana: University of Illinois Press.

Birchall, Annabelle. 1990. "Kinder Ways to Kill." *New Scientist*, May 19, pp. 44–49.

Boggs, Donald L., and Robert A. Merkel. 1984. *Live Animal Carcass Evaluation and Selection Manual*. 2nd ed. Dubuque, Iowa: Kendall/Hunt.

Broadway, Michael J. 1990. "Recent Changes in the Structure and Location of the U.S. Meatpacking Industry." *Geography* 75(1):76–79.

Broadway, Michael J., and Donald D. Stull. 1991. "Rural Industrialization: The Example of Garden City, Kansas." *Kansas Business Review* 14(4):1–9.

Carnes, Richard B. 1984. "Meatpacking and Prepared Meats Industry: Above-Average Productivity Gains. *Monthly Labor Review*, April, pp. 37–42.

Center for Rural Affairs. 1990. *Competition in the Livestock Market, Report of a Task Force*. Walthill, Neb.: Center for Rural Affairs.

Fund, Mary, and Elise W. Clement. 1982. *Distribution of Land and Water Ownership in Southwest Kansas*. Whiting: Kansas Rural Center.

Garden City Telegram. 1991. "Three Workers Found Dead at Liberal's National Beef Packing." *Garden City Telegram*, June 10.

Gottesman, Ronald. 1985. "Introduction." In Upton Sinclair, *The Jungle*, pp. vii–xxxii. New York: Penguin.

Green, Hardy. 1990. *On Strike at Hormel: The Struggle for a Democratic Labor Movement*. Philadelphia: Temple University Press.

McGraw, Mike. 1991. "A Case of 'Very Vested Interest.'" *Kansas City Star*, December 10.

McGraw, Mike, and Jeff Taylor. 1991. "Deadly Meat: Poor Inspection Exposes Public to Health Risks." *Kansas City Star*, December 10.

Mooney, Rick. 1989. "The Strong Arm of Earth First." *Beef Today* 5(7):12–13.

NCA Beef Industry Concentration/Integration Task Force. 1989. *Beef in a Competitive World*. Englewood, Colo.: National Cattlemen's Association.

Personick, Martin E., and Katherine Taylor-Shirley. 1989. "Profiles in Safety and Health: Occupational Hazards of Meatpacking." *Monthly Labor Review*, January, pp. 3–9.

Remy, Dorothy, and Larry Sawers. 1984. "Economic Stagnation and Discrimination." In *My Troubles Are Going to Have Trouble with Me: Everyday Trials and Triumphs of Women Workers*, edited by Karen B. Sacks and Dorothy Remy, pp. 95–112. New Brunswick, N.J.: Rutgers University Press.

Seibert, Gale. 1989. Class Lecture for Meat and Carcass Evaluation, Garden City Community College, January 31.

Sinclair, Upton. 1985. *The Jungle*. New York: Penguin, 1985 (first published in 1906).

Skaggs, Jimmy M. 1986. *Prime Cut: Livestock Raising and Meatpacking in the United States, 1607–1983*. College Station: Texas A&M University Press.

Slayton, Robert A. 1986. *Back of the Yards: The Making of a Local Democracy.* Chicago: University of Chicago Press.

Stull, Donald D., and Michael J. Broadway. 1990. "The Effects of Restructuring on Beefpacking in Kansas." *Kansas Business Review* 14(1):10–16.

Stull, Donald D., Michael J. Broadway, and Ken C. Erickson. 1992. "The Price of a Good Steak: Beef Packing and Its Consequences for Garden City, Kansas." In *Structuring Diversity: Ethnographic Perspectives on the New Immigration*, edited by Louise Lamphere, pp. 35–64. Chicago: University of Chicago Press.

Tabor, Mary B.W. 1991. "Poultry Plant Fire Churns Emotions over Job Both Hated and Appreciated." *New York Times*, September 6.

Thompson, William E. 1983. "Hanging Tongues: A Sociological Encounter with the Assembly Line." *Qualitative Sociology* 6:215–237.

U.S. News & World Report. 1990. "On-the-Job Straining: Repetitive Motion Is the Information Age's Hottest Hazard." *U.S. News & World Report*, May 21, pp. 51, 53.

U.S. Department of Labor, Bureau of Labor Statistics. 1989. *Occupational Injuries and Illnesses in the United States by Industry.* Washington, D.C.: Government Printing Office.

Wood, Charles L. 1980. *The Kansas Beef Industry.* Lawrence: Regents Press of Kansas.

4   Guys in White Hats: Short-Term Participant Observation among Beef-Processing Workers and Managers

Ken C. Erickson

There were five plate boners on the line, and the Hispanic guy across the conveyor from me seemed pretty new at the job. He had a stack of four or five untrimmed plates teetering on the cutting board next to him, the cutting board that should have been the work station of another plate boner, but we were running short crewed. Short crewing was the usual state of affairs on this new and brightly lit packinghouse processing floor. He also had a big stack of ribs next to him, a two-foot-high pile of uncleaned bones; he had boned the meat off them but had not finished trimming the meat from between the ribs. And Robert, the tall plate boner working next to me, kept hollering "Joe! Pull, Joe!"[1]

"Look at that guy." Robert leaned down and shouted above the din of saws and conveyors, pointing at Joe and his stack of untrimmed ribs. "They just put him on there and already he's having to pull count. He's all stacked up. That's why they lose people."

I nodded up at Robert, who was easily a head taller than me, and who was breezing through a plate every forty seconds or so, meat hook in his left hand, knife in his right, sharpening steel and ceramic rod hanging from one of the lightweight chains we wore as equipment belts. I glanced at Joe across the conveyor and watched him "steeling" his knife on his steel, but he couldn't finish to his satisfaction, and I saw him mouth an epithet as he reached with his meat hook to pull in another plate that was about to move by him on the clattering plastic scales of the conveyor.

I finished up the last bit of trimming between the ribs of a plate and held the bones over my head to push them onto the overhead

78

conveyor. I had been on the line for about two hours, and I had learned the basic moves in boning the plate, but my arm and wrist were already sore. Stretching to reach over my head felt good, though I had to stand on my tiptoes and flick the bones onto the conveyor with slippery, greasy-gloved hands. I yelled at Robert, whose earplugs dangled next to his shoulder-length brown hair, which was curled up in the obligatory hairnet. "What did you do before you started working here?"

"Worked in a pork plant. Ran the computer in the cooler."

"You like this better?"

"Hell no. But I just bought a house, and I have a wife and a kid at home. I want to be a greyhat. Then I can get off this line!"

Greyhats are trainers, but Dupaco, the Norfolk, Nebraska, packing plant that had asked me to look into its new-hire training efforts, was running a turnover rate that was so high they could not afford to take anyone off the line to do training.[2] My own trainer was a man whose arm was in a sling. He was the only greyhat I saw doing any training.

After about three hours of working next to my mentor, I was pulling half count. Joe, the Hispanic plate boner down the line from me, was stacking up my extras to do later, but smiling at me and banging his hook on his cutting table when I'd finish boning a plate and reached out with my hook to pull another off the conveyor.

A plate is a curved quadrangle of beef, about the size of a suitcase, twenty centimeters thick—the distal part of the dorsal side of usually seven ribs, either left or right, from just below the sternum to the last rib. It's covered by a tough skin, or "skirt." By the time it gets to our station on the processing line, a worker standing next to the "break line" where the carcass is broken into primal cuts makes a cut with an electric saw through the four largest, most proximal rib bones, along a line halfway down the plate, but stopping before the fifth bone. These four bones are the "short ribs."

I had to learn how to make a cut up along the fifth rib, setting the four short ribs apart from the others, then stand the plate up, held steady with the meat hook in my left hand. Sitting on its sternal side on my cutting board, I leaned the plate away from me and worked the knife up from the end of the saw cut, but like the saw cut in the middle of the plate, up but not through the skirt. I extracted the steadying hook, and the plate thumped onto the white plastic cutting board, short ribs still attached. Next, I hooked the corner of the short rib where I started the cut and pushed with the butt of my right hand, still holding the knife, against the oppo-

Boning and trimming subprimal cuts of beef on the boning line. (Photograph courtesy of MEAT&POULTRY Magazine)

site corner of the plate. I yanked with my left hook-holding hand in and away, hooking the already sawn and now sliced short rib, pulled and pried down, over the edge of the greasy plastic cutting table, and ripped the short rib from the back skirt of the plate. The short rib came away from the plate with a tearing sound, more imagined than audible through the plastic earplugs, and above the clatter of hooks and knives, conveyors, and saws.

Robert and I worked a while in silence, while Joe tried to catch up on his work. The line's supervisor, in his yellow hardhat, took an empty station across from Joe and started in on the stack of plates that Joe had been accumulating.

I was in the middle of working the short ribs off a particularly cold (and therefore tough to cut) plate when my hook slipped out, the short rib fell on my foot, rolled off the nonslip footing, and slid a little way on the tile floor. What should I do? Robert, my mentor, glanced over between long, smooth, arcing cuts, his knife feeling along the rib line, peeling meat and skirt cleanly away from bone. With his ceramic sharpener and superior knife-sharpening skills, he avoided some of the trauma to his hands felt by new workers.

He smiled as I tried to retrieve the short rib from the floor, which put me about ten feet away from Robert, too far for verbal communication.

Robert hollered something I couldn't really hear and indicated the metal sink behind him. "Just rinse it," he seemed to be saying. I did, and Robert motioned for me to toss the short ribs back on the conveyor.

By that time, I was glad that I wore a sweatshirt—I could see my breath in the refrigerated atmosphere of the "fab" floor. I tried to flex my hands between plates, remembering the story that the company safety director had told me during the ride to Norfolk from the Omaha airport.

Larry, the safety director, was a career packer, fairly close to retirement, a big man who had worked a good many years on the processing lines in Dupaco's pork plants in Iowa. On the ride from the Omaha airport to the Nebraska plant where I was to look into new-hire training, he told another consultant and myself about a processing worker's responsibility for his own job safety.

"There was a clod puller, new on the job, who came in and said he had a problem with his hand. Clod pullers don't work at a cutting table, but cut meat on foot, working on clods that hang from a moving chain. I asked him: 'Have you done the exercises that we told you to do, at night, for your hand? And have you read the little book that we gave you?' And the fellow says 'Yes.' Maybe he wasn't telling the truth, anyway. So I asked him, I says, 'When you go walk to the next piece, do you hang up your hook after each time? On the loop on your belt? That is what it is there for. And do you flex your hand while you walk back to the next one?' and he says, 'No.'"

"See, we don't hand out Pampers here" Larry said. "And we don't change 'em for 'em either. You have to make it on your own."

I didn't want to be among those workers needing disposable diapers, and thanks to Robert, Joe, and our yellowhat helping me with my workload, I was sometimes able to flex both hands between plates. But the cutting was tough going. There was more to boning a plate than just taking off the short ribs, and after learning how to make the cuts on pieces of meat from the left side of the animal, along came plates from the right side, and all my cuts had to be made in reverse. The geography of the plate was puzzling, and I interrupted Robert a lot in the early going, asking for directions. Had I been a new immigrant in Garden City, Kansas, and not an English speaker, I would have understood Robert's answer just as well—he didn't talk, he demonstrated with his knife, pointing out the lines of the cuts with his knife, and then, with his hook steadying the cold slab of beef, he made quick, precise cuts that revealed clean, white rib bones. But making the right cuts was not the most difficult part of the job.

After the short ribs had fallen on the floor and had been re-trieved, I found the knife more and more difficult to push through the meat. Though it started the day with a well-honed edge pro-vided by the man who trained our little group of new hires, it was no longer cutting smoothly. I tried "steeling" the knife, carefully monitoring the angle of the blade on the steel, doing my best to imitate Robert's light touch and smooth stroke. The knife still felt dull; the handle was transmitting a lot of pressure to my fingers and wrist as I cut along the rib line through the plate meat.

Robert noticed my trouble. "Lemme see your knife a second." He lifted his ceramic rod from his side—new workers are not given ceramics, and are told not to buy them "until you know if you're going to stick around or not." He quickly worked the blade back and forth along the ceramic. Then he switched to his steel. My knife came back to me with a sharp, centered edge, and my hand appreciated the lowered stress as I worked it through the meat along another set of ribs.

All together, two people had quit or were absent out of the seven or eight who should have been working on our end of the rib line. The supervisor, still helping Joe, began to bone plates furi-ously, while Joe and another worker yelled and banged their meat hooks on their cutting boards, a helmeted cheering section. We are doing about 200 head an hour, shorthanded. The supervisor's bar-room brag that he could make all fourteen cuts on a plate in twelve seconds seemed to have been a reality, as his knife fairly flew through the meat.

After another hour of trying to keep up with Joe, Robert, the yellowhat, and the other two athletic plate boners, my arm and shoulder began to feel heavy and weak. I was no longer chilly in my sweatshirt. Underneath the rubber apron, the chain-mail pro-tective apron, and the white frock, I was sweating. As the knife began to get dull again, the handle slipped in my grip, I scraped my plastic wrist guard and dropped the knife on the nonslip foot-ing. As I picked it up I noticed that the meat had stopped coming down the line. I looked over my shoulder and saw Tam, the Tai-Dam chuckboner, ascending the ladder to the catwalk behind our line.[3] He was waving at me to come to lunch. The break line, where primal cuts are taken off the carcasses after a twenty-four-hour stay in the cooler, and just to the right of Robert, was empty—no one at the hand-operated saws, no carcasses swinging slowly along the chain. The break line had stopped for lunch, and we were next in line to break, too.

Besides a fifteen-minute morning break, the half-hour lunch break is the only time a worker has to exchange a dull or pitted knife, use the restroom, visit the drinking fountain, or just pause for a few minutes to relax. One refugee packinghouse worker in Garden City, whose brother was soon to arrive from Vietnam, explained to me why he did not want his family working in the packinghouse, and in so doing he retold what must be one of the most common tales of the processing floor (see also Stull et al. 1990).

"When I first started on the line, I had to go to the bathroom, but the supervisor wouldn't let me off the line. My supervisor wouldn't listen to me. And if you leave the line they fire you. So I had to, excuse me, pee my pants. But after about a year I learned something. And I had to go to the bathroom, and the supervisor wouldn't let me, and so I walked over to the bulletin board, and I showed him the sign, you can't discriminate. And I told him if he wanted to we could go talk about it with the shift supervisor. And he let me go, 'cause I knew something, then. I don't want my brother treated like that, just because he don't speak English." As an English-speaking consultant at Dupaco, I had the option of quitting early, but at noon, I followed Robert up the slip-proof, green plastic stairs, onto the catwalk, and up to the lunchroom.

Upstairs in the hallway I stood in line at the door of the laundry and drew off greasy cotton gloves to trade them in for clean ones. I left my hardhat and my grimy frock on and walked into the men's locker room to get my sack lunch from my locker. I stepped gingerly in the narrow isle, moving sideways, stepping over the long bench that ran the length of the row of lockers to get around two Mexican workers who were getting their lunches. It was cramped, but brightly lit and clean. I kept the protective Kevlar glove on my right hand and unstrapped the stainless-steel mesh left-hand glove from the plastic wrist guard. I was hot, sweating even after I took off the chain mail and the yellow rubber apron. My hand was a bit numb, fingers and palm swollen; my left middle finger had a sore area where the meat hook hit it.

My locker was next to Steve's, one of the two newly hired beef packers I had trained with the day before. Steve was struggling with his rubber apron.

"The damn thing's bass-ackwards," he said, untangling his arms from the criss-crossed straps that held the heavy apron in place under the white frock. I noticed that Steve wasn't wearing any chain mail under his apron.

"Where are you working today, Steve? I didn't see you after

they sent me over to bone plates." I was trying to get my combination lock opened, while the *Mejicanos* next to me were whooping it up in Spanish. They had more energy than I did, and I had only started boning plates an hour before the morning break.

"They put me on a squeegee, cleanin' floors."

I kidded him about his good luck, getting assigned to a light-duty job. Although it pays less, after an employee has passed the low-wage probationary period, it is something that packers in the processing section often seek out, especially after they have been hurt on the job. A worker who has been injured will often come to work with a doctor's recommendation to engage only in light-duty work. If none is available, the employee is sent home. The plant has no legal obligation to keep an injured worker on the job. They sometimes try to find a light-duty job for a valued worker, but they might not do so if a qualified new hire is available.

The lunchroom was barely large enough to hold all the workers. The floor was cement, one wall lined with vending machines selling canned stew, snack cakes, candy, and soft drinks. Hispanics, some of the high-spirited workers I had seen in the men's locker room, grouped themselves near the vending machines. They filled about one table—significantly fewer than in the plants in Garden City—and were speaking Spanish. Tai-Dam and Lao workers claimed the space in one corner, the six or seven of them taking up about three-quarters of a table and sharing communal plastic containers of rice and black pieces of dry, jerked backstrap meat.

I notice that Tam was sitting away from the Asian group, next to an Anglo chuckboner with several United Food and Commercial Worker's union stickers on his hat. Like Tam, most people seem to be sitting with their work groups. I put my sack lunch down next to Tam and found a place in line in front of one of the soft-drink machines, remembering how Larry had made a big point of the low prices at the vending machines. "The boss, he decided we weren't in the soda pop business. We're in the beef business, so he keeps the price low." We three new hires nodded our approval. But while I noticed one of my fellow new hires sitting down to a lunch of vending-machine Dinty Moore beef stew, the Lao and Tai-Dam meat packers did not frequent the vending machines. They were intently working their way through their large plastic container of rice. When I came back with my soft drink, they recognized me from a previous Friday night visit to one of their homes, and without a word they pushed a small plastic sandwich bag full of jerked backstrap meat across the table in my direction.

Two weeks before, on a Friday afternoon after my first visit to the Dupaco processing plant, I met Somphet, a Lao meat cutter who had agreed to my request to visit him at his apartment after work. I had spent Friday afternoon tabulating daily absence data from Gwen's computer files in the personnel office and had taken the company car I had been given to Somphet's apartment. The apartment was almost entirely empty, without a stick of furniture except a kitchen table and chairs. On a blanket on the floor of the living room was Dinh Dung, a Vietnamese man I had seen in the lunchroom earlier that day, the only Vietnamese in the plant. Somphet suggested we go buy a six-pack of beer. Dung said he was too tired to go with us. I drove Somphet to the store, where he and the clerk had made familiar and friendly conversation while I picked up the tab. "People are friendly here. They smile and say hello on the street. I like the small town," said Somphet.

On the way back to his apartment, Somphet suddenly asked, "You want to meet some other Lao people?" I must have passed some kind of test. I said yes, and Somphet directed me to turn the car around, and we drove to another apartment a few blocks from his own.

Here was a Lao home on the range in northeast Nebraska. The familiar green-patterned plastic matting was spread on the living-room floor, the Lao functional equivalent of the obligatory coffee table that appears in Vietnamese living rooms. In one corner was a folded *bau cua* mat—a Vietnamese gambling game used with three special dice with symbols of *bau* (a gourd) and *cua* (a crab) among four others, matched by symbols on the mat on which players lay their money. A woman and a man were playing cards, seated on the floor by the *bau cua* mat. They barely looked up from their game while I removed my shoes and settled into a place at the edge of the mat.

There was another woman in a *sarong* in the kitchen, a young man asleep on a mattress in another corner, and another man chopping up and blending what looked—and smelled—like marijuana and cigarette tobacco on a small kitchen cutting board with a beef packer's knife.

The man with the knife looked up at Somphet and then at me, and got into a heated discussion with Somphet, apparently about my presence in the house. I assured Somphet that I was not offended by the weed and that I wasn't a cop. The young man loaded the bong with a single very small bowl of the mixture and smoked it in one puff.

The woman playing cards turned out to be related to a Lao

man from Garden City. We discussed this fact; it seemed to put the room at ease. I explained why I was in Norfolk, and that I worked with refugees in Garden City, but I was at Dupaco to help with training ideas. She told me about problems in the plant: that most people were quitting or getting fired or laid off. Her boy friend (the fellow with the bong) was going to quit. And the other man in the house, the one asleep in the corner, just got fired. The plant requires a doctor's slip for any absence, she said. "But Lao people don't want to go to a doctor. We have our own medicine. We like it better. Just stay home, and get better."

After a few moments, and after being offered two steamed buns to go with the beer, Tam came in. Tam was the Asian man I had seen boning chucks from my first day's observation post on the catwalk above the processing floor, the man that the maintenance supervisor had said was as good a chuckboner as I'd find. Tam used to work for Dupaco in Iowa and had moved to Norfolk when the plant in Iowa shut down. Tam seemed to be the management "contact" to the plant's Asian staff. He speaks Lao, but he is Tai-Dam. The talk about bad working conditions slacked off when he arrived. But then Tam started complaining about the company and then everyone in the room began to air their complaints: the familiar litany of high line speed, write-ups for no doctor's slip, and short crewing.

So during my next visit to the plant, two weeks later, the Lao workers in the lunchroom didn't include the woman's boy friend or the man asleep in the corner who I had seen at the apartment. The Lao workers' complaints were not specific to Asian workers; they were shared by other workers in the new plant. Seated across from Tam was an Anglo woman who worked on the hamburger line. The hamburger line was the fifth of the five "lines" in the Dupaco fabrication floor. IBP in Garden City, where fabrication is called "processing," has twelve lines. At both IBP and Dupaco, people who can't or won't do heavier boning jobs are often placed on the hamburger line. There, while the work is not as heavy, the risk of carpal tunnel syndrome may be even higher because workers use motorized "round" knives, whose vibrating handles are said to be more injurious than the knives the boners use (UFCW 1988).

I introduced myself to the woman and explained that the company had brought me in to come up with some ideas to lower worker turnover. (I didn't bother explaining that this was a negotiated role—at first they wanted me to "find them some Vietnamese.") Between bites on a sack-lunch sandwich, she was quite willing to tell me what she thought of the plant.

"This place is pretty screwed up. And they won't listen to me. I worked in a plant in Iowa, before, but I quit, because there was too much crap getting into the hamburger, and they wouldn't do nothing about it. This place is the same way. You want to do a good job, but they won't let you. Line runs too fast." She voiced the same concerns about line speeds and short crewing that I had heard from the Asian workers.

Studying Up and Studying Down: Packinghouse Entrée

My working on the line for Dupaco in Nebraska came about as a result of a call from a labor recruiter. It was June 1988, and I was a practicing anthropologist—the administrator in charge of refugee services at the Kansas Department of Social and Rehabilitation Services (Erickson 1990). My job was to write and administer federal grants for social services and English-language training for refugees. I had already worked closely with Michael Broadway, Don Stull, and Janet Benson (other contributors to this volume) in evaluating and designing social service programs for refugees. When Don Stull learned that we might all work together as part of the national Changing Relations Project (with Arthur Campa's, José Cintron's, and Mark Grey's invaluable help), I negotiated with my boss to spend part of my time in research. It was after the project began that I received an interesting phone call, a call that provided access to both management and workers in the packinghouse in Nebraska.

"Can you help us find some Vietnamese?" The man on the phone had been an employment director at one of the packing plants in southwest Kansas and now he was a labor recruiter. "They are just starting up, there in Norfolk. They've had Vietnamese work for them at their other plants. Maybe you know some Vietnamese who'd like to move up there. It's a good company, but they're just short of workers."

I declined to become a body hunter, but later convinced the owner of the chain of Iowa and Nebraska plants that I should come up to the Norfolk facility, visit with workers and management, and make some recommendations on staff training that might lower the plant's high turnover rate. (All new beefpacking plants seem to suffer from very high turnover—8 to 10 percent weekly is not unheard of). The entry to the processing plant provided an opportunity to work on the line, a chance to conduct, for a short while, the participant observation on the processing floor that had been denied our research team in Garden City (see Stull et al. 1990; Stull, Chapter 3 in this volume).

The short-term participant observation in the Dupaco plant

filled in details about work on the processing floor that were not directly available to us in Garden City. My experience, however brief, "running a knife" in a Nebraska plant helped the team of Changing Relations Project researchers understand what any new plant worker must go through in starting a new job at the packing plant. As Thompson (1983) has shown from his experience "hanging tongues" in the slaughter side of a beef plant, interviews with plant personnel are no substitute for direct experience with packinghouse work. They do not provide the intimate contact with sore muscles and demanding production schedules that participant observation in the workplace offers.

In addition to a close-up view of the processing floor, the Nebraska fieldwork provided a better understanding of turnover. In Garden City, the "man in the snakeskin boots" wouldn't talk about staff retention (Stull, Chapter 3 in this volume). At Dupaco, however, the corporate personnel manager was spending weeks at a time interviewing new hires. He told me he did not enjoy spending so much time away from his home and family in Omaha. Plant and corporate managers at Dupaco were bothered by their turnover problem, in contrast to Dupaco's owner, who saw the issue as a recruiting problem. Access to the processing floor in Nebraska highlighted the hierarchical nature of the workplace noted by the other researchers in Garden City. But it also brought to light a supervisor's need to help line workers pull count—to be collaborative and supportive in the face of demanding line speeds. Dupaco helped the research team avoid a monolithic view of plant supervisors and managers.

The work in Nebraska was different, in some ways, from shop-floor work that might have been conducted in Garden City. First, the ethnic mix of the community was different. While I met new-arrival Hispanics in the hallway outside the personnel office at Dupaco, they were from Grand Island, Nebraska, and were just looking for work at Dupaco. Norfolk did not have the long-standing Hispanic community that was present in Garden City. Instead, it had a growing Black community, thanks to the labor-recruiting efforts of IBP's pork plant located just south of Norfolk in the small town of Madison. Norfolk had a small but growing population of Hispanics drawn from other packinghouse towns in Nebraska, like Grand Island.

The plant's records showed that 84 percent of the workforce was "Caucasian," 5 percent was Spanish surnamed, 5 percent American Indian, 4 percent Asian/Pacific Islander, and 2 percent Black (using the terms employed by the plant's personnel department).

Of Dupaco's 416 processing employees in June 1988, only 65 were non-Anglo. If Dupaco wanted to be like IBP or Monfort in Garden City, then the company engineer's perception of the company's need becomes understandable. He put it rather bluntly: "We need to get us a minority group in here."[4]

While the plant did not have the rich ethnic mixture present in Garden City, it had a handful of Lao and Tai-Dam workers who had been with the company's defunct Iowa plant, and the company was seeking more Asian workers. "They come to us, they show up, they stay with us, they work hard and we know we can rely on them" said the company's personnel manager. I had asked him why he wanted Vietnamese workers. It turned out that one of the company's plants, in Omaha, had a high Vietnamese population, and, in the company's eyes, fairly low staff turnover.

IBP in Garden City has the same interest in Asian workers, and it demonstrated its continued interest in this labor source (see especially Benson 1992) by keeping one Lao and one Vietnamese personnel specialist on the payroll at their corporate offices. These men were often found visiting in the Vietnamese and Lao trailer houses in Garden City, making friendly visits to the homes of processing workers, listening to worker concerns, and sometimes working to resolve issues that workers had with the company. During labor shortages, they joined other company personnel department staff and traveled the United States as labor recruiters.

The Norfolk plant was different in two other respects: It was a "start-up," and it was a union shop. The stresses that IBP placed on Garden City when it opened its second shift in 1981 is the stuff of Kansas legends. New workers in Garden City were living in tents at the highway rest area on the western edge of town. People in Garden City still talk about "planeloads" of new Vietnamese workers, and while there appears to be no evidence that IBP actually flew in Vietnamese workers, start-up was a peak time for new-worker immigration to the community. The IBP that was operating during the time of the Changing Relations study was much more stable, with monthly turnover running near 7 percent. At Dupaco, weekly turnover was much higher. (Curtis, the plant manager at Dupaco, had been in a management position with IBP in Garden City during its start-up; while he never said exactly what his position was, he did say that he knew what start-ups were like, and that they were always rough going.)

DJ, the corporate engineer at Dupaco, had filled me in earlier on the plant's turnover rate. "The time clerk keeps the figures for me on the PC," he told me. "I can look at them daily. I took a five-week average. I show an average of 10.2 percent per week. The last week of April it was 11.7. Then in May, 9.8, 11.8, 11.8 and 8.0, IBP is about 6 percent per month in Madison." This means that out of the approximately 416 employees at Dupaco, nearly 42 workers were leaving (or getting fired) each week.

Second, Dupaco was a union shop. The slaughter side of the plant had been union before it was purchased by Dupaco, and the company had told the local business community that fabrication would not be a union shop. But the United Food and Commercial Workers Union (UFCW) started early to organize the fabrication side of the Norfolk plant. Some former UFCW members and shop stewards had moved to the Norfolk plant from the old Iowa facility, and the union had enough members who had "signed the card" to challenge the company for a contract. Dupaco agreed without calling for a vote because it was clear that the union would win anyway.

IBP, in contrast, had staunchly resisted unionization efforts in Garden City. In an interview with a UFCW official at union headquarters in Washington, D.C., I was told that the end of the union's campaign in Garden City was not due to a lack of new-immigrant union members but to internal union politics. By November 1988, UFCW was said to be six members away from having enough people to vote for a separate local for Garden City, and one Vietnamese labor organizer told me he believed that "most" Vietnamese had been willing to sign the card. The UFCW brought two Vietnamese labor organizers into Garden City, one from a packinghouse and one from a food-processing plant, both in Nebraska. And they hired a former IBP packer who had injured his hand. Along with an organizer from their national headquarters and a Hispanic organizer, UFCW, at least for a time, made a serious effort to organize IBP. In response, IBP brought in Anglo and Southeast Asian personnel and employment division staff from plants throughout the United States to make home visits and talk to employees in group meetings at the plant. For a while, both IBP and UFCW Lao and Vietnamese staff were to be found on weekends in the trailer park, making friendly visits, underwriting informal parties, and poviding helpful interpretation and translation services to maintain good relations in the community.

At Dupaco, I never met an Asian or Hispanic union member, and while this could have been an artifact of my short stay in the plant, the small population of Asians and Hispanics made it possible for me to visit with nearly all of them. Certainly none of them were sporting UFCW stickers on their hats, except for Tam, the

Tai-Dam chuckboner, and he said he did so to "keep the union guys away from me."

Besides working next to other whitehats on the line, I also had access to the offices that overlooked the packinghouse floor. So in addition to gaining some understanding of the workers' point of view, I came, insofar as was possible over three weekend visits and several long phone calls, to appreciate the point of view of the plant's management. Because my role as "consultant" was one that was understood by plant managers and workers alike, I had easy and fairly equal access to both strata of plant employee. The result was a short-term ethnographic encounter that studied both "up" and "down" at the same time.[5]

Participant observation of workers and management at Dupaco would not have been possible without prior familiarity with the packinghouse setting. Our research team had been working in and around Garden City in one capacity or another for up to three years. Besides our research connection, I had a family tie to the industry. My nephew had worked in the front office at IBP for a time, after working as an hourly laborer in the cooler for several months. And as Stull and Benson point out in Chapters 3 and 5 in this volume, all of our research team members toured the plant often; we discussed the implications of packinghouse work incessantly (though as Benson notes, we did not always share the same perspective). The background work in the Garden City community provided the interpersonal connections that led to a request to visit the plant from a labor recruiter. Our earlier work provided an understanding of the "lingo" of the packinghouse. Without this prior familiarity, short-term participant observation at Dupaco could not have taken place, and access to management, aside from Broadway's lucky interview with one packinghouse owner (Stull et al. 1990) probably would have been impossible.

Studying Up

Laura Nader (1969) sounded the call to arms for anthropologists studying complex institutions in industrial societies. The ethnographer needs to match her interest in and concern for disempowered others with scientific attention to powerful people if we are "serious in terms of developing adequate theory and description" (Nader 1969:290). It is often easier to study students, peasants, and factory workers than school administrators, landowners, or packinghouse managers. But in Nebraska, access to both workers and management was possible, and my familial connection to IBP provided an early example of management's view of processing workers.

In 1988, the UFCW had opened a union hall in Garden City and had employed two Vietnamese and one Hispanic union recruiters, pulled in from UFCW plants in the region. It was a period of intense union activity in Garden City and elsewhere. For a time, the union struck the IBP plant in Dakota City, Nebraska, and IBP was responding to the Garden City membership drive with posters and information meetings in the plant to discourage membership. By that time, my nephew had been pulled off his job in the cooler and had been advanced to a management position in the front office of the Garden City plant. He called me at work one afternoon, and asked if I knew "what they were thinking. You know, the Vietnamese."

I suggested that he was just a short walk away from the production line and that he could ask one of the company's workers just as well as I could. The call illustrated the "us" versus "them" thinking that sometimes characterizes relations between a packing plant's management and its workforce. Management at IBP evidently thought they needed an inside view that they could obtain only by going outside their own plant. At Dupaco, despite amazingly high worker turnover, management's behavior provided further evidence of the distance between workers and management. But it also provided some counterexamples that showed individual managers' recognition of a worker's value to the company.

Somphet was an outstanding example. He had been in a wreck a few weeks after the Dupaco plant had opened, and he was jailed for drunk driving when Curtis, the plant manager, came to the rescue. Curtis proudly told me how he bailed Somphet out of jail, thereby demonstrating the value of a skilled chuckboner.

A few weeks after my visit to Dupaco, I called Somphet at home to see how things were going. Somphet was not at home, but his wife was. "He almost quit on Saturday," she said, "because they asked him to help out on another line. But after that, his supervisor saw him, and he was sharpening his knife, not on his line, and the supervisor said, 'Are you here to work or are you here to sharpen your knife?' So he get mad. You can't work with a dull knife. So he walked off the line. The shift supervisor came and got him back again." For anyone else, walking off the line would be the end of the job, but not for this experienced chuckboner.

More often than not, however, management does not have time to look out for the needs of its staff, especially when those needs are complicated by language differences. But not all office staff act in company-specific, monolithic ways. When one manager will not help, another office worker may step in, as I learned during one afternoon at Dupaco.

The administrative offices at Dupaco are located along the hall across from the lunchroom. Just opposite the lunchroom's vending machines is the cramped personnel office, housing Gwen, the personnel director, and Jill and Barbara, the two clerical workers. Unlike the supervisor's office, the engineer's office, and the plant manager's office, the personnel office had no window looking down on the workers on the processing floor. Personnel was cluttered, with three desks and several file cabinets jammed into just enough space for people to squeeze from one desk to the next.

Gwen was constantly smoking. She handled a constant stream of phone calls from absent workers, a river of paperwork for new ones, and managed payroll for the entire processing staff, apparently all at the same time. While I was standing beside Gwen's desk looking at some absentee data, a Lao worker came in. He could not find his time card, and he seemed to be worried about not being paid for his work.

"You have to find it," said Gwen. She stayed in her seat, busy with her bookwork.

"I can't find it."

"Well, have your supervisor help you find it." Gwen sounded impatient. The man looked back at Gwen without saying anything. He didn't seem to understand what she had just said. Barbara, one of Gwen's clerical staff, looked up from her desk behind Gwen and asked, "What color is your card?"

"My name is Thavone," said the man.

"What color is your card?" she asked again, coming around from behind her desk.

"My name is Thavone."

"No, what color? What color is it?"

Again the man looked puzzled. Barbara stepped out into the hall, where workers' time cards are stored on racks on the wall. Thavone followed her. In a moment, she returned.

"It was behind one of the other cards. We found it." She was speaking to me. Gwen had not looked up from her paperwork.

While dealing in a sensitive way with language diversity was not quite routine at Dupaco, dealing with injuries most certainly was. On my first visit to the plant, before I went through training with the new hires and learned to bone plates, Gwen came into her office from across the hall in the lunchroom. She had been explaining some paperwork to a small group of new hires; I was sitting at her desk, going over the plant's ethnic composition from her employment lists. As I collected my computer printouts and vacated Gwen's desk, a fellow came in who appeared to be in his early twenties, not wearing his packer's frock. His left hand was locked in a clenched fist, his forearm was swollen and a bit discolored.

"I don't understand it," he said. "I was cutting good all last week, but it locked up on me this morning." He held up his arm and looked at it as though it were disconnected, not a part of him.

"You better head over and see the nurse," Gwen said. She wrote a note on a slip of paper, and he made his way down the hall and around the corner to the dispensary. I took my paperwork out to the lunchroom—there was no other desk for me to work at in Gwen's cramped office. The man with the swollen hand came in, noticed me sitting at one of the lunch tables, and said he had worked in a pork-processing plant for a long time and that he had not had much trouble with his hand, but it just locked up. "I'd done the hot wax," he said. "But here it is, a locked-up hand." [6]

The nurse came in from the hallway. In her packer's white frock and her white hardhat, she was dressed like most of the other plant management. Except for personnel staff, who rarely visit the shopfloor, upper management employees wear white hardhats, the same as the workers; the absence of safety gloves, rubber aprons, and bloodstains marks the difference.

But management at Dupaco all have experience on the packinghouse floor. Gwen had been a personnel manager at an IBP pork plant in Madison, Nebraska. My nephew's college degree did not exempt him from working in the IBP cooler before management considered him for an administrative position; the safety director had been a hamboner. And in Nebraska, Curtis, the plant manager, had been with IBP in the early days of the Garden City plant start-up; he too had worked on the line. Curtis was in his late thirties, proud of his "open door" policy, his efforts to retain good line workers, his desire to work his processing line fewer Saturdays, and willing to detail his frustrations with the plant's owner. His clean and quiet office upstairs, a few steps down the hall from personnel, offered a sharp contrast to the noise, wet floors, and rapid activity of the fabrication floor. From the spartan, cement-floored offices upstairs, plant managers can observe the work taking place below through picture windows that overlook the shopfloor. When they want a closer look, they can and do venture out onto the catwalks that run above the five lines. During my first few hours of work on the training table, I had frequently noticed shadows moving across the table in front of me. Only after several hours of work did I realize that the shadows were made by Curtis and the corporate engineer, who were watching me from the catwalk.

After several hours of trimming random pieces of meat from a a seemingly bottomless plastic barrel most of the morning and early afternoon, I used my status as a visiting consultant to walk off the line and spent some time in Curtis's office. My short visit there brought to light an important ethnographic moment. Curtis had wanted me to visit with the corporate engineer. The engineer's name was DJ. Curtis said that DJ's mother was Hispanic, and Curtis relayed his belief that DJ's Spanish abilities were becoming more and more helpful as the plant hired more Hispanics.

I asked Curtis about the Hispanics on the floor and mentioned that I had greeted two Spanish-speaking job applicants out in the hall that morning. I wondered aloud if there could there be people in the plant who could work as trainers of Spanish-speaking workers. If, as DJ had said, the company was planning to hire more Hispanics and Asians, they would need trainers who could communicate. Curtis said he had used one worker as an interpreter who might work out as a trainer. I said that I might like to visit with him. Curtis said he'd call him up to the supervisor's office next door, where we could talk.

The engineer was evidently in a joking mood and comfortable acting out in the presence of Curtis and myself. After Curtis called one of the line supervisors on the radio, DJ took a boning knife out of a nearby cabinet, put it between his teeth like some white-frocked pirate, and, with his back to the wall and his eyebrows arched, pretending to be lying in wait for the unsuspecting worker, he said, "Don't tell him why we want to see him, Curtis!"

The engineer's mock threat, like the position of the office high above the shopfloor, dramatized one kind of relationship between workers and plant management. It illustrates the packing-plant *machismo* that the men in the "snakeskin boots" express, themselves former packers who have escaped the daily strains of production-line work. The corporation's Omaha-based assistant personnel director, insulated from the day-to-day work on the fab floor by her distance from Norfolk, expressed a somewhat different view in a telephone interview.

"People don't understand how tough it is," she said. "It's a totally different world. $10.96 was a top rate when I started to work. That lasted until 1981. Then they did the rollback, rolled back to $9 and now it's $8 per hour [the top wage after six months]. Interesting, too, to look at the change. In one plant, we have 1,400 retirees, out of Dubuque [Iowa]. I've been talking to a lot of them.

None of them, not one of them, have any kids who are in the industry. And 60 percent of them have put their kids through college, any way they could, however they could. I had one man come in and cry, when we were closing [the Iowa plant]. It broke my heart, like I had to cry, too. You know, I'd love to be behind the desk at personnel and have two people in there wanting my $10 per hour job, instead of going begging for people."

The forces that drove wages down in the 1980s were beyond the control of collective worker efforts to maintain them (Green 1990), just as workers were powerless to resist the contraction in wages that paralleled the declining economy of the early 1920s (Barrett 1987). As Broadway (1992) notes, the reasons for the more recent decline transcended the national economic picture and resulted from strategic efforts by the industry to lower costs in an environment of technological change. Studying the plant in Norfolk did not bring these macro-level factors into clear focus, but the results of decisions made outside the plant clearly affected both workers and managers at Dupaco.

Today's packinghouse floor responds to marketing decisions made by managers outside the plant. The kind of cuts that workers make, the amount of "bone-in" or "bone-out" product, and hence the stress and strain on workers' hands, have to do with daily changes in the boxed-beef market; fluctuations in demand from restaurants, supermarkets, and exporters; and the ability of the plant to maintain a fully crewed processing floor. The forces that drive the relations of production in the modern beef "fabrication" floor (at Dupaco) or "processing" floor (at IBP) can therefore lead to sudden changes in production schedules. At Dupaco, Curtis told of frequent instances in which the plant's owner would call and order that an afternoon's production be increased significantly, work changed from bone-in to bone-out product, and result in faster line speeds and overtime for a staff already short crewed and bone tired by late afternoon on a Saturday.

While I completed several short reports to the plant's owner, and made suggestions about a training video, about ways to treat new workers, and (somewhat idealistically) about the need for full crews and reasonable line speeds, only the video came to pass. At one point, Curtis sent me a copy of a memorandum from the owner that said, "Since Erickson began his program, turnover is up." But my suggestions about line speed and short crewing had been ignored (although they were as much Curtis's suggestions as my own). Later, I learned the plant was "on the block." Dupaco sold to a consortium of out-of-state investors less than six months after my short foray into the noisy world of conveyors, saws, and knives. At this writing, the Norfolk plant is still the second-newest beef-processing facility in the United States. (IBP's Lexington, Nebraska, plant holds first-place honors.) The new name of the Norfolk plant, this place that needed to find some Vietnamese who would stick with them, is emblematic of the time-honored role of the packinghouse in the lives of new immigrants to the U.S. The new packinghouse in Norfolk, Nebraska, is none other than Beef America.

Notes

1. Robert and Joe are pseudonyms, as are all names in this chapter. The plant's identity is not concealed here, however. As the only large start-up in the industry in 1988, trying to hide the plant's identity would be futile. It would also unfairly deprive plant owners and management of the opportunity to comment on the description presented here.

2. While the colors of trainers' hardhats vary, white hardhats for line workers and upper management seem to be a consistent industry pattern.

3. Tai-Dam are members of a highland ethnic group from North Vietnam that fled into Laos during the French war in Vietnam. Most Tai-Dam people in the United States live in Iowa. None lived in Garden City during our research, although many Lao, Vietnamese, and Khmer refugees did.

4. I conducted a study of a convenience sample of twenty-four Wednesdays and Fridays from the plant's absence records and found no substantial difference in absenteeism among Asians, Hispanics, and Anglos. The sample was too small to be statistically significant, but Asians were marginally more prone to sick leave, contrary to management's apparent belief that Asians were less often absent.

5. Because it is based on short-term fieldwork, this chapter is also part of a growing body of rapid appraisal work in anthropology (Van Willigen and Finan 1991). But unlike most rapid appraisal work, it does not rely on questionnaires or focus groups. While "rapid" methodologies are becoming important as anthropologists are more and more frequently called on to consult in a variety of social settings where extended field research is impossible, our research team's experience with the packing plant spanned several years, so while the experience at Dupaco was brief, it was supported by intensive and extensive work in the beefpacking and immigrant-worker arena. It is likely that most rapid appraisal work owes its success to just this kind of long-term involvement with a research arena (see, for example, Hess 1991, who reports on "rapid" assessment work that is, in fact, grounded in many years of professional practice in Chicago public schools).

6. Beef plants at the time of my visit were still maintaining a kettle of melted wax for workers to dip their hands in when they experienced joint pain, something that the UFCW's health experts say is a bad practice (UFCW 1988). Experts recommend heat for muscle sprains only, not for problems that in-

clude inflammation at the joints (OSHA 1990). While the hot-wax procedure produces some temporary relief, it stimulates circulation in the affected area and can increase the speed with which calcium is deposited in the carpal tunnel, speeding up the nerve-pinching disease.

Bibliography

Barrett, James R. 1987. *Work and Community in the Jungle: Chicago's Packinghouse Workers 1894–1922.* Urbana: University of Illinois Press.

Erickson, Ken C. 1990. "New Immigrants and the Social Service Agency: Changing Relations at SRS." *Urban Anthropology* 19(4):387–407.

Green, Hardy. 1990. *On Strike at Hormel: The Struggle for a Democratic Labor Movement.* Philadelphia: Temple University Press.

Hess, G. Alfred. 1991. "Using Time-effective Ethnographic Evaluation to Reshape a Private–Public Partnership." In *Soundings: Rapid and Reliable Research Methods for Practicing Anthropologists*, edited by John Van Willigen and Timothy Finan. NAPA Bulletin 10. Washington, D.C.: American Anthropological Association.

Nader, Laura. 1969. "Up the Anthropologist—Perspectives Gained from Studying Up." In *Reinventing Anthropology*, edited by Dell Hymes. New York: Pantheon.

Occupational Health and Safety Administration (OSHA). 1990. *Ergonomics Program Management Guidelines for Meatpacking Plants.* Washington, D.C.: U.S. Department of Labor.

Stull, Donald D., Janet Benson, Michael J. Broadway, Arthur L. Campa, Ken C. Erickson, and Mark A. Grey. 1990. *Changing Relations: Newcomers and Established Residents in Garden City, Kansas.* Report No. 172. Lawrence, Kans.: Institute for Public Policy and Business Research.

Thompson, William E. 1983. "Hanging Tongues: A Sociological Encounter with the Assembly Line." *Qualitative Sociology* 6(3):215–237.

United Food and Commercial Worker's Union (UFCW). 1988. *Hand and Wrist Problems: Carpal Tunnel Syndrome.* UFCW Job Hazards Fact Sheet. Author's files.

Van Willigan, John, and Timothy J. Finan, eds. 1991. *Soundings: Rapid and Reliable Research Methods for Practicing Anthropologists.* NAPA Bulletin 10. Washington, D.C.: American Anthropological Association.

5   The Effects of Packinghouse
Work on Southeast Asian
Refugee Families

Janet E. Benson

My first insight into the "objective conditions of existence" experienced by refugee packing-plant workers came during the summer of 1987 when I conducted research on refugee day-care needs for the Garden City area office of the Kansas Department of Social and Rehabilitation Services. Together with my six-year-old son, I had arranged to live in Garden City for ten days as the paying guest of a Sino-Vietnamese couple with two young children. Both Tinh and his wife, Mai, worked at IBP, Garden City's largest packinghouse employer, though during my stay Mai was on leave because of recent childbirth. Tinh had been employed at IBP for approximately four years but was worried about disability (specifically, carpal tunnel syndrome) because his wrist was bothering him. Tinh and Mai were extremely hard-working and future-oriented; they had already established an impressive savings account for their children's college education.

To my surprise, when I left, the couple presented me with many gifts: little stainless-steel coffee brewers, chickory coffee, and a large, handsome mat. I protested that I would be seeing them again, but Tinh replied that the future was uncertain. He and his wife could lose their jobs at any time. The gifts symbolized his gratitude to America and Americans for accepting him as a refugee.

Although I thought that his fears were exaggerated, Tinh's prediction was correct. In fact, Mai lost her job soon afterward, perhaps not coincidentally just before she was about to reach seniority. As they later described the situation to me, poorly trimmed meat piled up on the wife's line due to a shortage of workers. Mai

99

was asked to stay and finish slicing off the fat. Because a sitter was caring for her children, and she and her husband were in a car pool with others, she declined—and was fired on the spot. The family subsequently moved to another state in search of employment and training; Tinh planned to have Mai do piecework for a garment factory at home while he studied drafting.

By its rigidly scheduled, physically exhausting, highly production-oriented nature, industrial work such as meatpacking places constraints on family life that are very different from those experienced by white-collar or professional employees. At the same time, it is a means of economic survival, and sometimes capital formation, for non-English-speaking immigrants and refugees. This case clearly illustrates some of the "contradictions and tensions at the intersections of home, the informal sector, and the formal sector" (Ward 1990:3). In this chapter I look at the consequences of such work for Southeast Asian refugee family life. I particularly focus on family economic strategies and women's role in production. I argue that when family members participate in meatpacking, especially in large plants using many refugees and immigrants, the family subsidizes costs of this industry to an unusual degree (Griffith 1993; Griffith and Runsten 1988). Family socioeconomic strategies represent attempts to adapt to corporate policies of the past two decades involving mobile capital, plant closings, and cutthroat cost-cutting measures, a phenomenon dubbed "the deindustrialization of America" by some authors (cf. Bluestone and Harrison 1982) and "low-wage labor processes in advanced capitalism" (Griffith 1993:28) by others.

Most of the following data were collected over nearly ten months' residence in Garden City during 1988–1989; some case-study material comes from subsequent research in other southwest Kansas beefpacking towns. Between 1987 and 1989, I spent varying periods in the households of four Vietnamese families containing packinghouse workers, while I was the guest of an established Mexican American family during the summer of 1989. During 1988 I lived in two large mobile home courts that contained the densest local populations of Southeast Asians and spent much time visiting families, interviewing, and observing. During the Ford project, I focused on Vietnamese and Laotian refugees, their interactions with established residents, and gender issues. During the two-year project period, I interviewed refugee packinghouse workers, school administrators and teachers, service providers, mobile home dealers, and park managers. My son was enrolled during fall 1988 at Victor Ornelas, a large new elementary school with a 56 percent minority

population, primarily the children of packinghouse workers. I tu-
tored Laotian and Vietnamese families in English, attended most
public events in Garden City, and observed or participated in
Southeast Asian ceremonies and activities, including Têt (Vietnamese New Year) celebrations and a Laotian "party," or public
dance. Although residence with households was difficult to arrange, the insights I gained into the relationship between work and
home could not have been easily obtained by any other fieldwork
method.

Gender also had an effect on ethnographic focus and perspective. I was the only woman on the research team, and the only
individual with child-care responsibilities. It was easier for me to
interact informally with women than with men, which biased me
originally toward the study of families, rather than single males; on
the other hand, male researchers could socialize more freely with
male workers and tended to adopt male perspectives. We disagreed
for some time on how to characterize packinghouse work in reference to gender. While the male researchers tended to discuss it as a
single-male occupation, I was struck by the almost universal participation of Laotian and Vietnamese women in packinghouse employment.

Dramatic increases in school district enrollments since 1980
also indicated an influx of worker families; minority enrollment in
Garden City schools had reached 36 percent by 1989 (38 percent in
the elementary schools), and many of these were immigrant children. By the beginning of the 1989–1990 school year, the school
district had enrolled 359 children categorized as "Asian or Pacific
Islanders" (mainly Vietnamese and Lowland Lao), while 13 children (mostly Vietnamese) were enrolled in Catholic schools (Stull et
al. 1990). As the Monfort data finally indicated (Bustos 1989; Stull
et al. 1990, 1992; Broadway interview 4/29/89:11), though male
workers still predominate, women form an increasingly significant
proportion of the southwestern Kansas packing-plant labor force
today. At Monfort, which had very few Southeast Asian employees
in 1988, it was Anglo women whose numbers were increasing,
while Southeast Asian women (and men) usually worked at IBP.
The trend toward more female employment in meatpacking is
likely to continue as the proportion of available Anglo male workers
declines relative to women, immigrants, and minorities (see Griffith
1993; Griffith and Runsten 1988; Remy and Sawers 1984:99).

Theoretical Focus: Women, Work, and Family

As anthropologists have reexamined earlier notions of gender and turned to studies of industrial societies, it has become increasingly necessary to acknowledge the relationship between family organization and work outside the home. In an effort to bridge this gap, a number of feminist theorists (Caplan 1985; O'Laughlin 1975; Vogel 1983; Westwood 1985) have applied the Marxist concept of reproduction to the analysis of women's status in both Western and non-western societies. Other researchers (Benson 1990; Lamphere 1987; Safa 1983; Safilios-Rothschild 1976; Sanjek 1982; Zavella 1987) have used the concept to discuss household functions or home–workplace relations within a capitalist mode of production.

Reproduction in Marx's sense includes much more than childbearing and is intimately related to production outside the home. By "reproduction," Marx refers to a condition of production that requires the replacement of labor power and associated social relations (Vogel 1983:139). In addition to replacing tools and maintaining a set of social relations at work, this means providing the conditions under which workers sleep, eat, have clean clothes, and maintain livable housing. It also means that dependents must be maintained and the next generation of workers raised (Lamphere 1987:25). Historically, women have been associated more with these maintenance activities (housework, child care, socialization) within the home, men more with wage labor (Lamphere 1987:25). But, women have also worked for wages, and this is a familiar pattern in industrial societies today.

Vogel makes the useful point that the family is not the sole site of maintenance of labor power or replacement of workers; for example, dormitories or households of single males may carry out maintenance functions, while replacement workers arrive through immigration as well as biological reproduction (Vogel 1983:141). Nevertheless, this chapter focuses on family households containing women and the impact of packinghouse work on families.

Production and reproduction (in the Marxist sense) are contingent on each other. For example, kinship and friendship networks among Southeast Asian refugees draw new workers to Garden City, constantly replenishing the labor force. Male and female activities within the household are shaped by the needs of workplace production, while worker requirements for rest and maintenance (as well as existing laws) place limits on what the factory can demand. But in the context of a seasonal, low-profit-margin industry such as meatpacking, management strategy (at least in the largest plants) involves demanding the maximum production from workers with minimal concessions to household needs (see Stull et al. 1992). As long as sufficient numbers of new workers can be recruited, that is, as long as potential workers have limited options elsewhere, management will exert the tightest possible control over workers' time. Members of worker families, in turn, must devise strategies to cope with these demands on and off the job.

From Macro to Micro: Bridging Levels of Focus

According to Lamphere (1987:26–27), several processes in the history of capitalism in the United States have affected women in the labor force: workforce expansion, mechanization, increased concentration, and deskilling as the division of tasks in industrial work becomes increasingly complex. All but the first of these trends have been well documented for the meatpacking industry (Broadway and Ward 1990; Remy and Sawers 1984; Skaggs 1986; Stull and Broadway 1990; Stull et al. 1992). In addition, as the proportion of white males in the U.S. labor force has declined, beef and poultry processors have increasingly turned to women, minorities, and immigrants as employees (Skaggs 1986:108; Stull et al. 1992).

These trends should not be viewed in isolation but are related to large-scale changes in the U.S. economy since the 1960s: loss of international competitiveness, increasing pressure for cheap labor, the deregulation of many industries, loss of union strength, and the proliferation of part-time jobs (Bluestone and Harrison 1982; Harrison and Bluestone 1988; Skaggs 1986). While the packing industry has always used immigrant labor to some extent, the socioeconomic characteristics and gender composition of the labor force vary over time and according to the needs of employers (see Griffith 1993; Remy and Sawers 1984).

The Meatpacking Industry

The effects of industrial employment cannot be understood without reference to the demands of the specific industry. Meatpacking, of course, shares some characteristics with other industrial work but has unique features as well (described in detail by Don Stull, Chapter 3 in this volume). Characteristics relevant to families include (1) deskilled operations (since women usually have less opportunity for extensive training than men); (2) increased mechanization, especially in the larger plants, reducing the number of jobs requiring great physical strength; (3) the need to attract labor from any possible source, since today's lower wages, as well as the difficult working conditions, have reduced the attractiveness of the industry for established male Anglo Americans; and (4) probably most crucial from management's perspective, the industry's low profit margin (Stull et al. 1992). In short, the larger meatpackers, such as IBP, have recently sought women as a source of cheap labor, replacing more skilled, highly paid men wherever possible.

Southeast Asian refugee labor has been highly valued by packinghouse managers for many of the same reasons as have women. Although slighter in build than many other ethnic groups, size and physical strength are less important with greater mechanization, and refugees have a reputation for hard work. Southeast Asians also have the fewest alternatives of all employees; in most cases, they cannot go home again, while many have minimal English skills and a low educational level. Working-class Anglos can seek other employment options because of their English fluency and familiarity with the culture; Mexican immigrants can, and frequently do, return to Mexico. Although I focus on Laotian and Vietnamese families in this chapter because of my responsibilities during the Garden City project, I do not mean to imply that families from other ethnic groups—Anglo, Mexican, African American—are not similarly affected by the same labor processes. The discussion here primarily refers to workers "on the line," although limited mobility to supervisory positions is possible for bilingual employees, including women (Stull et al. 1990).

Women's Roles in Production and Reproduction

Women play an important role in production and reproduction from the perspective of both packinghouse managers and the Vietnamese and Laotian workers themselves. From the managers' viewpoint, women workers provide a needed labor source, add stability to the workforce, and are reputedly more docile than men. Both federal legislation and greater mechanization since the 1960s encourage increasing reliance on female workers. From the perspective of Vietnamese and Laotian refugees, married women form the nucleus of the family and, ideally, household (Benson 1990; Erickson 1988; Rynearson 1984). Single males new to the community join the households of married relatives or friends whenever possible. All-male households are a matter of expediency and often transitory in nature. For both economic and social reasons, single-

A Vietnamese family relaxes at the Lee Richardson Zoo in Garden City, Kansas. (Photo by Janet Benson)

person households are almost nonexistent; therefore, the question for most refugee workers is not whether they should share a household with others, but with whom among friends and relatives they should share.

Women Workers

In addition to managing and provisioning a household, Vietnamese and Laotian women work in meatpacking plants. The fact that Asian women work outside the home, either in their countries of origin or as immigrants, is not new (Haines 1986, 1989:60;

Westwood 1985; Yamanaka 1987); in fact, the relative economic success (or economic self-sufficiency) of Southeast Asian refugees in the United States has been attributed by several authors (Dunning 1989; Kibria 1989; Rumbaut 1989; Whitmore et al. 1989) to a multiple wage-earner strategy in which women play a prominent role. Dunning (1989:69), for example, notes that in his 1980 sample of Vietnamese and Sino-Vietnamese refugees, women frequently worked outside the home, and median household income increased systematically with household size. While some studies indicate that refugee women are less frequently employed than men and receive lower wages (Bach 1985:31–32), this is not a major problem in Garden City. It is true that women are still relatively handicapped by childbearing, child-care responsibilities, and assignment to "lighter" and lower-paying jobs within the plant; however, the male–female differential in wages and opportunities is less than in many other occupations. For example, paraprofessionals, almost entirely female, working for the school district in 1988 could earn a maximum of only $4.90 per hour, while IBP processing workers started at $6.40. Males injured at "heavier," more highly paid jobs are switched to "lighter" tasks within the plant, where females predominate, and women may bid for higher-paying jobs. Although meatpacking is "low wage" when yearly incomes are considered, the pay is relatively good considering other local options for non-English-speakers. Interestingly enough, when IBP originally opened, the Holcomb plant did not intend to allow both husbands and wives to work; the management quickly changed its mind when it found itself short of labor.

Individual refugee women in Garden City may or may not have had prior experience at wage work in their countries of origin, depending on age and socioeconomic background. Vietnamese in particular refer to a middle-class ideal in which the wife does not work outside the home. In addition, many refugee women were too young to have worked much in either the formal or informal economy before their U.S. arrival. The literature on Laos and Vietnam, however, as well as some refugee women's work histories, indicates that by the 1970s it was not unusual for women to participate in formal or informal economic activity outside the home (see Haines 1986); the idea of women contributing to the household budget is not new. For example, one interviewee had worked as a telephone operator; another had experience in a garment factory; one had served as an elementary school principal. Lack of formal education was not necessarily a barrier to employment. For example:

At my neighbor's trailer we found Noi trying to iron, an unfamiliar enterprise. Her household had used charcoal irons in Laos and other family members had done the ironing there anyway. Her husband had owned five trucks and run a big logging operation; she marketed the family's fruit and was too busy to stay home doing housework. (Benson fieldnotes 7/24/88).

Women packinghouse employees work outside the home for the same reasons as married men do, that is, to support the family. And many Laotian and Vietnamese women work as hard as men for this purpose. For example, 1988 school district data for the two Garden City elementary schools with the largest Vietnamese and Laotian populations indicate that in the majority of cases for which information is available, both husband and wife were packing-plant employees. The mother's place of work is consistently underreported for all ethnic groups. But, among Vietnamese and Laotian parents, very few women indicate having occupations (including "housewife") other than meatpacking, while a disproportionately large number of "Asian" children (the school's broad classification, primarily Laotian and Vietnamese) have mothers who work at packing plants.

For example, in school A, of an estimated twenty-four Asian families for which the father's employment was known, all worked at a packing plant. Of the mothers, sixteen were at the same plant, the workplace of five mothers was not noted, two (Koreans) worked at the local hospital, and one mother was at home. Of children reported to have mothers who worked at packing plants, 55 percent were Asian (34 of 62), while the proportion of Asian children to all children at this school was a little less than 20 percent (77 of 394).

At school B, of an estimated sixty Vietnamese or Laotian families for which the father's occupation was known, all but one worked at a packing plant. Information was lacking for ten mothers, while two were at home. In four other cases, information was available for mothers but not fathers; this may indicate single-parent households or simply that the information was not recorded. In forty-seven of the sixty-four cases, both parents were listed as packing-plant workers. This was probably an underestimate due to underreporting of mothers' occupations. Asian children constituted 23 percent of the total student population at this school (112 of 484) but 66 percent of all children (83 of 125) with mothers working outside the home.

The fact that a high proportion of Laotian and Vietnamese

children live in families where both parents are packinghouse employees has important consequences for children and schools, as is discussed in a later section of this chapter.

Mothers' wages are very important to the family economy. Wages vary according to such factors as seniority and specific job within the plant, but the average Garden City worker makes about $12,000 to $15,000 in take-home pay per year. Even with low-cost housing in mobile homes, this is not sufficient to support a family containing several dependents or to accumulate capital. Refugee workers agree, however (and wage data suggest), that the average husband and wife, working overtime, can bring home $30,000 or more per year. According to Loc, a Vietnamese Catholic familiar with many refugees in the area, dual-worker families are common:

> That's the only way you can save some money, because if only one income, you cannot save that much. . . . Many people want to get a little bit more money, to save. . . . In five years . . . if both husband and wife work, and they don't gamble . . . they can save up to seventy, eighty thousand dollars. (Benson interview 6/19/89)

Wendy, a young Vietnamese woman from a meatpacking town an hour's drive from Garden City, discussed her own and her parents' income:

> Most Vietnamese packing-plant workers take the night shift [as they do in Garden City] in order to receive the $3.60 per hour overtime. This plant pays $6 per hour as a beginning wage, $7.35 as the highest salary. Wendy's husband made $16,000 last year, $15,000 this year. A couple can earn $30,000 in take-home pay; however, fewer hours have been available recently, only 35.5 hours (of which 24 would be overtime) rather than 40. Wendy herself holds down a part-time white-collar job. Her father and mother earn about $370 (net) per week together, or $1,480 per month; her father's salary is $7.20 per hour. If they work 40 hours, the father, who claims deductions for family members, gets $260 gross per week and the mother, who claims no deductions, receives $210 (the deduction is worth $100 per week in tax savings). Their two grown children (including Wendy, who is married) also work, but do not pool their money with the parents. Van, a colleague of Wendy's, says that when he worked at the same plant, his take-home pay averaged $175 per week, or about $700 per month. Since he is single, he received no family deductions and taxes were higher. (Benson fieldnotes 3/15/91)

Because one income is not sufficient to maintain a family with several dependents, most refugee women who can meet the employer qualifications enter packing-plant work. Except for a few families with business or professional backgrounds, and a small minority receiving public assistance, the only exceptions among Garden City refugees occurred if the wife had recently given birth, was waiting for her application to be accepted, or had several very young children. Women in those situations often provided babysitting services for other workers and were able to contribute to the household budget in this way. The migration history of one refugee family illustrates a persistent search for the wife's employment, regardless of her reproductive status:

> Mr. Tuan and his wife Thu first arrived in the U.S. in 1978 and stayed in Washington, D.C., for several years. Mr. Tuan worked as a busboy at first, while Thu was in housekeeping at the same hotel. Then they found better jobs in Maryland, paying about $7 to $8 per hour. They moved to Wichita, Kansas, in 1980 expecting to live near a friend, but he had already moved to California. Mr. Tuan left his wife behind temporarily in Wichita and went to Dodge City, having heard of jobs at the Excel packing plant. [Meatpacking and aircraft industries in Wichita were laying off workers at this time.] His starting wage was $5.44 per hour. After five months Thu joined him, and although two or three months pregnant, secured a job mopping floors at the plant. When she became sick, however, the foreman fired her. Tuan worked for a total of one year at Excel but remained dissatisfied because he wanted a job for his wife. Tuan and Thu moved to Denver to apply for jobs, having heard of packing-plant employment, but were unsuccessful and returned to Garden City in 1981; by this time the wife's baby was two months old, and she went to work with her husband at IBP near Garden City. By 1984, the family had accumulated enough capital to invest in a small fishing boat, and the husband left for Texas to fish. In 1985, however, he returned to southwest Kansas and soon purchased a business in the area. During my fieldwork in 1988, the couple continued to work six days a week at IBP while a relative managed the business. When asked why they continued to work at the plant, the husband said that they had to save for the children's college education. This kind of capital accumulation would not have been possible without a second income. The family also regularly sends clothes and medicine to both the husband's and the wife's parents in Vietnam. (Benson interview 7/23/88)

If women cannot work because of illness, failure to pass plant tests, or child-care responsibilities, the family may be severely handicapped. For example, Somsak, a Laotian father with seven children aged six to seventeen in 1988, discussed his family situation and work history as follows:

Like many Garden City refugees, Somsak came first to Wichita, where his in-laws lived. He was in Wichita from 1980 to 1984, studying English at an adult learning center until the government assistance money for refugees ran out. He was required to look for jobs, but could not find one which met his family's living expenses. Somsak's wife was home with young children during this time. Then he moved to Dodge City where he worked at Excel for one year and also translated for a public agency. However, this income still did not meet family needs. Somsak desperately wanted some other job besides meatpacking, but finally gave up the search and moved to Garden City in 1985 to work at IBP, which paid more than Excel. Somsak was able to get by because his brother lived in the household and shared expenses. By June 1988 Somsak's wife, whose youngest child was now school-aged, had started working at IBP. Having three earners in the household has meant more temporary financial security, if not necessarily a more certain future. (Benson interview 11/29/88)

In addition to providing for their own families, both husbands and wives have commitments to their natal families. As indicated in the Tinh's migration history, refugees frequently arrange for shipments of goods or transfer of funds to relatives abroad, including those still in refugee camps. Mai, frequently ill and in danger of losing her job at IBP, told of sending her family in Vietnam $500 every few months. In another case, money remitted to a younger brother in Vietnam by his sister Phung Thi allowed him to marry and start his own family.

As refugees become citizens, they sponsor kin, who then become their economic responsibility on arrival, often funneling them into the same industries. Friends and relatives already in the country may arrive to share the household and receive free food and lodging initially. These obligations constitute yet another reason for women's employment.

The case studies given above also make the point that economic survival, or self-sufficiency, is not the only goal motivating refugee worker families. The majority of family households seek capital accumulation if at all possible, realizing that the only route out of this demanding, stressful, potentially disabling work is to acquire the funds for a new start elsewhere. Some refugees, especially those from professional backgrounds, seek more training or education; others purchase their own businesses or fishing boats; still others have given up hopes for their own advancement, but will invest the money in college education for their children. Capital, therefore, plays a central motivating role at the household as well as the corporate level, and working women are essential to the accumulation

process. From a macro perspective, the search for capital has penetrated the family in a fundamental way, shaping its goals and organization (Griffith 1990).

Finally, women work outside the home so that the family not
only survives but can also participate in a culturally and socially
desirable lifestyle. Haircuts by professional beauticians, fashionable
clothes, new cars and vans, microwaves, and expensive television
and stereo sets are not "needed" for physical survival but are certainly part of refugee worker (as well as established American) expectations. New refugee arrivals, or those too impoverished to acquire these status symbols, may be ridiculed by other members of
the refugee community, and refugee women find it hard to resist
the social pressure to enter packing-plant work.

Time and Labor Control

The view of meat cutting as essentially male employment seems
to persist in the meat industry today despite federal legislation requiring equal opportunity for both sexes, increasingly mechanized
plant operations, and a dearth of Anglo male workers. Plant schedules are designed for maximum production, without any concern
for family needs. At IBP, the main employer for Southeast Asians
in Garden City, most refugees prefer to work "B" shift (3:05 P.M. to
midnight) because of the extra overtime pay. If husband and wife
work on the same shift, however, children may be left without supervision. Working on different shifts creates other problems, as
discussed later.

From a management perspective, time is literally money. Consequently, workers' time is monitored as closely as possible to keep
the chain speed high and production on schedule (see Erickson,
Chapter 4, and Stull, Chapter 3, in this volume). This constant
pressure places workers under great daily stress while exacerbating
scheduling conflicts between work and children's school or other
tensions arising within the family. Labor availability is controlled as
much as possible both on and off the job; for example, in the slack
season, workers never know until the last minute whether they will
be called to work on Saturdays or not, as this depends on what
orders for processed beef come in.

Rigid control of workers' time has many implications for family
life. In dual-worker families, for example, it affects what and when
family members eat. Typically, if a mother is working the evening
shift, she will cook a meal in late morning before going to work,
then heat up food after returning from the plant at 1:00 A.M. (Men

sometimes cook as well.) When a mother goes to work, the diet may suddenly change from nutritious Vietnamese meals to high-sodium packaged noodles or American "fast foods." Parents working the evening shift chat and socialize between 1:00 and 3:00 A.M., with or without the children, while mothers sleep late and children are expected to get themselves off to school, often without breakfast, the following morning. (This is not entirely the result of schedules, since the American-style breakfast is not customary for most refugees.) Because so many children were not receiving breakfast at home, at least partly because of working mothers, the Garden City school district has now instituted a school breakfast program. Bottle feeding, which puts children at risk for poor nutrition, diarrheal disease, and dental caries, is encouraged by mothers' needs to return to work within two months of childbirth or lose their jobs.

Workers in a difficult, stressful job like meatpacking tend to sleep more than usual and wake late in the morning if they are employed on the night shift (earlier for mothers with infants). This leaves them only three or four hours a day, six days a week, in the busiest season, between waking and returning to the factory to conduct all household maintenance activities: shopping, cooking, cleaning, child care, house repair, paying bills, visiting the post office or the hospital, helping friends or neighbors, and so on. Understandably, parents often do not attend school events, which may take place when they are working. Sunday is the only day free for relaxed socialization (as well as laundry, ironing, and shopping) with friends and family. Workers can summon little time or energy to pursue English study or vocational training even if they have the ambition and the educational background to do so.

Family Economic Strategies

How do refugee workers adapt to, exploit, or resist the management control I have outlined? Here I am primarily concerned with family economic strategies and their consequences. These can be understood only in the context of mobile capital and restructured industries based on low-wage labor. As Bluestone and Harrison (1982:18) note: "The newly enhanced ability to move capital between regions within the same country provides corporate management with the necessary economic and political clout to insist upon reductions in local taxation, and therefore cuts in community services and the social safety net."

Along the same lines, Griffith notes that "firms in low-wage labor industries depend on formal and informal social support mechanisms to subsidize the costs of reproducing labor and maintaining labor during off seasons or periods of economic crisis" (Griffith 1993:227).

Vietnamese and Laotian families, households, and the "ethnic community" in its broadest sense—a local and national network of relatives and friends—must provide much of the "social safety net" when workers are fired or become disabled. This frequently occurs, given the hazardous and insecure nature of packing-plant employment (Griffith and Runsten 1988, Stull and Broadway 1990, Stull et al. 1992). Although refugee workers have a legal right to unemployment benefits and workers' compensation if disabled, management tactics often render it difficult or time-consuming for workers to exercise these rights. As a result, families often give up and move elsewhere in search of employment. A worker who has lost a job in one southwest Kansas plant will often attempt to qualify for work at another; his or her relatives provide support in the interim. From the family's point of view, its social network provides essential assistance in the form of information about jobs or welfare benefits, offers of housing, and other help. From management's perspective, network recruiting provides a steady stream of workers from the same ethnic group.

Two points should be made here. First, as noted earlier, postwar industrial restructuring in general and the highly competitive nature of meatpacking in particular affect workers of all ethnic groups, established residents as well as newcomers. Immigrants and refugees, however, are more vulnerable than established residents because they have not yet attained citizen status, lack English fluency, and are subject to local antagonism. Particularly in the small towns of southwest Kansas, very few employers are willing to hire Southeast Asians for work outside the packing plants. Ethnic antagonism (see Wallimann 1984) helps confine most to the slaughterhouse. With few exceptions, refugees who come to Garden City must adapt to the management demands of meatpacking and to economically viable options regarding household arrangements (see Griffith 1990).

Second, while Vietnamese and Laotian refugees are like all other workers in having to adapt to specific conditions of production, distinct cultural values reveal themselves in family goals, concepts of kinship and marriage, and models for economic survival. First-generation Vietnamese families, for example, respond to the same working conditions and family tasks in different ways from those of Anglo families. The strategies discussed next, then, are both a response to the local labor market and an attempt to restructure lives in culturally meaningful ways.

Housing

All newcomers face the initial problem of housing. Refugees arriving in Garden City during the early 1980s, shortly after the opening of IBP, discovered a tight and discriminatory housing market for low-cost renters (see Broadway's discussion of housing patterns, Chapter 2 in this volume). Many local landlords would not rent to Laotians or Vietnamese, who were stigmatized not only because of their foreignness and association with the Vietnam war but because of their large families. Rents were high in relation to salaries. Initially, people slept in cars or shared available housing with numerous members of the same ethnic group, as this account indicates:

[Bounlian is a Laotian woman packing-plant worker, age 54.] When Bounlian first came to Garden City in 1981, there were six or seven in her household including four daughters and herself. Renting a house was too expensive: four people had to deposit $450 for an apartment and the monthly rent was $450 for a total initial outlay of $900. About twenty Laotians stayed in a big pink house downtown. Part were on "A" shift and part on "B" shift so that if the landlord came, he wouldn't see too many people at one time. For a while, her family did share a Holcomb motel room (now in ruins) with another family. Then in 1983 she bought the mobile home and moved to Garden City. (Benson fieldnotes 7/25/89)

To help remedy the initial insufficiency of low-cost housing, IBP, which wanted to start a second shift in its new Holcomb plant (see Benson 1991), brought in an Iowa developer to start up a mobile home court, East Garden Village. IBP initially owned mobile homes there and deducted rent directly from workers' paychecks. By the summer of 1988, however, privately owned units at this park (still known informally as "IBP" by Vietnamese) greatly outnumbered rentals; most residents had accumulated enough capital to purchase their own mobile homes. This is a common strategy because of the relatively high cost of rent. Laotians and Vietnamese also share a cultural preference for outright ownership. In 1988, for example, rentals at "IBP" ranged from $240 to $320 per month plus $70–90 for gas and electricity, or a total of $310 to $410 in monthly expenses, excluding cable television and telephone. Most utilities required sizable deposits because of the transient population.

The housing costs detailed here are relatively high for a single worker or single-earner family with a paycheck of less than $1,000 per month, particularly when car payments and insurance are added to the budget. Newcomers also have difficulty paying deposits. Both individuals and families, therefore, try to identify friends or relatives in Garden City (before moving, if possible) with whom they can live while accumulating enough funds for a mobile home of their own. Close relatives might not be asked to pay anything, at least initially, because, as one Laotian worker explained:

> Lao people have different customs than American people. If you're my cousin, and you don't have a job, you live with me about two months, eat with me free. I take care of you, you don't pay nothing. Like I came to my brother's, my brother took care of me for about two months. I don't pay for food, nothing; I can sleep at his house free. [Second speaker:] No rent, nothing. You can stay in the home until you find your own job. You help them for a while to get the things they need, then they can start their own way. For a while when they come, they don't know anything. I mean all Lao people they help in that situation. (Benson interview 10/16/88)

Vietnamese also often let newly arrived relatives stay rent free. Nonrelatives, however, paid approximately $200 per month per individual or $350 for a family of four during the late 1980s. This amount usually covered both food and lodging and implies that adult married women are present in the household to cook, clean, and provide for others. Single males must take turns cooking or eat out, less efficient and more expensive options, and divide household expenses equally; they also spend more on cars, gas, and luxury items than families. Loc, the Vietnamese Catholic refugee cited earlier, felt that households composed of single males were rare, despite the demographic imbalance in their favor (see also Erickson 1988): "Usually they live with some of the families. The reason is that in Vietnamese tradition, the males, we don't cook. We don't know how to cook. So if we just live together, I think that is a tremendous problem. Nobody cook. So that is the reason they live with a family with a lady" (Benson interview 6/19/89).

The practice of taking in boarders allows newcomer families to save considerably on expenses so that they can put funds aside for rental and utility deposits of their own, a car (essential for transportation to the plant), or a mobile home. Used mobile homes can be purchased for a few thousand dollars, leaving families with only lot rent (approximately $100–125 per month), utilities, and property tax to pay. Having established itself in its own housing, a family that once boarded with others may in turn accept paying guests (see Gold 1992:115).

Another way of looking at this strategy is to say that household members engage in self-exploitation, subsidizing moving expenses, food, and housing costs that the plant would otherwise have to pay in the form of higher wages or the community in the form of increased social services. Because workers' living standards are culturally and socially determined, and refugees will tolerate conditions, such as substandard housing, that established American workers are likely to reject outright, they offer a prime target for plant recruitment (Griffith 1993; Walliman 1984).

Child Care: Production versus Reproduction

Families, as opposed to single workers, shoulder child-care responsibilities as well as other household maintenance duties. The Garden City plants do not provide day-care facilities, and workers must arrange their own child care as best they can. Difficulties are compounded for Lao and Vietnamese refugees, a young population demographically speaking, because they tend to have larger families than the American norm (Rumbaut and Weeks 1986; Zaharlick and Brainard 1987). Paid child care becomes prohibitively expensive when more than two children per family are involved. The use of American day care is also undesirable because parents want children to learn Vietnamese or Laotian as the first language.

Parents attempt to cope with this situation in various ways. If children are very young, and no other household members are available to caretake, they arrange for paid sitting with an otherwise unemployed woman. This may or may not be satisfactory from the standpoint of children's health or safety. Most sitters are unlicensed and do not meet American care standards. Lily, a well-educated, English-fluent, white-collar worker, complained that her son spent the day in a mobile home with more than a dozen other children and came home black and blue from being pinched or hit. She tolerated it only because she and her husband wanted him to speak Vietnamese as a first language. Aside from possible fire or tornado hazard to mobile home residents, children are sometimes fed poorly, suffer abuse, or develop bottle-mouth from propped-up bottles.

Another child-care strategy is to ask any unemployed member

of the household, male or female, relative or nonrelative, to watch young children, subordinating customary gender roles to the needs of production. If there are older children in the household, they will be expected to care for younger siblings (see also Erickson 1988). This, again, may or may not serve the purpose adequately. In one case observed during fieldwork, a toddler's teenage stepbrother locked his charge in the house and left on an errand. When darkness fell, the child began crying, and concerned neighbors tried fruitlessly to contact the parents at IBP. One problem resulting from packing-plant work is that in emergencies involving children, it is difficult or impossible to locate parents at the plant, and parents who do leave work in these cases run a strong risk of being fired. In this instance, the stepbrother eventually returned.

Finally, if all else fails and parents cannot find satisfactory child care, mother and father will take different plant shifts so that one parent will be home at all times for the children. This is not easy to arrange, complicates transportation (normally husband and wife ride together), and lowers income, since only one spouse can then collect overtime. It also greatly reduces communication between husband and wife, creating more problems in the long run. Mai, a Vietnamese woman worker, described her near-heroic efforts to transport her children to school and back lacking bus service or a second vehicle:

> Mai and her husband, Vinh, have worked different shifts at IBP for about two years, since the time her eldest daughter began attending school. At that time the family was living in a mobile home in a locality not visited by the school bus. Vinh worked the first shift, rising at 4:30 every morning. Mai would walk her daughter to school and bring her home when she was through, leaving for work at 2:00 P.M.; Vinh returned from work by 4:00 and stayed with the children in the evening. Transportation, however, was a major problem in winter during the cold and snow. Her daughter's teacher advised Mai to send her daughter in a taxi, so she began having the taxi transport her daughter to and from school. This cost between $30 and $40 per month, and was not very dependable. Sometimes her daughter waited outside the school for hours, without the staff's knowledge: "She *very* cold." Because the family owned only one car, Mai had to join a neighborhood car pool and pay $30 per month for daily transportation to the factory. (Benson interview 11/6/88)

Even very young children, by American standards, may be left at home alone or in the care of slightly older children. For example, summer school teachers reported occasionally accepting nonenrolled siblings in their classes rather than condone young children staying by themselves. Of course, standards of child care vary among Laotian and Vietnamese refugees, the more highly educated parents in particular being more concerned about child-care arrangements; but the main point is not that refugees do not care about their children—in fact, parents often literally "live for their children"—but that child care must be subordinated to the requirements of work. Most families cannot afford the luxury of an unemployed wife. The needs of the plant, and the goal of capital accumulation for families, often override other concerns.

Effects of Packinghouse Work on Families

What are the implications of packinghouse work for refugee families? Parents face an acute child-care dilemma when their work situation is so inflexible; an emergency or constraint due to children, as in the first case discussed in this chapter, can easily result in parents being fired. Given the lack of work options for those other than established Americans in a small town like Garden City, unless a worker can obtain a job at Monfort or another plant within driving distance, the family usually must move. This may take place virtually overnight, without regard to the school calendar, because the family must support itself. Although disruptive of children's education and social adjustment, frequent moves, both nationally and within southwest Kansas, were characteristic of all refugee workers interviewed. For both financial and social reasons—lower rent, purchase of a trailer, quarrels with relatives sharing the household—families frequently change residential locations even within the community, further adding to members' stress. Established Americans in schools and other local agencies are often concerned about refugee children's care and supervision to the extent, in some cases, of individuals voluntarily assuming semiparental roles.

While child-care issues are particularly important among refugee parents with young children (the most common situation), different problems arise with unsupervised youth. If both parents work on the night shift, the typical pattern among Vietnamese and Lao, children may be unsupervised from the time they return from school until after midnight and, during the busiest season, on Saturday afternoons and evenings. Instances of rape, teenage pregnancies, theft, and other offenses have taken place in the absence of adult supervision. Although the subordination of children to parental authority is an important value among newly arrived refugees, it may be difficult to enforce when parents are absent for long hours. Another problem is that a significant generation gap develops as children become accustomed to American culture in the schools. Cultural loss takes place because parents have neither the time nor the energy to teach their children to read and write in the native language. At the same time, children below driving age cannot participate fully in American culture by attending sports and other events and so tend to be stigmatized and isolated within their schools (Grey 1992).

Although juvenile authorities were not aware of many delinquency problems with local Laotian or Vietnamese youth during 1988–1990, this partly reflected underreporting and partly the fact that most refugee families are still relatively young. Several incidents did occur during fieldwork, and local authorities agreed that as more refugee children became teenagers, delinquency among this population is likely to increase. When a juvenile committed an offense (e.g., shoplifting), and both parents were working, I was told that the judge would ask the mother to quit her job—hardly a viable option for worker families.

Health-care issues also affect families, which require more medical care than single males. Initial coverage is one problem; workers cannot enroll until four to six months (depending on the plant) after they are employed. At some southwestern Kansas companies, only the worker is covered; insurance for other family members must be paid separately. Even if insured, family members may fail to seek treatment because they cannot afford deductible amounts.

Lack of prenatal care for low-income women was a major, publicly recognized problem in Garden City during the 1980s. Since pregnancy is considered a "preexisting condition" under insurance rules, women tend to conceal their pregnancies, consequently receiving little or no prenatal care. Local physicians were overburdened and would see only a few indigent patients per month. In 1987, 25 percent of women who gave birth in the local hospital had received no prenatal care at all (Stull et al. 1990). Local agencies and institutions have struggled to fill the gap by creating prenatal programs, some specifically aimed at Vietnamese, and a health clinic for those without medical coverage.

The threat of disability for line workers is another constant feature of packing-plant work. As one lawyer commented:

Where else can these people earn $6 to $7 per hour? It [the packing plants] must seem like manna from heaven to them at first. Then they get injured. They can't do any more heavy lifting, they don't have their GED [high school equivalency], and they've lost their manual labor capability. The work is hard and fast. They can be refused a job if they have a workers' compensation case in the courts [due to employer ignorance about insurance law, he says]. (Benson fieldnotes 11/22/88)

To avoid employee insurance claims, companies commonly find excuses to fire workers who show signs of debilitating injury. This practice leads to underreporting and lack of treatment, exacerbating any existing problem. Refugees quickly become aware of the work's stressful, hazardous nature and health tradeoffs (insurance coverage versus possible worker disability), as the following case study indicates:

Chin, who is Vietnamese and a former packing-plant employee, was injured when a side of beef fell on him. He says he is often in pain and unable to sleep. Although he had a medical card at the time I met the family, his nonworking wife and three children had no medical coverage. They said that according to the rules, they could not qualify for aid without incurring over $2,000 in bills; then they would have to pay part and Social and Rehabilitation Services would pay part. The procedure is complicated. Whether his wife, Phung Thi, should go to work at a local plant was a bone of contention between the couple. Chin said that Phung Thi had tried to work when they were living in Liberal, but her hands were injured after nine days and the family had to pay $150 for medical treatment. If she works for IBP, he doesn't think she will be able to hold the job very long. Right now, however, they have no medical coverage for the children, and the youngest boy alone needs nearly $900 worth of dental work. (Benson fieldnotes 11/28/88, 12/1/88)

Phung Thi did seek a job at IBP, held it through the six-month waiting period, and was able to pay the dental costs for her children. Three years later, however, she was complaining of pain in her arms, which she was afraid to report, and husband and wife were planning to move elsewhere. In another case, both husband and wife were incapacitated:

Long, a Vietnamese father of six, was disabled after five years' work at IBP. The family is arguing that his severe mental problems are due to a plant accident, while IBP's attorney claims that he has been seen driving his car around town and that the problem is due to a preexisting condition. While I interviewed his family, Long remained curled in the fetal position in an armchair, pushing a pencil through a sponge-rubber ball over and over again, oblivious to his surroundings. According to the Vietnamese interpreter, no one can communicate with him. Long's wife worked for IBP for two and a half years but then developed health problems herself and is currently home under doctor's orders. The family is on food stamps and probably cash assistance but has not received any disability payment from IBP as the case is still in dispute. (Benson fieldnotes and interview 11/12/88)

In addition to health concerns, packing-plant work raises gender issues. Relations between husband and wife are changing, as well as those between parents and children. The possibility of communication gaps between spouses on different shifts has already been mentioned. In addition, traditional authority bases, particularly among Vietnamese, are threatened by wives interacting with strange men in the workplace and bringing home relatively large sums of money in their own name. Role asymmetry may now favor the wife as she receives opportunities to attain a higher-status job position than her husband:

> Phung Thi says that Thu, Anh's wife, is very busy training to be a blue hat [assistant to line supervisor—see Stull, Chapter 3 in this volume]. Her husband doesn't like it, although the pay is 20 percent higher, because people in authority positions have a lot of headaches dealing with other employees and the management. (Benson fieldnotes 11/21/88)

A working wife supporting a dependent, homebound husband is of course an extreme case of role reversal given conventional middle-class Vietnamese values.

Several times during fieldwork, Vietnamese men spontaneously voiced their concerns about the frequency of divorce in America; refugees recounted stories of unfaithful wives who left for a new lover, taking a husband's cash. From a male point of view, the family, a central institution in Vietnamese life, is fundamentally at risk. Men find life without their children inconceivable. Most strikingly, men fear being replaced by other men with higher incomes. What seems to be happening is that wives, who traditionally held a central domestic role, are now rapidly expanding their already considerable power and autonomy into new areas. Although first-generation refugees still value marriage and the family, husbands and wives are renegotiating their relationships (Benson n.d.; see also Kibria 1990). While an increased incidence of divorce cannot be attributed to meatpacking alone, the transience and insecurity of jobs available to refugees is unlikely to contribute to a stable home life.

Conclusions

Griffith (1993) and others have shown how low-wage industries in advanced capitalism depend on reproductive labor. The specific economic adaptations of marginal households are central to understanding low-wage labor processes (Griffith 1990:5), for these strategies allow plants to pay the wages they do and continually recruit under conditions of high turnover. Too much turnover, however, threatens production. By summer 1991, for instance, the personnel manager of a Dodge City packinghouse, an hour's drive from Garden City, was concerned enough about worker turnover to discuss publicly the need to attract more families. Because they must support children and other dependents, and are presumably less mobile than single male workers, plant managers increasingly find family households desireable. Families involve more potential costs for companies than single workers, but these can be minimized if housing, child care, health care, education, and other services are provided largely by the family itself or the local community.

The work schedules and company policies described in this chapter do not sufficiently explain refugee workers' adaptive strategies and responses. Another factor that specifically affects refugees, as opposed to established Americans, is the U.S. government's policy of early economic self-sufficiency for refugees. Funding for an initial period of refugee adaptation, including English classes, has steadily decreased (it was down to twelve months for new arrivals in 1988), while pressure to obtain jobs of any kind has helped push newcomers into a low-wage job market that affords few resources for additional language learning or training. Once in this market, it becomes very difficult for workers to move into more permanent jobs with better working conditions (Bach and Tienda 1984; Finnan 1981; Haines 1987). While family reproductive labor helps subsidize packing-plant costs, Vietnamese and Laotian families may view this work, at least initially, as "easy money" and an opportunity for capital accumulation. As children grow older and enter employment themselves, a family may become relatively affluent. But not all families are this fortunate. As the case studies indicate, injury robs some households of adult wage earners. For example, three workers, including a Laotian refugee, were killed during the summer of 1991 in Liberal, a southwest Kansas packing town not far from Garden City. Even if workers escape serious injury or disability, families inevitably pay a price in terms of domestic stress, inadequate health treatment, substandard housing and child care, and other problems resulting from their incorporation in a labor system that places overwhelming emphasis on production.

These managerial practices and government policies have broad implications for issues of ethnicity and gender in the U.S. workforce. With regard to Lao and Vietnamese refugees, insecure, low-wage industrial jobs encourage the creation of a highly mobile ethnic enclave within the American working class. Factory employment of women has also created changes in family relations, in many cases transforming families from rural backgrounds into an industrial proletariat. Women's new potential for economic independence in a work setting outside the home is reconstituting husband –wife roles in a more competitive, although more consensual, mode. This chapter has been a contribution toward understanding the impact of restructuring on gender and ethnicity in a specific community and labor market.

Acknowledgments

This research was conducted with funding from the Ford Foundation Changing Relations Project, the American Ethnic Studies Program at Kansas State University, and the KSU Bureau of General Research. Funding from the Kansas Agricultural Experiment Station (Project No. 839; Contribution No. 93-112-B) allowed continuing research on immigration into southwest Kansas after the completion of the Ford Project. I owe a major debt to the many Garden City residents, especially Lao and Vietnamese, who generously shared their lives with me. I am particularly grateful for the help of Ms. Jenny Tran, Mr. Ban Vu, and Ms. Bouala Baccam. This work would not have been possible without the cooperation of USD 457, the Southeast Asian Mutual Assistance Association, and the staff of the Adult Learning Center.

All personal names are pseudonyms, and in some cases details have been changed so that individuals cannot be identified.

Bibliography

Bach, Robert L. 1985. "Labor Force Participation and Employment of Southeast Asian Refugees in the United States." In *Aspects of Refugee Resettlement in the United States*, pp. 1–96. Washington, D.C.: U.S. Department of Health and Human Services, Office of Refugee Resettlement.

Bach, Robert L., and Marta Tienda. 1984. "Contemporary Immigration and Refugee Movements and Employment Adjustment Policies." In *Immigration: Issues and Policies*, edited by Vernon M. Briggs, Jr., and Marta Tienda, pp. 38–82. Prepared for the National Council on Employment Policy, Washington, D.C., Salt Lake City, Utah: Olympus.

Benson, Janet E. 1990. "Households, Migration and Community Context." *Urban Anthropology* 19:9–29.

————. 1991. "Good Neighbors: Ethnic Relations in Garden City Trailer Courts." *Urban Anthropology* 19:361–386.

————. Forthcoming. "Reinterpreting Gender: Southeast Asian Refugees and American Society." In *Identity, Ethnicity, and Change*, edited by Linda Camino and Ruth Krulfeld.

Bluestone, Barry, and Bennett Harrison. 1982. *The Deindustrialization of America*. New York: Basic Books.

Broadway, Michael J. 1989. Interview, April 29, 1989. Changing Relations Project Files, Lawrence, Kansas.

Broadway, Michael J., and Terry Ward. 1990. "Recent Changes in the Structure and Location of the U.S. Meatpacking Industry." *Geography* 75:76–79.

Bustos, Tony. 1989. Personal communication. Changing Relations Project Files, Lawrence, Kansas.

Caplan, Patricia. 1985. *Class and Gender in India: Women and Their Organizations in a South Indian City*. London: Tavistock.

Dunning, Bruce B. 1989. "Vietnamese in America: The Adaptation of the 1975–1979 Arrivals." In *Refugees as Immigrants: Cambodians, Laotians, and Vietnamese in America*, edited by David W. Haines. Totowa, N.J.: Rowman and Littlefield.

Erickson, Ken C. 1988. "Vietnamese Household Organization in Garden City, Kansas: Southeast Asians in a Packing House Town." *Plains Anthropologist* 33:27–36.

Finnan, C. R. 1981. "Occupational Assimilation of Refugees." *International Migration Review* 15:292–309.

Gold, Steven J. 1992. *Refugee Communities: A Comparative Field Study*. Newbury Park, Calif.: Sage.

Grey, Mark A. 1992. "Sports and Immigrant, Minority and Anglo Relations in Garden City (Kansas) High School." *Sociology of Sport* 9:255–270.

Griffith, David. 1990. "Consequences of Immigration Reform for Low-Wage Workers in the Southeastern U.S.: The Case of the Poultry Industry." *Urban Anthropology* 19:155–184.

————. 1993. *Jones's Minimal: Low-Wage Labor in the United States*. Albany, N.Y.: SUNY Press.

Griffith, David, and David Runsten. 1988. *The Impact of the 1986 Immigration Reform and Control Act (IRCA) on the U.S. Poultry Industry: A Comparative Analysis*. Report prepared for the Bureau of International Labor Affairs, U.S. Department of Labor, Washington, D.C.

Haines, David W. 1986. "Vietnamese Refugee Women in the U.S. Labor Force: Continuity or Change?" In *International Migration: The Female Experience*, edited by Rita James Simon and Caroline B. Brettell, pp. 62–75. Totowa, N.J.: Rowman and Allanheld.

————. 1987. "Patterns in Southeast Asian Refugee Employment: A Reappraisal of the Existing Research." *Ethnic Groups* 7:39–63.

————. 1989. "Introduction." In *Refugees as Immigrants: Cambodians, Laotians, and Vietnamese in America*, edited by David W. Haines. Totowa, N.J.: Rowman and Littlefield.

Harrison, Bennett, and Barry Bluestone. 1988. *The Great U-Turn: Corporate Restructuring and the Polarizing of America.* New York: Basic Books.

Kibria, Nazli. 1989. "Patterns of Vietnamese Refugee Women's Wagework in the U.S." *Ethnic Groups* 7:297–323.

———. 1990. "Power, Patriarchy, and Gender Conflict in the Vietnamese Immigrant Community." *Gender and Society* 4:9–24.

Lamphere, Louise. 1987. *From Working Daughters to Working Mothers.* Ithaca, N.Y.: Cornell University Press.

O'Laughlin, Bridget. 1975. "Marxist Approaches in Anthropology." In *Annual Review of Anthropology,* edited by Bernard J. Siegel, Alan R. Beals, and Stephen A. Tyler, pp. 341–370. Palo Alto, Calif.: Annual Reviews.

Remy, Dorothy, and Larry Sawers. 1984. "Economic Stagnation and Discrimination." In *My Troubles Are Going to Have Trouble with Me: Everyday Trials and Triumphs of Women Workers,* edited by Karen Brodkin Sacks and Dorothy Remy, pp. 95–112. New Brunswick, N.J.: Rutgers University Press.

Rumbaut, Rubén G. 1989. "Portraits, Patterns, and Predictors of the Refugee Adaptation Process: Results and Reflections from the IHARP Panel Study." In *Refugees as Immigrants: Cambodians, Laotians, and Vietnamese in America,* edited by David W. Haines, pp. 138–182. Totowa, N.J.: Rowman and Littlefield.

Rumbaut, Rubén G., and John R. Weeks. 1986. "Fertility and Adaptation: Indochinese Refugees in the United States." *International Migration Review* 20:428–465.

Rynearson, Ann M., and Pamela A. DeVoe. 1984. "Refugee Women in a Vertical Village: Lowland Laotians in St. Louis." *Social Thought* 10:33–48.

Safa, Helen I. 1983. "Women, Production, and Reproduction in Industrial Capitalism: A Comparison of Brazilian and U.S. Factory Workers." In *Women, Men, and the International Division of Labor,* edited by June Nash and María Patricia Fernández-Kelly, pp. 95–116. Albany: SUNY Press.

Safilios-Rothschild, Constantina. 1976. "Dual Linkages between the Occupational and Family Systems: A Macrosociological Analysis." *Signs: Journal of Women in Culture and Society* 1:51–60.

Sanjek, Roger. 1982. "The Organization of Households in Adabraka: Toward a 1Wider Comparative Perspective." *Comparative Studies in Society and History* 24:57–103.

Skaggs, Jimmy M. 1986. *Prime Cut: Livestock Raising and Meatpacking in the United States, 1607–1983.* College Station: Texas A&M University Press.

Stull, Donald D., Janet E. Benson, Michael J. Broadway, Arthur L. Campa, Ken C. Erickson, and Mark A. Grey. 1990. *Changing Relations: Newcomers and Established Residents in Garden City, Kansas.* Report No. 172. University of Kansas: Institute for Public Policy and Business Research.

Stull, Donald D., and Michael J. Broadway. 1990. "The Effects of Restructuring on Beefpacking in Kansas." *Kansas Business Review* 14(1):10–16.

Stull, Donald D., Michael J. Broadway, and Ken C. Erickson. 1992. "The Price of a Good Steak: Beef Packing and Its Consequences for Garden City, Kansas." In *Structuring Diversity: Ethnographic Perspectives on the New Immi-*

gration, edited by Louise Lamphere, pp. 35–64. Chicago: University of Chicago Press.

Vogel, Lise. 1983. *Marxism and the Oppression of Women: Toward a Unitary Theory.* New Brunswick, N.J.: Rutgers University Press.

Wallimann, Isidor. 1984. "The Import of Foreign Workers in Switzerland: Labor-Power Reproduction Costs, Ethnic Antagonism and the Integration of Foreign Workers into Swiss Society." *Research in Social Movements, Conflict and Change* 7:153–175.

Ward, Kathryn. 1990. "Introduction." In *Women Workers and Global Restructuring*, edited by Kathryn Ward, pp. 1–22. Ithaca, N.Y.: ILR Press.

Westwood, Sallie. 1985. *All Day, Every Day: Factory and Family in the Making of Women's Lives.* Urbana and Chicago: University of Illinois Press.

Whitmore, John K., Marcella Trautmann, and Nathan Caplan. 1989. "The Socio-Cultural Basis for the Economic and Educational Success of Southeast Asian Refugees (1978–1982 Arrivals)." In *Refugees as Immigrants: Cambodians, Laotians, and Vietnamese in America*, edited by David W. Haines, pp. 121–137. Totowa, N.J.: Rowman and Littlefield.

Yamanaka, Keiko. 1987. "Labor Force Participation of Asian-American Women: Ethnicity, Work, and the Family." Ph.D. dissertation, Cornell University.

Zaharlick, A., and J. Brainard. 1987. "Demographic Characteristics, Ethnicity and the Resettlement of Southeast Asian Refugees in the United States." *Urban Anthropology* 16:327–373.

Zavella, Patricia. 1987. *Women's Work and Chicano Families.* Ithaca, N.Y.: Cornell University Press.

MIAMI

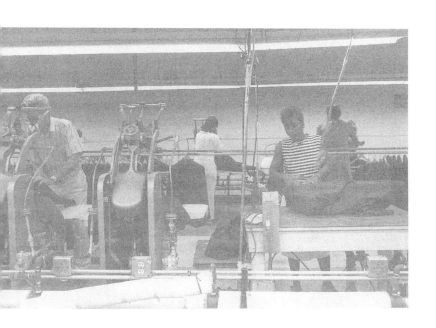

6   Miami: Capital of Latin America

Alex Stepick

I have been after the *Herald* ten times to do a story about millionaires in Miami who do not speak more than two words in English. "Yes" and "no." Those are the two words. They come here with five dollars in their pockets and without speaking another word of English they are millionaires.

—Joan Didion, *Miami*

The bosses should be looking out for the people who have lived here for years. They shouldn't allow those foreigners to come here and take our work

—Geoffrey Biddulph, *Miami Herald*

Since 1960, immigration has transformed Miami[1] as much if not more than any other major U.S. city, recasting it from a southern U.S. retirement and vacation center to the northern capital of Latin America (Garreau 1981; Levine 1985). By 1980, Miami had the highest proportion of foreign-born residents of any U.S. metropolitan area, proportionally 50 percent more than either Los Angeles or New York (see Figure 6.1).

But it is not simply the number of foreigners that makes Miami the capital of Latin America. Even more important is who and where the Latins are and what they are doing in Miami. While Miami has only 5 percent of the total U.S. Latin population, it has close to half of the forty-largest Latin-owned industrial and commercial firms in the country. There are more than twenty-five thousand Latin-owned businesses in Dade County. Its mayor, city manager, county manager, and one of its representatives in the U.S. House of Representatives all are foreign-born Latins. Elites from throughout the Caribbean maintain houses and bank accounts in Miami. Its community college has more foreign students, mostly Latin, than any other college or university in the nation. One of the two Spanish-language local television newscasts has more viewers than those of any single local English-language television station.

Cubans fleeing Fidel Castro's Cuba began arriving in significant numbers in the 1960s following the failure of the Bay of Pigs invasion. The immigration came in waves according to the tenor of relations between the U.S. and Cuban governments. In general, the upper classes, those most directly affected by Castro's socialist revolution, arrived in the early 1960s. In the mid- and late 1960s professionals and others from the urban middle class followed on U.S.-government-sponsored "freedom flights." During the early 1970s the flow gradually broadened to include a social spectrum of Cubans, although the immigrants still came primarily from urban backgrounds. In 1980 the flow peaked with the *Mariel* boatlift, which brought one hundred twenty-five thousand Cubans to the United States, many from more humble backgrounds than the earlier arrivals. Regardless of the immigrants' backgrounds or when

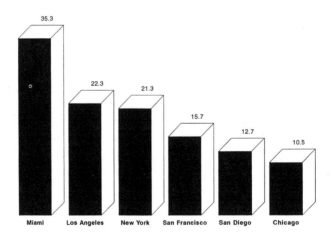

Figure 6.1. Percentage of foreign-born population in major U.S. cities. *From* U.S. Bureau of the Census figures, 1980.

they came, the flow has been largely one way. Once Cubans come to Miami, very few return. The resulting population contrasts with most contemporary immigrant flows to other U.S. cities. Miami's Cuban community contains all levels of the sending society from the elite to the working class, but the upper and middle classes are disproportionately represented.

While Cubans constitute nearly two-thirds of Miami's new immigrants, their relative proportion declined during the 1980s as immigrants from other national groups began settling in Miami. The *Contra* war in Nicaragua pushed more than seventy thousand Nicaraguans to Miami, and smaller numbers from other Central American nations also settled there. As with the Cubans in Miami, Nicaragua's elite arrived first, followed by the middle classes and lastly the working classes.

In the late 1980s, Latins became Miami's demographically dominant group, surpassing "non-Hispanic whites" (i.e., Anglos and Jews). By 1992, Latins established an absolute demographic majority, not just in the inner city, where the change is even more dramatic, but throughout the metropolitan area including all the suburbs and Miami's elite residential areas (See Figure 6.2).

A second major newcomer group is African Americans from various Caribbean islands. By the early 1980s, Greater Miami be-

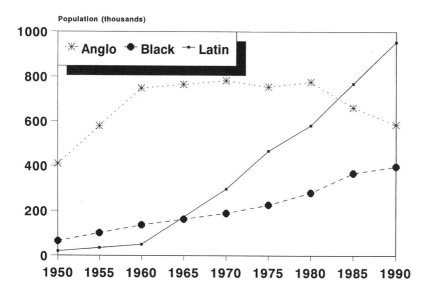

Figure 6.2. Population and ethnicity in Dade County, 1950–1990. *From* Metro-Dade Planning Department, 1984.

came one of only sixteen metropolitan areas in the United States with more than three hundred thousand African Americans. Between 1970 and 1980, Dade's African American population grew by 47 percent, a growth rate exceeded only by Atlanta's.

Bahamians have always constituted a significant component of Miami's African American population. Indeed, before the railroad brought southern U.S. African Americans in 1896, Bahamians were the only African Americans in Miami. And they have remained a major presence as those descended from the earliest immigrants maintain a Bahamian identity and commonly differentiate themselves from U.S. African Americans.

In the 1970s, after the civil rights movement had abolished legal segregation, other Caribbean African Americans, many of whom had settled in the northeastern United States, began to move to Miami. The largest concentration is of Haitians, who number approximately seventy thousand in the Greater Miami area. Between 1977 and 1981, approximately sixty thousand Haitians arrived by boat in south Florida, with the peak coinciding with the 1980 Cuban *Mariel* inflow.

Miami had a peculiar profile even before the arrival of the newcomers. It was a fundamentally southern city, but with a largely northern U.S. population. Its original population of southern whites and Bahamian and southern U.S. African Americans was supplemented from the 1920s onward by a large, transient population of tourists and retirees from the Northeast and Midwest, many of whom were Jewish. Jews went from less than 1 percent of the population in 1926 to a peak in 1975 of just under 20 percent, after which there was a relative and absolute decline to an estimated two hundred forty thousand, or 13.2 percent of the total Dade County population in 1987. The Jewish population is primarily elderly, with 53 percent over age fifty and 36 percent over sixty-five.[2]

This diverse ethnic mix has confused ethnic labels as language, race, and nationality all independently vary. The majority of Cubans are phenotypically white and refuse to be contrasted with "white" Americans. Moreover, a high percentage of Cubans are U.S. citizens, and even for those who are not, Cuba is still geographically a part of the Americas. Thus, for Cubans, "white" or "white Americans" includes them. Most Cubans identify themselves simply as Cubans, just as Nicaraguans and other Latins commonly refer to themselves by a national label. There are also subgroups within each nationality. Miami has a community of Latin Jews sufficiently large to support two synagogues, and there are also Black Cubans. Latin Jews commonly refer to themselves as Cuban-Jews (or more colloquialy as Jubans), Argentinian-Jews, or whatever-nationality-Jews. Similarly, Latin Blacks refer to themselves as Black or Afro-Cubans. In contrast, Hispanic has emerged as an ethnic identity only among a few, primarily highly educated and politicized Cubans or other Latin Americans who seek affiliations outside the Miami Cuban community. The word *Latin* is used almost exclusively by the Anglo elite, and virtually no one uses *Latino*.

In contrast, native white Americans do not wish to be identified by the residual category, "non-Hispanic white." For most native white Americans, "white American" does not include Cubans or other Latins and is the most appropriate label. Some refer to themselves as Anglo, but the term cannot be extended to include Miami's significant Jewish community.

Similar categorical difficulties exist among African Americans. The term African American has the same problem as white American because virtually all African Americans in Miami are from the United States, the Caribbean, or Central America, all part of the Americas. As with Latins, national identities predominate, such as Haitian or Jamaican. Even those descended from Bahamians recognize themselves as different, even if they and their parents were born in the United States.

Because of this complexity, whatever labels we use will either be confusing or arbitrarily simple. We have decided to use *Latins* for all those who themselves or their ancestors come from Spanish-speaking countries. When important, we will distinguish among Latins by national and racial attributes, such as Cuban Americans for those born in the United States or Afro-Cubans. Non-Hispanic whites we will refer to as *Anglos*, unless we need to distinguish them from Jews. *African Americans* will refer to all who are phenotypically Black, and national labels will distinguish among them, such as U.S. African Americans.

From its inception at the turn of the century until World War II, Miami was a frontier city in search of a destination. Decades before Walt Disney arrived in central Florida, the laissez-faire political policies of the South allotted northern entrepreneurs enormous latitude to remake the native Everglades swamp and coastline into fantasy commercial ventures. Venetian, Arabian, and Spanish housing developments emerged, while the indigenous mangrove coast was plowed away to make room for wide, vegetation-free beaches. When the ocean washed away the beaches (since the trees were no longer there to hold the sand), hotel proprietors arranged for sand to be pumped back onto the beaches.

As the proportion of tourists declined and that of retirees increased, which occurred especially after World War II, Miami became more of a settled community. The proportion of workers directly involved in the tourist industry declined, but the economy remained service oriented. Construction proceeded with only minor dips in response to U.S. recessions. Some light, locally oriented industry emerged, yet the economic and civic focus remained firmly on attracting more northerners and servicing those who brought money from elsewhere.

But at the end of the 1950s, the Miami economy confronted a crisis. The opening of new air routes to the Caribbean provided competition for the tourist industry. An especially cold winter in 1958–1959 and a national economic recession combined to bankrupt numerous hotels, creating disturbing ripples for the rest of the local economy. While most Miamians paid little attention to the revolution that had occurred just ninety miles off the southern coast of Florida, the Miami business and civic elite welcomed the revolution's first refugees. The new residents, who were primarily upper and middle class, pumped the economy and were expected to return quickly to Cuba as soon as Fidel fell.

Instead, the arrival of the Cubans launched a shift in Miami's service-centered economy from the Northeast and its sojourners toward the countries to the south. During the 1960s, Miami displaced New Orleans as the U.S. principal trade outlet with Latin America. By 1982, Miami stood second only to New York as an international banking center. By the mid-1980s, Miami International Airport was the ninth-busiest airport in the world in passengers and the sixth-largest in air cargo tonnage. About one hundred sixty thousand workers, one-fifth of the labor force in Miami, were directly or indirectly employed in airport and aviation activities. Moreover, the port of Miami provided a base for over eighty-five steamship companies and was the largest cruise-ship port in the world (Mohl 1985).

By the late 1980s, Miami's industrial profile was similar to that of other newer American cities where the economy was led by services: wholesale trade, finance, insurance, and real estate. The biggest occupational increases in the 1980s came among executives and in sales (Metro-Dade 1988). Overall, white-collar jobs were increasing, while blue-collar jobs declined (Cruz 1990). The recession of the early 1980s hit Miami, as it did the remainder of the United States, and sectors tied to Latin America were severely affected as the U.S. recession coincided with even more severe economic difficulties in Miami's economic backyard (i.e., the Caribbean and Latin American economies, which confronted a profound debt crisis).

Nevertheless, the area's economy proved resilient, exhibiting a relatively low 5.2 percent unemployment rate in late 1988.

The early 1990s recession, however, severely damaged Miami's economy. The nationwide banking crisis consumed two of Miami's largest savings institutions, along with a few smaller ones. Both Eastern Airlines and Pan-American, which concentrated in Miami because of its links to Latin America, disappeared. Miami's unemployment rate surpassed the nationwide average, and only its links to Latin America's by then recovering economies kept it from becoming even worse.

Geographically, Miami is a typical post–World War II sunbelt city, dispersed over a broad area in which it seems virtually impossible to get anywhere without a car. Bus service exists, along with a single rapid-transit rail line (Metro rail), but public transportation either does not go where most people want to go or it takes nearly forever to get there. Public transit is thus used only by the poor and a fortunate few who live close to Metro rail and work in the central business district. Miami, like all U.S. cities, is segregated. Blacks live next to downtown and north, with scattered small enclaves in the southern part of the county. Latinos live immediately west of downtown and spread out like a fan toward both the northwest and southwest. Anglos concentrate in the extreme northeast and southwest. While overall segregation in Miami, especially between Anglos and Latins, is less than in other major U.S. cities (see Massey 1990 and Boswell 1987), the geographic diffusion of the city fundamentally conditions interethnic interactions and the construction of communities. The apparel, construction, and hotel and restaurant workers described in the following three chapters are unlikely to encounter one another across ethnic lines outside of the workplace. There is no bar such as Tom's Tavern in Garden City, Kansas, where workers from even one of these worksites interact socially and informally. Geographic segregaton partitions workplace relationships from other social interaction.

An Ethnic Economy

In Miami's early years, the relationship between ethnicity and work was straightforward. As a southern city, Miami reserved the worst jobs for African Americans. When the railroad was extended south to Miami in 1896, many of the laborers were African American. They tilled the fields and harvested the vegetables. They dug the ditches that defined the streets, then cleaned the streets, drove the cars of white people, hauled their garbage away, were nannies to their children, maids in their homes, and washerwomen for their clothes. While they often were working for northerners who had migrated to Miami, the southern legacy meant they were still treated like "niggers." Segregation was the law, and generations of policemen and sheriffs repeatedly harassed, beat, and even killed African Americans to keep them in their place (Porter and Dunn 1984: Chap. 1).

At the dawn of the 1960s, just as African Americans had begun to achieve victories in civil rights and had forced the local Anglo elite to begin to redress a half century of discrimination, a group of white foreigners arrived, Cubans, whom the government greatly welcomed and soon classified as minorities, eligible for the civil rights protections and affirmative action programs that emerged. But these new arrivals were different from other minorities in the United States. Not only were they white, but also the Cuban early arrivals were predominantly middle or upper class. In spite of these differences, new Cuban immigrants had special programs created for them and qualified for minority set-asides and other affirmative action programs.

Because of the relatively privileged background of the first Cuban arrivals and the assistance from the U.S. government, Miami is the only U.S. city where Latin immigrants have created a successful and self-sustained ethnic economy. The Miami Cuban enclave is much more than an ethnic neighborhood containing ethnic businesses. It is an economically complex ethnic community in which individuals have a high likelihood of being able to work with fellow ethnics in enterprises owned by fellow ethnics, shop in stores owned and operated by fellow ethnics, and obtain professional services from these ethnics. In Cuban Miami, one can be born in a Cuban American hospital, be attended by Cuban American doctors and nurses, register the birth with a Cuban American bureaucrat, attend Cuban American schools, work in a Cuban American firm, do all one's shopping in Cuban American businesses, obtain the services of Cuban American lawyers, vote for Cuban American politicians, and be buried from a Cuban American funeral home.

But Cuban American economic activities are not limited to those that serve solely the local Miami Cuban community. They figure centrally in the role Miami plays as capital of Latin America. Cubans frequently head the import and export companies, the banks that finance the transactions, and the smaller transportation and service companies that allow goods and services to migrate.

The vast majority of the more than twenty-five thousand Latin businesses in Dade County at the end of the 1980s were small businesses, the true engines of Miami's economic growth (Satterfield 1987). Moreover, as mentioned earlier, while Miami has only 5 percent of the U.S. Hispanic population, it has close to half of the forty largest Hispanic-owned industrial and commercial firms in the country. By the mid-1980s, 40 percent of Miami's banks were owned by Latins (Botifol 1985). There were Latin insurance companies, shipping firms, and innumerable import and export establishments. Some of the most important developers were Latins, one having become in the late 1980s the first Latin head of the Greater Miami Chamber of Commerce. As Figure 6.3 demonstrates, between 1970 and 1980 the number of Spanish-origin professionals in Miami more than doubled, and Spanish-origin executives nearly quadrupled.

These figures should not lead one to conclude that all of Miami's Cubans are successful businessmen or even that Latins dominate the summit of Miami's occupational hierarchy. Figure 6.3 indicates that the Anglo abandonment of Dade County that began in the 1970s was class selective. Anglo laborers and production workers left in great numbers, while higher-class workers, notably executives and managers, remained or moved into Dade County. Although Latins and African Americans expanded their presence

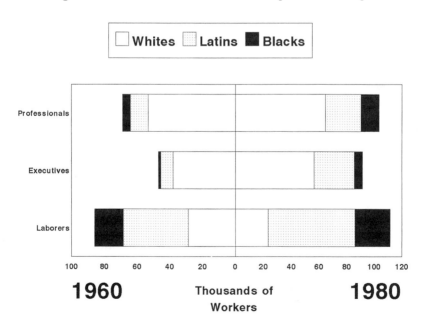

Figure 6.3. Ethnicity and occupation in Miami: professionals, executives, and laborers, 1970 and 1980. *From* Metro-Dade County Planning, 1984.

among executives, managers, and professionals during the 1970s and 1980s, Anglos still outnumbered both of them together. Similarly, the largest employers in the private sector, the electric and phone companies, also remain Anglo controlled.

Even the fact of business ownership is somewhat misleading. Of the nearly twenty-five thousand Latin-owned and -operated business in 1982, only 12 percent had paid employees, and together they generated a total of only 18,199 paid jobs (Diaz-Briquets 1984). In fact, the occupational profile of Miami's Latins, in some ways is nearer to that of Miami's African American community than to anything else. Latins as well as African Americans are underrepresented in Miami's fastest-growing industries, especially financial services, which are dominated by Anglos (Cruz 1990:17). Correspondingly, Latins and African Americans in Miami are over-represented in manual occupations and work as laborers, craftsmen, and service workers. Blue-collar workers constitute the largest occupational sector among Latins and African Americans (Grenier 1992). Moreover, most of the Latin employment growth during the 1970s was directly attributable to population growth.

The arrival of one hundred twenty-five thousand Cubans in 1980 and another hundred thousand Nicaraguans throughout the 1980s significantly added to the proportion of working-class Latins. These newer arrivals, especially in the first few years after arriving, tended to take what appear to be low-wage, unskilled positions that are often part of the informal economy, that is, terms of their employment in some way violate wage and labor laws.[3] They commonly worked as dishwashers, busboys, or waiters and waitresses in Cuban restaurants, in the apparel industry, in construction, and as flower vendors on street corners (see Portes and Stepick 1986; Stepick 1989). Yet by 1986, the vast majority of *Mariel* Cubans, six years after their arrival, had graduated from informal or lower-echelon jobs in the enclave economy. Moving into the positions they vacated were the more newly arrived Central Americans, especially Nicaraguans. Two Miami industries in which informal activities surged in the 1980s are those detailed in later chapters, apparel and construction, which reveal that Miami's Latin informal economy did not begin in the 1980s. Instead, the enclave itself began with many informal businesses that subsequently grew and expanded into the enclave and larger Miami economy (see Stepick 1989). Their success opened opportunities for later-arriving *Mariel* Cubans and Nicaraguans.

An Enclave Community

The importance of an enclave community for new immigrants is most obvious in language use in Miami. Insead of fading away, Spanish in Miami has become an important second language. Even at work, the language most frequently spoken by Latins in south Florida is Spanish (42.2 percent), up from 36.6 percent in 1980 (Strategy Research Corporation 1989). At worksites, language is the first social divider, then nationality, and then race. When new workers arrive at a local apparel plant, during breaks the first task is to determine if they speak Spanish, then their nationality, which is closely tied to the food they eat. On one occasion, a long-time Cuban American apparel worker addressed a new hire whom she thought was Colombian, "Oh, you're eating yellow rice. Colombians don't eat yellow rice. We Cubans do." The new arrival replied, "Yes, but I'm married to a Cuban." "Oh, how nice!" responded the first woman.

Knowing Spanish is an asset in the job market. With the plurality of the population Hispanic and with so many being first-generation immigrants, employers recognize that a good proportion of their market is Spanish speaking. They commonly prefer bilingual employees, as shown in a 1989 study that found 11 percent of help-wanted ads in the *Miami Herald* referring to bilingualism as a qualification for employment. The figure may be an underestimate, since bilingualism may in some instances be a factor in employment but not be listed as a qualification in a newspaper job advertisement (Castro 1992).

The benefits of the enclave, however, embrace only Latin immigrants. Others, most notably Haitians, have integrated themselves into the local labor market in an entirely distinct way, different from Latin immigrants and different from U.S. African Americans. It would not be entirely misleading to state that the primary mode of incorporation of Haitians is *no* incorporation, that they remain outside the normal local labor market. In 1983, just three years after the largest influx of Haitians, unemployment among the recent arrivals was nearly 60 percent. In 1985, involuntary unemployment had decreased to 24 percent, a significant improvement but still triple the figure among the Miami economically active population and double that reported by the census for Haitians nationwide in 1980. In 1985–1986, typical jobs for recent Haitian immigrants were kitchen helpers (8 percent), maids (12 percent), janitors (9 percent), gardeners (6 percent), seamstresses (9 percent), and agriculture (7 percent). Median earnings were

$680 per month. The *average* hourly wage was $3.96 among Haitian refugees who found some form of paid employment, and 11 percent received less than the legal minimum wage (see Portes and Stepick 1987; Stepick and Portes 1986).

While figures for other undocumented immigrant groups are less representative and are not always directly comparable, Haitians appeared to be faring worse than *Mariel* Cubans who arrived at approximately the same time, Dominicans in New York City (Grasmuck 1984), undocumented aliens in northern New Jersey (Papademetriou and DiMarzio 1985), and documented Vietnamese refugees in southern California (Montero 1979). Moreover, improved education or skills does little to improve Haitians' chances of either getting a job or earning more money. Indeed, the only thing that seems to make a significant difference is gender—females have it much worse than men (Stepick and Portes 1986).

As with the *Mariel* Cubans and recent Nicaraguan immigrants, Haitians have responded to these difficulties by engaging in informal-sector work, either as wage laborers or entrepreneurs (Stepick 1989, 1990). As informal-sector wage laborers, they are most likely to work in apparel, construction, hotels, restaurants, and agriculture. If they become informal-sector entrepreneurs, the most likely activities are dressmaking and tailoring, commerce, food preparation, child care, transportation, and the provision of semiskilled services in such areas as construction work, auto repair, and electronic repair. Most Haitian informal entrepreneurs drift back and forth between wage labor and self-employment. Generally, they do not leave wage labor voluntarily in favor of their own informal business. Instead, informal enterprise provides a supplement to, not a substitute for, wage labor. Haitian immigrants usually become full-time informal entrepreneurs when they have no choice, for example when they lose jobs or cannot obtain regular employment. These activities clearly are survival strategies. They only indirectly articulate with the broader market, and only indirectly benefit the larger economic system.

Conclusions

This brief overview of the restructuring of Miami's economy reveals the fundamental impact immigration has had. Without the Cuban revolution, Miami would probably appear similar to Tampa or St. Petersburg, primarily dependent on retirees from the northern United States, instead of being the capital of Latin America with a service economy oriented to the south. Not only has immigration fundamentally transformed Miami, but it has also recast it in a mold quite distinct from other U.S. cities affected by immigration. African Americans still are overrepresented at the bottom of Miami's occupational hierarchy, just as they are in any U.S. city. Similarly, Anglos remain overrepresented at the top, but in Miami those Anglos in the middle and at the lower ends have abandoned the entire urban area. They have not just fled to the suburbs, as has occurred in many other U.S. urban areas, but in Miami they have deserted the whole county.

Whereas cities such as Philadelphia were built on the backs of immigrants, primarily unskilled and semiskilled labor, many of Miami's immigrants directed and controlled the process of change, creating an economic and social environment that eased the integration of later-arriving immigrants. What distinguishes Miami, then, is not simply the relatively high proportion of successful Latin immigrants. The Latin Miami enclave does not consist exclusively or even primarily of businessmen. Latins in Miami are primarily blue-collar workers who, unlike most U.S. immigrants, work for Latin entrepreneurs, shop in Latin-owned and managed stores, watch and read Latin media, and listen to and vote for Latin politicians. Many of the businesses originated informally, breaking U.S. labor law in some way, thus prefiguring one aspect of industrial restructuring that later became widespread in the United States. In Miami, however, this industrial restructuring occurred within an immigrant Cuban community that maintained tight ethnic solidarity that offered a training ground to future ethnic entrepreneurs who both displaced Anglo entrepreneurs and advanced a vibrant local economy

Miami's largest non-Latin immigrant community, the Haitians, has assumed an entirely different role in Miami's restructuring. With a smaller proportion from advantaged economic backgrounds and having received a rejection rather than a welcome from U.S. authorities, Haitians in the early 1980s were largely excluded from the broader labor market. In response they created an informal sector that simply provides survival and not the opportunities for growth of the Latin enclave. By the mid-1980s, the majority had been absorbed into the local labor market, but almost exclusively in its lower echelons, in positions traditionally occupied by Miami's U.S. African Americans. Both are most likely to work for Anglos, and Anglos are more likely than anyone else to hold the top positions in the most important companies.

In short, the creation of the Latin Miami enclave economy has meant that ethnicity, as expressed particularly through language and race, fundamentally partitions Miami's labor market and the workers within it. Because of the likelihood of Latin managers, Miami also exhibits differing forms of managerial control that reflect not only differences in work processes but also ethnic differences. We particularly examine how ethnicity affects managerial control in Chapter 8, which discusses Miami's apparel industry.

The primary importance of ethnicity in Miami does not denote that work environments are entirely segregated by ethnicity. The Miami work environments we examine in later chapters have an ethnic mix of workers. Yet, while different ethnic groups share a work space and sometimes cooperate across ethnic lines, our examination of the apparel and construction workplaces demonstrates that, most of the time, workers maintain high ethnic solidarity and interact primarily with fellow ethnics.

Notes

1. The term *Miami* can have a number of referents. Most narrowly, it means the City of Miami. It also can refer to the broader urban area encompassed by Dade County or the Miami SMSA. In some cases, it even loosely refers to all of south Florida including Fort Lauderdale and farther up Florida's east coast. We use Miami to refer to the contiguous urban area in Dade County.

2. Estimates developed by Ira Sheskin, University of Miami, quoted in Castro and Yeaney 1989: Chaps. 2, 7–8.

3. Using the most common definition of informal economic activity as one that evades government regulation (see Portes, Castells, and Benton 1989: Chap. 1), the dividing line between an enclave and informal economic activity in Miami Cuban businesses is constantly shifting and ambiguous. In restaurants, for example, the restaurant will be licensed and inspected by the state, but the newly arrived Central American employees often receive less than the minimum wage. In the apparel industry, the larger factories usually pay at least minimum wage, but there is also considerable subcontracting for work done at home. Under U.S. law, this subcontracting is illegal. In construction, most workers receive the minimum wage, but a significant pool of casual day laborers developed to whom unscrupulous employers sometimes paid less than the minimum wage. Also, during the 1980s, street vending, especially of flowers, became widespread. All these vendors were self-employed or were paid on commission. A flower seller, for example, would sell a bunch for $5, of which $2.50 was returned to the wholesaler.

Bibliography

Biddulph, Geoffrey. 1989. "Blacks Feel Left Out as Refugees Get Jobs." *Miami Herald*, January 20.

Boswell, Thomas D. 1987. "Racial and Ethnic Change and Hispanic Residential Segregation Patterns in Metropolitan Miami: 1980." Occasional Paper Series Dialogue, Latin American and Caribbean Center, Florida International University, Miami. June.

Botifol, Luis J. 1985. *How Miami's New Image Was Created.* Occasional Paper 1985-1, Institute of Interamerican Studies. Miami: University of Miami Press.

Castro, Max. 1992. "The Politics of Language in Miami." In *Miami Now!* edited by G. Grenier and A. Stepick. Gainesville: University of Florida Press.

Castro, Max, and T. Yeaney. 1989. *Documenting Dade's Diversity: An Ethnic Audit of Dade County.* Miami: Greater Miami United, January.

Cruz, Robert David. 1990. "The Industry Composition of Production and the Distribution of Income by Race and Ethnicity in Miami." Paper, Department of Economics, Florida International University, Miami. July.

Diaz-Briquets, Sergio. 1984. "Cuban-Owned Businesses in the United States." *Cuban Studies* 14(2)(Summer):57–68.

Didion, Joan. *Miami.* 1987. New York: Simon and Schuster.

Garreau, Joel. 1981. *The Nine Nations of North America.* New York: Houghton Mifflin.

Grasmuck, Sherri. 1984. "Immigration, Ethnic Stratification, and Native Working Class Discipline: Comparison of Documented and Undocumented Dominicans." *International Migration Review* 18(3)(Fall):692–713.

Grenier, Guillermo. 1992. "The Emerging Voice of the Working Class: Ethnic Solidarity and the Cuban-American Labor Movement in Dade County." In *Miami Now!* edited by G. Grenier and Alex Stepick. Gainesville: University of Florida Press.

Levine, Barry, B. 1985. "The Capital of Latin America." *Wilson Quarterly*, Winter, pp. 46–73.

Massey Douglas S., and Mitchell L. Eggers. 1990. "The Ecology of Inequality: Minorities and the Concentration of Poverty, 1970–1980." *American Journal of Sociology* 95(5)(March):1153–1188.

Metro-Dade. 1984. "Changes in Employment and Occupations: Dade County, Florida: 1980–1987." Paper, Metro-Dade County Planning Department, Miami. September 14.

Mohl, Raymond A. 1985. "An Ethnic 'Boiling Pot': Cubans and Haitians in Miami." *Journal of Ethnic Studies* 13(2)(Summer):51–74.

Montero, Darrel. 1979. "The Vietnamese Refugees in America: Patterns of Socioeconomic Adaptation and Assimilation." *International Migration Review* 13(4)(Winter):624–648.

Papademetriou, Demetrios G., and Nicholas DiMarzio. 1985. "A Preliminary Profile of Unapprehended Undocumented Aliens in Northern New Jersey: A Research Note." *International Migration Review* 19(4)(Winter):746–759.

Porter, Bruce, and Marvin Dunn. 1984. *The Miami Riot of 1980, Crossing the Bounds.* Lexington, Mass.: Heath.

Portes, A., M. Castells, and L. Benton. 1989. *The Informal Economy: Studies in Advanced and Less Developed Countries.* Baltimore: Johns Hopkins University Press.

Portes, A., and A. Stepick. 1986. "Unwelcome Immigrants: The Labor Market Experiences of 1980 Cuban and Haitian Refugees in South Florida." *American Sociological Review* 50(August):493–514.

———. 1987. "Haitian Refugees in South Florida, 1983–1986." Dialogue No. 77, Occasional Papers Series, Latin American and Caribbean Center, Florida International University, February, pp. 1–13.

Satterfield, David. 1987. "Growth Is on Rise; Focus Is in Dade." Special Report: Outlook '87. *Miami Herald,* January 19, pp. 29–31.

Stepick, A. 1989. "Miami's Two Informal Sectors." In *The Informal Economy: Studies in Advanced and Less Developed Countries,* edited by A. Portes, M. Castells, and L. Benton, pp. 111–131. Baltimore: Johns Hopkins University Press.

———. 1990. "Community Growth versus Simply Surviving: The Informal Sectors of Cubans and Haitians in Miami." In *Perspectives on the Informal Economy,* edited by M. E. Smith, pp. 183–205. Washington, D.C.: University Press of America.

Stepick, A., and A. Portes. 1986. "Flight into Despair: A Profile of Recent Haitian Refugees in South Florida." *International Migration Review* 20(2) (Spring):329–350.

Strategy Research Corporation. 1989. "Survey of Language Use among Hispanics in Dade County." Unpublished paper. Miami.

7   Brothers in Wood

Alex Stepick and Guillermo Grenier, with
Steve Morris, and Debbie Draznin

Yeah, there's always going to be prejudice, but it's not that bad here.
Everyone's in the same boat. Everyone gets sweaty, dirty and smelly.
—A young Cuban American carpenter.

Pretty soon they'll be no whites in this trade. It won't be worth it. You
can't make a living. You can't buy shit—a nice house, a new car. Shit,
you can't even go on a fucking trip when you get time off. Pretty soon
the fucking Cubans and sambos will take it over. They know how to
live on less.
—A middle-aged Anglo carpenter.

During 1987, the Miami Beach Convention Center was the
largest single building being constructed in Dade County. It was
being built solely by union labor, an anomaly in Miami's primarily
nonunionized construction industry. Thirty years ago, however, before the Cubans took over most of the industry, the convention
center would not have been such an aberration. Then, the unions
controlled most of the industry, and virtually all the workers were
white Anglos, with the exception of African American laborers.
Now, things are different. Not only have the unions lost control of
most of the industry, but among the workers there are nearly as
many Latins as whites, and among the Blacks, many are immigrants from the Caribbean, especially Haiti.

Immigration has assuredly restructured Miami's construction
industry. Not only has there been deunionization and the penetration of immigrant workers, but also immigrant-owned firms control

145

a large portion of the industry that has been divided into union, nonunion, and informal firms. Immigrants have penetrated each of these sectors, although unevenly, predominating in nonunion firms. As the two quotes that open this chapter reveal, the immigrants' impact is mixed, with some American workers blaming them for a decline in the industry and others maintaining that solidarity persists regardless of a worker's origins.

This chapter examines these trends based on an analysis of secondary sources and fieldwork. Steve Morris worked for one summer as a carpenter's apprentice at the Miami Beach Convention Center. Debbie Draznin worked out of the Carpenters' Union Hall for two summers. Alex Stepick and Guillermo Grenier conducted interviews of union officials and managers and owners of construction firms. We first describe the transformation of the industry wrought by immigration and then the actual relationships within the workplace, the resistance of workers to management, and the conflicting forces of solidarity and autonomy among workers themselves.

The Building Trades in Miami

Between 1940 and 1960, Dade County's population increased by nearly 90 percent every ten years. For the following twenty years, the rate declined but remained a significant 30 percent per decade. Correspondingly, the construction industry boomed. Until the late 1960s, unions controlled 90 percent of all housing construction in Miami. This changed as the first wave of Cubans inundated the local labor market.

The refusal from the 1960s until the mid-1970s of local building trade unions to accept Cuban workers fundamentally transformed, rather than preserved, the construction industry. The false security created from a near-monopoly of the industry combined with nativist sentiments to create an implicit policy of exclusion. One of our Cuban respondents tried to join the Carpenters Union in 1969. He had to pay $25 to take a test in English, a language he did not speak at the time. He failed the test and was denied entrance. A few weeks later, he responded to a newspaper advertisement announcing openings for carpenters through the union. This time he did not take the test or pay any money. They simply refused to allow him in. The third time, he finally got in the union because he had married an Anglo woman whose father was a member of the Carpenters Union. His new father-in-law recommended him, and the union's business agent helped him pass the test. Subsequently, he consciously devoted himself to bringing

more Latins into the Carpenters Union and urged them to become
involved in union politics.

In short, recruitment patterns did not change; they still relied
on personalistic ties. The only difference was that through marriage one Cuban penetrated those networks and then expanded
them to include more Cubans. He later became an important officer in the union and explained his role thus: "The way I see it, it is
my job to give Latins a chance. If you are no good, you won't stay
long, but I will always give a Latin a chance to prove himself."

Unlike many other U.S. minorities, Cubans rejected by the
unions did not simply return to low-wage, unskilled work. Instead,
Cuban immigrants began creating their own, nonunion firms and
competing for housing contracts. Meanwhile, unionized construction workers focused on higher-paid jobs building condominiums
in Miami Beach and office buildings in downtown Miami. Then the
1973 recession, which severely depressed the construction industry
(see Table 7.1), impelled many Anglo construction workers to

Table 7.1. Miami's Construction Industry: Employment, Earnings, and
Firms, 1973–1989

	Number of Employees	Annual Payroll ($1,000)	Number of Firms
1973	44,707		2,544
1974	47,662	482,194	2,694
1975	30,992	331,140	2,362
1976	25,250	309,068	2,486
1977	26,614	330,021	2,675
1978	33,135	402,963	2,702
1979	37,993	486,112	2,854
1980	41,959	612,907	2,967
1981	44,716	701,896	2,950
1982	38,117	642,732	2,770
1983	35,834	640,081	3,220
1984	37,363	668,069	3,234
1985	37,039	645,637	3,328
1986	36,325	654,192	3,428
1987	38,609	708,510	3,689
1988	37,612	755,767	3,606
1989	37,532	783,600	3,581

Source: County Business Patterns (Dade County). Bureau of Economic
Research, Gainesville, Florida. Annual Reports 1974–1990.

abandon Dade County altogether, leaving a void that newer, non-union Cuban firms began to fill as the recovery began in the late 1970s.

When the unions finally recognized that excluding Cubans was a mistake, it was too late. The number of unionized carpenters declined from a high of ten thousand to a low of three thousand in the late 1970s. The 1980s were especially hard on construction unions. Throughout the United States, construction unions suffered some of the most severe economic conditions since the 1950s. On top of this, mismanagement and corruption in Miami's Carpenters Union forced the International Brotherhood of Carpenters to assume control of the Miami area local Carpenters Union. The union began to recapture some membership, but the influx of more than one hundred twenty thousand Cubans and another twenty thousand Haitians during 1980 provided more workers willing to work for nonunion wages. Then the early 1980s recession reduced the amount of work. The most recently hired were the first to go. As an Anglo leader of the Plumbers Union stated:

> We are a pretty red-neck union. . . . At first, we wanted to keep them out. That was OK with my members. I was one of the few that wanted them in anyway. Then, we decided we had to let then in . . . so we loosened up and set up some training . . . so, then the contractors put them on but they are the first ones out when the job gets done. . . . The contractors are red-necks, too. . . . To keep working, then they go work non-union. You can't blame them but that's our problem. (Grenier 1992)

In contract negotiations in the mid-1980s, the unions were forced to accept wage cutbacks and relinquish their right to strike. By that time, the Latin Builders' Association, thoroughly nonunion, had emerged as one of the most influential forces in Dade County politics, and Cuban firms, mostly nonunion, controlled more than 50 percent of all Dade County construction and nearly 90 percent of new housing, the fastest-growing sector of the industry.

When Cubans first began penetrating the construction industry in the 1960s, informal practices predominated in Cuban construction firms. Small-scale entrepreneurs operated out of the back of their trucks, accepting cash for payment and paying their workers with cash. As the industry and the number of Cuban firms grew through the 1970s, work relationships became regularized. Larger firms began subcontracting with smaller Cuban firms. By the 1980s, most larger firms paid by check, as did many of the subcontractors, who also generally made all the appropriate deductions. Wages were assuredly lower, approximately by one-third, than union wage scale, but they remained far above the minimum wage. The Cuban construction industry, in short, started informally and then became formalized.

In the wake of the 1980 *Mariel* influx and then again in the mid-1980s when working-class Nicaraguans began settling in Miami, small-scale subcontractors exploited the unemployed new immigrants by offering lower wages, hovering near the minimum wage, paid in cash without any deductions. Since 1980, many subcontractors, especially smaller ones, have no longer paid time and a half for overtime and have falsified records to conceal the true number of hours worked.

The ethnic composition of the labor force, seen in Figure 7.1, further reflects this transformation. The proportion of Latin construction workers doubled in the 1970s, from 20 percent to nearly 40 percent. Latins achieved this relative growth primarily at the expense of Anglos, many of whom, as mentioned earlier, were packing up and leaving Dade County and whose relative numbers in the construction industry declined from 60 to 44 percent.[1]

Immigrant penetration of the construction industry did not affect all sectors of the industry equally. Nonunion work is obviously more likely to be Latin dominated. But unionized work has also been affected. Different construction trades tend to be dominated by particular ethnic groups. They are also stratified in terms of prestige by race and as a result of previous political gains. The Black tradesmen, Laborers,[2] are exclusively African American and Haitian. At the other end of the scale, workers whose trades re-

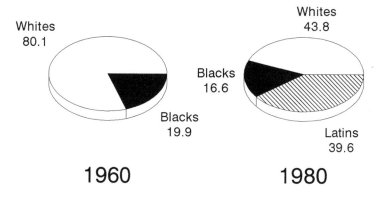

Figure 7.1. Ethnic employment percentages in Miami's construction industry, 1960 and 1980. *From* U.S. Bureau of the Census figures, Florida.

quire state licensing, for example Electricians and Plumbers, receive the highest wages and have the highest prestige. These trades are not only virtually all white but have also been the slowest to admit Latins. Carpenters fall in the middle of this hierarchy. Latins have significantly increased their percentage in the Carpenters Union, giving it the highest proportion of Latins among the unionized trades.

Unionized Latin Carpenters do mostly "inside work," that is, cabinet and door shops, where they probably constitute about 70 percent of the overall unionized workforce. In "outside work," Anglos continue to hold on. Nevertheless, even in unionized work, the trend is clear: Latins are increasing, while Anglos are declining.[3]

At the worksite where Steve Morris conducted his fieldwork, Carpenters were more or less evenly balanced between Anglos and Latins, although among all the trade workers at the site, Anglos predominated. Out of a maximum of seventy-five Carpenters working at once, there was only one African American. At the entire site, there were approximately seventy Blacks, nearly all of whom were Laborers. Laborers were further divided informally into African Americans (about three-quarters) and Haitians (about one-quarter).

Immigration, then, has dramatically affected the ethnic composition of the Miami construction industry, not only through the penetration of immigration workers, but also and even more significantly through the creation of immigrant, that is, Cuban firms and the establishment of an informal sector of construction work. This resulted from the forces described in Chapter 6 that created the Miami Latin enclave. In the construction industry, the usurpation of the majority of the industry by Cuban firms was greatly advanced by the exclusionary policies of Anglo-dominated unions. Although the unions subsequently reversed their policies, the example cited of a Latin joining the Carpenters Union through his Anglo father-in-law's intercession reveals that discriminatory, Anglo-dominated recruitment patterns persisted. Cubans simply penetrated the networks and used them to incorporate fellow ethnics.

Workers' Attitudes and Relationships

The nature of construction work directly affects construction workers' control of their labor, their consciousness, and the perception and nature of class conflict. Unlike most employees in modern industrialized society, construction workers, especially those involved in "outside" work, such as the site where Steve Morris worked, maintain a high level of independence and autonomy. Owning their tools, construction workers are freed from the technological dependence found in occupations alienated from the means of production. In Applebaum's (1981) and LeMasters's (1975) analyses of construction worker autonomy, independence among workers was found to extend through the entire process of construction work, including control over one's managerial supervision, the ability to regulate which partners to work with, and the sovereignty to decide whether or not to work in adverse environmental conditions. In Miami, we found all this to be true. But we also found that ethnic changes wrought by immigration have introduced variation in management–labor relations while complicating and apparently partially eroding solidarity among the workers.

In contrast to the workers in Miami's apparel industry, construction workers are defiant and resistant toward management. A Haitian recalled his experiences constructing the Hyatt Regency in Coral Gables. "They [the owners] wouldn't even let me go through the front door. Once we bust our balls and finish a building, the guys who own it think we are not good enough to walk in the front door. People might see us or something. What bullshit! They even told us we would get fired if we did."

Workers are especially likely to confront and resist management on safety issues. For example, an Anglo supervisor, Mark, wanted an Anglo Carpenter, Willie, to build a soffit (the underside of an enclosure to conceal air-conditioning ductwork) with a two-foot span between the studs that framed it. Willie thought a two-foot span was unsafe and directly told Mark that he would not build it to those dimensions. Mark meekly conceded and indicated that Willie could build it as he saw fit.

Another time, Alberto, a Cuban Carpenter in his fifties, had been working alone, about a hundred feet from the ground, framing the sides where the ceiling met the walls. To reach the third-story scaffolds, he had to carry ten-foot studs in one hand up a ladder. About 2:00 P.M., Steve Morris went to the gang box to get a chop-saw blade. When he arrived, he noticed that Alberto was visibly upset, sweating profusely, red in the face, shaking his head as if it bothered him, and nodding his head as if in disgust. Just then Dan, an Anglo supervisor, walked up, put his arm around Alberto's neck, and asked what was wrong. Alberto responded in English, "Danny, you know I'm a good worker. I do what you tell me. But now, I have to say something. That scaffolding is dangerous. I can't work up there alone. How do you expect me to carry materials up there and do my job? I need someone to help me. Get me someone quick or else I'm leaving. This job ain't worth dying for. You guys are the ones who talk about safety. It's in the contract. This is bullshit." Dan responded coolly, "Calm down Al, I'll get you another guy. Just take it easy." Alberto, shaking his head, said "You know I work hard, Danny. I don't want to start trouble. But this is too much." Dan answered, "OK, Al. I'll send someone right over."

Construction workers plainly believed that they were far more concerned with safety than management was. Their antagonism toward, and derision of, management was most obvious during safety meetings, which were held every few weeks. At one meeting, a superintendent for the electrical engineering contractor began by stating, "Remember, safety is our first concern." Instantly, the workers jeered in response. "Yeah, that's bullshit." An Anglo Carpenter commented to those closest to him, "Shit, I'd rather get to work than sit here and listen to this." The supervisor in charge of one meeting had to chastise workers three times to "keep it down."

To management, it seemed as if the workers were unconcerned with safety, since they frequently ignored management-imposed safety rules, such as commands for everyone to wear a hardhat at all times. Jim, an Anglo Carpenter, did not wear a safety hat because, he maintained, it caused him to lose his balance when climbing or on a scaffold. Miguel, a young Latin, explained that "they [hardhats] do no good. They're hot and get in your way. They're a hazard." At one meeting, a supervisor threatened, "If you don't wear your hardhats here, you have no business working for this company." The rule, however, was never enforced. Similarly, Jack, a young Anglo Carpenter, commenting on why he did not wear a mask for dust and fumes, claimed, "You know, us Carpenters are ignorant. Anyway, if you had to do this shit for a living, ten years off your life is a blessing." Another Carpenter declared that he did not wear gloves because "they get in the way. Shit, you can't feel what you're doing. That's downright unsafe."

Nevertheless, at one safety meeting, after management discussed its safety rules, the supervisor asked for complaints. The workers quickly obliged: debris not cleaned up, unsteady makeshift ladders to the upper storeys, unclean Port-o-Lets, and no water coolers around the site. After another meeting, workers asked no questions but spoke among themselves of safety issues, particularly the "trash," ceiling insulation sprayed on during working hours. Jim commented, "We should not have to be contaminated by that shit. It should be sprayed on at night and cleaned up before we get here. It could kill us. Who knows what's in that stuff."

The dangers, of course, are real. Accidents do occur. In one two-day period, three Carpenters were injured, one requiring twenty stitches on his sliced hand. During break one morning, Miguel and Ignacio came walking toward Steve and Jim. Ignacio was holding the side of his head. Jim asked, "What the hell happened to you?" "Miguel dropped the fucking screw gun on my head," Ignacio responded. Miguel added, "It was an accident, man." "Well, are you gonna live?" Jim asked. Ignacio retorted, "Fuck you, beer belly." And both laughed. Ignacio complained, "My head feels like a fucking Yo-Yo. Goddam, I'm lucky I wore my hardhat or I'd be dead right now." Manny claimed, "Yeah it saved your freaking life." Jim, who never wears a hardhat, changed the focus. "Shit, you know what this means, guys, don't you? You got it, another safety meeting." After everyone sat down, Jim added, "Hey, Ignacio, you shouldn't have worn your hardhat. You could be getting workers' comp right now. Instead, you got to work like the rest of us slobs; what a pea brain." Everyone else seemed more concerned with Ignacio's health and ignored Jim's comment.

This incident reveals some underlying elements of construction workers' response to the dangers of their trade: individual autonomy and different ethnic responses to danger. First, as Ignacio stated, people should wear hardhats, "It's for their own good. But if they don't wear them, that's their problem." To the men, the key issue was that it should be the worker's choice. The foreman or supervisor should not tell the workers what to do.

Second, workers from different ethnic groups respond differently. In a nonrandom sample of Latins, Anglos, African Americans, and Haitians observed the day after a safety meeting five of ten Anglos, seven of ten Latins, ten of ten U.S. African Americans, and ten of ten Haitians were wearing hardhats. In short, African Americans obeyed management completely, Latins usually, and Anglos only about half the time.

Anglo workers openly criticized their supervisors, who were all Anglo. When Jim and Steve were erecting a wall frame, Steve was cutting 35-foot metal studs to 34 feet 6 inches with a chop saw, a 20-pound, 2-foot by 1 foot heavy-duty circular saw. It was heavy work turning the 150-pound studs while sitting, then, after cutting them, lifting them into place while Jim on a scaffold screwed the tops onto a metal crossbeam. Steve was exhausted by mid-morning, and Jim commented that they needed three people on the job. "That's it. It's ridiculous that you're working like a dog when we could get another guy out here and do the job in half the time." Jim got off the lift and told Steve to wait. About ten minutes later, Jim came back with Dan, the supervisor. "We need another guy out here. This kid is killing himself for nothing. With three guys, one could cut, the other could lift the studs, and the third would be on the scaffold." Dan nodded his head and said, "You don't need three guys to do this job." He then went over to the chop saw and said, looking at Jim, "This is how you do it." Dan grabbed a stud, barely able to lift it off the ground, placed it on the chop saw, cut it, then dragged it over to the lift, hoisted it up over his head, and attached it to the hook on the lift. Jim was obviously not impressed: "Sure, Danny. That's what the boss does when he wants to show that he's right. But do that for eight hours a day and see if it works." Dan's whole face turned red. Before leaving, he loudly declaimed, "Just make sure you make it work." Jim, turning to Steve, responded, "Danny's pissed, but I don't care. He knows he's wrong, but he's just too stubborn to admit it." Then, after a pause, he added, "That fucking redneck." A week later, Dan passed by and asked Jim if he needed a third man. Jim replied, "Danny, don't trouble yourself. We're doing fine." After Dan left, Steve angrily asked why Jim didn't request a third person. Jim responded, "I wanted to bust his balls. Dan's stubborn. He always wants it his way. If he can get a ten-man job done by busting one guy's ass, he'll do it." The next day, they had a third man on the job.

In contrast, Latins seldom criticized supervisors to their face, but they disparaged them frequently behind their backs. While Steve, Domingo, and Al were working on a door frame and soffit, Dan passed by to inform them that he wanted the entire structure reframed; the dimensions were off to the left by two inches. Domingo and Al merely nodded their heads and replied in English, "OK Dan." After Dan left, Domingo and Al started their criticism in Spanish, "That dick! First he tells us he wants it this way. Then he tells us he wants it that way. Why can't he make up his mind. They [the foremen] never get anything straight." They recounted the incident to every other Carpenter they encountered that day and continued to insult Dan and the other foremen for the remainder of the day. They did, however, rebuild the door frame and soffit.

In south Florida, the birthplace of the contemporary language restriction movement in the United States (Castro 1992), language use is the focal point of considerable conflict. Language is a metaphor, an emotionally charged emblem of identity and power that can easily antagonize management. At one nonunion construction site, managers posted a sign inside their office declaring that any telephone conversations must be held in English. At the unionized site where Steve worked, a Haitian Carpenter who spoke virtually no English was fired because he worked too slowly; he stapled studs on only one wall in two days, a job that should have taken one day at most. He had worked alone, and Steve observed him looking around as if to find someone to explain to him how to staple the studs properly. But there were no Haitian carpenters to help. Another time, two Latin sheetrockers were applying sheeting to the studs with three-quarter inch screws. The supervisor, Dan, came up to them after they had spanned half of a hundred-foot wall, to tell them to use one-inch screws. Despite his efforts at using sign language, Dan could not get his point across. His face became red with frustration, and he shouted that everyone should have to understand English if they wanted to work there. Finally, Ed, a bilingual carpenter, intervened and translated Dan's orders. The sheetrockers understood and began taking down the sheeting. Dan thanked Ed and left.

In short, non-English speakers did not confront management, but antagonized management when they could not complete a job as management wanted it. Spanish speakers commonly had co-workers available to assist them with translations. Haitian Creole speakers, at least those who were Carpenters, were not so lucky. If they did not learn English or Spanish, they were likely to be fired. English speakers, both Anglos and bilingual Latins, had the advantage of understanding management's directives and the ability to resist and defy them verbally.

While English-speaking ability permitted workers to argue with management directives, race, more than language, determined workers' responses to management. Haitians and African Americans were the most respectful and careful with supervisors. They usually did not speak with any supervisors or even other workers, except when it related directly to work. For example, Dan, the supervisor, would tell Daniel, a Haitian Laborer, to get studs for Domingo and Steve. Daniel would respond with a nod and "OK" He would never question what size studs or the safety of moving them or indicate that he was in the middle of doing something else. Never once did Steve observe African Americans publicly questioning management's rules about safety or anything else.

While language differences often alienate management, their effect among workers is more mixed. First, English deficiencies are not as common or as detrimental as one might expect. Joseph, a Haitian Carpenter who spoke perfect English, noted, "If you speak the language, that's your first step to making it. You can't advance without knowing the language." Virtually all construction workers understood and spoke enough English to get along, although they spoke among themselves in their native languages. An Anglo Carpenters Union business agent, David, conjectured that language was not as much a problem in construction-related industries because the workers know a specific trade or craft; it is their skill that earns them money.

Second, language in and of itself does not cause conflict. The inability to communicate one's needs and intentions does. At a worksite, if one can find a common language, cooperation usually follows, and the potential for hostilities and tensions is reduced. Many times, Steve observed a Cuban Carpenter unable to find the right word in English "signing" or miming for a tool and receiving it from an Anglo co-worker.

Even more common were multilingual interactions. While walking to the third-story bay windows, Steve noticed Frank, an Anglo, address Alberto, an older Cuban sheetrocker, in Spanish. "Hey joven!" Alberto responded in English. "Hey Frankie." A few minutes later, Alberto was hugging another Anglo Carpenter, saying in English, "How's the kids?" The Anglo responded in English, "They're fine, buddy. How's Marie?" At a lunch break, seven Cubans and one Anglo were eating together. They were all talking about the Anglo's girl friend as one of the bilingual Cubans simultaneously translated for the Anglo.

Haitians are even more likely to engage in multilingual conversation. Daniel, the Laborer's foreman, would give instructions to another Haitian Laborer in Creole. But to the older Cuban Carpenters, he spoke Spanish, while he spoke English to Anglos, including the supervisors. One day, Alberto walked up to an unknown Haitian Laborer and put his arm around him. The Haitian responded in Spanish, "*Que pasa*, man?"

Still, language can cause a chasm between members of different ethnic groups. As one Anglo Carpenter put it to a Cuban co-worker, "Just shut up. I can't understand a word you're saying." Moreover, there is a generation gap between Latins that is reflected in language use. Younger, bilingual Cubans frequently use English as a form of authority and status over older Cubans, who only speak Spanish. One day, for example, when Steve was working with Fred and Ignacio, Alberto asked in Spanish for advice about framing a wall on the second floor. Fred and Ignacio gave him their opinions, but they did so in English.

Nevertheless, Spanish has penetrated so deeply among all workers that being monolingual in Spanish is seldom an obstacle, especially for relations among co-workers within the Carpenters Union. In contrast, Haitian Creole is truly a minority language spoken solely among native speakers. Haitians have responded to this reality by learning both English and Spanish.

Workers versus Union Bureaucrats

Carpenters extended their antimanagement sentiments to union bureaucrats. Jack, an Anglo and the Carpenters Union steward, proclaimed, "We should start a civil case against the union for violating our contract. The members didn't want to take a wage cut, but we got it anyway. Shit, you can't take your grievances to the contractor or you get on the shit list. The union doesn't do shit about this. We fucked ourselves in a lot of ways. We gave away our bargaining power—the right to strike." Jim, another Anglo carpenter added, "The union is just going down hill . . . . Reps are only in it for themselves. They only care about securing their own ass. That's the only incentive they have to protect the union. They protect the union, they guarantee themselves a job." Jack added, "They know what we want, but they're not on our side. When are you guys gonna face that fact? They're not working with us. They're working against us." Bill, another Anglo, declared, "You got that right. I'll tell you what. I'm sick of this shit. If they negotiate us out of one more benefit, I'm out of here." Mark, an older Anglo, shook his head and insisted, "Come on, guy. You're an old-timer just like me. We're both lifers. We'll be buried with hammer in hand."

One time, Jim, the union steward, found himself battling both management and the union as he tried to protect a young Nicaraguan who had been working as a sheetrocker for four years, having been paid as a journeyman the last two years. When the subcontractor found out how young the Nicaraguan was and that he had not passed the apprenticeship program, he wanted to reduce him to apprentice wages. The Nicaraguan spoke little English and could not understand what the supervisor was saying to him. When Ignacio, a bilingual Cuban American Carpenter, translated, the Nicaraguan threatened to walk off the job. Jim claimed, "They're really trying to fuck that kid. Look at this kid. He's getting screwed. He's got a family to support. That's the problem we got down at the hall; we got a bunch of chicken shits who are afraid to stand up for what is right." Later the same morning, addressing Dan, the supervisor, Jim asserted, "Hey, Danny, this kid's been working for you for about a year now. All that time he was getting paid journeyman's scale. He's doing good work. So what's this shit that you're trying to pull. I know it's the [union] hall's fault, too. They fucked up. They couldn't even get the kid's work status right. But shit, just because the system's a pile of shit doesn't mean this kid should get the shaft. It really burns me up. The hall is so full of shit. Shit, you don't get to be an apprentice for four years before you start putting up rock. You can learn that shit in a few months. I bet none of these guys [other Latin sheetrockers] ever worked for such shit wages."

Ethnic and Racial Tensions

Ethnic and racial tension pervade Miami. Race riots convulsed the city three times during the 1980s. We have indicated how Anglos sought to exclude Latins from construction unions, how Latins subsequently transformed the industry, and how African Americans remain the industry's worst-paid workers, on the lowest-prestige rung. We might expect, therefore, that relationships among construction workers would be infused with tension and resentment and predominantly segregated by ethnicity and race. While these characteristics are present, they do not dominate construction workers' interaction. The situation is more complex. Workers transform their alienation from the policies of employers and their own union representatives into a strongly class-based view of society, viewing themselves as thoroughly working class with both lower earnings and less prestige than others. Domingo, an older Cuban Carpenter, advised Steve, "Don't get into this trade, there's no future in it for you. You make no money. You get no respect." And, John, an older Anglo Carpenter, added, "Can't make a decent living at this shit anymore, not even piecemeal work pays. Whatever you do, don't do this. There is no future in this. You get paid shit. You get cut up." Much of the time workers manifest solidarity as workers, regardless of race and ethnicity. As quoted at the start of this chapter, Frank, a beginning young Cuban American Carpenter, stated, "Yeah, there's always going to be prejudice, but it's not that bad here. Everyone's in the same boat. Everyone gets sweaty, dirty, and smelly."

Bob, an African American born and raised in Miami, refrained from criticizing any group. In response to comments that Miami must have changed a lot in his lifetime and that there were many more Latins now, he replied, "Hold on, Steve. Even when I was a kid there were plenty of Latins down here. They used to come from Cuba to invest their money and travel. It's just a media thing to make it seem like just recently all these Cubans are coming in. They have always been here. . . . I've seen the world ten times over [referring to his time in the navy]. What's funny is that no matter

Blacks and whites work on the same job, but they take their lunch breaks separately. (Photo by Peggy Nolan)

what anybody tells you, people are more alike than they are different."

Morris, an African American, commenting on nonunion immigrant workers, maintained, "Shit, I don't mind. They're trying to make a living anyways they can. They don't take away our jobs, shit. It's supply and demand. If you can work and no one else will do the job, go for it. There's a lot of work out there anyway. . . . The problem is all those greedy contractors who hire those nonunion guys."

Nevertheless, unionized workers brandished union symbols such as union T-shirts and bumper stickers: "I'm proud to be union." Moreover, they strongly believed in "buying American." Steve's survey of the construction workers' parking lot revealed sixty-four American-made cars (including fifty-one pickups), one beat-up Toyota pickup, one Subaru, and one Honda Accord, the last owned by a Haitian who carefully covered it every day when he arrived at work. A fellow worker told Steve that in the past workers had "egged" foreign-made automobiles.

Miami's unionized Latin construction workers assuredly do not fit the stereotype of immigrants as docile and complacent in the workplace. As one Anglo union business agent described them: "Man, are they radical. You can show them a contract and talk to them about language but if they think that an injustice has been done, they figure it's the union's job to undo it. They always want the union to step in and fight. They drive me crazy" (Grenier 1992). In spite of the ideology and objective reality of workers' autonomy, individuals become acquainted and can become friends regardless of ethnic differences. As one Anglo Carpenter stated about a Cuban co-worker, "I've known that son-of-a-bitch for years; we're brothers in wood." Jack, another Anglo, stated, "I know a lot of Cubans." Pointing to David, an older Cuban, Jack added, "I've worked with him for years. We borrow each other's shit all the time."

Borrowing "each other's shit," (i.e., tools) is a mark of trust and cooperation, When a tool is requested, the borrower presumes a level of trust. The lender is expected to give the tool to the person who asks on the condition that it will be returned in the same condition or replaced if lost or broken. Occasionally, the lender does not fully trust the borrower and asserts the primacy of autonomy, as Steve discovered one day when he needed some channel-lock pliers to loosen and replace his chop-saw blade. He asked an Anglo pipe fitter to loan him his channel locks. The pipe fitter stared at Steve and replied, "What would you do if I didn't bring my own tools with me—-you'd have to go out and buy your own, now wouldn't you?"

More important than ethnicity in regulating social interaction is a worker's trade affiliation. As briefly discussed earlier, immigrants have unevenly penetrated the construction industry, producing an ethnic segregation within the industry by trades. At the worksite where Steve conducted fieldwork, this segregation was further emphasized by the spatial dispersion of workers across the massive site, which was larger than many city blocks. Interaction among people of different trades was thus minimal and largely coincidental to one's work.[4] But even when cross-trade interaction did occur, trade affiliation seemed to take precedence. For example, two African Americans, one a Carpenter and the other a Laborer, were engaged in conversation during a break. A Haitian Laborer approached the African American Laborer and asked a brief, work-related question. The African American Carpenter quietly slipped away and did not come back even after the question was answered, even though it was still not time to return to work. Instead, he joined a group of fellow Laborers, all African Americans.

Among Anglos, stories of how things used to be better before the Cubans came aboard. Anglos, however, are not the only ones who assert that Cubans fundamentally transformed Miami. Cubans are just as likely to take credit. Ethnocentric remarks such as "the Cubans made Miami" are common, not only among Cuban Carpenters but throughout the Cuban community.

Conclusions

Immigration has fundamentally transformed Miami's construction industry, but not entirely in expected ways. Immigrants have penetrated the industry and contributed to deunionization and a decline in wages. But the unions themselves are probably more responsible for their loss of power than the arrival of immigrant workers. Not only did Anglos exclude Cubans from the unions through the 1980s but unionized Cuban workers are apparently even more radical than their Anglo counterparts.

There are, nevertheless, ethnic differences in responses to management control. Anglos are more likely to resist and confront management verbally, and at unionized sites management is most likely to be Anglo. Latins criticize management covertly, while African Americans and Haitians ostensibly obey management directives. In short, race and ethnicity fundamentally determine relationships. Not only do they affect responses to management, but nearly everything else, thus producing an uneven penetration of immigrants into the construction industry. Immigrant Blacks, for example Haitians, occupy the same low position, Laborers, as African Americans. White immigrants, for example Cubans, have the most varied positions. In the 1960s and 1970s they created an informal sector in the construction industry. The peculiarly favorable characteristics that Cubans enjoyed in the United States helped convert these informal firms into formal ones that began to take control of the new housing market. Subsequently, large influxes of immigrants in the 1980s produced a reemergence of informal labor practices in construction at the same time that other Latins gained entry into unionized work, particularly among Carpenters. By the late 1980s, Latins occupied all levels of the construction trade occupational hierarchy from poorly paid informal workers to owners of large firms that exercise significant political influence in Miami. In contrast, Anglo construction owners have not proven to be the primary beneficiaries of immigration and the associated deunionization of the construction industry. Indeed, their activities have been increasingly limited as Cuban firms gain control.

The workers themselves, at least those unionized workers we

came to know well through participant observation, inhabit a para-
doxical world. Social-class differences are fundamental, especially
between management and labor, where management from their
viewpoint includes not only company supervisors but also their own
union representatives. Among themselves, workers seemingly inhabit a world permeated by contradictions between profound solidarity and cruel contrasts associated with an ideology of individual
autonomy. Solidarity prevails not only in contexts where workers
are opposed to management but also surrounding worker-safety
issues. Harmony during workdays also predominates as long as
workers abide by their unwritten rules of "not messing with each
other's shit" and reciprocity in access and tool sharing. Although all
construction workers are relatively autonomous in their work, and
those engaged in outside work move from job to job, workers still
create and maintain friendships as they work with some of the
same people in different jobs. The trade segregation, which seems
to dominate informal relationships, implies that workers in integrated unions are far more likely to interact and come to know
each other personally. Among the Carpenters this included not
only tolerance but also genuine interethnic friendships that overcame language differences. The higher-prestige, higher-paid licensed trades remain predominantly Anglo, and the workers in
those trades act in the most ethnocentric and exclusionary fashion
as they attempt to intimidate minorities.

Notes

1. While the proportion of Blacks dropped from 19.4 percent in 1970 to
16.6 percent in 1980, the absolute numbers of both Blacks and whites increased
as the total construction labor force grew during the 1970s from 36,000 to
almost 50,000, according to U.S. census figures for Florida in 1970 and 1980.

2. When referring to a particular union or member of that union, we have
chosen to refer to it as a trade and to capitalize it: for example, Laborer and
Laborers Union. Some would not consider unskilled Laborers to have a "trade,"
but our research reveals that they view their work, and especially union work,
differently.

3. While the ethnic composition has been transformed dramatically, construction in Dade County remains an utterly male-dominated industry. During
more than six months of fieldwork, we found only three female construction
workers, two U.S. African Americans and one white American with one U.S.
African American doing "inside" work and the other two on the "outside."

4. A similar pattern of ethnic segregation also appears among Carpenters
engaged in "inside" work. Fieldwork among the unionized "inside" shops revealed a tendency for Anglos to hold management positions, except in the few

firms owned by Latins. Moreover, the few remaining Anglo Carpenters tended to dominate the higher-skilled jobs. Even when Latins had skilled positions, they still tended to work with other Latins.

Bibliography

Applebaum, Herbert A. 1981. *Royal Blue: The Culture of Construction Workers.* New York: Holt, Rinehart and Winston.

Castro, Max. 1992. "The Politics of Language in Miami." In *Miami Now!* edited by Guillermo Grenier and Alex Stepick. Gainesville: University of Florida Press.

Guillermo Grenier. 1992. "The Emerging Voice of the Working Class: Ethnic Solidarity and the Cuban-American Labor Movement in Dade County." In *Miami Now!* edited by Guillermo Grenier and Alex Stepick. Gainesville: University of Florida Press.

LeMasters, E. E. 1975. *Blue Collar Aristocrats: Lifestyles at a Working Class Tavern.* Madison: University of Wisconsin Press.

U.S. Bureau of the Census. 1963. *Census of Population, 1960.* Vol. 1, *Characteristics of the Population, pt. 11, Florida.* Washington, D.C.: Government Printing Office.

———. 1973. *1970 Census of Population, General Social and Economic Characteristics, Florida.* Final Report. Washington, D.C.: Government Printing Office.

———. 1983. *1980 Census of Population, General Social and Economic Characteristics, Florida.* Washington, D.C.: Government Printing Office.

8 Grounding the Saturn Plant: Failed Restructuring in a Miami Apparel Plant

Guillermo Grenier and Alex Stepick, with Aline LaBorwit

Behind tall fences and barren walls in the northwest section of Greater Miami are many small apparel firms, the epitome of sunbelt industry. There are no smokestacks or grimy buildings, just low-lying concrete-block rectangles joined by acres and acres of pavement covered with thousands of automobiles. Inside the buildings is the sunbelt's most attractive economic asset: abundant, mostly nonunion, mostly female, low-wage immigrant labor.[1] In Miami, nearly fifteen thousand women, almost all immigrants and primarily Cuban, cut and sew the latest in fashions.

When the national Chicago-based corporation bought the Miami apparel firm, they had big plans. They intended it to be at the cutting edge of the industry, both technologically and in labor–management relations. They originally called it the Saturn plant, named after General Motors still-experimental Saturn automobile plant. Borrowing somewhat from Italian manufacturers and adding some of their own innovations, they conceived of a new way of producing a man's sport coat, formally called two-shell construction and informally known as the "60-minute coat." Some lower-quality materials were used, but the real saving was to be in labor, in deskilling the most skilled apparel product, a top-quality man's sport jacket. These $400–600 coats would be made on an assembly line, actually two parallel assembly lines, one for the inner part and another for the outside shell. The two parts of the coat would proceed down the two parallel assembly lines to be merged about halfway through and emerge on average 95 minutes later (in spite of

164

the 60-minute moniker), compared to 135 minutes by the old, more skilled manner. The process would be the same as that for KMart dresses and jeans, but the quality, they anticipated, would be comparable to a tailor-made sport jacket.

Competition prompted the innovation, not from the offshore assembly plants of Asia or Latin America that compete with most of the U.S. apparel industry, but from Italian companies that capture the high end of the men's clothing market through a combination of quality and, as one of this company's managers put it, "charisma," the prestige of having clothes made in Italy. The corporate headquarters manager overseeing the Miami experimental plant attributed Italian high quality to a craftsmanlike attention to production that permeates all levels of the workforce. He claimed that such an attitude is regrettably and noticeably absent among U.S. workers. He incidentally mentioned that Italy was "quasi socialistic" with long vacations and high benefits, and found it inexplicably curious that "quasi socialism" exists in conjunction with craftsmanship. The U.S. corporation presumed that restructuring production through deskilling was the only way to beat the Italian competition.

They selected the Miami plant primarily because of its immigrant labor, Cuban women, whose deft and quick hands had created Miami's apparel industry in the 1960s. They had a reputation that pleases all employers: They were good, and they worked cheap. The plant would be far from the rest of the corporation's production facilities, which are located primarily in a triangle made by Chicago, southeastern Missouri, and Georgia, thus adding at least an extra dollar in transportation costs to each coat. But in the end, corporate headquarters could not ignore the advantage of low-wage, skilled labor, and they began their experiment with enthusiasm and elevated aspirations in the mid-1980s.

Their plans failed. In 1992 the corporation announced the imminent closing of the Miami plant. At the last moment, they found a buyer who promised to preserve at least some of the plant's approximately 250 jobs. But the men's sport coat "Saturn" plant dream dissolved, and not because the plant could not produce quality coats. Everyone agreed that the quality was equal to that in their other plants. The two-shell method worked fine. It was the sixty-minute part that was the problem. They could not produce the coats fast enough to keep labor costs per coat as low as they wanted.

The immigrant workers quietly but determinedly resisted management's plans. This chapter recounts the failed experiment, examining the restructuring of Miami's apparel industry since the 1960s and the particular venture at this one plant.

Immigrants Create the Industry

The garment industry in Miami shares similarities with others in Chicago, Los Angeles and New York (see Fernández-Kelly and Sassen 1991; Waldinger 1988). It is dominated by females; the work is considered unskilled machine labor, and it offers basic employment opportunities for new immigrant workers. As in other garment towns, new immigrants continue to be the preferred workforce. While garment is a traditionally unionized industry, in the sunbelt and elsewhere, it has suffered deunionization in the process of economic restructuring.

Table 8.1. Miami's Apparel Industry Employment, Earnings, and Firms, 1973–1989

	Number of Employees	Annual Payroll ($1,000)	Number of Firms
1973	20,567		532
1974	22,346	113,707	572
1975	18,846	111,363	595
1976	21,064	125,571	606
1977	23,006	147,626	702
1978	24,819	160,082	724
1979	24,441	169,496	693
1980	23,697	169,739	670
1981	20,707	174,839	671
1982	20,618	175,351	634
1983	20,278	192,191	708
1984	21,536	192,061	718
1985	19,546	192,315	724
1986	20,160	198,146	717
1987	18,982	216,369	702
1988	18,429	224,085	687
1989	19,019	237,231	670

Source: County Business Patterns (Dade County). Bureau of Economic Research, Gainesville, Florida. Annual Reports 1974–1990.

Miami's apparel industry has its roots in the 1940s diversification of the local economy, but its biggest boost came in the late 1960s. Many New York, primarily Jewish, manufacturers relocated in Miami in the face of threatening unionization in the Northeast and attracted by the labor force made available by waves of Cuban immigration in south Florida. Overall employment rates peaked in the late 1970s, but earnings continued to increase even after the number of employees declined (Table 8.1). Miami's apparel firms are almost all small, family-owned enterprises. Of the nearly 750 firms, only 20 percent have more than twenty workers, and the average number of employees is thirty.

While overall employment has been steady, the ethnicity of workers has changed dramatically. As Figure 8.1 indicates, thirty years ago employees were nearly 95 percent white; many, although by no means most, were unionized. Today's apparel workers are 85 percent Hispanic women, and far fewer shops are unionized.

In the mid-1980s, Miami manufacturers had difficulty finding new workers to replace their aging and retiring female Cuban workers. The economic success of the Cuban community permitted the second generation of Cuban women to forsake the low wages of the apparel industry, while the virtual elimination of Cuban immigration reduced new supplies of workers. Although Haitians and Black Americans provided a potential solution, manufacturers were reluctant to incorporate them. Instead, by the late 1980s, newly arrived Central and South Americans replenished the supply of women willing to work at tedious, repetitive tasks for low wages.

In response to the challenge of imports from Third World nations, Miami firms restructured by dividing into three types: (1)

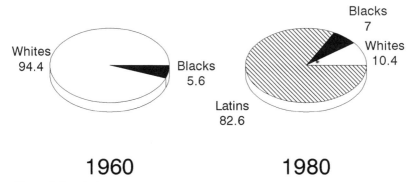

Figure 8.1. Ethnic employment percentages in Miami's apparel industry, 1960 and 1980. *From* U.S. Bureau of the Census figures, Florida.

completely above-board, legal firms with factories obeying all or most labor laws; (2) firms with factories that attempt to avoid labor laws; and (3) firms that specialize in putting-out, or homework (see Fernández-Kelly and Garcia 1989; Stepick 1989, 1990). The firm we studied falls into the first category, legal firms. Foreign competition and New York City's Chinatown garment district hit these firms the hardest, especially those concentrating on children's or women's wear. Many closed shop in Miami, some completely closing down operations and others resettling abroad. Union membership, which was concentrated in the largest firms, fell from five thousand in 1978 to one thousand in 1986.

The other two types of firms not only survived, but even flourished through the 1980s. In 1980, the U.S. Department of Labor, stating that Miami was swiftly becoming one of the sweatshop capitals of the United States, formed a strike force that found labor violations totaling $180 million in owed wages to over five thousand workers in 132 firms (Risen 1981). A good portion of the violations consists of homework, illegal in the U.S. garment industry, although it is estimated to incorporate between 30 and 50 percent of local production. The U.S. Department of Labor claims Miami homeworkers actually earn at least the minimum wage.[2] It is also asserted that garment workers prefer homework (see Fernández-Kelly and Garcia 1989). Nevertheless, homework in the apparel industry is illegal in the United States, and it does lower overhead costs even when workers receive the minimum wage.

Plant History

The apparel plant we studied is a subsidiary of the largest U.S. clothing manufacturer, which purchased the plant in 1985. Previously owner operated, the plant has been in existence since the early 1960s and at the time of the research in the late 1980s employed approximately 250 operators, most of whom were older Cuban women. Haitian workers have been increasing since the early 1980s and more recently Central Americans, especially Nicaraguans, have been hired. There are also sprinklings of Black Americans and other Latins.

The Amalgamated Clothing and Textile Workers Union (ACTWU) has represented workers since the plant's opening. The ACTWU has been associated with the Chicago-based corporation that owned this plant since the early part of the century when the two organizations joined ranks to develop some of the most progressive collective bargaining agreements of the time. Since that time, the union has also been one of the most active organizers of immigrant and female workers, groups considered by many to be the most difficult to organize. Perhaps because of this long tradition with female immigrants, all the employees of the three ACTWU plants in Miami belong to the union. This level of voluntary membership in a labor organization is a notable anomaly in a right-to-work state.

Guillermo Grenier and Alex Stepick conducted extensive interviews with all managerial personnel, interviewing the regional vice-president and the regional division chief. The managerial interviews lasted from forty-five minutes to three hours each. We also participated in various plant rituals and regularly walked the floor, talked to operators, and visited the lunchroom during the three different lunch periods. In addition, two research assistants worked as operators in the plant. Bernadette is a middle-aged Haitian woman with some experience in the apparel industry; Aline is a Jewish American who speaks fluent Spanish.

In 1981, it seemed that the plant would have to close. Mr. Elman, the plant's owner and manager at the time, addressed the workers and supervisors with a recommendation that they work without benefits for a certain amount of time. In an emotional appeal from the steps leading to the production floor, he informed the workers that they had a choice. Their benefits could be paid for the current period, but the plant would have to close for a while because of that expenditure. Or, if the workers agreed to work without benefits for an undisclosed amount of time, the plant could continue to operate. He put the issue to a vote, vowing to comply with the voice of the majority. With the union's approval, all employees, including nonunion management employees, voted on the issue. With only twelve opposing votes, the employees voted to work without benefits.

In spite of the evident sacrifices workers endured, employees cherish these memories, referring to Mr. Elman's tenure as the period of *huevos de oros*, "golden eggs." Workers uniformly remember Mr. Elman fondly as an accessible man who knew the names of all his employees, who cared if someone was sick, who would always keep his door open to workers, someone who attended to his workers' concerns beyond the workplace. He permitted a flexible, warm working environment. Workers could have their own radios, their own hotplates, or enjoy a snack while at their machine. After hours, they could use the company's presses or sew for themselves. As the production control manager put it, "Mr. Elman knew the names of all the workers. He talked to every new [employee]. . . . People worked because we wanted to protect him. . . . He had charisma."

Initially owned by a Venezuelan Jew, the plant formed part of a local manufacturing process, surviving largely on individual contracts established with outlets, retail, and specialized customers. This type of contract work continued into the tenure of the subsequent owner, a Colombian, and to the immediately previous owner, Mr. Elman. During the Elman period, from 1974 to 1985, the plant was a flexible production plant. Contracts for nun's habits, children's clothes, and other items were produced for as many as twelve contractors at one time.

Previous plant management exercised direct, personalistic control. One supervisor who had worked at the plant since 1965 maintains that the Colombian owner had a very "familial managerial style." Subsequent owners followed this style, culminating in the period of the illustrious Mr. Elman, the last owner before the present management, who seemed to have elevated paternalism to an art form.[3]

In exchange for certain personal considerations from their employer, workers were loyal, dependable, and understanding of the firm's needs. This tradeoff between personal considerations and company commitment appealed to the mostly Cuban workforce. As the union representative reported, Mr. Elman knew how to treat Latins: *Sabia como pasarles la mano*," ("he knew how to pat them"). This "patting" included sending employees to his personal physician when they needed medical care.

When Mr. Elman sold the plant to the present conglomerate, management–labor relations utterly changed. In reporting what the arrival of the new management meant to all the employees accustomed to Mr. Elman's style, one supervisor reported, "It was like giving children a new father."

Restructuring the Plant

After approving plans for the innovative Saturn-like apparel plant, Chicago corporate headquarters hired a well-known apparel management consulting team and assigned two of their own industrial engineers to implement their vision. Their initial impressions of the plant disenchanted the visionaries. One of the corporation's industrial engineers, who later became the in-plant industrial engineer, bluntly called the plant "a pigsty." The other industrial engineer, who became the plant's manager, expanded, describing it as "filthy, disorganized . . . with not clean engineering and off-standard discipline."

They envisioned a thorough restructuring of the labor process, ceasing flexible production and replacing it with their innovative two-shell process, which would also incorporate many of the methods in labor relations in the 1980s, including work teams, quality circles, and an abandonment of piece rates, an unprecedented step in the modern apparel industry. The corporation had already created work teams and quality circles in other plants, achieving higher output levels with acceptable quality.

While the two-shell process was an innovation, assembly-line construction is not at all new in the apparel industry (Lamphere 1987; Waldinger 1988). It has dominated the apparel labor process for over one hundred years, and previous management employed it at this particular plant from its beginnings in the 1960s. An extreme division of labor characterizes the process. Each worker performs a minute task repeatedly, hundreds of times a day. Almost all workers are paid a piece rate. The more they produce, the more they earn.

The task of the new corporation and its management team was to adapt the already entrenched assembly-line method to their product. This required three kinds of changes: reconfigured tasks and piece rates appropriate to the high-quality sport coats that would be produced; some new state-of-the-art machinery; and most important, substitution of the bureaucratic labor–management control for the simple, paternalistic relations previous management enjoyed with the plant's workers.

The industrial engineers intensively analyzed all the operations required to produce the coat, designing new operations and revising the piece rates earned by workers. The thrust of constructing the new sewing operations for the two-shell design was deskilling the process into simpler, more repetitive tasks. Workers, however, did not necessarily consider the tasks simple. Our research assistant, Aline, trained on one of the new machines, the "chopper."

> The "chopper" sews as it cuts, they said. Until I saw it work, I was completely baffled by the apparent paradox. But it does just that—it cuts off the ragged sides of the seam that is being made. I will be sewing an inside part of the shoulder of the jacket. . . . First, A. had me learn how to thread the machine, by watching her, then by doing it myself over and over again several times. Then she showed me the way to put the piece in the jacket. But she had me simply practice using the machine on pieces of plain cloth, without the chopper. I had

a terrible time the entire day getting control over the foot pedal—it is delicate enough that with a not-so-delicate touch of the foot, the thing flies. All the jokes from everyone not to get my fingers sewn together and not to get my fingers under any needles really weren't funny today. It all seemed very possible.

Even while in training, Aline described the work process as a demanding physical task. Operators are required to be at their machines when the break bell rings, "not running back." The constant reminder by her supervisor that she was working too slowly combined with the physical demands of the machine to make the production process "totally nerve-wracking. My shoulders are aching—and so is my ass from sitting on this hard chair the whole day." All talking and looking around was discouraged. All efforts focused on the task at hand: *dominar*, dominating, or mastering, the machine. The training director walked the floor timing new and old operators, to "save the company money and help the workers."

Helping the workers meant helping them operate the machine faster to increase production. To this end, the workers were not taught to sew but to operate a specific machine that performed a specific task. Each machine had a different "personality," and it was the operator's job to learn it. After the training period was over, the operator and the machine were moved out to the floor together, each knowing the other's quirks.

Each job was learned as a series of distinct steps, each of which had to be mastered. After two weeks on the job, Aline had developed a list in her head of the "little shit" that had to be done perfectly:

1. Smooth the lining and continue to do so before each section is sewn.
2. Go around the little curve slowly at the top.
3. The piece being inserted is a little longer than the shoulder because it is supposed to make the shoulder full—so you have to push the piece gently to add fullness.
4. But it can't be pleated.
5. Going around the curve, the material can't be cut, just the left over edges.
6. Sew in the middle of the foot, not too far to the edge or the inside.
7. Don't catch up the inside of the material as it rolls up.

Aline found that each step had to be done perfectly or the operation would not come out right. And if it did not come out correctly, "You have to do it again and again and again." To make

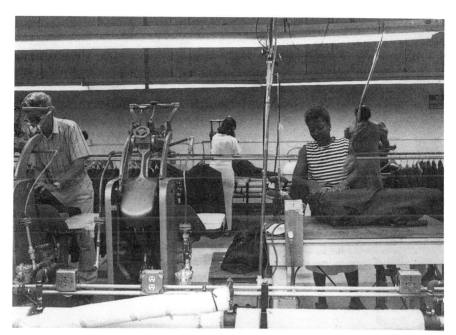

Haitians and Cubans working side by side. The individual and intense nature of the work limits interaction. (Photo by Peggy Nolan)

money, she learned you must also do it very fast. While the training period allowed Aline time to chat as her quality was checked, such "down time" was almost nonexistent for the operators on the shop-floor. Our Haitian research assistant, Bernadette, had worked previously in other Miami apparel plants, but she found this work more demanding.

As she described the conditions of her job, "I will not have the time to talk to people because I am worrying about the job, so that I can make more. Well, I could do it. But when I see people working, they are going fast. I would like to work like them, so that I can make a lot, too. I am rushing, I want to make a lot, too. But Fritz [the Haitian supervisor] said no. If you are rushing to make a lot, you are not going to make them well, because you don't know the work yet." As Bernadette said to a co-worker, "The work is easy for you, but it is difficult for me." The co-worker replied, "Don't worry, don't trouble yourself because you are going to find that the work is not easy until you have three months." Bernadette thought to herself, "Until I have three months, that is when I will find it easy. I told myself, three months! Until three months?"

Along with devising a new set of purportedly deskilled operations, engineers determined how much workers would be paid for each operation. The piece rates under the previous management were a complete mess, according to the new management. They seemed to have little relationship to the work performed, as similar and sometimes even the same operations were paid at different rates. In fact, there were almost as many piece rates as there were workers. Through re-engineering the tasks, the new management attempted to standardize work and wages through methods common throughout the industry. For each of the 130 operations that the new two-shell method contained, a 100 percent "base rate" would be established, the rate of an allegedly average worker, expressed in terms of how many pieces should be produced per hour or day. If the worker performed at 100 percent, then she or he would earn the standard hourly rate, which in this plant in 1988 was slightly under $5 per hour.

All workers believe, nevertheless, that the supposedly "average" base rate is too difficult to obtain and that correspondingly the piece rates are too low. Moreover, some materials are easier and faster to work with, yet the piece rates recognize only one distinction, that of plain and plaid materials. Workers vie to obtain bundles of easy materials that are paid at the same rate as slightly more difficult materials. It is the responsibility of the supervisor to regulate this competition among workers. While workers performing the same operation compete to obtain easier-to-work-with materials, those at subsequent operations depend on others to work efficiently enough to supply them with a constant stream of bundles for their work. As one of our researchers reported, "There's a lot of discussion about whose job is the hardest and how fast people are working."

Usually couched in the rubric of equity and improving working conditions, management bureaucratized worker relations. When workers had a problem under the previous owner, they walked directly into the owner–manager's office. He was the only boss. There was no personnel manager or payroll clerk, just one manager assistant who checked time cards, processed production sheets, and cut checks. Under the new regime, labor relations became considerably more complex with a many-leveled hierarchy.

Directly above the shopfloor operators, the new plant appointed supervisors who almost exclusively had worked their way up in the same factory. They spoke Spanish (or, in one case, Haitian Creole) and presumably workers could relate to them better.

Workers henceforth could no longer address the manager directly. He no longer listened to workers' problems, neither work-

related nor personal ones. One had to go through the floor supervisors, then the area supervisors, perhaps the personnel manager,
proceeding to the union representative, a filed grievance, and finally, an audience with the plant manager, who might still defer a
decision "upstairs," to corporate headquarters in Chicago. Chicago
even performed many accounting and inventory details, transmitting the results back to Miami by computer.

The chain of command was clearly hierarchical. The union grievance procedure was presented as the method through which all
workers must express their complaints. This significantly enhanced
the roles of both the union's and management's supervisors. Indeed,
the plant manager viewed himself as one of the strongest supporters
of the union because he emphasized the union as a stabilizing force
within the production and organizational structure.

Snacks at the machines were no longer allowed, and neither
were hotplates. The company put a new microwave in the lunchroom and encouraged its use during breaks. Individual fans and
radios were replaced by plantwide air conditioning and piped-in
music. (According to the production manager, the station played
alternates between American and Latin songs. "You can't please
the Haitians on this one." The radio, however, is played only on
Saturdays when a few people come in to do makeup work.)

Management conceived of these changes as beneficial to both
them and the workers. Consistent rules that applied equally to everyone and working through the union were "fairer." Having
Spanish-speaking supervisors fostered better communication. Ban-
ning fans would deter the spread of potential fire and keep pieces
of material from blowing into a worker's eyes. Forbidding food
from the floor would keep mice away.

Workers, however, resented the changes and employed their
resentment to sabotage the visions of corporate headquarters. The
workers produced acceptable-quality coats, but they did not produce them quickly enough; overall output struggled to achieve 80
percent of management's goals. According to the quality-control
manager, who had worked nine years at other plants for the corporation, "The people [at other plants] are more easy to control than
here." The highest management official we interviewed, the Chicago-based executive vice-president, believed that workers self-con-
sciously resisted change by work slowdowns. One of the locally
promoted Spanish-speaking supervisors claimed that the low production resulted from the management's bureaucratization. "People are still pissed, even three years later." Some workers labeled
the new management rules "totalitarian." Two other respondents

mentioned that new management was making the factory "just like Cuba" and that "this is becoming like a dictatorship."

Workers commonly ignored bureaucratic procedures. The payroll manager, another locally promoted Spanish speaker, still had Haitians storm directly into her office when their checks did not match their expectations. Workers did not care that floor supervisors spoke their own language. They wanted to address the plant manager directly. Moreover, unwittingly management selected floor supervisors who were not really representative of the majority of workers. Many were Spanish speakers, but were non-Cubans or from the earliest immigrant, slightly higher-class Cubans, and they maintained condescending attitudes toward those under them.

Whereas workers previously volunteered overtime for Mr. Elman, under the new management absenteeism became a continuing problem. Some workers snuck radios in under their blouses and listened to them through a small earphone.

Worker resistance was not organized by the union, but more informally. Some of it, such as sneaking in radios, was individual, but much of it came through informal social groups of workers, women who worked in the same area or had worked together in the plant for numbers of years. As in other apparel plants and female-dominated workplaces (Lamphere 1987), informal social interaction commonly focused on celebrations such as birthdays, showers, and retirement parties. While the intensity of work limited socializing when one was working, during breaks (one in the morning, lunch, and another in the afternoon) workers would gather in small groups. These activities provided the basis for resistance. They were the context in which workers remembered and reconstructed their relationship to Mr. Elman, a relationship that assuredly exploited labor more, but which in their restructuring assumed more positive tones. At the same time, workers critiqued the new management, the revised piece rates that could not be adjusted simply by visiting the manager's office but had to be addressed through a complex, multistaged grievance procedure.

All managers shared the belief that the new owners imposed their "northern, Anglo" management techniques too quickly and brusquely on an immigrant workforce that had been accustomed to, and worked well under, the paternalistic, less bureaucratic approach of the previous owner. The on-site Anglos assigned to Miami by corporate headquarters tended to recognize that they made errors in implementing changes, but they remained convinced that things would be better overall if the Latins and Haitians became more like them, instead of returning to the former paternalistic management styles.

The Latin managers, in contrast, believed that not only did the new Anglo managers make mistakes but that they changed and became a lot more like the Latins. By 1990, the plant manager had learned that he had to talk to people at all levels to get them to work for him. During his first year, he seldom communicated with the workers and took little advice from the older, middle-management group. Perhaps learning from the personalistic practices of his predecessor, he allowed a supervisor to use his condominium while he was out of town. But his adaptation was too little, too late. Corporate headquarters' impatience at achieving their dream plant finally forced the abandonment of the Miami experiment.

Conclusions

The structure of Miami's apparel industry, the nature of work in it, and the ethnic composition of the workforce are all similar to patterns in the apparel industry throughout the United States, both contemporarily and historically. An abundant supply of immigrant Latin, nonunionized women attracted manufacturers from the Northeast. Through these women's long hours and quick hands, the industry flourished through the 1960s and 1970s. The 1980s brought competition that restructured the local industry, closing some shops, forcing others abroad, and driving still others to bend the labor laws or go underground.

The particular shop we studied sold out to a national firm with an ambitious vision of restructuring. Their strategy included incorporating new machines, but also sought to recast labor relations contrary to the general restructuring trends in the industry. Flexible specialization was abandoned and replaced by concentration on a single product, men's sport jackets. The management eschewed the trends toward deunionization and informalization. Instead, they dismissed the allegedly inefficient prior paternalism and imposed a rigid, hierarchical bureaucratic structure, what one supervisor referred to as the "Americanization of the plant." One middle-level manager who had worked under both regimes succinctly expressed the nature of this dynamic interrelation: "I have fewer responsibilities now. Part of the reason for this is that the company produces less variety of products. Mr. Elman had to hustle whatever work we could get. When [new management] came in, we were producing twenty-one different types of garments! Everything from nuns habits to flight attendants uniforms. . . . Also, Mr. Elman had no personnel department. We all got involved with the workers." Under the new regime, the division of labor and responsibilities became much more specific and rigid.

For the workers, the new rules meant a depersonalization of control through integration into a rationalized, bureaucratic management structure that limited interactions between managerial and floor employees, restricted shopfloor behavior (no radios, hotplates, fans), and increased production requirements (higher quality was demanded, even if the units per hour remained approximately the same).

Now, not only did the workers have to follow a variety of new rules and regulations, but the on-site management also had to defer major decisions to an office in Chicago. As one supervisor said, "Mr. Elman was the only boss. He never told us he had to check with 'upstairs' to make a decision."

Workers resisted, complaining about and refusing to abide by the new rules. Management soon abandoned hopes of forming quality circles and concentrated on the more traditional forms of bureaucratization. But workers never produced up to management's expectations, and ultimately management conceded defeat. In 1992, seven years after beginning the experiment, management announced the closing of the plant, which was subsequently sold to a local investor.

The unusual aspects of this case—a unionized apparel plant that attempted to comply with all labor laws and fulfill the American ideal of bureaucratized labor relations—reveal both the force of macrostructural factors and the power of local labor resistance. The recession of the early 1990s damaged all of Miami's apparel industry. Those most able to survive relied on a combination of flexible specialization and the informalization of work relationships, particularly the use of homeworkers. While working conditions are uncertain and pay is low, workers may actually prefer these conditions to the bureaucratized relations of the plant we studied. Homework permits women to mix domestic chores with earning money, while the direct control of nonbureaucratic relationships in Miami, and apparently in southern California (see Fernández Kelly and Garcia 1989), provides for personal relationships with employers.

The workers in the plant we studied resisted quietly, indirectly. There were no strikes or formal work slowdowns. Informal social groups articulated their grievances, and individual workers complained to management and failed to work as quickly as management desired. The force of the macro factors, particularly the recession of the early 1990s, nearly cost them their jobs, and still might. Workers and management found themselves caught in the same vise, with structural factors pushing for lower wages and harsher working conditions and a management incapable of realizing their dream of a Saturn apparel plant.

Acknowledgments

The authors would like to thank the owners and managers of the apparel plant we studied. We would especially like to thank Tom and Frank, whose openness and generosity far exceeded what we expected. Without their assistance, this study would have been impossible. We would also like to thank all the workers, both in management and on the floor, who cooperated with us. Our two research assistants, Aline and Bernadette, both deserve to be co-authors. Bernadette, however, prefers to remain anonymous.

Notes

1. Low corporate tax rates are another attractive feature of sunbelt states.

2. Because wages are based on piece rates, and garment homework is illegal, it is impossible to verify this claim.

3. Paternalism is understood to mean a system of control in which the owner–manager has final and arbitrary authority but whose actions are constrained to some extent by an implicit understanding of the rights and obligations of the employees. One important characteristic of paternalism is the personal relationship between owner and employee.

The concept of paternalism dates from the Weberian presentation of "traditional" authority (Weber 1947). Bendix (1956:17) expanded the concept to include the dynamics of worksite control by arguing that traditionalism "frequently facilitated the management of labor" by establishing a familial structure of reciprocal loyalties (47). Bendix added that because of its exploitative nature and inefficiency, paternalism would decline in importance in capitalist development. More current studies, however, argue that paternalism is an important technique in controlling and motivating workers in small firms. These studies reveal that despite low wages and stagnant working conditions, many workers exhibit a surprisingly low level of alienation or resentment and often express loyalty to the firm and high levels of identification with the interests of the firm.

Bibliography

Bendix, Rhinehart. 1956. *Work and Authority in Industry*. Berkeley: University of California Press.

Boswell, Thomas D. 1987. "Racial and Ethnic Change and Hispanic Residential Segregation Patterns in Metropolitan Miami: 1980." Occasional Paper, Series Dialogue, Latin American and Caribbean Center, Florida International University, Miami, June.

Ferdández-Kelly, Maria Patricia, and Ana Garcia. 1989. "Informalization at the Core: Hispanic Women, Home Work and the Advanced Capitalist State."

In *The Informal Economy: Studies in Advanced and Less Developed Countries*, edited by Alejandro Portes, Manuel Castells, and Lauren Benton, pp. 247–264. Baltimore: Johns Hopkins University Press.

Fernández-Kelly, M. Patricia, and Saskia Sassen. 1991. *A Collaborative Study of Hispanic Women in the Garment and Electronics Industries: Final Report presented to the Ford, Revson, and Tinker Foundations,* New York: Center for Latin American and Caribbean Studies, New York University, May.

Lamphere, Louise. 1987. *From Working Daughters to Working Mothers: Immigrant Women in a New England Industrial Community.* Ithaca, N.Y.: Cornell University Press.

Risen, J. 1981. "Sweatshops Pervasive in Miami." *Miami Herald,* May 18, pp. 6–7.

Stepick, Alex. 1989. "Miami's Two Informal Sectors." In *The Informal Economy: Studies in Advanced and Less Developed Countries,* edited by A. Portes, M. Castells, and L. Benton, pp. 111–131. Baltimore: Johns Hopkins University Press.

———. 1990. "Community Growth versus Simply Surviving: The Informal Sectors of Cubans and Haitians in Miami." In *Perspectives on the Informal Economy,* edited by M. E. Smith, pp. 183–205. Washington, D.C.: University Press of America.

U.S. Bureau of the Census. 1963. *Census of Population, 1960.* Vol. 1, *Characteristics of the Population,* pt. 11, Florida. Washington, D.C.: Government Printing Office.

———. 1973. *1970 Census of Population, General Social and Economic Characteristics, Florida.* Final Report. Washington, DC.: Government Printing Office.

———. 1983. *1980 Census of Population, General Population Characteristics, Florida.* Washington, D.C.: Government Printing Office.

Waldinger, Roger. 1988. *Through the Eye of a Needle.* New York: New York University Press.

Weber Max. 1947. *The Theory of Social and Economic Organizations.* Fairlawn, N.J.: Oxford University Press.

9   The View from the Back of the House: Restaurants and Hotels in Miami

Alex Stepick and Guillermo Grenier, with Hafidh A. Hafidh, Sue Chaffee, and Debbie Draznin

At the meeting, all the Haitians—Sam, Edmond, Bobier, Joseph, Bobby, Lucy, and many others—sat at one long table. Lucy was the only female. We did two separate evaluations; the second one gave us the opportunity to rate each manager individually. Bobby did a quick translation for the Haitians, but I knew he was speaking too quickly for Lucy to write because her writing skills are not that good. I took the second paper from her. I filled out the top, the part where it asked for your occupation in the restaurant. I wrote "kitchen worker," then I filled in the names and gave it back to her. During the test, she turned to me and whispered, "Sue, why you don't put 'pantry' instead of 'kitchen'?" I whispered back to leave it alone so that they wouldn't know it was her evaluation. As we were driving home from the meeting, she told me she had made her own column next to categories 1, 2, 3, and 4. "On Vance's paper, I made a big zero and underneath it a whole row of little zeroes—because he's a bad person and they supposed to know that! Then I put down 'pantry' next to where you put 'kitchen.' Yes! I want them to know it was me who put that. Vance no good, he has no respect for people. He know my husband out of work and he's supposed to give me back my hours but instead he give my job to Isaac and that other stupid man, Smith. I So I gave him all zeroes."

Lucy and Sue had just attended a staff meeting of the Miami seafood restaurant where they worked, a meeting whose primary purpose was to obtain individual, anonymous staff evaluations of management. Vance is the restaurant's general manager. Lucy and

181

he have been engaged in a protracted struggle that encapsulates many of the themes of management–labor relations in Miami: ethnic succession and conflict, management's mix of bureaucratic and personal control, and workers' struggles with one another and against management.

This chapter examines those trends based on research conducted by three graduate assistants—an African male student, Hafidh A. Hafidh, and two American white females, Sue Chaffee and Debbie Draznin. Hafidh worked for three years as a server in a major national-chain hotel restaurant, both before and after being a graduate student. Sue similarly began as a server before becoming a graduate student, working in a popular seafood restaurant that is one of a chain of five in the southeastern United States. Debbie worked full-time as a cashier in the lobby gift shop of a Miami Beach luxury resort hotel.

Miami's Tourist Industry

Tourists, other temporary visitors, and the hotels and restaurants they spawned have fundamentally propelled Miami's history. When Miami incorporated itself into a city, at the end of the last century, its most massive building was a sprawling hotel adjacent to the Miami River and Biscayne Bay. The first major population influx occurred two years later when military troops trained in Miami Beach before embarking for Cuba and the Spanish-American War. By the 1920s, Miami had become a thriving center of winter tourism for northeasterners and midwesterners. World War II again found troops stationed and trained in Miami. Many remained or returned to settle at the conclusion of the war. During the 1950s, nationally popular entertainers such as Arthur Godfrey and Jackie Gleason became Miami Beach fixtures, and massive luxury hotels dominated the beachfront.

The post–World War II wave of permanent residents initiated a long-term relative decline in tourism, from about 35 percent in 1940 to about 10 percent in 1979. The recession of the late 1950s combined with new direct air service from the northeastern U.S. to the Caribbean sent many smaller, locally owned hotels into bankruptcy. The 1970s emergence of DisneyWorld and central Florida as tourist destinations further eroded Miami's tourism (see Table 9.1). Many hotels became condominiums and rest homes. During the 1980s, Miami's leaders became obsessed with creating a positive image for Miami as refugees, many branded as criminals and mental cases from Cuba, flooded the city, the cocaine trade spilled into

Table 9.1. Miami's Hotel and Restaurant Industries: Employment, Earnings, and Firms, 1973–1989

	Number of Employees	Annual Payroll ($1,000)	Number of Firms
1973	55,900		2,260
1974	60,131	219,076	2,270
1975	48,244	227,708	2,313
1976	52,948	248,163	2,370
1977	54,433	244,986	2,066
1978	57,573	270,881	2,260
1979	56,091	315,639	2,321
1980	58,770	372,655	2,373
1981	37,261	230,488	1,962
1982	56,081	408,865	2,459
1983	56,032	410,448	2,881
1984	60,793	455,662	2,939
1985	61,015	498,551	3,060
1986	41,911	324,675	2,717
1987	64,896	598,416	3,261
1988	63,980	364,550	3,149
1989	68,321	629,178	6,454

Source: County Business Patterns (Dade County). Bureau of Economic Research, Gainesville, Florida. Annual Reports 1974–1990.

shopping-center shootouts, and major Black uprisings shook the city three times in the decade. Through glitzy national advertising campaigns, the Greater Miami Convention and Visitors' Bureau struggled to create alternative images and attract conventions and tourists.

After three decades of decline and difficulties, tourism again thrust Miami to national and even international attention in the early 1990s as the rediscovered 1920s and 1930s Art Deco architecture became fashionable. The attention remodernized the first-settled South Beach section of Miami Beach, filling it with art galleries, boutiques, and, of course, hotels and restaurants, which were populated primarily by Latin American and European tourists.

Unlike in Miami's construction and apparel industries, restaurant and hotel unions played a small role in the growth or decline of the local hotel and restaurant industries. The climate, not the opportunity to escape unionization in the North, created these industries. Some immigrants may have been excluded from unions, as they were from the building trades, but so few hotels and restaurants were unionized that the effects were nowhere near as important as they were in construction.

By the 1990s, Miami's tourism stood much where it was one hundred years earlier, at the dawn of the city—small compared to the overall economy, but highly significant symbolically to local leaders and outsiders.

In 1991, the local chapter of the National Association for the Advancement of Colored People (NAACP) had volunteers disguised as tourists and maids visit 125 hotels and restaurants in Miami and claimed to have found Blacks employed at only 41 of them. One prominent African American asserted that "they've been boycotting Blacks in the tourist industry for twenty years" (Rowe 1990:14).

Both Miami's African Americans and its white Americans claim that Latins have displaced African Americans in the area's hotels and restaurants.[1] To be sure, Latins have become an important presence. In the hotel restaurant where Hafidh worked, nearly 80 percent of the more than a hundred employees were Latins, while less than 25 percent were Black. Overall, in 1980, Latins held 40 percent of the hotel and 30 percent of the restaurant jobs. Blacks had 23 percent of the hotel and just 9 percent of the restaurant jobs (see Figure 9.1).

While Latins certainly have more jobs in the industry than Blacks do, it is not at all clear that Latins have displaced Blacks. In 1960, white Americans overwhelmingly dominated both hotel and

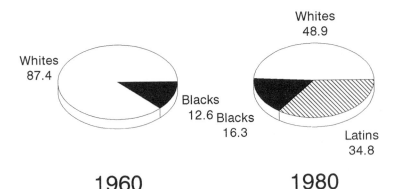

1960   **1980**

Figure 9.1. Ethnic employment percentages in Miami's hotel and restaurant industries, 1960 and 1980. *From* U.S. Bureau of the Census figures, Florida.

restaurant employment. From 1960 to 1980, the proportion of Blacks in both industries held steady, while the absolute numbers increased because of overall industry growth, but both the absolute and proportional numbers of white Americans declined drastically.

The key to the apparent contradiction between the facts indicating Black stability and the perception of Latins displacing Blacks is that the jobs Blacks hold in the industry are overwhelmingly in the "back of the house," in menial, unskilled positions such as dishwashing and housekeeping, largely out of the public's view. The U.S. Equal Employment Opportunity Commission calculated that while Blacks accounted for 22.2 percent of Miami's tourism workforce in 1988, they held only 5.1 percent of the jobs requiring a college degree (Tanfani 1991). Another observer claimed they hold less than 4 percent of management positions (Smith 1992). The Miami Beach resort hotel where we conducted research had no Blacks in management positions until 1992 when one was hired just before a convention of an umbrella organization (headed by an African American) of philanthropic corporations. Haitians, nevertheless, dominated the resort's housekeeping department. In the

The back and the front of the house. A white waitress attends to customers; a Black kitchen helper does not interact with customers. (Photo by Peggy Nolan)

seafood restaurant where we conducted research, management, waiters and waitresses, and cashiers were all Anglos or Latins, while Blacks worked as busboys and assisted in food preparation. Similarly, in the airport hotel, the top three management positions—general manager, food and beverage manager, and executive secretary—were all Anglos. The sales office was headed by a Jewish American woman, and the kitchen was managed by a Jewish American man. The banquet and front office departments were headed by Indian nationals, while a white male from Chile headed the maintenance department. Only in housekeeping did a Black appear—a Latin Black had replaced an Anglo in 1990.

Blacks are primarily confined to the back of the house, and even there an appreciable number of them are Haitian immigrants. The penetration of Haitians started in the early 1980s when Haitian arrivals in Miami peaked. Soon they acquired the reputation typical of new immigrants: hard-working and uncomplaining. Although a Haitian tuberculosis scare in 1979 and AIDS in the early 1980s (both of which were subsequently disproved) deterred many employers from hiring Haitians, their numbers continued to increase in the back of the house.[2] In the seafood restaurant, virtually all the busboys and pantry workers were Haitians.

Management Strategies

The most widespread method for maintaining low labor costs in Miami's hotels and restaurants is through using part-time instead of full-time workers. Aside from management, few workers work forty hours a week, and those who do constantly worry that their hours will be trimmed back. One of the most important weekly rituals at every worksite is the posting of the weekly schedule.

Almost immediately after arriving in mid-1991, a new management team at the seafood restaurant announced a set of cost-saving measures, including reduced hours. Lucy complained, "How am I supposed to feed my children?" Management responded that workers not willing to conform to the changes should feel free to leave and look for another job. After several weeks of receiving reduced hours and reduced paychecks, Lucy informed Sue, "Vance [the new manager] is no good. The Lord gave everyone a mouth and everyone is supposed to eat. Vance doesn't care what happens to Haitians because he has no respect for Haitians. He only wants white people in the restaurant."

In the following weeks, not only did Lucy work reduced hours, but Vance also frequently asked her to leave an hour and a half before she was scheduled to leave. On two successive Saturdays, when told to leave early, she grabbed the bag that stored her walking shoes and personal belongings, angrily talking to herself in Creole, punched out, and proceeded out the front door to catch a bus home. On the third Saturday she was ordered to leave early, she ignored the order and continued scooping lettuce out of the bin and filling bowls with salads. Vance soon confronted her, loudly demanding that she "punch out immediately!" Lucy later claimed Vance's "having no respect made her crazy." She erupted verbally as best she could in English, telling Vance that he was no good, had no respect for Haitians, and only wanted white people working in the restaurant. While Lucy was the only one to make these claims publicly, all the Haitians working there apparently concurred.

At the airport hotel restaurant one week, management cut everyone's hours, prompting immediate and loud complaints. The full-time employees reminded the food and beverage manager of their long commitment to the hotel restaurant and the hotel's policies that had always allowed full-time employees to choose shifts according to seniority. The food and beverage manager surrendered, but at the expense of cutting part-time employees' hours even further. Marta, an immigrant Latin, asked the food and beverage manager why her hours were cut so radically, from twenty-four to sixteen hours, when full-time servers lost no more than three or four hours. After receiving an unsatisfactory reply, she publicly proclaimed, "Men are pigs. They have always been." She continued by recounting her two failed marriages, as she had put it, "to pigs just like him [the food and beverage manager], because they had me to kick around and do their dirty work while I am out there working."

Perhaps the second-most-pervasive management technique for maintaining low costs comes through various violations of labor laws, including paying less than the minimum wage, not paying time and a half for overtime, making illegal deductions (such as for breakage), and not meeting health and safety standards. Many large restaurants concentrate their resources up front, in style and decor. The shadows and doors to the kitchen obscure the savings achieved by violating health and safety standards. These same restaurants are also most likely to deduct from a worker's wages fees for uniforms or breakage, which is illegal.

Employers particularly appreciate the work ethic of new immigrants. Charlie is a Haitian who has been working at the seafood restaurant since 1980. His brother-in-law has worked there for more than ten years and his brother for six years. Another brother-in-law, another brother, and a nephew all worked there at some time during the 1980s. Management considered all of them, especially Charlie, excellent employees. Charlie is a hard worker who keeps to himself and does not bother anyone. He never talks back to the boss. Indeed, he seemingly never talks to anyone while working. He just minds his business, paying attention to his work and nothing more. After more than five years of Charlie's exemplary work, the kitchen manager asked, "Charlie, you think your madam would like to work here in the pantry?"

The following day, Charlie's wife, Lucy, took the bus to the restaurant where the manager, according to Lucy, told her, "'Lucy, how about you work today and fill application tomorrow?' And that's what I did." Soon after that, the manager asked Charlie, "Charlie, do you have any sons old enough to start work?" One son, Vernet, then started working there. All the other Haitians told Charlie he was crazy to let Vernet be a busboy because they did not treat Haitians fairly in the front part of the restaurant. But Vernet proved to be like his father, resilient and compliant. Other sons followed—Edmond, Sam, and finally Patrick.

In the early 1980s, Latin restaurants hired either Haitians or *Mariel* Cubans for their back-of-the-house positions. By the late 1980s, Nicaraguans or other Central Americans replaced the *Mariel* Cubans. The more recently arrived Central Americans and Haitians were willing to work as dishwashers for $200 a week, while the earlier-arriving Cubans would not settle for less than $300 a week. The newer immigrants also accepted cash, off-the-books payments with no federal income tax withheld or social security deductions—and no benefits. In the mid-1980s, these practices were so pervasive in the restaurant industry, especially for Haitian employees, that the U.S. Department of Labor organized a special local task force to work with Haitian community organizations to educate Haitian workers about their rights.

Restaurants also lower their wage bill and control labor by deskilling, reducing the complex task of preparing and serving food to a series of relatively simple tasks assigned to separate individuals. Fast-food restaurants—America's most important contribution to international cuisine—maximize the technique, deskilling the entire process and requiring integrated, complex skills only from the franchise manager (Cobble 1991). Full-service restaurants have a division of labor where relatively unskilled, lower-paid employees prepare salads and desserts, while others clean and set the tables. At times, individual managers may attempt to save even more by hiring unskilled help for skilled positions.

The hotel restaurant's food and beverage manager replaced a formally trained chef with an untrained cook he labeled kitchen manager. In the midst of catering to a group of three hundred, everyone discovered management had gone too far. Arrangements and preparation of even the smallest details, involving the entire staff from the hotel's general manager down to the servers and busboys, had been completed at least two weeks earlier. When the function began and excitement consumed the staff, something was amiss. As the main meal was served, word spread like wildfire that the chicken, the meal's main course, had gone bad. The majority of the guests hardly touched it, and those who did complained about it. The general manager was present, but quiet. The food and beverage manager and the kitchen manager were clearly agitated and sweating. Who would be held responsible?

Staff knew that the general manager and food and beverage manager, both Anglos, were close friends, having worked together at a number of hotels before this one. The New York Jewish kitchen manager was a new hire, recently moved from New York and not yet well connected to management. Employees were certain that the banquet disaster would provoke some terrible response for some employees, and they predicted that the food and beverage manager's friendship with the Anglo general manager would save him. They were right. A week later, the kitchen manager lost his job.

Personal relatonships may conflict with bureaucratic rules in labor–management relations as workers frequently find themselves torn between management's efforts to control employees and limit expenses and workers' resistance. Once, in the hotel restaurant, a server ordered a lunch for himself, which the cook made for him. While the server was eating the lunch at a back-of-the-house kitchen table, a room-service waiter noticed that he was having a full lunch and apparently reported the infraction. The food and beverage manager soon appeared and asked what the server was doing. The server used the most popular excuse, "This was a bad order, a mistake." When asked, the cook confirmed the server's assertion. Nevertheless, management billed the server $6, which it deducted from her tips that day. Later, the "whole house," all of the staff on duty, came down on the room-service waiter, verbally attacking him for having informed on the server.

At the seafood restaurant, the manager suspended a cook for three days after seeing him eating a piece of fried chicken he had not paid for. When Sue arrived at work, she found Lucy surrounded by a group of co-workers, all visibly upset, angrily discussing the suspension. One Haitian man remarked to Sue, "Bobier [the suspended cook] has worked here for seven years. He worked a ten-hour shift today with no food and no breaks. The man was hungry, so he has every right to eat. Vance is the only person I know who would put a man on vacation for that."

Mabel, an immigrant Latin server at the airport hotel restaurant, was seated at a kitchen table one morning eating breakfast. The food and beverage manager came in and asked if she ordinarily got breakfast. Management served only one free meal, lunch or dinner, to the employees per shift. Any other food had to be paid for at half the menu price. Nevertheless, it was not uncommon for employees to convince cooks to prepare them something and not to charge them.

Mabel simply replied, "I was starved." The food and beverage manager retorted firmly, "Fine, madam, I just want to be fair. Continue eating and when you are done, pay $5.50 for the breakfast to the cashier."

When word got around about this confrontation and the verdict, the general feeling was "these people [management] are cheap." A fellow server, Diana, an Anglo, asked, "Does she [Mabel] know the lines? Why didn't she say it was a wrong order?" The workers consider pilfering food legitimate and informally regulate the amount of food servers and other workers can "fiddle," or steal.

Workers most commonly resist management by conspiring to get an extra break from their work. Sometimes workers help each other in routine tasks, act as "lookouts" while others take a break during slow periods, "cover" for each other when someone is absent or late, and sympathize with a co-worker in a stressful or traumatic situation.

Demaris, a server, may say to her co-server, Janet, "I can't stand it anymore. I have to run to the ladies. Please see to my customers." Or, "Will you do me a favor? Give me a hand here. Hold that door for me. I can't handle this alone." Or, "Refill that customer's cup, over there. I have to run back to the kitchen."

Amalia, the cashier, might say to Susan, a server, "Please come over and stand by the register. I am starving. I have to eat something." Or, "Would you mind bringing me singles [one-dollar bills] from the front-desk? I am running out of them here."

When the restaurant is "dead," managers may sneak out of the hotel, and two, three, or more workers from the restaurant-kitchen area may sit around joking and gossiping. They may convince a cook to make them a nice dish. One worker stands at a strategic location, looking out for an approaching manager or customer. On these rare occasions, the chit-chat makes the rounds, more often than not including some individual self-acclaim, family reminiscing, past romances, and dietary matters. The workers concentrate on social and economic issues immediate to themselves, hardly ever addressing political issues. From these superficial intimacies, loose, flexible alliances among workers may arise. They provide support for those within one clique, but also take the tension and frustration created by the job and management demands and direct it toward co-workers through back-biting castigation that blames other workers for problems on the job.

Workers generally view management as incompetent and incapable of doing the "real work" that staff does.

On a particularly busy morning at the hotel restaurant, servers are trying hard, and succeeding very well at, bringing out the breakfast orders. Mark, the restaurant manager, notices the general manager (GM) strolling into the restaurant. Walking straight through to the kitchen, the GM talks to no one. Mark follows, abandoning whatever he was doing, and assumes a position between the kitchen line where meals are prepared and the servers' receiving area. Mark orders the servers to stand aside so that he can control the placing of meal orders on the turnstile. The servers and cooks complain, but Mark does not listen. According to him, unless he controls the whole work process, no orders will ever get to the table. Instead, Mark's assertion of authority only delays service by confusing the two cooks and the three servers.

On another busy morning, Mark noticed that Diana, an Anglo server, had not yet put on her bow tie, which is part of her uniform. He reprimanded her severely. Later, when the restaurant had become extraordinarily busy, Diana complained,

Christ! why do they [management] always pick on us for small things like bow ties and stuff instead of like right now? Christ! These people [management] never let off. As long as they are around here, why the hell don't they let us do what we are supposed to? And they do their work, which is never much anyway. If you only know how I feel. There are times I never want to come back to this hole of a place. You hardly do anything without one of them picking on you.

In contrast to carpenters, who can defy management and prevail, restaurant workers, especially new immigrants, are more vulnerable. Management will likely dismiss restaurant staff who defy them directly. Lucy and Charlie, for example, did not tell the seafood restaurant management about their son Patrick because they felt "Patrick might give them [both the restaurant and the parents] problems." Patrick is the most headstrong of the family's sons, the one with the fiercest pride, the one most likely to object to management's efforts to control and abuse them. But Vernet, Patrick's brother, asked the restaurant's managers if his brother could work there and "sure enough, Patrick had problems with Michele [an Anglo server] because she wasn't treating him fairly, so he left." Lucy's defiance of Vance similarly resulted in her having her hours reduced drastically.

Lucy expressed her frustration and resistance directly at management. But because workers are so vulnerable, such feelings are just as likely to be expressed toward and against fellow workers. On one occasion, Hafidh, our server–researcher in the hotel restaurant, was in the kitchen when a customer sat at one of his assigned tables. Instead of calling him, the other server, a Latin woman, worked the table. This infuriated Hafidh so much that he retreated to the lounge and staged a sit-down strike to protest his co-worker's invasion of his territory. Only after the restaurant was almost filled, and after being asked many times to resume his duties, did he return to the floor. The offending server greeted him with an apology and a hug.

Workers similarly compete for tips. "Mr. Ben" was a wealthy white businessman from the Caribbean. He stayed in the airport hotel four days a week and flew back home every Friday to spend the weekend with his family. He was a generous patron, far beyond the usual 15 percent tip. In return, he expected prompt and quality service of the standard set for domestic servants in upper-class homes of the past and many contemporary Third World homes: "unobstructive, meek, and respectful" (Cobble 1991:47). The three servers who generally worked when he ate, two Anglos and one Latin, fought each other to attend to Mr. Ben, trying to convince the cashier and Mr. Ben himself to sit at one of their assigned tables.

Tips are the servers' most important income, and they protect them assiduously. The biggest server sin is pocketing someone else's tips. In the hotel restaurant, servers deliberately left a large tip on the table to test a newly hired server. Fortunately for her, she passed the test, turning the money over to the cashier.

Workers may also argue over who should do what. Julie was already at work at the hotel restaurant when Demaris arrived one morning. As Demaris prepared to set up her station, Julie reminded her not to forget to bring out the backup items, to get the iced tea going, to bring out fruits and juices and whatever else would be used. Most mornings, Demaris would have quietly complied. But this morning, something inside told her to resist. She wondered if she was going to do all those tasks. What had Julie been doing for the last hour before Demaris came in? When Demaris asked Julie, "How come, were you late this morning?" Julie defended herself:

> "Come on now, Demaris, don't I always do most of all that stuff [an assertion that was not true]? What of this telephone—never off the hook from the minute I walked in here? I tell you, the cashier should either open or I be paid extra for all this. Why, I brought out the bread, but I just couldn't get around to get the other stuff out."

Demaris first set up her own station, had a cup of coffee, and then, grumbling and silently cursing Julie, she brought out the required items.

During rush periods, servers frequently scrawled, misspelled, or failed to use accepted menu acronyms, thus confusing cooks and delaying orders. Servers insistently urged the cooks to hurry, complaining to each other, "What a pain, what a slow cook." The cook retorted, "Write English." Or, "Better get back to school." "This is not Haiti." "Where are you fellas from?"

One day in the hotel restaurant, Sam, an African American cook, and Memo, a Latin pre-cook, quarreled when Memo insisted that he did not understand Sam's shouted instructions. A few minutes later, after tempers had cooled, Sam informed Hafidh, our African server–researcher, "The Spanish have taken over everything in Miami. And now they want to impose their language."

Hafidh gently replied, "Say, Sam, you were really harsh on Memo. What if he truly did not follow what you were saying?"

"I don't care. The guy is pretending. How does he talk to the chef in English? Besides, what I wanted him to bring out from the freezer is stuff he always handles and he knows."

Hafidh then asked Sam if he remembered Kamena, an immigrant Latin pre-cook, who used to say, "We are all the same, all God's children." Kamena spoke little English, and Sam never let him alone, claiming that Kamena was stubborn and would not listen to a Black, no matter what. After a few months of working together, Kamena quit, claiming that he could not work with Sam. The staff suggested that the physically imposing Sam had threatened Kamena, frightening him into quitting.

Sam recalled, "I remember him. But, hey, this is the U.S.A. When you come here, it is English." Sam indicated that he had little contact with Latins. Before moving to Miami, he had lived in Atlanta; referring to the *Mariel* refugees imprisoned there, he joked, "All the Cubans we know [in Atlanta] are in jail anyway." Surprisingly, Sam's "lady," his girl friend, is Latin, a Puerto Rican, and she and her sister are the only Latins with whom Sam has any informal social contacts. Not surprisingly, Sam's "lady" and her sister both speak English.

This prejudice between Blacks and Latins can even lead to some Latins claiming that Blacks cannot be Latins. In the hotel restaurant, a Cuban waitress was mystified by a Black who spoke English with an African American accent, but also spoke Spanish with a proper Spanish accent. She questioned the Black, "How come you speak Spanish?" He replied, "Because I'm from Honduras." She retorted, "No, you can't be." And he explained, "Yes, I was born in Honduras, but my parents brought me to the United States when I was twelve and I learned English in New York City." Later, after he left, the waitress turned to Hafidh and asserted, "No, it can't be true. He's lying. He's from Suriname."

Conclusions

Working in a restaurant or hotel, especially in the back of the house, has never been a great job. Restaurant work has always been arduous and ill paid with virtually no opportunities for advancement and with workers subject to immediate and arbitrary management discipline. Restructuring has had little effect on the nature of restaurant work, except in fast-food restaurants. Nevertheless, in Miami restructuring has changed the ethnicity of the workforce. While the perception remains that immigrant Latins have displaced native African Americans, the reality is that Latins have primarily displaced unskilled native whites, many of whom have simply abandoned the Greater Miami area. Top management remains dominated by native whites, but Latins have filled many of the remaining positions. In the process, many Latins, who in Miami are overwhelmingly white, have leaped over Blacks, who remain out of sight, in the back of the house. Many of the Blacks are Haitians, new immigrants, hardworking and compliant. Yet, even in the back of the house or perhaps because they are there, Haitians remain vulnerable. False health scares more than once dislodged them. Many employers unscrupulously exploit them. If they dare complain, such as Lucy did, no bureaucratic mechanisms or workers' organizations protect them. Management simply and directly controls them by reducing the worker's hours.

Workers can only feebly resist management's often arbitrary and capricious power over them. On occasion, they conspire to pilfer a meal, but almost as frequently a co-worker informs against them. High worker turnover, the extensive employment of part-time workers, and extraordinary direct control by management all subvert worker cooperation and resistance. As previously found in the U.S. restaurant industry (Cobble 1991:33), the resulting extreme competition among workers allows them to emphasize ethnic differences among themselves and further subvert worker solidarity, fashioning more individualism than in both the other Miami industries we studied and in restaurants in other parts of the United States.

Notes

1. Because of the perception that African Americans have been displaced by Latins from Miami's hotels and because of the industry's visibility, African Americans have targeted the industry in their protests against local racial discrimination. In 1990, South Africa's Nelson Mandela swung though Miami on his tour of the United States. Miami Cuban politicians, objecting to Mandela's praise of Cuba's Fidel Castro for having supported the anti-apartheid movement from the beginning, pointedly refused to welcome Mandela to Miami. In response, African Americans organized their own welcome of Mandela and a convention boycott of Miami hotels. By November 1991, they had convinced twenty-two national organizations to cancel conventions scheduled for Miami, representing an estimated $38 million in lost revenues. To answer the African Americans' complaints, Dade's hoteliers and the city of Miami offered nearly $100,000 to fund scholarships for twenty-five local Black students to attend Florida International University's highly acclaimed school of hospitality management (Tanfani 1991).

2. In 1979 and 1980, community health personnel indicated that a high proportion of arriving Haitian boat people had tuberculosis, a disease still widespread in Haiti. Some politicians called for health tests for all Haitians, particularly those working in restaurants. The cries eventually subsided as it became recognized that tuberculosis was not rampant among Haitians in south Florida and that there were serious concerns about issues of civil liberties and discrimination in subjecting only Haitians to such tests. When AIDS first became a national concern, the U.S. government's Centers for Disease Control (CDC) identified Haitians as one of the primary groups at risk. The others were homosexuals, intravenous drug abusers, and hemophiliacs. The Haitian community objected strongly, claiming that it was another example of racism they faced in the United States and that the stigmatization would further impede Haitian efforts to adapt to U.S. society. After much debate, some study, and

intense Haitian lobbying, the CDC removed Haitians from the official list of groups at risk.

Bibliography

Cobble, Dorothy Sue. 1991. *Dishing It Out: Waitresses and Their Unions in the Twentieth Century.* Urbana and Chicago: University of Illinois Press.

Rowe, Sean. 1990. "The Quiet Riot," *New Times*, September 26–October 2, pp. 12–22.

Smith, H. T. 1992. "Boycott Miami." Speech to the Public Citizenship Forum, Florida International University, Miami, February 22.

Tanfani, Joseph. 1991. "Hotels Offer Scholarships For Blacks." *Miami Herald*, April 21, pp. 1B, 2B.

PHILADELPHIA

10 Polishing the Rustbelt: Immigrants Enter a Restructuring Philadelphia

Judith Goode

In the early 1990s, pessimism about the future of Philadelphia was frequent in everyday conversations and newspaper editorials. This once-mighty city had been a major port during the colonial period and the largest industrial center in the United States until the construction of the Erie Canal. Our two years of research in 1988 and 1989 preshadowed the fiscal crisis. Doomsday discourses about the state of the city were constantly heard on the street and in the media. As the city publicly revealed its fiscal crisis in September 1990, citizens were not surprised. According to one auto repair shop owner, "The city's not going down the tubes. I think it went already" (*Philadelphia Inquirer* 1990). As the reporter who was interviewing described it, this citizen's disgust had now reached the point where he desired "to bail out of a neighborhood where he has spent his life and raised four children," to move to the suburbs, which he has never even visited.

During two years of fieldwork in three similar parochial neighborhoods in 1988 and 1989, we heard similar refrains. But our encounters were in neighborhoods that had already lost many of their long-term residents. The people we came to know were those who were still digging in their heels. They talked in military terms about "taking a last stand" or "standing their ground" as the inexorable forces of crime, drugs, and blight (trash and graffiti) approached or invaded their communities. Most of them had childhood friends and relatives who already lived in the suburbs and or in the Northeast (an internal suburb) who were encouraging them to leave.

199

While Philadelphia has obviously been affected by the general forces of deindustrialization common to declining centers of the Northeast–Midwest rustbelt, it has several features that set it apart. In the following overview, we look more closely at the region's history in order to provide a specific context for the three case studies that follow.[1]

Our research dealt with settings in which relationships between new immigrants and established residents in Philadelphia are affected by the shift in the political economy of the city. In the past fifty years, the city has experienced significant deindustrialization and the loss of stable, unionized factory jobs. Today, more and more Philadelphians work in the service sector, which includes information and people processing in expanding corporate, health-care, and educational organizations, as well as retailing and commerce. The new jobs have different consequences for wage levels and job security and different patterns of employment of women, minorities, and immigrants. This overview provides a history of the relations between economic transitions, immigration waves, settlement patterns, and politics in Philadelphia. After we describe the twentieth-century city in terms of the Euro-ethnic/African American dyad, we analyze the entry of recent immigrants.

Always a city of divergent interests and heterogeneous populations, earlier forms of economy created local linkages that held the city together. The new postindustrial economy, oriented to national and international systems of exchange, no longer provides these linkages. Recent changes in the city have been shaped significantly by intended and unintended effects of public policy as well as the forces of capitalism (Adams et al. 1991).

A Picture of Decline

Recently, the Philadelphia Standard Metropolitan Statistical Area (PSMSA) as a whole has lost jobs and population to other regions of the country and to other countries as a result of deindustrialization. This was followed by an economic restructuring in the region (Summers and Luce 1988). Yet this restructuring has benefited mainly the suburbs, further widening the gap between them and the central city. The misfortunes of the city, symbolized by a fiscal crisis in 1990, have generated class conflict usually expressed as city versus suburb, downtown versus neighborhood, and race against race.

Philadelphia has been harder hit by decline than other rustbelt cities because of the nature of its manufacturing, the degree of suburbanization and the degree of fiscal dependence on state and federal resources. The former manufacturing base of the city relied largely on the production of nondurable goods. These enterprises were more sensitive to labor costs and had more movable infrastructures than durable goods. In 1950, 30 percent of the city's manufacturing jobs were in nondurable goods, as opposed to 19 percent for the national average (Summers and Luce 1988).

The impact of suburbanization is relatively greater here than elsewhere. Much of the city's population, jobs, and tax base have relocated to the seven counties surrounding the city in the PSMSA. While this pattern of dispersal is typical of old manufacturing cities, a recent comparative study shows that Philadelphia has lost many more economic activities to the suburbs than forty-two comparable SMSAs nationwide (Summers and Luce 1988). Between 1970 and 1980, the city lost 11.9 percent of its jobs, while there was an overall gain in the SMSA. This compares poorly to a 6.2 percent average loss for central cities nationwide, showing that suburbanization has had a greater impact in Philadelphia. The exodus has left the city with a population that is older, poorer, and more nonwhite than the suburban ring. The resulting shrunken tax base was coupled with a drastic decline in federal funding during the Reagan and Bush years.

In 1979, federal revenues amounted to 25.8 percent of the city's tax base; in 1988, they were only 7.5 percent (Peirce 1990). This fact, plus a low rate of state legislative support, brought about a fiscal crisis in fall 1990 that necessitated drastic bailout policies. One contributing factor was that Philadelphia relied more on its local tax base (as opposed to state or federal monies) than all the other large cities in the United States. In fiscal 1986, 72 percent of the city's budget was financed by local taxes, compared to 37 percent for Boston, 43 percent for Baltimore, 54 percent for New York, and 65 percent for Chicago (Pennslyvania Economy League 1986).

Hard hit by decline, the city also faces difficult obstacles as it plans for restructuring. With the exception of the enterprise zones, most of the current development strategies relate to high technology and the service sector as the areas of greatest growth potential. Philadelphia is using the same strategies to combat deindustrialization as similar cities with which it is in competition. Once again, the region's history illuminates some unique features that limit the possibilities of high technology or service restructuring.

One feature is the poor position of the city vis-à-vis other cities in the Northeast megalopolis. Philadelphia competes for a dependent hinterland with obviously stronger economic and political centers, such as nearby New York City and Washington, D.C., in many potential service industries. In competing with other cities, it has not been able to turn its central location in the megalopolis into an advantage. Instead, in an international strategy to revive import–export, location has become a disadvantage as air transportation favors the nation's capital and New York City.

Unlike Pittsburgh, the second-largest city in the state, Philadelphia does not have a clearly defined region to serve that would enhance its position as a corporate control center and help it retain locally oriented financial and manufacturing institutions. Moreover, because of a long-term negative relationship with the state legislature, the construction of statewide road and rail systems has left Philadelphia poorly situated as a port or major transportation node for the region in comparison with smaller cities of the region, such as Baltimore. In attempts to revive decaying ports, New York City and Baltimore have an advantage because of the highway linkages initially created by state legislative action (Boldt 1991).

In tourism, Philadelphia lags behind Washington, D.C., Baltimore, New York City, and Boston. The city currently has an inadequate supply of hotels and convention space compared with other major cities. A new convention center opened in 1993, which attempts to redress this. The high-tech strategy of creating a research-and-development center, as in Boston and Raleigh/Durham, has aided the suburbs (as in the Princeton corridor and the new industrial parks of Route 202 near King of Prussia, a secondary Central Business District or CBD), but not the city.

Finally, the history of political interest groups in the city, the breakdown of important alliances, and the unintended outcomes of particular local policies have softened the glue that once held the city together. Here again, while Pittsburgh has been able to forge public–private alliances to retain local capital investment, Philadelphia has been less successful.

Decline in the city has not had a uniform effect on all neighborhoods, groups, and industrial sectors. Declining markets create opportunities for new investment in housing and small retail businesses for some newcomer groups. Housing-cost increases serve to stem the flight of population and neighborhood turnover. Smaller, more flexible manufacturing has expanded, creating jobs for many displaced factory workers. There are many bright spots in the overall picture of gloom and sliding indexes.

Rise and Decline

The political–economic history of Philadelphia has been well documented in the works of Warner (1968) and Hershberg et al. (1981) in terms of several transformations. Each period of economic transformation has been characterized by different patterns of immigration and spatial patterns of settlement. Seen from the perspective of the immigrant, each wave of newcomers has entered a different opportunity structure in terms of the labor and housing markets.

There are two reasons to talk about these demographic facts. First, they give us a larger view of the emerging social interest groups in the city by showing many significant shifts: from the dominance of industrialists to bankers and insurance firms, from locally oriented capital to conglomerate capital managed elsewhere, from unionized industrial workers to nonorganized, increasingly part-time, minimum-wage service workers (professional and minimum wage). Second, these trends have an impact on individual career directions, on the way people perceive opportunities for themselves and their children, and on the way they view competition with other groups.

Originally a colonial port city, the center of trade with the motherland, Philadelphia developed its spatial center with residences and economic activities densely packed along the Delaware River. The original city, laid out by William Penn, was made up only of what is today considered the downtown area and is popularly known as Center City. The industrializing city (1830–1880) contained one of the largest concentrations of textile, garment, carpet, printing, publishing, foundry, and machine manufacture on the Atlantic littoral (Hershberg 1981). Industrial development was confined to the original city and to areas along the two rivers. In the east, industry stretched out along the Delaware River, just north (Northern Liberties, Kensington, Richmond) and south (Southwark, Moyamensing) of the original city. The neighborhood names refer to once separate municipalities that existed before the city's consolidation. Other industrial activities clustered along the Schuylkill River, farther west in Manayunk. These original milltown areas have remained working-class enclaves.

Immigrants from northwestern Europe entered this expanding job market, with the Irish and Germans coming in large numbers. By 1880, 30 percent of the city's population was Irish and 16 percent was of German stock. Entering the densely packed area of the old city along with rural–urban migrants from outside the city provided no opportunity for ethnic clusters. Instead, the population "filled in" wherever vacancies could be found. Ethnic heritage was relatively unimportant in accounting for settlement patterns (Greenburg 1981).

By 1880, the city had shifted from an "industrializing city" to a full-fledged industrial city with newly rationalized production systems, innovative technology, and large-scale bureaucratic organizations with a growing managerial class. Philadelphia's self-image as a center of industrial innovation was symbolized by the Centennial Exposition in 1876.

In the 1870s, massive homebuilding occurred in delayed response to the population influx of the previous decades. The existence of horse-drawn omnibuses and new practices of multiple-home construction (tract development) enabled a rapid expansion of the housing stock in bedroom communities or "streetcar suburbs" to the north and west of the former population concentration. The new middle classes that emerged to manage the increasingly large manufacturing and financial institutions began to move away from the noise and nuisance of the industrial area to the newer, larger housing. The vast majority of current housing units in the city were built between 1870 and the Great Depression.

The new streetcar suburbs were in sections of the city that had been consolidated in 1854 when the city boundaries were enlarged to include the entire county. With this annexation, today's city limits were created. The late nineteenth century saw the development of citywide systems in the enlarged territory. The police system and the school system originated at this time. With transportation networks developing around the horse-drawn omnibus and later the electrified trolley, the new city continued to develop.

During this period, as the labor market expanded, great immigrations from southern and eastern Europe occurred, transforming the space and society of the city once again. These immigrants clustered in ethnic enclaves around their industrial worksites. Local parishes offered Catholic Mass in native languages, and the parish served as a base for the proliferation of such neighborhood institutions as clubs, shops, and newspapers (Golab 1977).

In hindsight, the demographic trends of deindustrialization can be noticed in the 1930s. Analysis indicates that the city reversed its manufacturing growth trajectory during the depression. Industry revived briefly during World War II, but in the postwar period it continued to decline (Adams et al. 1991; Binzen 1970).

The city reached its population peak in 1950 with a total of 2.1 million. By 1970, population was down to its 1930 size of 1.95 million, and it has continued to fall with each census. This trend shows an alarming persistence. In 1940, six of ten people in the eight-county metropolitan region lived in the city. Today, three of ten do so. The city lost 10 percent of its population between the 1970 and 1980 censuses and appears to have lost another 9 percent since then (*Philadelphia Inquirer* 1990).

Job loss lagged behind population redistribution but was equally significant. Although the city contained almost 50 percent of the employment in the eight-county SMSA in 1970, its share had decreased to 40 percent in 1980 and 35 percent in 1986. Moreover, this loss affected every industrial sector but one. Only in professional services was there less than the nationwide average loss of jobs in Philadelphia (Summers and Luce 1988).

Population and job loss were not matters of noticeable governmental or popular concern until the late 1960s. In industrial Kensington, where the largest factory made Stetson hats, employed five thousand people, and occupied five square blocks, the factory's closing at the end of the 1960s was seen as a turning point, even though the downturn was several decades old. The blight that accompanied the closing of factories in Kensington—high turnover, housing abandonment, dirt, vandalism, decay, graffiti—entered public discourse in the 1970s (Seder 1990).

During the Great Depression, when economic expansion in the city was waning, a massive in-migration of African Americans from the rural South was under way. While Blacks had always lived in the city, this movement significantly accelerated in the 1920s and continued for the next four decades. Blacks accounted for 221,000 city residents in 1930 and as many as 654,000 in 1970. Since the total city population was the same in both years (1.95 million), the contrast in the proportion of Blacks in the city is striking. In 1930, one-tenth of the city was Black; by 1970, Blacks accounted for one-third of the population. The white population disproportionately left the city for the suburbs, and by 1980, the Black population rose to 40 percent. By 1990, the Black population in the SMSA had risen another 5 percent and had increased slightly in the city itself. The proportional increases in the last two censuses are not due to in-migration but to the continuing abandonment of the city by whites.

The in-migration of African Americans from the South occurred at the same time as the opportunity structure of the city constricted. Moreover, employer discrimination throughout the history of the city meant that Blacks were never important in the expanding industrial economy (Hershberg 1981). It is ironic that this pattern has been reversed only since whites have left the city and the remaining industry has begun to recruit Blacks as industrial labor. At the very point when employment in manufacturing has become most vulnerable, Black workforces have expanded in industry. Thus they are less likely to benefit from the security and income gains of earlier labor movements.

Manufacturing was hit hardest, with a loss of 75 percent of the jobs from 1955 to 1975 (Adams et al. 1991). The severity of the loss is partly exaggerated by the recession of the early 1970s, but 35 percent of the manufacturing base was lost between the 1970 and 1980 censuses.

Some of the loss of industry has occurred because of general trends in global and national economies. Many analysts point to the 1970s as the point at which a new global economic integration markedly changed the nature of the American economy (Goldsmith and Blakely 1992). This can be seen in Philadelphia as locally owned firms are bought by multinational corporate concentrations of capital, or decisions are made to seek cheap and nonunionized labor by relocating offshore or in the sunbelt. Other firms, severely affected by global competition, have simply closed down. The garment industry has been particularly affected by both trends. The impact of style changes and imports led one of Philadelphia's largest men's suit companies, Botany "500", to close down. Another, Louis Goldsmith, was the victim of conglomerate relocation as first Kaiser-Roth and then Gulf Western acquired the plant, downsized it, and moved operations elsewhere.

An analysis of half of the 126,000 jobs lost in Philadelphia between 1969 and 1979 revealed that while conglomerate, multinational, and absentee-owned firms accounted for about half of all industrial jobs, 68 percent of the job losses were incurred in such firms (Hochner and Zibman 1982). Once a core sector of Philadelphia industry, in 1880, 40 percent of the workforce in Philadelphia was employed in textile and clothing manufacture (Adams et al. 1991). In the late 1960s, there were still seven hundred apparel firms in Philadelphia with a workforce of forty-eight thousand. In 1989, there were only fourteen thousand workers in two hundred firms (Haines 1982; *Philadelphia Inquirer* 1989).

Other losses occurred as local firms moved to the suburban ring of the city in search of cheaper land to accommodate new production technology and less tax pressure (Byler and Bennett 1984). The labor force was also moving to the suburbs. Well-acknowledged public policies accounted for much of the redistribution of population to the suburbs in the postwar period: investment in new roads and corresponding disinvestment in public transportation; favoring new home construction by federal mortgage subsidy programs and the corresponding redlining or disinvestment in city neighborhoods. Ultimately the loss of population and jobs to the suburbs critically wounded the city's tax base, creating a decline in the quality of life.

The Restructured and Restructuring Economy

The economy of Philadelphia is both declining and restructuring. In the early 1990s, 75 percent of the workforce was engaged in tertiary activities in what is confusingly referred to as the service sector. This shift is less true of the suburbs, where relocated manufacturing and new high-technology firms have increased the share of manufacturing there. Only 60 percent of the suburban workforce is not engaged in manufacturing.

Manufacturing

While manufacturing has diminished as a basic economic activity, it is still important as an employer in the city, especially for some groups. In fact, for the Puerto Rican population, it is the most important sector of the economy (Ericksen et al. 1985).

But manufacturing is vulnerable. Philadelphia is still important in petrochemicals and pharmaceutical manufacture, but these jobs tend to be disproportionately professional, managerial, and high-skilled technical. Furthermore, both worksites and corporate headquarters in this industry continue to move to the suburbs. ARCO petroleum relocated its headquarters to the suburbs, and Smith Kline and Beecham (pharmaceuticals) announced plans to relocate many white-collar and manufacturing jobs there.

Conglomeration, absentee ownership, and the threat of relocation remain. In the heart of the industrial zone in north Philadelphia, there are still many functioning factories. Some of them, like Summit Lighting, which was one of our research sites and is discussed by Carole Cohen in Chapter 11, used to be locally owned but are now owned by conglomerates. Summit, which had been taken over by a second conglomerate, was feeling the results of some relocation of functions and resulting layoffs. The workforce at Summit is typical of many large workforces in the city; it consists of whites, Blacks, and Latinos in order of seniority. Puerto Ricans are generally the last hired and first fired.

Two other kinds of manufacturing organizations remain important. One consists of firms that are still locally owned independents and are smaller and more specialized than other organizations. They have adapted to the changing economy by remaining small plants, making frequent changes in product lines, having short product runs, and subcontracting. Many are in the hands of families from the 1880–1920 immigration wave. Very few are minority owned. A typical metal-fabricating firm that employs between 150 and 200 workers recently celebrated its fiftieth anniversary, and its current operations are being shifted from a group of second-generation brothers to the third generation. A nearby metalworking firm is of similar age and history. These enterprises, while small, are larger than sweatshops and are unionized. Their workforces are similar in composition to those of the conglomerates: white, Black, and Puerto Rican.

These plants, along with several distributor–warehousing enterprises, are typical of participants in the "enterprise zones," a concept and strategy for providing incentives and tax benefits to entrepreneurs willing to locate near poor communities. Our field work in Kensington involved one of these zones. Chapter 13 discusses the problems it was having in relating to the surrounding community.

The other kind of firm includes small plants involved in metalworking, woodworking, and garment production. These enterprises are nonunion, pay piecework rates, and provide no worker benefits. These enterprises are significantly represented in the employment histories of Asian, Puerto Rican, Colombian, and Central American immigrants and Eastern European refugees. Some of them are located in the older industrial areas of the city, while others are found in the suburbs (Petras 1990).

A somewhat clandestine garment industry has developed based on Korean and Chinese capital and using newcomer Asian labor. Many Koreans initially worked in these firms in order to generate capital to open up small, family-run stores. Often, members of the family remain in these jobs when others in the family work in their shops. An article in the *Philadelphia Inquirer*, "Asian Immigrants Lend New Life to City's Sewing Industry" (Power 1988), quotes the president of the Korean Businessman's Association as aware of about thirty Korean-owned and -operated sewing businesses. Others are thought to be operating out of homes, basements, and garages. They are described as employing from twenty to fifty workers of Korean, Chinese, Vietnamese, and Cambodian origin. They often are subcontractors for Sears, Bloomingdales, the U.S. military, and New York City garment firms.

The Tertiary Sector

As the industrial base has declined, the nonmanufacturing sector has become more important as an employer in the city. There are five components of this sector: FIRE (finance, insurance, and real estate); and services (business, legal, health, education, and other); trade (wholesale and retail); construction; and TCPU (transportation, communications, and utilities). The first two are the only areas in which the city has grown or has held its own. Both areas are characterized by two-tier workforces composed of highly educated professional and managerial staff and deskilled, increasingly part-time clerical workers. Thus, for the kinds of people involved in our research who are likely to work in these clerical jobs or in service jobs of the retail sector or as skilled and unskilled workers in construction or transportation, these growth areas have not benefited them. Moreover, the continuing threat of the loss of corporate headquarters and the reorganization via mergers of the banking industry threaten continued growth. These five components today employ three-quarters of the city's population.

Philadelphia is especially important as a health-care center, in higher education, and in other professional and business services. The city is second only to New York City as a location for medical schools. Five large medical schools support more than twenty-five hospitals and ancillary institutions. Higher education is also a major industry. Philadelphia's largest employers are two major universities. The city also boasts a large community college and three Catholic colleges, as well as many others in the suburban rings.

The fastest-growing segment of the tertiary sector is services to business and legal services. These are related to the region's role as a corporate control center. Yet here there has been a constant threat of capital flight, and the credit market is less and less locally controlled as most major banks have been taken over by corporations headquartered in New York, New Jersey, and Pittsburgh.

These service activities are symbolized by skyscrapers that house large-scale bureaucracies. All these activities create large numbers of white- and pink-collar jobs (clerical and technical information-processing workers.) Most of the clerical staffs in these bureaucracies are either white or Black; they are not yet a significant source of employment for Puerto Ricans (Ericksen 1985). During our research, we encountered several Puerto Rican women employed in these corporate bureaucracies, most of whom went through CETA job-training programs in the 1970s. Interviews with high school students and counselors indicate that these are highly desireable jobs for contemporary Puerto Rican graduates.

Services to People

Service jobs outside the large bureaucracies of the financial, business service, educational, and health-care industries involve serving the needs of the residential population of the city. These include the large retail sector discussed in Chapter 12. A recent study revealed that 25 percent of the population in the region is employed in food-related industries (including agriculture, processing, wholesale, retail, convenience, fast food, and restaurants). Moreover, 50 percent of the trade sector is related to food markets and restaurants (Koppel 1988). The retail sector has been very volatile; between 1970 and 1980, the city and the suburbs lost 20 percent of the jobs in this sector. Two national department store chains, two large discount stores, and two major food chains closed down their operations in the region. Altogether, ten major retailers left, accounting for 10,000 of the 27,643 retail jobs lost (Moberg 1982; Steiner 1982). The major retail union, United Food and Commercial Workers, has lost significant membership. Sales jobs have also become increasingly part-time with two-tiered wage systems.

The structure of retail activities has shifted as well. The development of suburban malls that attract city residents has hurt both the center-city department stores and specialty shops and the local shopping strips in the city. The recent attention to the revitalization of the downtown and neighborhood strips by the Philadelphia Commercial Development Corporation (PCDC) and the development of in-city malls have provided incentives for independent mom-and-pop investors and small chains, often locally owned. Thus, in-city commercial activities are showing some new life after a long decline, especially in relation to frequently needed goods and services such as food, eating and drinking establishments, hardware, and dry cleaning. Immigrants are playing a major role here. Relationships between newcomer Koreans and other newcomer merchants and the established white and African American communities in which they open businesses are heavily influenced by these commercial encounters.

Direct social services to the local population by public-sector employees such as teachers, social workers, postal workers, police officers and firefighters, street and sanitation workers, and other government employees provide work opportunities to the populations we worked with. This job market depends on population size. As the population to be served and the tax base decline, so does employment in these jobs. Direct service jobs require some bilingual workers to serve the needs of the growing non-English-speaking populations. The Puerto Rican population is heavily employed in the nonprofit social service organizations for Spanish-speaking populations funded by public and foundation grants. As recent Human Relations Commission hearings demonstrated, however, Puerto Ricans are severely underrepresented in public-sector jobs, with few teachers, school administrators, police, firefighters, workers in the corrections system, and other municipal jobs. They are a growing presence as service recipients in these institutions. Even fewer Asians are in these jobs.

Construction in the region has grown in the past decade while it has declined nationally. But this growth is temporary. There has been an industrial growth spurt in the suburbs as well as a building boom in the center of the city and a lot of work repairing the decaying infrastructure in and around the city. Given the low occupancy rates in center-city office buildings, however, there is concern about overbuilding and a decline in the building trades. Suburban housing has been cyclical, following interest-rate cycles. Immigrants tend to be involved at the lower end of the construction chain in nonunionized subcontracting work. They work in monolingual work crews largely recruited through personal ties.

There has also been a general decline in transportation, communications, and public utilities, which directly followed crises in the public funding of transportation subsidies and the restructuring of the utilities. Although established African Americans have made some advances in public transportation and the postal service, there have been complaints about the underrepresentation of new populations.

Restructuring Social Space

The early-nineteenth-century immigrants were hardly clustered at all by nationality (Hershberg 1981). Those of the 1880s to 1920s were more clustered but did not live in census tracts dominated by particular groups. The typical Italian or Jewish immigrant inhabited a tract with many people of similar background, but not a majority. This was even true of Blacks, who had always been more clustered. In the earlier period, as Greenburg shows (1981), work locations dominated residential patterns more than ethnic heritage did. Today, as workplace and residence become less connected, class and race dominate residential patterns. Although Blacks were always more segregated than others, not until 1950 did census tracts appear that were more than 50 percent Black. This segregation was exacerbated by the racial polarization of suburbanization and the 1964 riots in North Philadelphia, which accelerated the exodus of white residents and businesses.

Today, the urban spatial structure is polarized by a racial dyad.

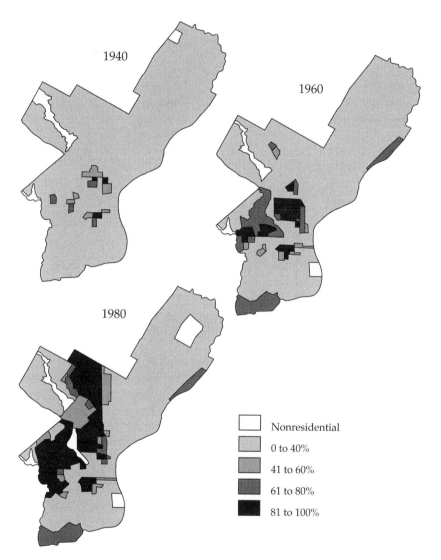

1940

1960

1980

Nonresidential

0 to 40%

41 to 60%

61 to 80%

81 to 100%

Figure 10.1. Proportion of Blacks in Philadelphia neighborhoods, 1940, 1960, and 1980. *From* Carolyn Adams et al., *Philadelphia: Neighborhoods, Division, and Conflict in a Postindustrial City* (Philadelphia: Temple University Press, 1991), p. 80.

By 1980, a map of the city (Figure 10.1) revealed a stark division between Black Philadelphia in the northwest and west and white Philadelphia in the east. The homogeneity of white, largely Catholic industrial areas and the river wards along the Delaware (Kensington, Port Richmond, Bridesburg, and Frankford) is striking. Formerly Jewish-dominated communities farther west were emptied by suburbanization, and Blacks moved into these newly available areas. The Northeast, an internal suburb built after the war, retains an all-white, suburban character and houses many of those who moved northward from the white river wards.

At the same time that workplaces and schools have become increasingly integrated in the city and more social contact occurs between whites, Blacks, Puerto Ricans (and other Spanish speakers), and Asians, there has been more resistance to integration in residential areas. Some neighborhoods reinforce their boundaries through violence to keep outsiders from entering. Other neighborhoods have been rapidly depopulated and reconstituted.

Overall, the index of segregation continues to increase in the city (Adams et al. 1991; Goldstein 1985) as many all-white areas close ranks and protect their borders through harassment of unwanted newcomers. The 1990 census again showed an increase in segregation; nearly three out of four Blacks in Philadelphia lived in neighborhoods that were at least 90 percent Black. This figure contrasts with a national figure of 30 percent, down from the 34 percent figure of 1980 (Borowski and Dubin 1991).

The city also has become more spatially polarized by class. The nature of the jobs in the restructuring economy increased the numbers of high-income and low-income workers, as well as the gap between them. The wealthy live increasingly isolated lives in the suburbs or in gentrifying areas adjacent to the city's center. Meanwhile, a recent study of the very poor in the United States has indicated that Philadelphia has fared worst of the fifty-largest cities in terms of the number of census tracts with high concentrations of the very poor (Hughes 1990).

Figure 10.2 indicates the distribution of housing by cost and reflects the division between old industrial housing, housing built in the late-nineteenth-century "streetcar suburbs," and the newest housing in the northeast, northwest, and gentrified areas around the center. Disinvestment and nonmaintenance of low-income housing areas in north Philadelphia have created considerable pressure on the border between Black north Philadelphia and the white industrial areas farther east as decay decreases the available housing stock there. The results of the 1990 census yielded the headline

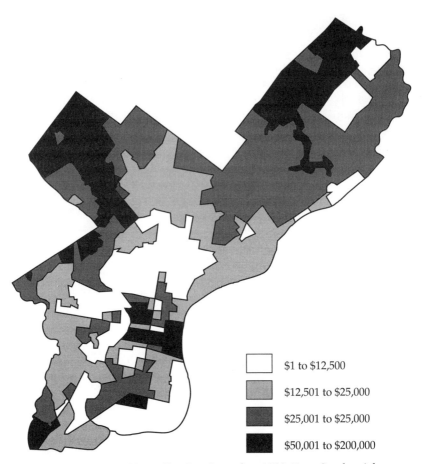

Figure 10.2. Philadelphia median housing value, 1980. *From* Carolyn Adams et al., *Philadelphia: Neighborhoods, Division, and Conflict in a Postindustrial City* (Philadelphia: Temple University Press, 1991), p. 71.

"Decades of Flight Turning North Philadelphia into a Ghost Town" in the *Philadelphia Inquirer* on April 12, 1991. Our study looked closely at three neighborhoods in the eastern Euro-ethnic Catholic zone; each responded differently to these pressures. They are described at the end of this discussion.

Recent Immigration

With the context complete, a picture of the currently fragmented city as Black and white, rich and poor, emerges. Into this structure a new immigrant wave is being incorporated. Engendered by the Immigration Reform Act of 1965, which prompted the Changing Relations Project, the impact of this latest wave of immigrants has been relatively small in Philadelphia, largely because of a declining labor market and poor opportunity structure. While ranked fifth in city size, the city is only sixteenth as the receiver of new immigrants. Philadelphia attracted an average of 7,117 newcomers each year between 1984 and 1986, as opposed to 92,345 for New York City and 57,912 for Los Angeles. Yet the numbers of people who define themselves as different nationally, culturally, and linguistically from the majority is considerably increased when Puerto Ricans (who are citizens and not technically immigrants) are included. They are the largest group of newcomers to the city.

While small compared to other cities, the newcomer Asians and Latinos[2] accounted for the fact that the Philadelphia metropolitan region sustained a population gain rather than loss in the 1990 census (Borowski 1991). In the city proper, whites declined 14 percent and African Americans 1 percent; Asians grew 145 percent and Spanish speakers 40 percent.

With the exception of Puerto Rican newcomers and rural refugees from Southeast Asia, many immigrants are arriving in Philadelphia with higher levels of education than did earlier waves (Young 1989). The entry of many of these immigrants is often not in unskilled manufacturing jobs, as was true for most earlier migrants and is still true for new immigrants elsewhere. Similarly, the location of settlement is often in newer suburban housing, rather than the poorest housing stock that was characteristic of earlier waves.

In Philadelphia, as in the United States generally, the post-1965 immigration is predominantly Latino and Asian. The largest Latino presence consists of Puerto Ricans, who began coming to the city before immigration reform. While a significant Puerto Rican presence in New York City dates to the 1920s, just after the Jones Act granted the islanders citizenship, the Latino community did not begin to form in Philadelphia until the 1950s. It remained small, localized, and generally invisible in the public life of the city for several decades. The following figures are considered undercounts: The Hispanic population in the city grew from less than 2,000 in 1950 to 7,000 in 1953, doubling each decade following. The population reached 14,000 in 1960, 28,000 in 1970, and 64,000 in 1980. The community assesses the real population today to be 120,000, but experts on census undercounts feel that 80,000 is a more reasonable guess. These figures are dominated by Puerto Ricans, who officially make up 75 percent of the total. Colombian and Central American immigrants, however, both legal and illegal, have also increased since 1980. Colombia was the only Latin American country represented in the top-ten feeder countries in the Immigration and Naturalization Service figures for 1984–1986, averaging 288 legal individuals per year (*Philadelphia Inquirer* 1988).

Among Puerto Ricans in Philadelphia, there are significant differences in the pattern of entry and experience. Looking at differences in place of birth and nature of social and economic ties to the island, three patterns predominate. First, home-grown Philaricans[3] are the offspring and grandchildren of those who came in the 1950s and 1960s and continuously stayed in Philadelphia. This group largely contains those whose family networks have been relocated on the mainland and whose ties to the island of Puerto Rico are somewhat attenuated. A second group are those who have maintained a pattern of movement back and forth to the island[4] over time and constitutes circular migrants. For example, as we tried to locate "newcomers" in the communities we studied, we became aware that everyone who had come recently from the island had been in the United States before and had networks of friends and relatives both here and there. In addition, many Puerto Ricans are secondary migrants from New York and New Jersey.

One study of Puerto Ricans in Philadelphia indicates that while Hispanics constitute just 4 percent of the population, their present age and fertility rate will make Puerto Ricans alone account for 8 percent in the year 2000 (Ericksen et al. 1985). Moreover, the Spanish-speaking population is clustered spatially to a very high degree. Fifteen contiguous census tracts account for 80 percent of the population.

The official number of Asians in the region listed for 1980 was 53,900, and this number had increased to 104,000 by 1990. In the city proper, there was a 145 percent increase, making Asians account for 3 percent of the population (Borowski 1991). This population stream is dominated by Koreans but also includes people from India, the Phillipines, China, Hong Kong, and Taiwan and refugees from Vietnam, Cambodia, and Laos (including the Hmong).

Koreans are still the largest immigrant group coming to the city. The Immigration and Naturalization Service study indicates that between 1984 and 1985, they averaged 1,082 newcomers per year. The next four groups were also Asian, with Indians averaging 738 individuals annually, China 458, the Phillipines 443, Vietnam 437. Cambodia ranked seventh with 380 (*Philadelphia Inquirer* 1988).

Other newcomers consist of refugees from Eastern Europe, Portuguese and Greek immigrants, as well as those from the Caribbean and Africa. Many are transnational in terms of residence and economic participation, meaning that their customary residence and social and economic connections are not concentrated in one nation but in two or more.

Economic Absorption

Given the economic decline and spatial restructuring of the city, how are newcomers competing with established residents for jobs and residential space? Although newcomers may compete with one another for some jobs, such as those in the competitive sector, they tend to be clustered in different sectors from established residents, overrepresented in some and almost absent from others.

Chinese and Koreans are heavily involved in enclave economies (retail activities and the garment industry), where they use their capital to leverage loans from banks and federal programs. They employ members of their community, themselves aspiring to be entrepreneurs in these activities. Chapter 12 describes some aspects of this. There is also a significant participation by Indian, Phillipine, Korean, and Chinese immigrants in the health-care and higher-education sectors.

For Puerto Ricans, manufacturing is the largest employer for both men and women (Ericksen et al. 1985). Puerto Ricans and other immigrants from Central and South America work in the primary and competitive sectors. In the primary sector they rank third in seniority to whites and Blacks, at a disadvantage in the multiethnic factories as they downsize.

These Latinos also work in monolingual settings such as small factories and construction crews of the competitive sector; for example, one established Nicaraguan informant in Philadelphia for twenty years had assembled a crew of recently arrived, undocumented Colombian men to work on a succession of suburban home subcontracts. University-educated Puerto Ricans are also concentrated in nonprofit service delivery areas where they tend to be segregated in jobs that serve Spanish speakers. They are underrepresented in public-sector service, as well as corporate jobs.

Are any serious issues of displacement specifically related to work? This does not seem to be true for Latino factory workers, who are last hired and first fired. It also appears that the Asian retail businesses have not displaced former merchants but have created a market for their stores as they retire. Nonetheless, both established whites and Blacks see Asians as taking over important features of their local neighborhoods.

Spatial Patterns

In the 1960s, Puerto Ricans began to occupy the buffer zone between the white Catholic industrial areas and the Black communities farther west, creating some Latino–white tension. Latino clustering in this middle zone of eastern north Philadelphia is marked. A narrow band of fifteen census tracts stretches north and south and observes the same class patterning as white settlement, with poorer households in the southern area and aspiring middle-class households in the north.

Other newcomer settlement is either voluntary or determined by agency-controlled placements in the case of refugees. Russian Jewish refugees are placed in the Jewish northeast, new Poles are placed in the center of Polish American areas like Port Richmond. Poor Asian refugees are frequently placed among poor Blacks in west Philadelphia and north Philadelphia, creating significant tension. The predominantly middle-class immigrants, Koreans and Asian Indians, are largely suburban bound. Those who live in the city initially settle in formerly Jewish areas vacated by suburban flight. In many cases, newcomer entrepreneurs—Koreans, Asian Indians, and Palestinians—are significant actors in the revival of abandoned and declining shopping strips throughout the poorer areas of the city. But while they continue to own shops, they rarely live in these communities for long.

Class, Race, Power, and Development Strategies

The economic trajectory of the city and present policy strategies to reverse decline have led to shifts in groups that have a stake in the city and the ways in which they form alliances and conflicts. Today the city is trying to develop political and economic strategies for development at a moment in time when few alliances exist.

As Warner (1968) points out, throughout its history as a port and an early craft-based industrial center, Philadelphia had local elites whose mercantile and industrial interests were tied to the locality and the collectivity. The city never created structures to link public and private interests, but the economic system of interdependencies provided the glue creating multiple ties between workers and patrons, elites and neighborhood leaders.

Later, in the period of expanding industrial capitalism, the rampant pursuit of private interests was mitigated by the Republican party machine, which brokered relations between elite owners and ethnic workers in the wards. Republican machine politics punctuated by short reform movements dominated between 1850 and 1950. The machine mediated between the ethnic working-class wards and the business elite by providing jobs, services, and favors to the former while both allowing private interests to shape the growth of the city and sending a strong protective tariff lobby to Congress (Adams et al. 1991). Philadelphia was also a strong union town during the heyday of industry. The labor council was an active player representing labor's interests in the city.

The Reform Movement and Its Aftermath

After World War II, several shifts occurred. First, public policy and planning emphasized the possibility of deliberately shaping cities. Second, the nature of economic change decreased the links between capital and local commitment. The reform movement of the 1950s was a watershed in Philadelphia that illustrates these shifts.

After the war, a major break with industrialist–Republican machine domination occurred with the reformist Clark–Dilworth mayoral regimes. The reform movement, while partly a reaction to the excesses of the machine, can also be seen as the takeover of control by emerging forces produced by the shift from industrial capital to corporate services. The powerful "downtown" interests involved in the reform were corporate elites in the rising service sector: banking, insurance, large-scale retailing, and real estate. The Greater Philadelphia Movement that represented them did not include the formerly important manufacturers, who were organized through the Chamber of Commerce.

The reform administrations of 1950 to 1962 held the postwar belief that technocracy could reverse negative trends in the economy. Reform officeholders and technocrats were aware of Philadelphia's declining economic position but were optimistic that an end to graft and corruption and the replacement of the machine by technically sophisticated economists and professional planners could change the direction (Berson 1982).

Representing the new corporate bureaucracies, they espoused an architectural and planning approach to revitalizing the "city," which for them meant the downtown area. Several plans were made to reconstruct a new center, the site of corporate headquarters, financial institutions, business services, and retailing, which would bring people back to the city as workers, shoppers, and residents. The assumption was that benefits accruing from the enlarged pie would eventually reach everyone. Optimistic planners predicted continued growth for the city (Adams et al. 1991) at a time before the recognition of the depth of national and global economic shifts and their effects: capital flight and deindustrialization.

For a brief period, the progressive technocrats were joined by segments of the traditional Democratic party long out of power, which represented the white working class (ward leaders and labor) as well as the emerging Black leadership. During the 1950s, these new Democrats took over city government and strengthened the charter. The heady days of the reform government were days of optimism in the city. A much-maligned machine was displaced by enlightened leaders who restructured the government bureaucracies. The moribund school district was headed by an innovative progressive, intent on change.

While Democrats have remained in control of City Hall, the reform coalition is no longer functioning. Over the past three decades, the nature of local elites and their ability to control local outcomes have changed. Very few local business elites have a serious investment stake in the city. As the economy of the city declines, major economic decisions are increasingly made by corporate decision makers elsewhere or by branch executive officers who view Philadelphia as just another step in a corporate career. More international money is invested in the city, and at the same time more Philadelphia money is invested outside the city for greater return.

The Fragmentation of Elite Leadership

The once mighty Greater Philadelphia Movement, a tangible network of influential, locally committed business elites of the reform period, has given way to a series of similar groups, but each successive group has contained fewer players with local interests from increasingly limited sectors of the economy: local real estate, local law firms, and the few remaining companies headquartered in the city. One journalist commented that only two of the twenty-two original members of the board of one of the groups formed in 1982 were still chief executive officers of the member companies: "That speaks volumes about the turmoil in executive suites here in recent years" (Binzen 1990).[5]

Those business elites who still have a stake in the city also exercise interest through the proliferating nonprofit corporations (public–private partnership authorities) that operate outside the system of electoral accountability and still play a major role in program and policy development (Adams et al. 1991).

As absentee owners turn their backs on city concerns, they receive more and more attention from city government. In the past two decades, the city has increasingly used tax incentives in order to attract or retain large businesses. In an effort to save jobs, city leaders have also courted and empowered locally based turn-of-the-century small industrialists with programs like the enterprise zones discussed in Chapter 13.

As Philadelphia becomes more influenced by nonlocal interests and banks and corporate headquarters leave, there is increasing awareness that the economic development strategies during and since the reform era favored elite downtown interests and failed to trickle down to working-class and poor neighborhoods. With increasing decline, the discourse on power relations in the city emphasizes oppositions between classes (popularly referred to as city versus suburb or downtown interests versus neighborhoods) or between racial groups.

Downtown versus the Neighborhoods

In the aftermath of the massive public and private capital investment in the new center, the conflict between downtown and the neighborhoods crystallized in public debate. As urban-renewal funds were utilized in the late 1960s and early 1970s, the city was seen as determined to bulldoze housing for the poor in neighborhoods around Center City in order to build housing for the rich and lay the groundwork for further gentrification. The attempts at reviving commerce in the center were seen as displacing jobs and enterpreneurs who had businesses on the neighborhood strips. In the 1970s, plans for a commuter tunnel that would link the two separate commuter rail lines to Amtrak and the airport were seen as providing benefits to suburban residents and downtown interests but as diverting federal funds from depressed neighborhoods. The same debate took place in the late 1980s and early 1990s around the construction of the convention center to abet the "tourism" strategy of development.

The neighborhoods movement in the city emerged in response to forces in the 1970s catalyzed by the pro-community impetus of federal antipoverty and community development block-grant funding. These generated localized centers of power as city agencies divided the city into Community Development Corporations (CDCs) and Neighborhood Action Councils (NACs). At the same time, the community empowerment associated with the work of Saul Alinsky in Chicago was institutionalized in training programs and organizing manuals used to develop common practices and strategies.

The expansion of business and legal services, health-care training and provision facilities, and higher-education institutions accelerated gentrification, or the transformation and takeover of deteriorating areas near the center of the city by upper-middle-class professionals. Awareness of the role played in the initial deterioration by redlining or disinvestment by banks and insurance companies grew. Local neighborhood groups in low-income areas organized to resist displacement and seek control over their housing stock. Nonprofits such as the Philadelphia Council of Neighborhood Organizations and the Institute for the Study of Civil Values formed to train neighborhood leaders and activists. Neighborhood groups formed alliances to fight redlining and downtown development. In the 1980s and 1990s, they asked for "linkage," a concept that, if implemented, would force those who benefit financially from development for the wealthier downtown constituencies to allocate a portion of their profits for the needs of the neighborhoods. It is these empowerment groups that object to the enterprise zone described in Chapter 13.

The neighborhoods movement is symbolic of the fact that the old economic networks and links between owners and workers, firms and industrial sectors no longer operate in the city. Those who remain in the city see themselves as unconnected by patronage in the workplace, labor unions, and the ward structures of the political machine.

Race and Politics

Religion, race, and ethnicity have always organized politics and conflict in the city (Davis and Haller 1970). In the nineteenth century there were anti-Catholic riots in the industrial zones along the Delaware as the Irish and German Catholics entered the labor force, and anti-Black race riots punctuated the century. Nativist violence occurred during the migrations of 1880 to 1920. In the long run, however, the political machine and later the reform movement provided a mode for allocating public goods among the groups. Blacks, however, have been involved in this distribution only since the civil rights movement.

During the reform movement in the 1950s and early 1960s, the races were linked in the reform coalition. The business elite of progressive technocrats, Blacks, and traditional white politicians in the working-class wards collaborated. This alliance has been credited for the rapid resolution of conflict after the 1964 riots in North Philadelphia (Moore 1991). By the 1980s, Blacks demonstrated that they could rely on their own machine and be more independent in their dealings with downtown elites. Traditional party discipline weakened as the 1950s coalition fractured (Adams et al. 1991; Morgan 1989).

During the 1970s, the combative years of the Frank Rizzo administration, racial polarization increased in the city. The battle over the charter change that would have enabled Rizzo to run for a third term proved to be the catalyst in the creation of Black political strength that undergirded the election of Wilson Goode as the first Black mayor. The 1991 mayoral election was frequently seen in terms of race. The Republicans who nominated former Democrat Rizzo were hoping to return to power as the voice of the white working class, while several powerful Blacks competed for the nomination, opening the way for a progressive white to be nominated and win.

Ironically, Blacks gained a political foothold in a declining civic order just as they had gained a foothold in a declining manufacturing economy. Moreover, while Blacks are more visible in some formerly white neighborhoods, manufacturing and clerical bureaucracies, and sectors of the service economy where they come into contact with the public (public-sector jobs, transportation, retailing), this is occurring simultaneously with the growth of increasingly poor Black and isolated census tracts.

In the early 1990s, contact between Blacks and whites increased in the workplace and commerce but decreased in residential communities. The inability to transfer successful interracial interactions from the workplace to the neighborhood has led to the kind of contradictory statements and ideologies reflected by the workers at Summit Lighting (see Chapter 11). Conflicts between whites and Blacks, whites and Puerto Ricans, Blacks and Asians, and Asians and whites are increasing (Philadelphia Commission on Human Relations 1990).

For many white city residents, the decline of the city is associated with the increasing Black presence in the city. The great population redistribution to the suburbs of the 1950s and 1960s was driven by many public policy decisions favoring investment in suburban housing and highways that made the suburbs cheap and accessible. Many experts comment on the process as "white flight." The loss of whites was a complex response to the perceived economic and social consequences of remaining in the city: a decline in housing values (losing one's investment in houses in redlined neighborhoods) and racially biased fear of social danger from Blacks as neighbors.

Today, the talk about resisting decline in neighborhoods and quality of life that characterizes the everyday preoccupations of those in the city sometimes continues to personify problems by attributing them to particular scapegoat groups. Our research, as well as a study of "talk radio" in the city (Logan 1990), revealed a significant amount of anger about affirmative action based on real experiences of competition in the workplace and hearsay and mis-understandings. Newcomer immigrant groups were often subject to the same kind of resentment about unfair access to housing and government programs as were Blacks.

More recent newcomers have yet to play a major role in city-wide politics. Latinos elected their first city councilman and state legislator in the early 1980s. An early attempt to develop a coalition with the Black machine has broken down. The number of Latinos precludes a widespread electoral strategy on their own, but their geographic concentration gives them control over some offices. Their predominant political strategy has been to seek patronage from mayors and governors through the mechanisms of commis-sions and task forces. Earlier attempts have involved polite petition-ing and have benefited a few individuals. Newer activities have been radically demanding and have pushed for collective benefits.

After some violent incidents in the summer of 1989, the Latino community demanded hearings by the Philadelphia Human Rela-tions Commission to investigate bias against the community in hir-ing for city jobs and in the criminal justice system, schools, and other administrative agencies. The period of our research was a period of heightened attention to the presence and plight of the Latino community in the city.

Koreans are the only other group who act on a citywide level. The Korean Businessman's Association has significant economic power. It represents seven subgroups based on the commodities involved and serves the higher-level banking, real estate, and bro-kerage entities in the community. Korean political participation has been largely limited to using their economic power to make politi-cal contributions to assure access to city government in order to protect local business interests. They have also tried to establish links with the Black political leadership to help ameliorate tensions between Korean merchants and Blacks.

In 1991, the first Korean ran for city office. His basic strategy was to form alliances with Black political groups he had come to know through his role as the major representative of the Korean community on several human relations commissions and task forces. He underscored the similarities between Koreans and Blacks as vic-tims of white racism.

For the most part, however, Koreans do not see themselves as underdogs. Korean leaders often see themselves as providing im-portant capital for the rebuilding of the Philadelphia economy. As one leader said, "We have come to make Philadelphia #1 city again." As a favored "model immigrant" group, Koreans are some-times seen as the hope of the city by public spokespersons for downtown interests. In an editorial about saving Philadelphia (Lipson 1989: 1), it was stated:

> In practically every neighborhood of Philadelphia, you will now find thriving Asian small businesses. The men and women who spend 18-hour days in these storefronts are driven by the ethic of hard work; they sustain themselves through close family relationships. People . . . marvel at how well their children do in school, despite staggering problems of language, culture and economics.

Asians are then contrasted to the poor (Blacks and Latinos) around them who perpetrate crime. The criminals are described as having limited education and employment and "hideously frac-tured families." Their concerns that immigrants are being unfairly helped by the government is described as "pathetic." The editorial ends by saying: "How do we save Philadelphia? Many Asian immi-grants are doing just that."

Neighborhood Differences

The recent political and economic restructuring of Philadel-phia did not have the same impact on all neighborhoods in the city because of local historical patterns of social turnover, economic de-velopment, and housing markets. Three distinct neighborhoods were included in our research. Their local differences play a signif-icant role in the social relationships described in the Philadelphia chapters.

Kensington, in the heart of the historic mill town, has been central to manufacturing since the early nineteenth century. This community is one example of those severely affected by plant clos-ings since the 1960s. It has experienced high rates of housing aban-donment, blight, and crime. Formerly a stable working-class area, it now houses a large percentage of households below the poverty line. This is an area of largely European American ethnic and La-tino households. It is perceived as divided into small block areas that are Spanish dominated (language on the street, control of or-ganizations) and English dominated. This area contains many of the central institutions of the spatially concentrated Latino commu-nity. Asian immigrants are a major presence in the commercial areas of the neighborhood, and Palestinians own businesses and a large share of the housing stock as well.

Social order between groups is maintained by shared views of who controls which areas. Conflict tends to occur as much within as between groups. Several organizations are trying to organize across group lines to empower the neighborhood as part of the neighborhood movement. They are trying to control the housing stock, improve their share of city services, and generate economic development. Many of them fear the forces of gentrification.

This is the setting for the American Street Enterprise Zone discussed in Chapter 13. Participants in the zone are seen by neighborhood empowerment activists as potential gentrifying outsiders. The entrepreneurs, shaped by their own interests, see the neighborhoods as dangerous and their role as that of benefactors. As a group of nonconglomerate entrepreneurs, they are using the program to seek prestige, power, and influence through their connections to government officials. They spurn the interest expressed by local minority entrepreneurs. The intended improvements in relations with the community (increased local employment, local cleanups) do not develop as expected.

The second neighborhood is Olney, an area of newer housing stock several miles north of Kensington. Olney was constructed as a streetcar suburb in the late-nineteenth and early-twentieth-century building boom. Rowhouses are larger than those in the industrial neighborhoods and have porches, bigger yards, and other amenities. Olney has always housed aspiring middle-class families moving up from Kensington and the older industrial locales. Today it is still attracting middle-class whites looking for affordable housing and good schools, as well as attracting middle-class Blacks. But the most notable trend in Olney is the presence of large numbers of newcomer group who have their community institutions centered here: Koreans, Portuguese, Asian Indians, Southeast Asians, and so on. This is also the destination of many aspiring middle-class Latinos from the industrial zone, although their central institutions remain farther south.

The community is undergoing massive turnover as newcomers move in and established residents move out. Much of the local dynamics are related to this turnover and the desire of established residents to maintain the existence of local institutions. Chapter 12 on the service sector looks at this neighborhood.

The retail economy is the site of many encounters between newcomers and the established residents in Olney. Unique aspects of the nature of service work affect the working out of relationships in both large corporate and small individually owned enterprises within this sector. The nature of the community also exerts an influence.

Kensington and Olney can be contrasted to Port Richmond,

which was also in the historic zone of industry. Unlike Kensington, Port Richmond has weathered the decline and is still a stable working-class area with almost no housing abandonment, well-maintained houses, and immaculate public space. Although the housing stock in Port Richmond is smaller and has fewer amenities than that of Olney, there is much more intergenerational continuity here than in Olney with its high rate of turnover. In Port Richmond, newcomers are kept out by harassment, and borders are occasionally contested. Bent on reproducing its local institutions and keeping outsiders away, the community has few links to city agencies and networks of neighborhood activists.

Port Richmond is the institutional center for the Polish American community in the city and houses its clubs, stores, schools, credit union, and beneficials. The skyline is dominated by four parishes based on nationality, a symbolic reminder that the social order is still structured by Catholic and Protestant church-related institutions. There are no empowerment movements.

The only newcomers in Port Richmond are Polish refugees. Some tension exists between the new Poles and their Polish American hosts. Newcomers often come from the intelligentsia and are seen as moving ahead too quickly, having different lifestyles and values, not willing to participate in local institutions, and likely to move. People from Port Richmond and similar communities work at Summit Lighting, described in Chapter 11.

At Summit Lighting, a factory that is downsizing, employees are European American, African American, and Puerto Rican. They come from each of the three study neighborhoods as well as the other parts of the city and suburbs and work together. The dominant group and those with the most seniority come from typically segregated Philadelphia neighborhoods such as Port Richmond, which have kept newcomers out, or from those who fled changing neighborhoods like Kensington and Olney. Few have accommodated to different groups in their residential communities as the residents of Kensington and Olney have done.

Workplace relations are shaped by what is happening to the corporation as well as the nature of particular tasks and the nature of control. These interact with their ideologies of race and class, which reflect the communities they come from.

Conclusions

Group boundaries and group power have been shaped by transformations in the political economy of Philadelphia. Places that different groups hold in the economy, geography, and the power structure of the city are strongly influenced by the nature of the structure at the moment they enter. Blacks have gained power in a declining city. New immigrants enter a transforming economy with a contested power structure.

The new service economy offers few opportunities for full-time jobs with security and benefits. The city has not only lost economic strength during the period of deindustrialization; there has been a parallel loss in linkages between interest groups. A recent analysis of the city argues that it cannot be saved by economic development alone. Increasing the pie will not be effective unless the fragmentation between classes, neighborhoods, and ethnic–racial groups in reversed. Unless there are more formal and informal structures of collaboration, cooperation, and linkage within the economy and power structure, there is no bright future for the city.

This overall city context frames interactions on the ground in specific local communities and workplaces. Each setting engenders different kinds of hierarchical and social interactions. Each workplace incorporates immigrants, minorities, and established ethnic groups differently in different positions of power: owner, supervisor, and worker. These very local micro processes, shaped by larger macrostructural forces, will contribute to the future development of linkages, cooperation, and conflict.

Notes

1. This overview has drawn heavily from Chapter 2 of Goode and Schneider (1994).

2. The largest group of Spanish speakers in Philadelphia are Puerto Ricans. We looked primarily at Puerto Ricans in our study, but other Spanish speakers often use the same services and share the same social space. When we refer to this larger collectivity of Spanish-speaking people in Philadelphia, we use the term "Latino," which is preferred by most individuals and groups.

3. "Philaricans" is a term recently coined on the streets of Philadelphia to parallel the widely used New Yorican. It refers to someone born and raised in a specific place on the mainland and is somewhat different from an island resident. The use of "Spanglish," a mixture of English and Spanish, is one example of the difference. Such differences and their conscious labeling make it harder for people to move back and forth between social networks.

4. "Island" and "mainland" are important terms of reference among Puerto Ricans to refer to differences in lifestyle.

5. As an example of this, consider that one of the central figures in the original coalition was an officer of the powerful department store John Wanamakers. Today, the chain is owned by an international retail conglomerate and is controlled from a distance.

Bibliography

Adams, Carolyn, David Bartelt, David Elesh, Ira Goldstein, Nancy Kleniewski, and William Yancey. 1991. *Philadelphia: Neighborhoods, Conflict and Division in a Post-Industrial City*. Philadelphia: Temple University Press.

Berson, Leonora. 1982. "The Reform Period." In *Capital and Community in Conflict*, edited by John Raines, Leonora Berson, and David Gracie. Philadelphia: Temple University Press.

Binzen, Peter. 1970. *Whitetown USA*. New York: Random House.

———. 1990. "A Quiet Influence on Philadelphia's Agenda." *Philadelphia Inquirer*, November 5.

Boldt, David. 1991. "The Main Line Isn't the Mainline and That's the Story of Philadelphia." *Philadelphia Inquirer*, March 24.

Borowski, Neill. 1991. "Minorities Account for Area Population Gain." *Philadelphia Inquirer*, February 20.

Borowski, Neill, and Murray Dubin. 1991. "Black Segregation Up in Philadelphia, Census Shows." *Philadelphia Inquirer*, April 11.

Byler, Janet, and Douglas Bennett. 1984. *Employment Trends in Southeastern Pennsylvania 1972–1982*. Working Paper No. 11. Philadelphia: Temple University Institute for Public Policy Studies.

Carvajal, Doreen, and Neill Borowski. 1991. "Asians, Latinos Flock to Philadelphia," *Philadelphia Inquirer*, March 3.

Davis, Alan, and Mark Haller. 1970. *The Peoples of Philadelphia*. Philadelphia: Temple University Press.

Dubin, Murray. 1990. "City Report on Latinos Is Delayed." *Philadelphia Inquirer*, December 9.

Dubin, Murray, and Neill Borowski. 1991. "Decades of Flight Turning North Philadelphia into Ghost Town." *Philadelphia Inquirer*, April 12.

Ericksen, Eugene, et al. 1985. *The State of Puerto Rican Philadelphia*. Philadelphia: Temple University Institute for Public Policy Studies.

Golab, Carolyn. 1977. *Immigrant Destinations*. Philadelphia: Temple University Press. 1977.

Goldsmith, William, and Edward J. Blakely. 1992. *Separate Societies: Poverty and Inequality in U.S. Cities*. Philadelphia: Temple University Press.

Goldstein, Ira. 1986. "The Wrong Side of the Tracts: A Study of Residential Segregation in Philadelphia 1930–80." Ph.D. dissertation, Temple University.

Goode, Judith. 1990. "A Wary Welcome to the Neighborhood: Community Responses to Immigrants" *Urban Anthropology* 19:125–153.

Goode, Judith, and Jo Anne Schneider. 1994. *Reshaping Ethnic and Racial Relations in Philadelphia: Immigrants in a Divided City*. Philadelphia: Temple University Press.

Greenburg, Stephanie. 1981. Temple University Press. "Industrial Location and Ethnic Residential Patterns in an Industrializing City: Philadelphia 1880." In *Philadelphia: Work, Space, Family and Group Experience in 19th Century Philadelphia*, edited by Theodore Hershberg. New York: Oxford University Press.

Haines, Pamela. 1982. "Loss in the Garment Industry." In *Capital and Community in Conflict*, edited by John Raines, Lenora Berson, and David Gracie. Philadelphia: Temple University Press.

Hershberg, Theodore, ed. 1981. *Philadelphia: Work, Space, Family and Group Experience in 19th Century Philadelphia*. New York: Oxford University Press.

Hochner, Arthur, and Ira Zibman. 1982. "Absentee Owners and Job Losses." In *Capital and Community in Conflict*, edited by John Raines, Lenora Berson, and David Gracie. Philadelphia: Temple University Press.

Hughes, Mark Alan. 1989. *Poverty in Cities*. Washington D.C.: National League of Cities.

Koppel, Ross. 1988. *Agenda for Growth: The Impact of Food and Agriculture on the Economy of the Delaware Valley*. Philadelphia: Mellon Bank Department of Community Affairs.

Lipson, D. Herbert. 1981. "Off the Cuff." *Philadelphia Magazine*, September.

Logan, Joe. 1990. "Study Criticizes 'Racial Divisiveness' of Radio Talk Shows." *Philadelphia Inquirer*, November 8.

Moberg, David. 1982. "A Big Step toward Worker Ownership." *In These Times*, June.

Moore, Acel. 1989. "The 1964 Riot: Twenty-Five Years After." *Philadelphia Inquirer*, April.

Morgan, P. 1989. "The Last L . . ." *Philadelphia Magazine* 79 (August).

Petras, Elizabeth. 1990. Personal communication.

Pennsylvania Economy League. 1989. "Taxes in Philadelphia Compared to Other Large Cities, 1980. Philadelphia: Pennsylvania Economy League, Eastern Division.

Philadelphia Commission on Human Relations. "Race Relations in Philadelphia: A 1989 Perspective, a 1990 Opportunity." 1986. Report by the Philadelphia Commission on Human Relations and the Temple University Institute for Public Policy.

Philadelphia Inquirer. 1988. "Metropolitan Business Report." September 12.

———. 1990. "Report on Early Census Statistics." September 16.

Peirce, Neil. 1990. "The City's Crisis Has Many Fathers." *Philadelphia Inquirer*, September 17.

Power, E. 1988. "Asian Immigrants Lend New Life to City's Sewing Industry." *Philadelphia Inquirer*, February 28.

Seder, Jean. 1990. *Voices of Kensington: Vanishing Mills, Vanishing Neighborhoods*, McLean Va.: EPM Publications.

Steiner, Robert. 1982. "123 Years of A&P: From Unprecedented Growth to Radical Corporate Surgery" B.A. thesis, Temple University.

Summers, Anita, and Thomas Luce. 1988. *Economic Report on the Philadelphia Metropolitan Area 1988*. Philadelphia: University of Pennsylvania Press.

Warner, Samuel Bass. 1968. *The Private City: Philadelphia in Three Periods of Its Growth*. Philadelphia: University of Pennsylvania Press.

Young, Robert J. 1989. "What Kinds of Immigrants Have Come to the Philadelphia Area, Where Did They Settle and How Are They Doing?" Paper given at the Conference "Who Are These Strangers Among Us?" Balch Institute. September 1989.

11 Facing Job Loss:

Changing Relationships in a Multicultural Urban Factory

Carole Cohen

The decline of Summit Lighting, a lighting-fixture plant, was obvious in 1989.[1] Signs outside the personnel department's outer door boldly announced, in English and Spanish, "No Jobs Available." By early 1989, only nine hundred workers remained of the more than one thousand five hundred employed less than four years earlier. Management had terminated not only production workers but also lower-level management. In the spring of 1989, they even eliminated their security department, contracting with an outside firm for part-time security officers. Machines sat idle, covered up, and permanently shut down. Instead of a manufacturing plant, it looked like a warehouse as more and more boxes filled aisles where in the past machines hummed and workers previously toiled.

Deindustrialization fundamentally affected workers' attitudes and personal relationships.[2] Insecurity permeated. Older, longer-term workers tended to accept management's explanations and efforts at ameliorating the effects of decline. Younger workers were more likely to resist. Everyone's social relationships were disturbed as many workers disappeared and others were moved to new departments. Among most workers, the decline produced a solidarity that overcame the racial and ethnic divisions churning and even shaking the rest of Philadelphia. This chapter first briefly examines our methodology and then provides a short overview of recent plant history. I then detail the social relationships within the plant, developing the argument that the plant's decline has fundamentally affected who workers affiliate with and why.

231

Examining Relations in the Workplace

Getting the Lay of the Land

Our connection with Summit Lighting began with interviews of factory managers in the late fall of 1988. We conducted the bulk of our research, however, from February through August 1989, when two fieldworkers, Jay Longshore and Carole Cohen, maintained regular weekly contacts with this plant. In addition, David Marin made several visits to assess the placement and relationships of primarily Latino plant employees.

Within the broad context of the factory, we carried out our research in three specific departments in central production: polishing, plating, and assembly. We had access to employees during their two ten-minute break times and thirty-minute lunch periods. While management did not permit worker contact during production time, we could observe the work process. I held my meetings with workers at the various sites in which they took their lunch breaks, conducting some interviews with only one worker, while managing others with groups of workers who were eating together.

Restructuring at the Local Level

Summit Lighting had a long history in Philadelphia dating back to before the Great Depression. It was owned and managed by a local family until, as has been typical for much light industry in this area, the takeover mania of the 1980s gobbled it up. Through most of the 1980s, it was owned by one of the largest conglomerates in the United States, which operated 155 other companies. In 1988, the conglomerate sold Summit to another large corporation. Each ownership change entailed management restructuring. In fact, as we began our fieldwork, new managers took over leadership of the factory. The long plant history also incorporated an equally long union involvement as most production workers were represented by the International Brotherhood of Electrical Workers.

These developments embody the effects of U.S. deindustrialization, as discussed in both the introduction to this volume and Chapter 10. In the case of Summit Lighting, some labor-intensive operations had been moved from Philadelphia to other regions of the United States and outside the country's borders. As recently as 1987, operations for glass staining had been moved to Mexico, and Summit's Philadelphia-based tiffany department was closed down. Other phases of production had also been transferred from Philadelphia to subsidiary plants in Montreal and in South Carolina, where the black molding for the lighting fixtures was produced. In addition, parts such as the decorative brass trimmings were being imported from Italy.

Summit Lighting's Philadelphia sales and manufacturing operations took place in a large building erected in 1936 that had over a million square feet. Plant operations were conducted on three levels, with offices, management, and sales on the top floor, while most production departments occupied the first floor. The lowest level was normally used for the boxing department and for storage.[3] This physical structure mirrored the plant's internal bureaucratic hierarchy, as production workers were supervised by team leaders, who were accountable to department supervisors and managers and ultimately to the plant superintendent and plantwide manager. Team leaders who had the lowest-level supervisory positions had the responsibility for the machinery and their small group of department workers. They were often in precarious situations as they frequently took the brunt of problems in production from high-level management.

In all its four plants, Summit produced more than fifteen hundred different lighting fixtures, including chandeliers, Tiffany lamps, and recessed lighting. At the Philadelphia plant in 1989, production departments included the press shop, paint shop, polishing, plating, subassembly, and assembly. The manufacture of these lighting products usually included a process that began in pressing, where metal sheets were bent into particular shapes. These shapes were taken to plating, where they were dipped into copper and brass coatings. Once coated, parts were polished and painted and readied for preassembly. Here, smaller pieces were connected, and some wiring was done. Finally, in assembly, all parts were put together and boxed in preparation to be sent to the shipping department.

The assembly department occupied the center of the factory floor with its conveyor belts spread throughout most of the floor. Close to the break area, an enclosed four-sided windowed office provided supervisors a strategically located view of all belts. Early in February 1989, assembly operated twelve belts. By mid-July that number had been reduced to six. After the plant's two-week July vacation, there were only four working belts. One supervisor stated that the situation was temporary as all workers had not as yet returned from vacation. By August, however, a group of workers from subassembly occupied one of the idle assembly conveyor-belt spaces. By spring 1989, only two hundred employees worked in this department, which had employed four hundred workers the preceding year. In addition, there had been three full shifts in

1985 with overtime commonly available to workers; by early 1989, there was only one shift in assembly and virtually no opportunity for overtime.

Characteristics of a Workforce in Decline

From 1985 to early 1989, the number of employees had been reduced by about 27 percent, and cutbacks continued during the course of our fieldwork. As Table 11.1 indicates,[4] in 1988 approximately 27 percent of the plant's 972 workers were female and were employed primarily as semiskilled operatives, office and clerical workers, and sales employees. Only about 10 percent of the officials or managers were women, and the factory had no women listed as skilled workers.

Almost 70 percent of the workforce was white; about 20 percent was African American, with the remaining 10 percent being Latino, all of them of Puerto Rican descent. Only 5.5 percent of the Latino's female. Among the white and African American workforce, the percentages were less dramatic; 28 percent were white females, and 30 percent African American females.

White males dominated the higher-paid and more prestigious positions. Among managers, eighty-eight white males were counted, compared to four African American males and three Puerto Rican employees. Only one African American woman was listed in this category. White males similarly dominated among the "skilled workers," holding 85 percent of those jobs with only 12.7 percent going to African Americans. There was one lone "skilled" Puerto Rican worker. In short, as in many other American workplaces, gender and ethnicity segregated occupations within this factory (cf. Lamphere 1987; Remy and Sawers 1984).

Analysis of job terminations over a two-year period in the late 1980s also indicates ethnic disparities: 35 percent of Puerto Rican jobs were lost, 28 percent of African American jobs, and slightly less than 20 percent of white jobs.[5] Layoffs obviously affected all groups, but not equally. The old lemma of "last hired, first fired" appears to account for the discrepancies. Terminations hit the Latinos hardest because, as a group, they had the least seniority and the lowest-level jobs. Because the white workforce had the longest history with the company, more workers of that group remained during the 1987–1988 period.[6] In general, plant cutbacks decreased the number of immigrant workers, including Jamaicans, Barbadians, Asian Indians, and Poles.

Age also differentiated workers at Summit. Though the plant had a few young workers, most employees were middle-aged, and a significant number were seniors. As with immigrants, the seniority

Table 11.1. Numbers and Percentages of Summit Lighting Employees, March 25, 1988

Categories	Total (B through G) A	Male				Female			
		White, not Latino (%) B	African American, not Latino (%) C	Latino (%) D	Other (%) E	White, not Latino (%) F	African American, not Latino (%) G	Latina H	Other I
Officials/managers	106	83.0	3.8	2.8	.9	8.4	.9	—	—
Professionals	22	59.0	—	—	9.1	27.0	4.5	—	—
Technicians	16	56.0	6.3	—	—	18.8	18.8	—	—
Sales workers	104	69.0	—	—	—	30.0	.9	—	—
Office and clerical	113	38.0	6.2	2.6	—	52.0	.9	—	—
Craft workers (skilled)	55	85.0	12.7	1.8	—	—	—	—	—
Operatives (semiskilled)	482	38.0	20.0	15.0	.21	16.0	9.0	1.0	.21
Laborers (unskilled)	64	37.5	26.5	15.6	—	12.5	7.8	—	—
Service workers	10	60.0	10.0	20.0	—	—	10.0	—	—
Total	972								

system first laid off employees in their late teens through early twenties. Many of the plant's long-time employees had begun their work at the factory when they were in their late teens, recruited through family connections, a common practice in U.S. firms (Newman 1985). In earlier years, whole families often worked together at factories like Summit, but by the late 1980s most workers had found other means to secure their jobs,[7] and working life and home life became more separated.

Dealing with Decline

While management decreased the number of workers, they also slashed benefits for the remaining workers. They lowered the amount of permitted sick time and instituted a new production system in which workers could be fired for accumulating twenty-one late arrivals or sick days.

While work at the plant was evaporating, management attempted to maintain a facade of continuity, of continued concern and attention to its employees. Before the decline began, management sponsored or promoted company picnics, Christmas parties, group trips, and retirement lunches. Individual groups of workers still planned and carried out life-cycle-event celebrations, such as baby showers and birthday parties. Activities such as repainting the cafeteria and company-sponsored educational and health programs gave the impression that business was going on as usual. One of the managers spoke with pride about a recent "smoking cessation" program, basic education classes, and a proposal to begin English as a Second Language (ESL) classes in the near future. Management also redecorated the cafeteria and occasionally lowered food prices on special days. One manager stated that the company had plans to bring cafeteria food to worksites so that workers would not lose time walking to the facility during their breaks.

Workers, however, clearly understood the cafeteria to be management's "place." On numerous visits to the cafeteria, I observed large groups of white males in suits seated at some tables, and groups of white females in fairly dressy clothing at other tables. Though pockets of production workers regularly ate lunch in the cafeteria, for the most part this establishment seemed to serve the better-paid, higher-status, and middle-class company employees. Even on the hottest summer days, when the cafeteria was an oasis of air conditioning in contrast to the hot and uncomfortable department break areas, managers outnumbered workers in the cafeteria.

Management also maintained the retirement party rituals, but employees now viewed them cynically. One female assembly worker commented that sometimes the retiree refused to be present at his or her party because of the hypocrisy of the event. Workers knew that they could be laid off at any moment. Management's policy was to provide workers only one-day's notice before terminating them.

Management's pretense of continuity and concern for their employees was overshadowed by a more general attitude toward decreasing costs while maintaining production. Jim,[8] a white male assembly worker in his mid-thirties, reported that Summit's management no longer emphasized quality in the manufacturing processes. All they cared about was "getting out the numbers." Jim claimed that neither he nor such big companies as Sears, J.C. Penney, and Kmart wanted Summit products.[9]

The International Brotherhood of Electrical Workers had long represented Summit workers, but the union could do little to reverse the fortunes of workers in Summit's Philadelphia plant. Many of the plant's younger workers claimed the union had sold out to management. They blamed the union for not standing up to management's new rigid policy concerning absences, the arbitrariness of some supervisors regarding workers' hourly rates, and discriminatory promotion practices against employees who did not support the union. Younger workers boycotted union-sponsored activities, such as trips to Atlantic City, arguing that they were management supported. More important, their frustration culminated in their initiating a lawsuit claiming fraud in the previous year's union election.

The union, however, was not without support. Many of the older employees were content with the union status quo. Because of the ethnic succession that had taken place in the plant, with white workers being the longest-working employees, union supporters tended to be white females who commonly were married and whose husbands also worked. In short, they were far less vulnerable. Their seniority would protect them somewhat, and even if they did lose their jobs, their family was less likely to suffer severely.

This division over the union embodied a first layer of discontent and alienation among workers. Workers of the same "political orientation" ate lunch together, avoiding those whose views they opposed. Regularly seated at lunchtime in the assembly department's snack area "corral" was a core group of two African American and three white, U.S.-born male workers. These men usually sat together on picnic tables, next to the large group of "dissident" union members. All these men had limited seniority, having worked at the plant for about six years. Each man had been "bumped down" from another department. Most had previously been employed in tiffany. These men supported each other in their feelings of loss for their old positions, as well as their insecurities about future job opportunities at the plant.

Differentiations among departments provided a second level of discontent and alienation. In general, the assembly department, which had the lowest wages and greatest diversity of workers, had the most widespread discontent. The plating and polishing departments, which tended to have both higher wages and more long-term workers, although of mixed ethnicity, tended to exhibit solidarity among themselves.

Bumping Down

With plantwide slowdowns and a decreasing need for workers in many departments, management frequently "bumped" employees to other sections, displacing those with less seniority. Those bumped down to assembly replaced employees who had no place else to go; usually, these workers were laid off entirely. Some workers were sensitive to the resentments and insecurities bumping provokes, and if they had other employment options outside the plant, they preferred to be laid off. Other employees, however, complained a great deal and alienated workers in their new department. Remy and Sawers (1984) suggest that by forcing workers to establish new social roots within a factory, learn new skills, and witness the devaluation of their previous skills from their old positions, bumping commonly leads to psychological problems. Our observations reveal that social problems and declining morale among co-workers are equally likely and important.

The assembly department's workforce was a microcosm for the entire plant as African American, white, and Puerto Rican male and female employees of different ages worked together on the same belt. Bumping males from specialty departments had transformed a formerly female department into an increasingly diverse mix. Workers in assembly earned among the lowest wages throughout the plant. The base pay was $8.07 per hour, compared to a plantwide average of $10 an hour. Assembly workers were paid by the number of boxes that went off a belt, and since rates were determined for whole belts and not individual workers, team cooperation among employees was necessary.

Formerly, the female-dominated department had achieved tremendous cooperation and interworker harmony. Team spirit from the work process often carried over to break time with mixed groups of workers eating together at their belts or at picnic tables in the assembly area. Only the assembly workers initiated Christmas parties. One particularly close team in the assembly area resolved differences among themselves during lunchtime and even pooled their money together for state lottery tickets.

The bumped workers disrupted the team spirit. Many of the bumped male workers, and other males throughout the plant, viewed assembly employment as female work.[10] Women were supposedly well qualified for putting parts together because of their "well developed hand–eye coordination."[11] Typical of the bumped employees was Martin, a white, middle-aged man who had taken a salary cut on his move down from tiffany to painting and finally assembly. He had been hired for work in the tiffany department about six years ago, before the relocation of tiffany to Mexico. He missed the status and camaraderie of the smaller, specialized department, claiming, "You just can't get to know people in assembly, since everyone is just too spread out at the different belts."

Worker Solidarity

The polishing department was different. First, the workers were all males. In 1989, the polishing department had twenty-seven male workers. There had been three women in the department in 1987, but two had since been laid off and the third had been transferred to another department. While all workers were males, they were ethnically diverse and primarily from immigrant backgrounds. Until 1985, the department's workforce was primarily Polish, either immigrants or people with family roots in Poland. By 1988, sixteen of the workers were Puerto Rican, three were immigrants from Poland, one was Jamaican, another was African American, and six were European American. The department was supervised by a U.S.-born man of Polish ancestry. In 1988, there had been a Puerto Rican assistant supervisor for polishing, but he had been promoted and transferred to the plant in Mexico.

Traditionally, new hires for polishing came largely from immigrants with no social ties to the factory. Rarely did workers from within the plant bid on polishing positions. Most workers in other departments considered polishing undesirable because of its health and safety risks. This relationship between racial–ethnic labor and "dirty work" has long been reported in reference to ethnicity and immigration (Newman 1985; Piore 1979).

As the belts structured the work process in assembly, the piece-rate system dominated work in polishing. Workers had an hourly average quota to maintain. For example, 189 small pieces of metal had to be polished to make the base pay of $8.07, which was expected of every worker. Employees who polished 400 pieces an hour, or 150 percent of the quota, would receive $12.40 an hour. Thus the work in polishing was structured by the economic incentive of higher wages and the concomitant threat of dismissal if the hourly quota was not met. With this system, supervisors in polishing did not have to watch over workers directly as they did in departments like assembly and plating (Longshore 1990). The piece-rate system allowed management to control worker output without physically looking over their shoulders.

Though the piece-rate system is designed to individualize workers and have them compete with each other, with increased tensions between workers and management the system was used by employees as a means of resistance. Workers often attempted to strike a balance by making as much money as possible without going too far over the quotas. In that way, management could not set higher limits for the base-pay rate. One U.S.-born Puerto Rican worker stated that when management timed employees to set new pay rates, it was important for younger workers not to speed along and raise the averages, forcing older or slower employees to produce at rates they could not meet.

Thus relationships in polishing were sometimes formed in opposition to management's pressure to increase production quotas. Workers also tended to come together at break time in accordance with the division of polishing in which they worked. This department was divided into three sections: one for small, hand-polished parts; another for larger parts, which were polished by machine; and a final section known as antiquing. Since antiquing had the most heterogeneous workforce with Italian Americans, German Americans, Puerto Ricans, African Americans, and Caribbean immigrants, this section had the most marked blending of different workers having break time together.

Finally, some workers in polishing were united by their shared pride in working at a dangerous job that required specialized skills and paid relatively well. The work in this department was dangerous because machines such as the "band belt" had to be operated with precision; workers had been known to cut their hands and stomachs if metal parts slipped. In fact, before our involvement at the plant, one worker was killed when a metal piece flew out of the machine and crushed his chest.

This pride in earning good wages at a difficult job did not always serve to bring workers together. Sometimes, the pride took on a special ethnic meaning. Nestor, a Puerto Rican small-parts polisher, stated that the department had the most Puerto Ricans because it was one of the highest-paid departments at the plant. Nestor believed that Puerto Ricans came to the factory because they were hard workers who wanted to make good money.

Camaraderie among plating's mostly all-male, U.S.-born African American and white workforce paralleled that of polishing. Again, the most obvious tensions were not directed against different ethnic groups but were aimed at management. Workers responded to the proportionally greater number of layoffs in this small department, and to a "speed up" employees were subjected to because management expected the amount of work to remain constant despite the decreased workforce. As workers were stretched to the limit to meet quotas, they felt the need of the support and solidarity of their co-workers. Employees in plating did in fact seek one another out for that purpose. Like many of the workers in assembly, those in plating spoke very openly among themselves about work-related concerns.

In May 1989 the plating department employed seventeen workers; nine were African American, six were white, and one was Puerto Rican. There was also one female employee of European American ancestry. The department was supervised by an immigrant South Asian Indian male.[12] This workforce, which had five teams in 1988, had been reduced to two teams in one short year. Apparently every plating employee with less than fifteen years' seniority had been laid off or bumped to another area of the plant.

The work process in plating primarily involved placing mostly steel parts onto hooks, which were then dipped by machine into a tub of copper or brass solution that gave parts their particular coating. Employees worked in one of two teams, and each subgroup was overseen by a team leader. Workers in plating experienced a decidedly higher degree of supervision than their somewhat more autonomous co-workers in polishing. The two team leaders and one department supervisor watched over these employees continually. This of course added to the division between workers and management. Platers were paid a flat hourly wage according to their job category and thus did not have the advantage of higher-wage possibilities created by the piece-rate system in polishing.

Ethnicity versus Worker Solidarity

Ethnicity seemed to be most important for those at the two ends of the occupational hierarchy—management and the Puerto

Ricans who tended to be the most recent hires with predominantly low-level jobs. Ralph, an African American team leader, felt that he was well qualified for the position of assistant supervisor, since he had worked in plating for seventeen years. He had applied twice, but each time a white male with much less experience had gotten the job. Jesse was the only Puerto Rican to hold the position of assistant supervisor, which he held for six years. A few months after our fieldwork ended, however, management laid Jesse off. Jesse was convinced that he was terminated because he was a Puerto Rican and appeared interested in filing a suit against management.

Puerto Ricans also demonstrated ethnic solidarity among themselves. Puerto Ricans are demographically the most significant newcomer group in Philadelphia. They are also those most likely to have been last hired in the plant. At the time of our fieldwork, a number of violent incidents in the city considerably heightened both awareness of Puerto Ricans and tensions between them and others in the city.

A group of about ten Puerto Rican men regularly ate lunch together in the aisle made by the crates adjacent to the assembly department's snack area. These men worked in different departments at the plant. Their backgrounds represented variations in English proficiency, class, and length of time on the mainland. Some who worked in such departments as maintenance, assembly, subassembly, and shipping lived in the same neighborhoods and spent time together outside work; others of the group did not.

Robert was one of the men who ate lunch with the group of Puerto Rican workers who gathered just off the assembly break area "corral." Robert was fluent in English and had worked at the factory for nineteen years. At the time of our meeting, he had worked among the primarily white workforce in the shipping department.[13] He was committed to his ethnic identity and hoped to return to Puerto Rico someday, a desire that caused conflict in his household because his wife and children were all born in the United States and had little interest in settling in Puerto Rico.

Yet not all Puerto Ricans interacted predominantly with other Puerto Ricans. Celia was a grandmother in her mid-fifties who had worked for wages since she was fifteen and who had come to the United States in 1960. Celia's husband had also worked at Summit and apparently had left her for another Puerto Rican woman he had met at the factory. Ironically, Celia began her employment after she and her husband had separated. Celia stated that she was not friendly with the other "Hispanic" women because they were in different departments. She reported that she basically kept to herself at the plant and generally ate alone in the cafeteria. Celia felt that the white workers were not friendly toward her at the factory. She also did not believe that the whites went out of their way for African American workers either. Celia was unhappy with her worklife at the plant and stated that she worked like an "animal." Her somewhat limited seniority probably made her work situation more difficult. She was frequently moved from one assembly belt to another as additional workers were needed. Her relative short tenure, frequent bumpings, and estrangement from her husband all combined to alienate her from both co-workers in her department and other Puerto Ricans.

Beyond the more general Puerto Rican pattern, ethnicity did not appear to be a dominant factor in organizing social relationships. Workers who had been in the plant longest and who had not been bumped were the most likely to spend their free time with workers in their own department. Most workers repeatedly stated that employees at the plant got along well, and they pointed to conflict only during tense times when quotas had to be met or the summer heat caused tempers to rise. For example, one African American female assembly worker, who had been employed at the factory for thirty-eight years, reported that her best friend at Summit was a middle-aged Puerto Rican woman who worked with her on the same belt. On most occasions these two women ate lunch together, though they did not socialize after work hours. In addition, the very mixed ethnic groups of workers in antiquing, including two Puerto Ricans, remained in that section at break time and shared their lunchtime together.

Ideology of Difference

Despite the fact that we never witnessed workers using ethnicity or race as a point of contention, employees had their private thoughts about the others, which they sometimes shared. Some of these thoughts expressed an "ideology of difference" that supported efforts for harmonious working relationships, while other thoughts needed to be repressed in the workplace if people were going to keep their jobs in these unstable times, and if, as was necessary in some cases, they were going to relate successfully together as a team.

Martin, the white, middle-aged man who had been at the factory for six years and was bumped down from the tiffany department, stated that "everyone had to get along in this country whether they wanted to or not." He went on to explain: "In the United States, people came from all over the world, and you couldn't avoid them." Martin suggested that this was why he got along with everyone. He further reported that a white woman in his somewhat racially homogeneous neighborhood near the city's northeastern suburbs had wanted to sell her home to African Americans, upsetting other white residents in the neighborhood. Martin claimed he would not be bothered by the sale as long as the African Americans on the street allowed him "his privacy." In other words, Martin could live next to "difference" as long as his personal space or lifestyle was not disturbed.

John, a German American worker in the polishing department, presented a different picture when he spoke about African Americans. He declared that he "would work with them, eat with them, but he would not live with them." Furthermore, when Jay Longshore told John and another polisher of Italian American ethnicity that he was looking for a house, both workers were quick to point out which areas were acceptable because they were all white residential blocks.

Also in contrast to Martin's approach was the rationale employed by a close-knit group of middle-aged, white ethnic women, all of whom were long-time workers at the plant. Nancy, the most vocal of this group of four women, wanted me to know how "workers" felt about paying taxes for "foreigners" and other Americans who were on welfare. Nancy separated the "real Americans," a group in which she included herself and her lunch partners, from those on welfare.

Mary, another member of this group, also discussed seeing a woman in the checkout line at the food store pay for her food with food stamps and then pay cash for Amore cat food, which she described as a gourmet cat food and twice as costly as other brands. Mary said she was so angry she just wanted to "wring the other woman's neck." Mary further reported that she and her husband, who owned his own business, struggled to make ends meet, and they were unable to buy their dog gourmet food.

At this point, Nancy went on to state that "there were plenty of jobs out there, and that if she was a government official she would make everyone go to work with the exception of those who had real disabilities." A third group member then stated that "she could not get on welfare if she wanted to because she was the wrong shade." This group discussion ended with talk about how those on welfare had lots of children, which enabled them to get more money from the government.

This conversation was interesting because, throughout, specific races or ethnic groups were coded by euphemisms, rather than direct labels. Additionally, African Americans and immigrants all appeared to fall in the same category, "others." Furthermore, these women had spoken to me on several occasions about the many layoffs at Summit Lighting and the fact that because there was no new hiring and those with the least seniority were let go, very few recent immigrants were working at the plant. This points to the contradictions people experience in their ideology, which often may not coincide with the everyday reality of their lives. All these women were well aware of how difficult it was to keep a job at Summit in recent years. It is also ironic that the same declining conditions that led these women to "blame" others for getting more "benefits," such as welfare and food stamps, were instrumental in producing at least surface harmony in the workplace.

The fact that for the most part daily interactions between workers at this plant were pleasant and cordial, and at the same time the workers continued to maintain negative sentiments about the "other," may suggest that people simultaneously construct distinct beliefs about difference when they relate to the individual and the group. Perhaps, too, people are more earnest about "defending boundaries" at home or in the community than they are at the workplace.

Relationships Outside Work

We found that among workers there was little after-hours socializing. Though many employees stated that most other workers did socialize outside the factory, the majority of those we questioned reported that they were the exception to the rule. Workers suggested that they had little time to socialize because of family or second-job obligations. Others stated that they did not spend time with co-workers outside work because they simply lived too far from their friends.[14] Finally, some workers simply voiced a lack of interest in socializing with co-workers, as they were simply "tired of seeing each other all day."

One example of cross racial–ethnic friendships that did continue after work hours was between a white Italian American male of middle age and a black male in his early thirties from Barbados. These two men worked together in the paint department and regularly ate lunch together in the assembly break area.

Louis, the man from Barbados, often went shopping with Paul and his wife on weekends and sometimes visited in Paul's home. Paul, the Italian American, lived in a middle-class neighborhood a few blocks from the factory. When I first met Paul, he was planning his retirement in the near future. After he finally did retire, I spoke again with Louis, who stated that he missed his friend, and though they continued to maintain telephone contact, he doubted that they would spend much time together because Paul no longer worked at the factory.

For the most part, camaraderie between workers of different races did not flourish outside work.[15] It was as if the factory was its own separate arena subject to its unique structure, and after work, people went about their lives as usual. This often meant living out segregated lives in which ideologies of difference flourished. For the most part, the phenomenon of working together on a daily basis brought people together because in many instances wages depended on teamwork, but also because the declining conditions encouraged employees to seek each other out as they shared in the insecurities concerning the future. This resulted in at least superficial benevolent relationships between workers of different races and ethnicities.

Conclusions

Until the early 1980s, Summit provided a stable and secure work environment to many residents of three Philadelphia neighborhoods. It also had a tradition of hiring newcomers, in the early part of this century white Europeans, then African Americans, and most recently Puerto Ricans. As one white, middle-aged woman put it, "Summit was one of the places you could always count on for work." According to Summit's workers, it was a good job, too, where workers cared about their product and where management treated them fairly and provided good benefits. In a very concrete fashion, Summit Lighting was a part of and contributed to the American Dream of self-advancement through work under decent conditions with good pay.

Prompted by acquisition mergers, the exporting of production, and general cost-cutting moves, the scene at the end of the 1980s was utterly different. Every few months, the Philadelphia plant pruned production and discharged more employees. Those still left with jobs got caught in the "stretch out," working to produce the same amount as in the past when the company employed more workers, but for the same or less pay under stricter working conditions. Some workers declared that they were like "animals" or "slaves" and that work was "just not fun anymore." The plant's changes and the workers' responses to them appear to be a typical response to industrial restructuring (cf. Newman 1984). These same forces affected workers' interrelationships more complexly.

Deindustrialization plainly altered workers' relationships to one another and to the plant. Insecurity and disaffection infused individuals and social relations. Marvin, an African American and a team leader in plating, stated that in the past he worked over and above what was required by his job description. When management no longer trusted nor took much interest in employees, however, he began to do the minimal amount of work just to get by and keep his job. Yet Marvin was lucky because his family was grown and he had prepared for work after Summit as a minister.

Others resisted the changes. Primarily younger, more recently employed workers, those with the least seniority and thus the most likely to lose their jobs, attempted to provoke the union to oppose management's policies more vigorously. In contrast, those with the most seniority and especially older white women who had spouses holding jobs outside Summit supported management. In short, deindustrialization magnified the importance of minor internal class divisions between those whose tenure and family income insulated them from disruptions and those more recently employed who depended more fully on working at Summit.

Most arrestingly, in distinction to the worksites studied in Miami, workers did *not* segregate themselves along racial or ethnic lines, in either their attitudes toward Summit Lighting or their affiliations with co-workers. African Americans and whites both resisted management and the union. At breaks and during lunch, workers gathered primarily by department. Although many white workers still articulated euphemistically shrouded racial and ethnic prejudices, they ignored these opinions when it came to co-workers. Their prejudices applied to people outside the workplace, not those whom they worked beside and came to know personally.

Puerto Ricans, contrary to the factory's general inclination, did segregate themselves. They spoke a foreign language, but more important, they were the most recent hires and thus had had the least opportunity to become incorporated into the plant's informal social relationships.

"Bumping" unsettled workers' informal solidarity based on departmental and working team affiliations. In departments or teams within departments where few had been bumped, workers cooperated closely, exhibiting a high degree of camaraderie. But bumped workers intruding on a department or team subverted departmental solidarity. The bumped worker both dislodged another worker, who commonly ended up without a job, and resented being placed in a new, lower-level department. The bumped employee remained apart from his or her new co-workers, generally not taking breaks with them or sharing in other group activities.

Other factors shaped relationships, too. Some workers belonged to the same organizations outside the factory, such as Alcoholics Anonymous. Others, such as Celia, simply preferred to be alone. Yet deindustrialization, workers' terminations, and insecurities most profoundly affected social relationships.

While workers' memories of the earlier days of Philadelphia's Summit plant are undoubtedly colored by nostalgia, there is no doubt that deindustrialization transformed not only production but also workers' attitudes and their relationships with one another. Workers did not collectively rise up and oppose management, nor did they fracture along racial and ethnic lines. While everyone resented the plant's decay, workers' reactions and their informal coalitions diverged according to minor internal class divisions and their historical relationship to the plant. Resistance was quiet, expressed through a boycott of management functions, disaffection with the union, alienation from one's co-workers, and disruption of former worker solidarity. These divisions and countervailing solidarities permitted management to continue with its depreciation of the Philadelphia plant and workers to establish and maintain social relationships that largely overcame the racial and ethnic divisions that characterized Philadelphia outside the plant. Ideally, urban enterprise zones, as discussed in Chapter 13, would re-create Summit Lighting as it used to be. But as this chapter demonstrates, simply producing jobs is not enough. To achieve worker satisfaction and solidarity among workers regardless of ethnic background, the jobs must be well paid, stable, open to all, and administered by managers whose concerns for maintaining low costs do not obliterate genuine attention to workers' individual and social welfare.

Acknowledgments

Since carrying out this study was a team effort, I am indebted to various individuals involved with the Philadelphia Changing Relations Project. I wish to thank Jo Anne Schneider, coordinator of the project, for making the initial contacts with the Summit Lighting factory and for her several extensive interviews with factory management. I would also like to thank Jay Longshore and David Marin, my fellow fieldworkers at the factory, for their discussions during the course of the research and for their invaluable notes. Finally, I am most grateful to the project director, Judith Goode, for her encouragement and assistance. Her support was crucial to me at the time of fieldwork and especially in the construction of this chapter. I must stress however, that the ideas discussed in this chapter are mine, and I hold final responsibility for them.

Notes

1. The name of the company has been changed to ensure confidentiality.

2. The theory of deindustrialization was initially developed by economists Barry Bluestone and Bennett Harrison (1982), who regarded the phenomenon as a more or less permanent fact of U.S. society.

3. Additionally, the first level was the site of the cafeteria, the infirmary, the personnel department, and a well-appointed showroom that displayed the full variety of lighting fixtures manufactured at this factory and its three subsidiaries.

4. Data for the table were taken from a report filed by Summit to the federal government to establish racial and gender breakdowns of plant employees. Figures were not available for 1989, the year of our fieldwork.

5. Though probably not all workers were lost to layoffs, the failure to replace workers and informant interviews indicate that management terminated the vast majority of lost workers.

6. Remy and Sawers (1984) discuss similar findings for females and African Americans in their meatpacking plant study.

7. Among newer workers, some people landed their jobs by "walking in off the street" or by making applications through such impersonal institutions as state employment agencies. In other cases, workers learned of their jobs through community or ethnic social networks. We were aware of several Italian Americans who secured their jobs through contacts at the Knights of Columbus.

8. This worker's name has been changed to assure confidentiality. I follow this practice throughout the paper.

9. The relationship between the neglect of quality production and the loss of pride among workers was one of the major findings of Katherine Newman in connection with her study of the Singer Company (1985).

10. Nevertheless, men with a long history of working in assembly were quick to point out that they would not work elsewhere because there were no hazardous chemicals or machines in assembly.

11. This ideology appears fairly universal. It has been well documented that male managers of subsidiary plants offshore employed this rational for hiring young women (Fuentes and Ehrenreich 1983; Grossman 1980).

12. This supervisor was one of the few workers from any part of Asia. It was, however, reported that many Asian Indians had been employed at Summit in the past.

13. It is worthy of note that I had never met any of the white shippers, but on occasion I had met two African American shippers. One of these workers frequently took his breaks in the assembly area. Since Robert regularly met with these Puerto Rican workers, this may have implied that racially different men preferred not to break with shipping's mostly white workforce.

14. Though plant workers lived in a variety of neighborhoods in the Philadelphia area, including the suburbs and southern New Jersey, many workers lived in close proximity to one another.

15. This does not include the examples of workers who had connections outside the work relationship.

Bibliography

Bluestone, Barry, and Bennett Harrison. 1982. *The Deindustrialization of America*. New York: Basic Books.

Fuentes, Annette, and Barbara Ehrenreich. 1983. *Women in the Global Factory*. Boston, Mass.: South End Press.

Grossman, Rachel. 1980. "Women's Place in the Integrated Circuit." *Radical America*, pp. 29–49.

Hochner, Arthur, Cherlyn Gransoe, Judith Goode, and Elaine Simon. 1988. *Job Saving Strategies: Worker Buyouts and QWL*. Kalamazoo, Mich.: UpJohn Institute for Employment Research.

Lamphere, Louise. 1987. *From Working Daughters to Working Mothers: Immigrant Women in a New England Industrial Community*. Ithaca, N.Y.: Cornell University Press.

Lamphere, Louise, Patricia Zavella, and Felipe Gonzales. 1993. *American Working Families: Mediating the Contradictions of Work and Family*. Ithaca, N.Y.: Cornell University Press.

Longshore, Jay. 1990. "Hegemony and the Labor Process." Manuscript, Temple University, Philadelphia.

Newman, Katherine. 1985. "Turning Your Back on Tradition." *Urban Anthropology* 14(1–3).

Piore, Michael. 1979. *Birds of Passage*. New York: Cambridge University Press.

Remy, Dorothy, and Larry Sawers. 1984. "Economic Stagnation and Discrimination." In *My Troubles Are Going to Have Troubles with Me: Everyday Trials and Triumphs of Women Workers*, edited by Karen B. Sacks and Dorothy Remy, pp. 95–112. New Brunswick, N.J.: Rutgers University Press.

12   Encounters over the Counter: Bosses, Workers, and Customers on a Changing Shopping Strip

Judith Goode

> This corporation is not a welfare system. Nobody should expect to support a family on a supermarket job.
>
> —Male supermarket executive

This comment was made in an interview with the Philadelphia regional head of a national supermarket chain. As Philadelphia shifts from a manufacturing to a service-oriented economy, the retail sector has become increasingly significant as a source of work. Yet pressures on the retail industry have decreased the reliance on trained, experienced, full-time workers with career ladders and has created stressful, high-turnover, part-time work. These pressures also have degraded the quality of work, which primarily entails social interactions with customers.

This chapter explores the way in which store interactions have been shaped by the exigencies of economic goals and strategies interacting with the pressures of a changing city's demography and economy. It shows how the nature of service encounters has been transformed as new populations have entered Philadelphia and new patterns of investment have altered the nature of retail jobs. It compares three different segments of retail trade. A large corporate-owned supermarket, typical of new trends in retailing, is examined and contrasted to two kinds of small, owner-operated stores: those owned by white ethnics and those owned by recent Korean immigrants. Each segment has used different strategies to respond to increased competition and changing customers and engenders different relationships between bosses, workers, and customers.

251

Retail outlets have always been highly competitive in nature because profit margins are very low (Hochner et al. 1988). In the postwar period, innovations led to a "retail revolution" (Bluestone 1981), creating larger, more centralized firms, discounting practices, and relocation to sites of concentration in large suburban and downtown malls. In northeastern cities like Philadelphia, markets became saturated, and the declining population (customer base) increased competitive pressure. In the 1970s and 1980s, many national chains left the Philadelphia region (Hochner et al. 1988). This created a decline in career opportunities for workers but created new possibilities for some small-scale operations, often immigrant owned, with lower bureaucratic costs.

In all three kinds of stores, owners–managers have been concerned with the same issues: increasing the volume of sales, decreasing the cost of labor, and reducing losses of stock through employee and customer pilferage and mistakes at the register.

As shopping patterns changed and stores began to stay open for more days and hours, staffing no longer involved nine-to-five hours, six days a week. Scheduling for twelve-hour days, seven days a week, exacerbated the problems related to unpredictable customer flow. Managers and owners increasingly relied on part-timers and passed on the costs of unpredictability to their workers. In most stores a core of regular workers linked by mutual boss–worker trust and loyalty gave way to part-timers with no job security or benefits (Hochner et al. 1988). In addition, in the prewar period, store workers needed knowledge and skills to demonstrate, remodel, and repair merchandise. Butchers cut meat, jewelers and clothing stores required craft skills. By 1960, retailing relied less and less on product knowledge and skill.

Service work involves social interaction, which is different in nature from that in the manufacturing settings described in most other contributions to this volume. Service encounters occur in jobs where people work "on people" as opposed to manufacturing or information processing (Leidner 1988).[1] Workers have to contend with customers as well as bosses in a triadic situation as customers become a major source of control in the workplace. The customer has been called "our friend the enemy" in one study (Benson 1986) and technically a "partial employee" in another (Rafaeli 1989).

The efforts to decrease labor costs have indirectly reduced the quality of social interaction in large outlets, since the industry has moved from cultivating repeat customers through high-quality personal service to increasing the volume of sales through mass advertising and promotions. Transactions are sped up and are more impersonal as orders are processed at the checkout counter. Small talk and personal interaction have been replaced by "Thank you" and "Have a nice day" emblazoned on store bags.

Yet, while cutting down on labor costs, self-service also created security problems. Displays that encourage browsing also facilitate shoplifting and increase the potential for confrontations and mistrust between owners–workers and customers.

The Decline of Local Strips

This chapter looks specifically at local shopping activities that have important consequences for neighborhood relations in Olney. In Philadelphia, centralized shopping in suburban malls and revitalized downtowns have dealt a heavy blow to local strips and traditional stores, forcing new ownership patterns and retailing strategies. Traditional owner–operators have retired and have been replaced by immigrant owners or absentee owners who manage from a distance. This has transformed the nature of the local retail business, affecting the investment patterns and the nature of jobs.

Yet local retail outlets are more than sites of economic transactions. While most of the literature on service encounters focuses on large enterprises characterized by anonymity, the everyday service encounters described in this chapter are heavily contextualized in a local neighborhood setting.[2] Commercial areas in neighborhoods tend to be symbolic public arenas where much time is spent and important events occur.

Retail strips have become contested spaces in rapidly changing neighborhoods.[3] Conflict within local stores between Korean immigrants and both African American and white customers has become a regularly reported event in many cities (Schmidt 1990). The shooting of a teenage girl suspected of shoplifting by a Korean proprietor contributed to the violence against Koreans in the Los Angeles riots of 1992. Similar violent confrontations between storekeepers, workers, and teenagers of different backgrounds were often observed or talked about in Philadelphia.

In the context of the increasingly multicultural neighborhood of Olney described in the overview of Philadelphia (see Chapter 10), the easily observed performances of economic transactions simultaneously supported or refuted neighborhood stereotypes about residents from different classes or ethnic–racial groups.

The Olney Strip

One local businessman referred to the Olney strip as "the last good strip in the city." Compared to other strips we studied, there were fewer abandoned stores and a more middle-class clientele.

The strip developed at the turn of the century to serve a newly built streetcar suburb. By 1988, only two stores were still owned by the original families, but many current businesses were directly linked by transfer to former employee–apprentices who bought thriving businesses from retiring founders. Others were passed down to distant family members.

Long-term owners and shoppers remembered the strip as a magnet for a chic gloved-and-hatted middle-class clientele that patronized the upscale stores specializing in men's clothes, women's dresses, millinery, handbags, lingerie, children's wear, and shoes. Dave, a long-term merchant, said, "Thirty-five years ago when I came to the strip, women dressed up to come shopping. The clerks wore black dresses and starched white collars."

At two recent points in time, in the early 1970s and the early 1980s, the strip faced the decline seen in many neighborhood strips as suburban and central-city shopping replaced local shopping. Retiring owners could not find buyers for their stores. Each time, a new market emerged for the businesses.

The first shift in the 1970s was to chain stores and absentee-owned stores carrying discounted merchandise. The second shift was to Korean (as well as other immigrant) ownership, which steadily increased during the 1980s. This change was more consciously recognized by residents than the shift to absentee ownership and discount stores.

Korean and other immigrant investors were greeted with ambivalence. Many merchants and the local business organization were relieved. They saw Korean investment as saving the strip through the creation of "a hot resale market" that saved their own investments. After complaining about his Korean neighbor, one merchant said, "Well, it's better than having an empty store [next to you]. Then there is vandalism and no customer traffic."

But established residents and merchants alike resented the "takeover" by outsiders. They talked about Koreans traveling the strip "with suitcases of money," trying to buy buildings. Stores that served Koreans only created a sense of exclusion and generated conflict (see later in this chapter). Koreans were also resented for their suburban residence and lack of local orientation. Korean merchants were publicly blamed for the trash problem on the strip. One local leader stated: "They leave the garbage out on Saturday [for Monday pick-up]. They live in the suburbs and are too lazy to come back on Sunday night, and they just don't care."

In January 1988, we undertook a survey of ownership, employment, and encounter patterns in ninety-one stores on the strip. Table 12.1 describes the stores on the strip at the beginning of our research. Fifteen Korean store owners were interviewed in depth. Weekly participant observation took place in stores on the strip for two years. One supermarket and one fast-food outlet were visited regularly. Participant observation involved observing encounters and casual conversations with customers and workers. The break room in the supermarket was open to us as well. Managers and workers at both chain outlets were interviewed.

A survey taken in August and September 1989 showed that heavy turnover continued over a twenty-month period. There were

Table 12.1. Stores on the Olney Strip

	European American	Korean	Other Newcomer	Total
Food related				
Grocery–deli	2	2	3	7
Meat stores	2	0	0	2
Fruit store	0	2	1	3
Bakery	3	1	0	4
Takeout foods/restaurants	6	3	2	11
Candy	1	1	0	2
Minimart/Gas station	0	0	1	0
Farmers Market	1	0	0	1
Miscellaneous				
Gift/card shops	6*	1	0	7
Bookstore	1	0	0	1
Hardware store	0	1	0	1
Discount store	4*	6	0	10
Video shop	2	1	0	3
Photo shop	4*	1	0	5
Sew and vac	2	0	0	2
Jewelry store	4	3	0	7
Clothing				
Women's clothes	4*	2	0	6
Men's clothes	4	0	0	4
Children's clothes	3	2	0	5

Note: The following one-of-a-kind stores were owned by established residents with two exceptions: fabric store, lumber, comic book, plumber, roofer, music, furniture, florist, office supply, hobby shop–check casher, army/navy, and cosmetics.

*For each of these categories, two of the stores were parts of chains.

thirty-seven turnovers as more than one-third of the stores changed hands. The main change was an increase in the number of Korean-owned stores.[4]

As old customers left the area, new populations arrived—African Americans, Puerto Ricans, Colombians, Koreans, Portuguese, Asian Indians, Vietnamese, and Cambodians, among others—becoming potential workers and customers on the Olney strip. Additional customer perspectives come from two years of attendance at a civic organization that devoted much of its time to problems on the strip. General household interviews involving all ethnic groups described shopping patterns and expectations from the customer's point of view.

The Chain Supermarket

The large supermarket we studied was controlled by chain headquarters that relied on standard industry strategies and practices and union contracts as they engaged in national corporate competition. The supermarket in Olney was located just off the strip. Built twelve years earlier as a large store to draw white middle-class shoppers from a wide area including the nearby suburbs, its nature had significantly changed. Mike, a high-level supervisor, commented: "Customers used to come from as far away as Cheltenham [a nearby suburb]. Then we had 70 percent white middle-class customers, while now we have 70 percent Blacks and foreigners." Customers have become poorer too.[5]

For workers at the store, the same forces affecting the Summit Lighting factory (see Chapter 11) are at work. City population decline has led to the closing of stores and the bumping of workers from store to store, based on seniority. This system has given white workers more security, creating tension with Black workers. Immigrant hiring is minimal, and those who are hired have little opportunity to rise through the ranks. In general, labor practices have forced the worker to absorb the strains of the workplace. All workers experience the store after dark, when crimes occur, while most customers are unaware of incidents. Workers also absorb the economic pressures resulting from fluctuations in demand. Competition for good work schedules and fear of criminal encounters preoccupy workers and distract them from good service.

Chains use a system of centralized hiring and flexible deployment. In Philadelphia, unions systematized staffing practices as well. During retail expansion in the 1960s, labor strategies created mutual chain-worker loyalty and career ladders (Goode and Simon

1993). Today, chains have significantly reduced the full-time core (Hochner et al. 1988). In order to contain labor costs, managers must keep the number of hours worked by staff in the store within certain prescribed limits depending on the volume of sales. This requires constant adjustment in the number of hours assigned to part-timers.

The supermarket had 141 to 151 workers between 1988 and 1990. There were 16 entry-level general clerks and 108 regular clerks, mostly part-time, with the rest being full-time supervisors. Entry-level workers came from the neighborhood. They were "jacks of all trades" who bagged groceries, cleaned up, carried heavy boxes, and filled in where needed. In 1992, pay rates for clerks ranged from $5.50 an hour for entry-level clerks to $13.80 for experienced clerks (Carvajal 1992).

Regular clerks were located in specific departments, and seniority was vested in the department.[6] Many of these workers hoped to "move up to full-time hours." Yet, to keep labor costs trim, there are never more than 35 percent full-time workers in the store, and the number of part-time hours available fluctuates. Because of this, turnover is high among recent hires. The manager estimated that some 60 percent of the store's workers had turned over during his two-year tenure. This high turnover included transfers made by the chain.[7] Those who wanted a career at the store had to decide if and when to pursue full-time hours as a general clerk or whether to move to a department that entailed a drop to the bottom of the seniority ladder. Only two young local male workers who began to work in the store while in high school had successfully negotiated the various ladders and were core workers in the store in 1988. Most of the core workers, department heads, and regular clerks with good hours had worked in the chain for at least ten years, in this and other stores.

Many part-time workers who had families to support had to rely on other jobs and were thus forced to negotiate scheduling with two bosses. Abby, a woman cashier, worked three such part-time jobs. Workers talked constantly about wanting more and better hours. We often heard complaints about declining hours and cutbacks in the break room or at the checkout counter. For example, Phyllis, a cashier, asked her friend Marge at the next register about a store meeting she had attended. Marge responded: "Oh, it was the usual; I wish instead we could talk about getting more hours." Yet one supervisor said that the reason for the meeting was to give workers a storewide perspective on staffing complexities so that they would stop complaining and asking for more hours.[8]

On a busy day before a major holiday, one group of workers stood near the registers loudly discussing the timing of their breaks and their schedules for the week as if this were the main business of the day. On busy weekends, the head cashier was usually up front attending to the rush and trying to maintain a smooth flow. She spent most of her time coordinating break times, which necessitated closing aisles and angering customers. Management needed to cultivate a trusted workforce in the context of severe staffing limits and therefore were often forced to pit the needs of workers against shoppers. They needed to "stand behind" their reliable workers in order to encourage them to be loyal in the face of fluctuating hours and a neighborhood perceived as dangerous.

Next to hours, managers and workers were most preoccupied with crime. Several violent incidents over the years were frequently recalled.[9] A series of letters to corporate headquarters asking for more security were on display in the break room. Field notes from the break room include the following comment: "From the way the workers talk about the store, it sounds like Beirut."

With one security guard on duty all the time, about twenty-five shoplifters were caught each week, but the manager estimated that, with more staff, "We could catch twenty-five a day." In fact, several features of design and location, rather than the nature of the neighborhood, have exacerbated problems not envisioned in the planning of the store.[10]

Hiring New Populations

While the supermarket made a commitment to stocking products desired by Latinos there were only seven Spanish-speaking workers and one Portuguese during our fieldwork, and only four of them remained at the end. All but two were in the entry-level category and only one was full-time. The full-timer was a bilingual woman who was considered indispensable by the manager, who said, "I could use a dozen like her." The constraints of personnel policies impeded this. The long probation period and the loss of hours entailed in switching from entry level to clerk precludes recruitment and retention.

Antonio's story provides a good example. Antonio, a Puerto Rican about forty years old, had worked for supermarkets as a traveling salesman on the island. He was fully bilingual. His attempts to translate his experience in the business into a full-time grocery clerk position failed. He was forced to enter as a general clerk. While workers and managers called him a "gentleman" and used his skills as a translator as well as his outgoing ways as an "ambassador" to customers, he did the same cleanup and bagging work as any general clerk. He did not advance much in terms of hours and rank. After a few months, he left for a factory job at the plant where his son worked and later returned to the supermarket as an additional part-time source of income.

The Racial Dyad

The store's labor force reflected the racial dyad of the city. Retail management has always been conscious of race in hiring. Acceptance of Blacks in the retail labor force was especially slow because it was thought that white customers would not like to be served by them (Westcott 1982). This was particularly true of food-related businesses.[11] The corporation did not assign Black staff to the store until six years before our fieldwork. The change was made in response to the changing local population. The first Black cashiers were greeted by some initial conflicts and complaints by regular white ethnic customers.

By 1990, the staff was roughly half white and half Black. There was a large cohort of recently hired Black workers. There was also a disjunction between the age and educational statuses of Black workers and their status in the store. One meat wrapper was the same age as the meat cutters in his department. Yet because meat cutting requires apprenticeship and certification in a separate union, he was relegated to the lower-status job of meat wrapper, a job often held by women.[12]

As at Summit Lighting (see Chapter 12) co-workers in the store had developed warm relationships within departments but not on a storewide basis. Departmental differences in work processes accounted for some differences. The isolated meat room with its cold setting and its financial clout in contributing to the store's bottom line developed solidarity. Relations between Black and white workers within the meat room were of a cordial nature. Black meat wrappers constantly joked with the white meat manager.

One day, three young male grocery clerks, two white and one Black, stood around telling jokes and jointly teasing their supervisor. Even up front, where work speed-ups (Rafaeli 1989), competition for schedules (Hochner et al. 1988), and the physical separation of checkout aisles might hinder cooperation and communication, cashiers developed solidarity relationships across groups.

Cashiers, when observed, all worked steadily until something broke the flow, for example, a spill requiring the borrowing of paper towels, or the need for a price check. Once engaged in interaction, cashiers engaged in conversations about people they knew in common or store gossip. After a brief exchange, they turned back to work. Cashier cooperation was most evident during times of heavy volume. Everyone worked cooperatively to locate prices, get more paper bags, or fill in as baggers on slow lines. At this time, general clerks were sent to the front to help out. They added to the noise level with their teasing chatter with the women cashiers, but the work did not stop.

But there was little carryover of cordial departmental personal relations in the storewide break room. The room was characterized by self-segregation by race, gender, and common work history. When the room was full, clusters of mixed-gender Blacks, white women, and white males sat in three groups holding separate conversations, with the white males loudly asserting control over space and Blacks most soft spoken.

The importance of this racial dyad was a reflection of the city's population and the recent insertion of the Black worker into an all-white workplace within the chain. The gender hierarchy was also characteristic of the retail industry (Goode and Simon 1993). The division between Blacks and whites was symbolized by an argument over music for the Christmas party. One white worker said to the Black woman in charge of music: "I hope you remember us and don't only play your kind of music."

Service Encounters

Since managers protected the loyal long-term core, which was largely male, the impact of pressures on labor costs and security concerns fell mostly on entry-level workers (young local workers and immigrants) and on women cashiers, who were almost all part-time.

Women checkers bore a large measure of the strains of interaction in the newly multicultural setting. In the gender division of labor in the retail industry, women are assigned the "social" work, since they handle customers at the checkout counter. They reported this aspect of work as most satisfying to them and as a reason to prefer retail work to clerical or factory work (Goode and Simon 1993). In this store, as the population changed and more transactions involved non-English speakers and enforcing the complex rules of government food programs, women workers had fewer of the friendly personal encounters they valued.

Constrained in their ability to give workers better hours and conditions, managers worked to maintain good relations with their customers in ways not dependent on the worker's goodwill. They established programs that reached out to white ethnic neighborhood leadership. Community leaders established a police ministation at the store, which is manned by local volunteers. The store provided the space as a service. A chainwide promotion offering computers to schools in return for register receipts led to schools organizing parents to collect receipts in a way that created the feeling that local schools and the store were collaborating. Early trouble with the local high school across the street was ameliorated through a new program.

The store also made significant attempts to provide Latino products. They had the largest shelf space devoted to packaged Latino products in the entire city (Rodrigues 1987). A large section of the produce department featured batatas, malange, melons, yucca, and other items. Baccala was ordered in large quantities from a special distributor. Spanish greeting cards were available, as were bulk quantities of rice and other staples. These products also attracted other Caribbean customers.[13]

Furthermore, because of the perfunctory social interaction at the checkout counter, the negative consequences of labor pressures had little effect on customers, who instead had a great deal of autonomy in creating the social order of the store. For established whites and Blacks and for immigrants, the store was a different social space, allowing them to meet their different needs.

For established white ethnic residents, the store was a community institution. Almost every established resident we knew who lived near the store shopped there. As a fieldworker, I was in the store more than thirty times, and I always met at least one person I knew. On my last visit, the day before Thanksgiving in 1990, the former head of one of the largest neighborhood organizations turned up in line behind me. As he filled me in on recent events, he was greeted by scores of other residents passing by.

Established residents considered the store a site under their control. Fifty percent of the volume of sales occurred on weekends, and 65 percent of the daily volume occurred in the evening. Most whites avoided these high-pressure times. For this reason, they did not share the "Beirut" image of the store held by workers. Whites claimed space by speaking loudly to one another across long distances. For many older residents, this was one of the community social spaces safe for interaction.[14] Older white ethnic men and women had long conversations with cashiers they knew, using first names and talking about mutually known neighbors. Ruth always sought out her two favorite cashiers. She told them about her personal life, hugged them and even gave them presents at Christmas. Teenagers who worked as general clerks often engaged in flirtatious chatter with girls they knew from the neighborhood as they went through the checkout line.

In contrast, new immigrants liked the impersonal anonymity of the store, the freedom to shop and avoid interaction. On weekends, the store was filled with immigrant shoppers. Many customers wore non-Western clothing: women in saris and a Buddhist monk in his robes. Many immigrants shopped in large, self-contained family groups speaking different languages. This insulated them from forced interaction with outsiders. They also used their children as translators in encounters. Unless a collision occurred, a conflict over place on line, or problems with coupons and food stamps, there was little contact and the need for English-language skills was minimal.

Occasionally, positive contacts with established residents occurred. Sometimes children broke the ice, as when a Black four year old traveling in a shopping cart reached out and took the hand of an Asian infant in another cart. The Black child said, "Hi, cute baby," and the mothers were forced to make eye contact and smile, as did everyone around them.

For many immigrants, this setting was the only one in which they mingled with the larger society. Inez, a Puerto Rican woman who has lived on the mainland for twenty years, brought her mother to the store every Saturday morning. The mother did not speak English, and this was the only time she was in contact with people outside the house. "It's good for her to get out; she looks forward to it all week." While her daughter and grandchildren did the shopping, the mother wandered down the aisles looking at the Spanish-language magazines and greeting cards.

As with workers in the break room, there was some social distance between white ethnic and established Black customers, and occasional incidents occurred between fellow shoppers or shoppers and workers. White ethnic residents would talk with each other in line, even if they were strangers. When customers were collecting register receipts for school computers, whites approached only other whites. Black cashiers who had experienced hostile encounters when they first came into the store tended to maintain a wary distance from all customers.

Conflict, while rare, was often related to the Black–white interaction. The only hostile incident we witnessed between customers occurred when a mature Black woman politely asked an older white man to move his basket out of the way, and he cursed, saying he would not move it. A reported incident of conflict between Black customers and store staff occurred late one night when two

Black teenagers accused of shoplifting were handcuffed to a shelf by a white supervisor in charge for two hours until the police arrived. Other Black customers angrily accused this store employee of brutality.

The checkout line served as a place to observe and comment on class and group differences as market baskets were emptied. Judgments were often made about the values and consumption behavior of others. One white ethnic informant expressed annoyance that "minorities" were buying luxury items with "my hard-earned money [taxes]."

The lengthiest transaction we observed provoked no overt hostility from either cashier or fellow customers. It involved a Black customer in the Women, Infants and Children (WIC) nutrition program and a market basket filled with WIC-related products. For each item, a form had to be filled out. A long line of customers watched the cashier struggle, albeit competently, to complete the complex paperwork. The interaction involved no small talk or smiling, but it was not hostile. The customers on the line were patient and made no comment. Nevertheless, the cashier and many customers registered annoyance silently.

In general, in an attempt to cut labor costs, the quantity of available work and the quality of worklife have been degraded for the supermarket worker. Seniority policies make it difficult for immigrants to advance. Nevertheless, the nature of impersonal self-service has allowed white and immigrant customers both to meet their shopping needs and to create satisfying encounters. Reflecting historical labor and residential patterns, Blacks were relative newcomers to the workplace and community and fared least well as both workers and customers.

Small, Owner-Operated Stores

In contrast to the supermarket, small stores responded differently to changes in retail competition and new populations. The small stores included in this discussion were all owner operated and catered to all groups. We excluded the small storefronts on the strip that are absentee owned[15] or that targeted an exclusive clientele.[16]

White Ethnic Merchants
The small stores owned and operated by families descended from turn-of-the-century European immigrants share much of their strategies of investment and labor practices through the ven-

erable Olney Business Mens Association, which has been in existence for over forty years. Many of the community ceremonials were part of a popular series of events sponsored by them. These included the arrival of Santa Claus at Christmas, a trick-or-treat night at Halloween when merchants gave out candy, and a visit from the Easter Bunny at Easter.

These events encouraged loyalty from local customers and counteracted the normal resentment found in poor and lower-middle-class neighborhoods from customers who believed that the merchants they were supporting "are getting rich from us." This class resentment occurred even when both parties come from the same racial and ethnic background.[17] Many association members expressed their activities in terms of reciprocity or "giving something back" to the neighborhood.

This community embeddedness made owner–operators with modest profits more likely to invest in additional property on the strip than to move or expand outlets elsewhere in a chainlike fashion. The business association served as a watchdog over the local investment scene and as a lobby group vis-à-vis city government.

Cultivating "Regulars"

These small stores on the strip focused on friendly personal service and relied on developing loyal, regular customers through word of mouth. In fact, price negotiations for the sale of such stores included an amount for "goodwill," which meant an established customer base.

Most small stores operated by white ethnic owners were still set up for personal encounters. When customers entered the store with a counter around three sides, they were immediately approached and offered help. This arrangement required interaction. At the minimum, an appropriate service encounter included a greeting, small talk, instrumental bargaining exchanges, and an exiting exchange.

The reliance on "regulars" in these stores affected the investment decisions of long-term white ethnic owners. For small owner–operators who were not ready to retire, moving entailed a major risk. In fact, in one case, a thirty-year-old business that moved to a mall was reported as a failure by another long-term merchant. The wife of the relocating store owner told us, "This place is going downhill fast. We have to get out." A few months later, his former neighbor reported that he was not doing well in his new location. "His son-in-law talked him into the move. I told him he would fail because he would lose all his regulars."

Labor in Small, White Ethnic Stores

Many traditional stores were caught in a financial bind. As their regular customers moved away, they could no longer afford to hire nonfamily labor. Yet they needed to hire immigrant labor to attract a new customer base. New immigrants who had difficulty speaking English avoided chit-chat and places that required close interaction unless someone spoke their language. The presence of immigrant employees signaled newcomers that they were welcome and that there was someone from whom they could ask advice on purchases. As operating hours decreased in response to business decline and the fear of danger after dark, however, most owners were able to cover their stores by themselves. Their first strategy to augment the labor force was to use kin. Many families used teenage and adult children or siblings. One man used both his mother and mother-in-law during times of heavy volume. Another couple hired a best friend.

Otherwise, they augmented staff by using local part-time help seasonally or occasionally throughout the week. The labor market in small stores was thus very constricted.[18] Dave, a long-term owner who had operated on the strip for more than thirty years, spoke of his former practice of hiring a local high school boy each year as a helper. He saw himself as a mentor and described several close and continuing relationships. The amount of "dead" time between customers, when bosses and workers could talk and socialize without the formality of bureaucratic work rules, gave their relationships a family-like closeness. Five years before our interview, he had cut back to using temporary help only during the Christmas rush. The short, episodic relationship with these workers precluded closeness. Creating minimal trust and loyalty to the store among workers who know they are dispensable was difficult.

Employers who used nonfamily workers sought out prospective employees who were not supporting families and who could be paid "under the table" and then laid off with less guilt: high schoolers, married women seeking part-time work, and retired people on social security. These were also the categories of workers who found it advantageous to work nights and weekends because of school and family schedules.

Local women often worked sporadically, depending on the seasonal need for help and the cycle of their own family crises. For example, Sally had held a series of jobs over a two-year period on the strip as a bank teller, a salesperson in the large, local Farmer's Market, and a clerk at Woolworth's before returning to the Farmer's Market. Each stint lasted a few months. Twice she was laid off, and twice she resigned because of family problems.

Immigrant Labor

Strategies for hiring immigrant labor were undeveloped by traditional merchants, even though they realized that immigrant employees could help cultivate a new customer base. Only eight stores on the strip had Spanish-speaking workers.[19] This was not the result of deliberate avoidance or exclusion. The financial limits on hiring nonfamily labor operated here, as well as a lack of knowledge about how to recruit Spanish-speaking workers. Two white ethnic merchants reported that they advertised for Spanish speakers but were unable to find or keep them. One said, "They all go to the chains where they can get more hours than I can offer them." And indeed, several absentee-owned chain variety and shoe stores on the strip employed mostly Spanish speakers, who were moving up career ladders in the corporation.

White ethnic owners knew little about the Spanish-speaking community, its brokers, and its word-of-mouth communication system. The traditional business association had little experience in hiring Spanish speakers and could provide no help. Many Spanish workers also preferred to work for Koreans because they feared white discrimination.

Yet the experience of one children's clothing store, in business for thirty-four years, demonstrates that the use of such labor can lead to a high volume of business for both white and immigrant customers when the store is set up for intimate personal encounters. The store advertised that Spanish and Portuguese speakers were available among the staff, and a serious commitment was made to keep workers who speak these languages as core workers. Merchandise efforts were made to appeal to these groups. The strategy succeeded at the same time that two other children's wear stores closed.

Service Encounters

For white ethnic owners, concern about language was more related to the inability to cultivate regulars and engage in an appropriately pleasant service encounter than to the instrumental transaction itself. Owners without Spanish-speaking staff accommodated Spanish speakers by learning some Spanish (particularly colors, numbers, and greetings) to help them get by. Often customers used their children as interpreters and communicated through them. One merchant talked about getting by with "sign language," and a lot of pointing and gestures were used on both sides of the transaction. Another said, "Somehow we manage to communicate."

Yet neither party was happy in these situations. Merchants

struggled to complete the expected small talk that made the situation uncomfortable for immigrants. Dave said candidly after a transaction that was instrumentally successful but in which he failed to draw a smile or friendly response, "This language business is really getting me down." Immigrant shoppers felt similar frustration and discomfort. In one case, a personal, friendly comment about an accompanying child was taken by Marisol, a Central American newcomer, as a criticism of the child's behavior.

Because Koreans have developed their own stores, which cater separately to their merchandise needs, white ethnic merchants expect them to "shop at their own kind."[20] Almost no attempt was made to target them as customers. Only one non-Korean store had hired a Korean, and that tenure was short-lived.

One merchant, who deliberately sought to appeal to Korean clients with the standard strategy of cultivating regulars, was especially uncomfortable in trying to enact what he saw as appropriate pleasant encounters because Koreans did not follow the "rules." He complained, "They don't answer when you offer to help, and they don't say anything when they leave the store."

He also saw Korean customers as violating the rules when they tried to bargain. He commented, "Even if it is on sale, they want to get a lower price." Nonetheless, he has changed his pricing practices. Without a Korean employee as a broker, he was unsure about whether he understood the community and constantly worried about generating a negative reputation that would destroy his business.

In contrast to immigrants, for many merchants, shifting to Blacks as regular customers was easy. Stores of all types recognized that Black shoppers account for a large proportion of their clientele. This led to store owners increasing their small talk and chatting with Black customers and precluded racist expressions and behaviors. Blacks understood the rules of service encounters. One storekeeper reported that he could recognize his white ethnic and African American regulars because he was able to chat with them about the weather, sports, and politics, but he did not recognize newcomers. Since they could not engage in small talk, he did not "know their faces" and could not cultivate personal relationships.

Ten percent of the stores had Black employees. One clothing merchant had changed his merchandising and labor strategies to cater to Black customers. He changed from conservative stock to "cutting edge" fashions that appeal to a young Black male clientele. Staffing shifted from a total reliance on family labor to include core Black workers with whom a close relationship developed.

Korean Merchants

More than half the Korean merchants were similarly owner–
operators who served the diverse population of the community.
But these stores were negatively affected by the presence of Ko-
rean-owned stores that were either wholesale firms that supplied
Korean retailers from all over Philadelphia and other parts of the
Middle Atlantic or "Korean only" retail outlets that restricted access
to Korean customers. Both these types generated a negative view of
Korean merchants in Olney.[21]

Many established Olney residents described exclusion from
these stores, which are kept locked and require ringing a bell for
entry. One recounted how she knocked at a wholesale store and
was told with a frown and wave of the hand, "No, no. Wholesale."
The rudest encounter reported occurred between a well-placed
community representative when she tried to enter a new, upscale
Korean dress store. She was refused access and was told that the
store was for Koreans only. Then she was told, "Besides, these
clothes are better than you wear. You couldn't afford them any-

Once a large, established Italian restaurant, this business is now Korean owned.
One side continues as a community pizzeria, while the other serves a Korean
clientele. (Photo by Melissa M. Forbis)

way." Since the established resident involved was influential in the community, the story of this encounter "made the rounds" quickly.[22]

Most business at wholesale stores occurred in the evening when merchants around the city were able to close their businesses and buy stock from wholesalers. Often large vans were seen double-parked in front of the wholesalers, loading and unloading boxes at night when the strip was closed down. These activities were seen as surreptitious and suspicious and were discussed at community meetings.

The Korean business community was well organized. A pattern of shared practices concerning investment, hiring, and handling customers developed and was transmitted by a tight-knit citywide business network that was in contact through newspapers and business links to Korean merchant communities in other cities.

There were several unique patterns in the Korean response to retail conditions in Philadelphia. Koreans often bought stores and then quickly resold them. This gave merchants fewer ties to any one neighborhood and in turn decreased the importance of long-term relationships with local customers and workers. The Korean pattern of business turnover and upward mobility was shaped by the opportunity structure on business strips throughout the city when they came. In the wake of the 1964 riots, white ethnic merchants were selling stores at "bargain prices." With a small investment, one could buy a store and save enough money in profits to sell it to a more recent arrival and move upward to a better store in terms of neighborhood, social rank, size, and/or the merchandise hierarchy. This practice, referred to by one community resident as "hit and run" tactics, shaped business strategies, stereotypes of customers, and the nature of service encounters.

Our interviews with Korean owners on three strips revealed this pattern of business turnover as immigration created a steady stream of incoming Koreans. Those arriving in the 1970s usually started by working for other Koreans and opened their first stores within eight years. By the time we interviewed them in 1989, many had owned three or more successive businesses. Unlike the white ethnic owner–operator, who retained a model of the family-owned business committed to serving loyal repeat customers and "giving back" to the neighborhood, many Korean merchants saw their current store as a rung on a ladder, a commodity to be bought and sold. In this way they were very similar to the absentee white ethnic owners, who saw the store as an investment and managed it from afar.

In another contrast with white ethnic owners, Korean linguistic difficulties and pressures from neighborhood activists led to a shared pattern of hiring non-Korean workers as a way to attract and serve customers. Koreans were pressured in their early years in Philadelphia to hire minority labor. At one of the major strips in north Philadelphia, a boycott of Korean stores by Black community groups in the 1970s forced Korean merchants to maintain the local minority workforces of the stores they bought. These experiences taught them the advantages of hiring local facilitators, patterns that they brought to other strips.

As one merchant recounted,

> when I first bought this store, I decided to fire all the former employees and replace them with Koreans. The previous owner . . . did not notify his employees that I would be taking over the store. Legally there was nothing wrong because employment of former workers was not considered in the contract between me and the previous owner. . . . So they were shocked to hear that I became the new owner and would fire them all. . . . I was new to the area and my previous business was a grocery store [small, family labor] so I could not image [*sic*] that I would leave cash registers to my non-Korean employees.

After placards and banners were prepared for a protest, he spoke to the leader of the community group and negotiated an agreement. It specified a freeze in wages, no vacations, and firing as permissible if the employee was caught stealing. "So I kept them all and it proved beneficial . . . because I was new to this [type] of business."

Koreans learned that workers from their customer groups could buffer unpleasant encounters. Mr. Park spoke of Black employees as buffers between "tough and bold" customers and the innocent and naive new arrival. While he could now handle his "headache" customers, less experienced owners should always rely on buffers. Over and over, Korean merchants said they were advised by experienced peers to hire people from other groups as workers in spite of the economic cost.

Korean owners hired white Americans as buffers against racism. Two food-service businesses kept their white staff intact when they bought their stores and maintained a low profile out front. One reported that his customers always avoided him and placed their orders with an American counterman. Others reported being taunted with racial epithets by teenagers.

Mrs. Kim said that for the first three months of business, she displayed American signs and merchandise, but customers would enter the store and then leave quickly when they saw she was

Asian. She ultimately created a display on the sidewalk and hired a white ethnic part-time worker to tend it.

Many Korean merchants successfully employed established Blacks and whites. One white formerly employed in a Korean store said, "I learned everything I know about business from working for him. He was like a father to me." Thus, in spite of the image of the Korean store as the quintessential family enterprise, many Korean merchants on the strip hired part-time employees, while this was becoming increasingly rare for white-ethnic-owned stores.

Moreover, Koreans have been more successful in hiring and retaining Latinos than their white ethnic counterparts. Two of the Korean stores had employed the same Spanish-speaking employees for more than two years as core workers, and relationships were excellent. One Colombian had been able to persuade his bosses, a Korean husband and wife, to hire a recently arrived compatriot as a favor to him. Another Korean couple trusted their Puerto Rican employee to do most of the transactions at the cash register. Still another Puerto Rican woman, who had worked in several Korean stores, said that her "Chinese" bosses were easy to work for and not "racist" like whites.

Relations between Korean owners and Latino customers were also successful. Fellow immigrants with less-than-perfect English were less threatening to both parties in the transaction.[23] Latinos also reported liking Korean merchants and searched for bases of similarity with them. One Puerto Rican customer said, "We both like fresh produce." Another indicated, "We are both victims of white racism."

Korean merchants learned to treat workers differently in the United States than in Korea. One owner said, "You can't treat workers the 'Korean way' [authoritarian] here," implicitly recognizing that strict hierarchical relations would not work in this new setting.

Service Encounters

For those Korean merchants who did not hire established Americans, it was not easy to fulfill the expected service encounter with Black and white ethnic customers. Those who spoke little English felt uncomfortable with the involved service interactions typical of small American stores. Consequently, many developed a layout for the store that minimized interaction. The arrangement in these Korean stores thus differed from the traditional white ethnic store. Merchandise was set up in aisles in a quasi self-service pattern. While these stores were set up for browsing to minimize verbal interaction, the fear of shoplifting led to surveillance, which violated the expected freedom of browsing. One white ethnic resident said, "I do not like going in there. He follows me around while I am looking."

This arrangement created different transactions from those of white ethnic owners, who tried to endear themselves to regular customers. Such patterns had mixed results, creating tension with potential established American customers used to personal encounters and very good relations with immigrants wishing to avoid complex interaction.

Moreover, freedom to browse implied clearly marked fixed prices. But Korean merchants often wanted to bargain. They offered to undercut a price seen elsewhere. One Black customer complained, "He asked me what the other Korean store was selling it at. He was willing to undercut his own." The strong myth of Koreans sticking together is nevertheless given grudging respect, and criticism follows when it is violated. Another customer was given a price she did not understand. When asked to repeat it, the merchant lowered the price, thinking this was bargaining. The customer was visibly flustered and left.

Other problems emerged from the practice of Korean merchants to establish themselves first in poor neighborhoods. Many security strategies, including bullet-proof barriers and keeping a gun visible, were developed, as well as the erection of social barriers through the use of toughness. Maintaining the upper hand was accomplished through stiff and erect posture and rigid, unsmiling demeanor. There was often no speaking, and transactions were perfunctory, while pointing and grunts were used to communicate. When one woman merchant was told that she was the friendliest Korean merchant on the strip, she shook her head sadly and said, "But friendly makes no good business, cold is better for business. I do not treat bad, but not too kind."

Such nonengagement is especially important for women store managers. More women were managers of Korean stores than in white ethnic traditional established stores. In most cases, their husbands had other full-time activities and helped out on weekends. Safety was a significant preoccupation for these women, who developed the technique of talking on the phone to relatives and friends between customers as a precaution. Their consequent inattention to entering customers further fueled the perception of unfriendliness.

In sum, many Korean merchants did not perform the expected pleasantries of the American service encounter. They were seen as "blunt" and "brusque" and rude. Yet Koreans who served Korean clients said that small talk and chatting was essential to maintaining regular Korean customers. One restaurateur who served a Korean clientele said about cultivating them, "I try to smile and not act like too much of a big shot." It was not traditional Korean mercantile "culture" that shaped distance in encounters but the strategy of self-protection in an alien world.

Shifting to American Strategies

At the end of our research in 1990, Korean immigration had shifted, as had the market for small retail stores. In response, more Koreans with experience were adopting the patterns of their white ethnic counterparts. The migratory stream also changed, with new arrivals bringing more capital and raising prices on the market.[24] The pool of available stores was shrinking. As one merchant said, "There are no bargains anymore."

Some Olney Korean merchants were aware that it was not possible to keep moving up. They began to see their interests as tied to the local community and their fellow white ethnic merchants and shifted their allegiance to this network. They spoke of having learned "American grass roots" ways. For them, strategies approximated those of white ethnic owners. Service with a smile and developing long-term relationships with a regular clientele were common. Two Korean sisters owned two stores in Olney. Both spoke English well. They smiled and were cheerful and had a loyal following.

At the end of our fieldwork, half the board of the strip merchant's association was Korean. This replaced a five-year pattern of two separate organizations with a single Korean merchant as liaison to the traditional white ethnic association. One of these locally oriented Korean merchants criticized the organized citywide Korean business leadership for actions that led to a public conflict in 1986, which exacerbated Korean–white tensions. He said the group had operated in the "Korean way" by dealing with city government officials rather than the local community. "'Korean way' is top down. That is what C [Korean leader] did [in regard to the incident]. In America that is not enough. Here you have to build good relations with neighbors. That is the grass roots. You have to lobby to be accepted."

Conclusions

The demographic and economic shifts in the city have engendered different social processes in three retail segments: corporate-owned supermarkets and white-ethnic and Korean-owned and -operated small stores. Two interrelated changes in retailing, increased pressure on labor costs and the shift from personal to self-service, have been important factors in the change. In each type of store, changes have been different because strategies are shaped by different goals and expectations.

Pressures on labor costs have severely constrained the labor markets in all these local retail enterprises. For all workers outside the high-seniority chain employees or small-store family workers, work is transitory, seasonal, and fraught with problems related to schedules, fear of crime, and distrust between bosses, workers, and customers.

Both small stores and chains offered less and less opportunity for reliable work or careers for either immigrant or white ethnic workers. Yet household interviews revealed that many women and teenagers still looked to the strip and the supermarkets to provide them with occasional and sporadic work when they wanted it. The supermarket, with its protection of seniority, offered little opportunity to newcomers. Furthermore, worker dissatisfaction increasingly focused on the erosion of schedules and fear of crime. Friendly encounters at the checkout counter, a major source of work satisfaction for women in the industry, were affected by the same forces that operated in small stores. Only white ethnic checkers and their counterpart customers engaged in small talk and pleasantries as immigrant customers insulated themselves in the face of language difficulties. Here, the tense relationship between whites and Blacks led to an avoidance of contact and occasional conflict.

The shift from personal service to self-service has had ironic and contradictory effects on relationships. On the one hand, this move has created tremendous security problems and distrust. On the other hand, it has given the customer the upper hand in shaping the store's social order. The chain store, rather than an impersonal space shaped by the bureaucratic pressures, is open terrain. Both white ethnic customers in claiming control and immigrants in avoiding interpersonal interaction have created pleasant and segregated spaces for themselves. In contrast, the workers bear the brunt of the changes.

The future of work in national chain supermarkets in the city is not secure. Since the early 1970s, increased competition has led two major chains to pull out of the area, and a third to forestall a pull-out by experimenting with a new labor contract that lowered wages and benefits in return for a QWL program (Hochner et al. 1988). The supermarket we studied was part of a chain that has had its Philadelphia stores up for sale for two years.[25]

Seniority rules under conditions of store closings favored white workers over Black and made it hard for entry-level workers to move up. Thus immigrants found little opportunity, and established workers were increasingly dissatisfied with their rewards.

In small stores, Korean owners had more success than white ethnics in dealing with other immigrant groups, as both workers and customers. These immigrant owners, concerned about being in an alien setting, saw buffer workers as essential in attracting and retaining customers. Early experience with neighborhood activists also taught them to hire workers from the same backgrounds as their customer base.

Yet tensions in dealing with both whites (seen as racist) and Blacks (seen as dangerous) were further exacerbated by a history of community conflict. White ethnic customers approached Korean stores with a negative image fueled by the hostile encounters in wholesale and "Korean only" stores. The ambiguous "self-service" design and other techniques of social distancing made Blacks and white ethnics feel uncomfortable in the stores.

As business declined for white ethnic owners, newcomer-worker brokers were too expensive and strategies to recruit them went undeveloped. Without buffer workers, the strong desire to cultivate regular customers and maintain the commitment to a long and pleasant service encounter was increasingly unattainable. Attempts at small talk were frustrating to both parties. While adjusting to Blacks as a new customer pool was an easy transition for many, this type of store is an endangered species, rapidly being replaced by immigrant or absentee white ethnic ownership.

At the same time, some Korean owners' investment patterns became more community oriented, more like traditional white ethnic owners, and they distanced themselves from those of the city-wide Korean merchants' groups. They talked about learning "grass roots" ways, they hired buffer labor, and they gave friendly service accompanied by small talk to cultivate regular customers. They also accepted leadership roles in the neighborhood business organization. The future for these stores depends on the continuing increase of new populations and keeping the loyalty of white ethnic customers, who see the strip as "going Korean."

Some Koreans have come to share the emphasis on personal service and "giving back" to local residents with white ethnic owners. White-owned small stores with absentee owners and the chains are similar to the "hit and run" stores of wealthier Korean investors. The critical difference is whether owners are locally embedded with limited capital or are large-scale investors with capital mobility who can easily take losses, pull out, and reinvest. These factors are more salient than cultural origins.

The retail sector is providing significant investment and work opportunities for middle-class immigrants like the Koreans in Philadelphia. Like much of the service economy, however, it is not providing the kinds of jobs being sought to replace the declining manufacturing sector. These jobs have become less skilled, less rewarding, less secure, and more stressful as the city continues to face a declining population and economy. Moreover, as sites of regular cross-ethnic and cross-class interactions, the encounters between workers, bosses, and customers have important implications for community relationships between increasingly diverse neighborhood groups.

Acknowledgments

I wish to thank Hong Joon Kim and Marilyn MacArthur for their insightful contributions to the analysis of Korean merchants. The initial store survey was organized and supervised by Jo Anne Schneider. It was carried out by Jo Anne Schneider, Cynthia Carter Ninivaggi, Saku Longshore, and the author. Marilyn McArthur undertook the follow-up survey.

Notes

1. There has been less research on the service sector compared to manufacturing. What has been done largely focuses on clerical work in large bureaucracies. In these cases, the use of technology and centralized corporate control makes this kind of work analogous to manufacturing. Much less has been done on work in organizations providing services to clients, including the retail sector.

Examples of research about service encounters include department stores (Benson 1986), restaurants (Bigus 1972; Butler and Snizek 1976; Mars and Nicod 1984; Paules 1992; Whyte 1948); fast-food (Leidner 1988, 1993), convenience stores (Sutton and Rafaeli 1988), supermarkets (Rafaeli 1989), and flight attendants (Hochschild 1983). These works are written from the point of view of the worker and focus on opportunities for autonomy and the ability to resist control from either management or customers.

Other works include those written from the perspective of management academics from a management point of view. They focus on rationalizing tasks, training, and worker control (Cziepel et al. 1985). Here, a main concern is developing techniques to improve the quality of "service" and control work and increase productivity.

2. Most studies are biased toward middle-class customers or do not mention social differences between owners–managers, workers, and customers in terms of class, race, or ethnicity. Many of the workplaces are located in center

cities (department stores) or serve national markets (airlines) and have a broad-based, nonlocalized clientele.

3. This conflict is exemplified in *Do the Right Thing* and was underscored by the 1992 Los Angeles riots. Documentaries on similar topics have been produced for public television in both New York and Philadelphia.

4. In sixteen cases, established American owners sold to Koreans; in six, Americans sold to other immigrants (two South Asians, one Puerto Rican, three Southeast Asian ethnic Chinese); and in six, Koreans sold to Koreans. Of the remaining five, there were three sales by American owners to other Americans, one sale of a chain store to another chain owner, and one sale by a Latino owner to a Jamaican. In the aftermath of a conflict incident in 1986, the resale market was viewed by many as "too hot."

5. There were fewer large-volume market baskets and many small transactions. The bulk of monthly sales occurred at the beginning of the month, when government checks arrive, and many transactions involved government food programs.

6. Grocery was the largest regular department with forty-five workers. In addition, there were thirty cashiers, ten night crew, fourteen in deli/fish, and nine each in the meat and produce departments. The other employees were administrators. Spatial arrangements and product knowledge led to social divisions.

7. These transfers were frequently made when openings were created when a store closed and senior workers from the closed store "bumped" workers at other stores.

8. The store had developed a QWL (quality circle) program to try in part to raise employee morale and as a tradeoff for contract concessions. They were attempting to imitate the success of another local chain with this strategy.

9. These included a stabbing and a mugging in the parking lot. Much of the danger was related to drug activity. Pairs and clusters of male teenagers were closely watched for covert actions and hand signals. They took Tylenol and Preparation-H, used by druggies, and other items that were sold on the black market.

10. This large and attractive store was built to be a high-volume store and the areal size created the atmosphere of an impersonal facility. Furthermore, it was located in an unprotected setting and was set off from the residential heart of the neighborhood by railroad tracks and overpasses. Its only immediate neighbor was a huge high school across the street, which was empty at night. Vandalism and parking lot incidents were frequent.

11. One local chain lost a major EEOC suit because of this. In earlier research in other supermarkets, workers were concerned when a Black was assigned to the deli department because "people will not want to take food he has handled."

12. Several Black workers had some college education and were in lower-level jobs than their less-educated white counterparts as a result of seniority.

13. The commitment to Latino/Caribbean products indirectly exposed established residents to new commodities. One day, two elderly white women

walked over to the shelves of Goya products. Looking at the variety of beans, one said, "Oh, look, this is the stuff that is supposed to be good. Look at how big the beans are." The display elevated these products to specialty ethnic status and reduced social distance abstractly if not concretely.

14. At the local McDonald's, the central space of the eating section was similarly controlled by older neighborhood residents, who used it as a hangout. The store even hired one of them to clean up, control the bathroom key, and maintain social control out front, in contrast to a mostly teenage minority food crew. The group spoke loudly to each other, claiming the space from outsiders, who still heavily used the outlet and sat around the periphery.

15. Absentee-owned stores were managed from a distance by larger investment groups. They were less committed to the neighborhood and less likely to join a local business group. They often appeared similar to "mom-and-pop" stores, but in practice they were more like chains. There were several examples of owners from as far away as New York or New Jersey. An even more common pattern involved stores owned by Philadelphia families who had expanded successful businesses to several Philadelphia strips and malls. In the initial survey, we found twenty-one absentee-owned stores and thirteen outlets of national and regional chains, compared to fifty-seven family-owned stores. This figure undercounts the number of Korean stores that were absentee owned and managed because the high turnover in Korean businesses made the absentee-owner rate difficult to calculate.

16. Among the traditional established stores, few outlets restricted access to a narrow group. In enterprises such as hairdressers and taverns there were often barriers to access, requiring one to be accompanied by a "regular." Some stores were locked and only open for preferred customers. Elsewhere, nonregulars were ignored and made to feel uncomfortable on entry. Some of these stores were part of the traditional strip, such as the "Irish" bars and a set of specialty stores that dated to the 1950s. These included a bookstore, bakery, deli, and two gift stores—all owned by people who arrived after World War II and were oriented to a German, Polish, Ukrainian clientele.

Other exclusive shops were new immigrant-owned stores on the strip that provided goods and services to their group. The new ethnic food stores and service outlets provide places for people to spend long periods of time and pick up gossip and information.

17. In Philadelphia, Black entrepreneurs have both privately and publicly (on the radio) expressed dismay that their customers avoid them; they also feel resentful that customers accuse them of exploitation.

18. Two shopkeeper surveys were done as part of the fieldwork, both during quiet times, January and August. Almost all single-family stores reported that they had nobody outside the family working at the time of the survey. In the January interview they talked about having just laid off Christmas help, and in August they said they were planning to hire for the "back to school" rush. In general, there was little margin in the bottom line, and hiring was deferred till necessary.

19. Many Latinos did their specialized shopping on the Latino strips farther south, but used the strip for many ordinary goods and services.

20. Thus most merchants claimed to have very few Korean customers. A

pharmacist talked about rare referrals from the Korean pharmacist, but only highly specialized services like tax preparation services, the lumberyard, men's clothing stores (no such Korean store on the strip), and Radio Shack reported a significant Korean clientele.

21. This area had been informally designated as the locale for the concentration of citywide services for the Korean community, a large component of specialized Korean businesses are here (see Table 12.1). Both "Korean only" and wholesale stores were part of a major conflict in 1986 that occurred when the community responded negatively to the erection of Korean street signs. Many felt the signs meant the Koreans were appropriating the strip and were intent on excluding local residents (Goode 1990).

22. One white ethnic resident who befriended a Korean entrepreneur and his wife told of admiring the wife's sweater and asking where she bought it. She was aghast when told that it came from a Korean store up the street and cost $100. She said, "I don't even spend that amount on clothes in a year."

23. The same phenomenon was reported in New York City (Park 1991).

24. The Korean government in 1989 raised the ceiling on capital that could leave the country. Newer arrivals were both bringing more money to the United States and moving into family networks that knew the city. They were becoming large-scale investors with several outlets. This created more strain within the Korean community and increased competition. One grocery owner at another strip told us about a Korean who began to remodel a store near him. "He told me it would be something else, but when it was done, it was direct competition to me. He had more capital and could undercut my prices, and I had to leave."

Another commented on the increased competition: [In Korea] "even desperate North Korean [refugees] still kept ethics and morals even though they were at survival level . . . but here there are no ethics anymore." A business broker reported: "When I first worked on contracts, between Koreans, they were only one page, they were not suspicious of each other. Now they are thirty pages long. Once they were willing to sacrifice to help less experienced Koreans. Now everyone is more profit oriented."

25. In contrast, nonunion stores were the fastest-growing segment of the industry. These included local chains and independent stores that share warehouses.

Bibliography

Albrecht, K., and R. Zemke. 1985. *Service America! Doing Business in the New Economy*. Homewood, Ill.: Dow Jones-Irwin.

Benson, Susan Porter. 1986. *Counter Cultures: Saleswomen, Managers and Customers in American Department Stores, 1890–1940*. Urbana, Ill.: University of Illinois Press.

Bigus, O. E. 1972. "The Milkman and His Customer: A Cultivated Role." *Urban Life and Culture* 1:131–165.

Bluestone, Barry. 1981. *The Retail Revolution: A Market Transformation*. Boston: Auburn House.

Butler, S. R., and W. E. Snizek. 1972. "The Waitress–Diner Relationship: A Multi-Method Approach to the Study of Subordinate Influence. *Sociology of Work and Occupations* 3:2209–2223.

Carvajal, Doreen. 1992. "Acme Clerks Concede on Wages, Bet on Renewal." *Philadelphia Inquirer*, December 14.

Cziepel, John A., Michael R. Solomon, and Carol Suprenant, eds. 1985. *The Service Encounter:Managing Employee/Customer Interaction in Service Businesses.* Lexington, Mass.: Lexington Books.

Destanick, R. L. 1987. *Managing to Keep the Customer.* San Francisco: Jossey-Bass.

Goode, J. 1990. "A Wary Welcome to the Neighborhood: Community Responses to Immigrants." *Urban Anthropology* 19:125–153.

Goode, J., and J. Schneider. 1994. *Reshaping Ethnic and Racial Relations in Philadelphia: Immigrants in a Divided City.* Philadelphia: Temple University Press.

Goode, J., and E. Simon. 1993. "Women's (and Men's) Work Culture and the Transition to Leadership in the Supermarket Industry." *Frontiers* 14(1).

Hochner, A., C. Granrose, J. Goode, E. Simon, and E. Appelbaum. 1988. *Saving Jobs in Supermarkets: Worker Ownership and QWL.* Kalamazoo, Mich.: Upjohn Institute.

Hochschild, Arlie. 1983. *The Managed Heart: Commercialization of Human Feeling.* Berkeley: University of California Press.

Leidner, Robin. 1988. "Working on People" Ph.D. dissertation, Northwestern University.

———. 1990. "Serving Hamburgers: McDonald's and the New Service Economy." PARRS Seminar on Work and Welfare, University of Pennsylvania.

———. 1993. *Fast Food, Fast Talk: Work and the Routinization of Everyday Life.* Berkeley: University of California Press.

Mars, G., and M. Nicod. 1984. *The World of Waiters.* Boston: G. Allen.

Park, Y. 1990. "The Korean American Dream: Ideology and Small Business in Queens N.Y." Ph.D. dissertation, City University of New York.

Paules, Greta. 1991. *Dishing It Out.* Philadelphia: Temple University Press.

Rafaeli, A. 1989. "When Cashiers Meet Customers: An Analysis of the Role of Supermarket Cashiers." *Academy of Management Journal* 32:245–273.

Rodrigues, G. 1987. "Goya Foods Take on Philadelphia." *Philadelphia Inquirer*, September 20.

Schmidt, William E. 1990. "For Immigrants, Tough Customers." *New York Times*, November 25.

Simon, E., and J. Goode. 1989. "The Constraints on the Use of Anthropology in Interdisciplinary Policy Studies." *Urban Anthropology* 18:219–240.

Sutton, R. I., and A. Rafaeli. 1988. "Untangling the Relationship between Displayed Emotions and Organizational Sales: The Case of Convenience Stores." *Academy of Management Journal* 31:461–487.

Westcott, D. N. 1982. "Blacks in the 1970s: Did they Scale the Job Ladder?" *Monthly Labor Review* 105:29–38.

Whyte, W. 1948. *Human Relations in the Restaurant Industry.* New York: McGraw-Hill.

13   Poverty and Politics: Practice and Ideology among Small Business Owners in an Urban Enterprise Zone

Cynthia Carter Ninivaggi

Almost every state in the United States during the 1980s designated enterprise zones in the hope that they would stimulate capital investment in economically and socially distressed urban areas. Proponents of enterprise zones believe that an easing of governmental regulations and tax burdens on business will create a friendly atmosphere for redevelopment and revitalization in specific areas of cities where unemployment is high.

The flurry of media attention and public debate devoted to enterprise zones had gradually waned by the late 1980s, until the Los Angeles riots in the spring of 1992 brought pressure to bear on Washington to formulate a plan for some sort of urban aid. In the postriot political turmoil that ensued, enterprise zones again appeared on the editorial pages, and a bill to create federal urban enterprise zone legislation emerged in Congress once more.

This chapter describes one of the oldest active urban enterprise zones in existence in the United States and addresses the question whether enterprise zoning brings about positive economic and social change in urban areas. What I have found is that the enterprise zone tends to exclude minority business owners and residents and that political antagonisms and ethnic and class divisions between different groups in the community are exacerbated by the structure of the zone program.

Instead of a mathematical model of fiscal impacts, such as that of Funkhouser and Lorenz (1987), I would like to present a less abstract picture of who the business owners of the zone are and how they perceive their role in the community studied in the

281

Changing Relations Project. In pointing out some of the contradictions of the urban enterprise zone, I criticize the program for failing to develop a means of fairly evaluating the costs and benefits of
the local zone. There is evidence to show that enterprise zones have
failed to create jobs in areas of high unemployment. Despite a bi-
partisan consensus among congressional leaders in Washington
that federally designated enterprise zones should be established,
evidence from already established zones indicates that enterprise
zoning at best creates an uncertain number of low-paying, unstable
jobs.

In addition, I propose that enterprise zones benefit only relatively privileged sectors of the business community. I argue that
enterprise zoning does not constitute a cost-effective means of preventing the kind of urban decay that led to the Los Angeles riots.
In addition, I propose that federal urban enterprise zone legislation will have a chilling effect on the rate of establishment of
minority-owned businesses in urban areas.

Historical Origins of the Enterprise Zone

Industrial subsidies of various kinds have been used since the
late nineteenth century to encourage industrial development (Cobb
1982:5). Enterprise zones offer many of the same kinds of financial
incentives to business owners as those seen in other subsidy programs. Urban enterprise zones are small, specific areas or zones in
cities that are targeted for certain subsidies.

In most American enterprise zones, including the American
Street zone that is the subject of this chapter, various tax abatements, low-interest loans, and other financial incentives are offered
to businesses willing to relocate or expand within zone boundaries.
These areas are targeted for such privileges because of high rates
of unemployment or economic and physical decline—what the
public policy literature refers to as "distressed" urban areas. What
areas ought to be designated enterprise zones, what incentives businesses there ought to get, and what the actual costs and benefits of
enterprise zones might be have been matters of lively debate since
enterprise zones were conceived in the late 1970s.

The history of the enterprise zone had its roots in Great Britain
and was the brainchild of the political scientist Peter Hall (1982).
Observing the rapid industrial growth in various Southeast Asian
countries such as Taiwan, Singapore, and Hong Kong, Hall suggested that First World countries attempt to re-create the conditions for development found in Third World countries in their

own distressed areas. Hall hoped that the industrial redevelopment resulting from the easing of governmental regulations and tax burdens, and providing cheap labor in these areas, would stimulate capital investment, revitalizing urban economies and relieving unemployment. At his boldest, Hall envisioned a kind of "takeoff" in which high-tech industries would gradually join low-tech firms within the zones, attracted by low property values, industrial parks, and other financial incentives.

This vision drew fairly sharp criticism from Hall's colleagues, who questioned his logic in assuming that the "Third World conditions" that fostered growth in Asia could be, or ought to be, recreated in an advanced industrialized country (Goldsmith 1982; Massey 1982; O'Dowd and Rolston 1985). They also pointed out that instead of creating an environment that would encourage "enterprise" and entrepreneurship, the more likely result would be a relocation of already existing industry (Bromley and Morgan 1985). Research on the fiscal impact of enterprise zones warned that these zones do little to create new economic development (Botham and Lloyd 1983; Funkhouser and Lorenz 1987; Gunther and Leathers 1987; Keating et al. 1984; Witthans 1984). Critics following the development and implementation of the program in Great Britain and Northern Ireland noted the political wrangling and tradeoffs that characterized the process of deciding which areas ought to qualify as enterprise zones. They saw that areas with greater political pull and better financial prospects for profitability were more likely to be designated than areas of desperate poverty, supposedly the original targets of the program (Barnes and Preston 1985; Bromley and Morgan 1985).

The enterprise zone concept was introduced in the United States by the economist Stuart Butler of the Washington-based Heritage Foundation, an influential, prolific, and traditionally conservative think tank. Enterprise zones have been offered as a political Band-Aid for all kinds of social ills, particularly those affecting urban areas. The zones have been offered as the solution for every kind of political problem from the demise of the family farm (rural enterprise zones, as George Bush called them in the 1988 Bush–Dukakis debate) to rising crime rates in urban areas (providing jobs will help reduce drug trafficking).

Enterprise Zoning in the United States

Creating an environment that will attract business by granting tax abatements and freedom from government regulation is a fairly traditional political program for attracting industry to a given area. The enterprise zones of the 1980s offered similar inducements to industry, and the political rhetoric associated with proponents of the zones echoed familiar themes of entrepreneurship, saving, risk taking, investment, and hard work.

Neoconservatives of the 1980s encouraged the private sector to take upon itself a considerably larger part of the economics of urban social conditions that seemed to grow more deplorable every year. Federal cuts to housing, urban development, and various social welfare programs left states and cities to finance such services as best they could. Despite social conditions in the cities, the Reagan–Bush administrations did not introduce any new federal urban program to address the problems of decaying urban centers and the poverty of their residents, except for enterprise zones, first introduced in 1981 as the Kemp–Garcia bill.

Various versions of this bill have since been reintroduced in Congress and rejected several times in the past ten years, and by 1990 the White House seemed to have lost interest. While Jack Kemp, an admirer of Puerto Rico's Operation Bootstrap program of the 1950s and the zone's most ardent lobbyist, gamely continued to push for urban enterprise zone legislation at the federal level, not until the Los Angeles riots in the spring of 1992 brought pressure on the White House to take some action on urban decay did enterprise zones again emerge as a focus of public debate. Under the rubric of job creation for the poor, the program serves as an elaborate rationale for government subsidies and regulatory relief provided to particular kinds of private businesses.

The failure of the federal bill to pass Congress has not prevented the establishment of urban enterprise zones in some thirty-seven states. By 1989, about fifteen hundred enterprise zones had been established in the United States (Guskind 1989). While most of these designated zones will become "active" immediately on passage of an enterprise zone bill, about five hundred are already active. That is, they already provide tax abatements, low-interest loans, regulatory relief, and other subsidies to business. Creating such an inviting atmosphere for industry is supposed to help stem the flow of capital and jobs from afflicted urban areas to the suburbs, the sunbelt, or the Third World. Enterprise zones are financed through sometimes quite intricate partnerships between federal, state, municipal, and private funding bodies and organizations.

Studying a Zone's Business Organization

In 1988 I had the opportunity to study an enterprise zone and its effects on the community of Kensington (see Chapter 10). In this enterprise zone the business owners' organization wished to fund a membership drive. They looked for a student to visit non-member businesses in the zone and convince them to join the organization. I was interested to see to what degree the enterprise zone actually did affect employment rates and the quality of life in poor inner-city neighborhoods. I was also interested in how the business owners who took part in the program saw their own interests as articulated with those of the other "receivers" of the policy, the local residents.

During the summer of 1989 when I worked for the business association, I had the opportunity to talk to 225 of the 420 small business owners in this "distressed" urban section of Philadelphia about their concerns, goals, and neighborhoods, and about how the enterprise zone project has affected them. In general, I found that there were two groups of business owners in the zone: those who were interested in political mobilization of the business community and attempted to "sell" zone benefits to others as an organizing tool, and other business owners who resisted joining the organization because they believed that the zone benefits were inadequate and the organization did not "do anything" for them.

In the zone, the "community" was always the "business community" or the members of the business association. Zone residents and employees remained invisible in the discourse about the zone between zone administrators, politicians, and business owners. The discourse was as carefully upbeat in tone as a business journal editorial on labor relations. Racism and poverty were simply not talked about.

My job at that time was to knock on the doors of businesses that had never joined the organization or that had stopped paying their annual dues and convince them to join, mostly by appealing to their self-interest. Business association leaders organized the membership campaign in this way because they felt that people in the business community would only respond to an appeal to their profits. Residents of the community, who are supposed to benefit from the jobs, did not figure very prominently in our discussions about ways to sell the zone to business owners. Encouraging membership in the business association was seen as very much analogous to advertising a product. A great deal of attention was paid to creating a brochure that would emphasize zone benefits to the business. It had to be colorful and professional looking, but very brief, because business owners were busy and could not afford the time to read a long brochure.

Once, during the time in which the brochure was being developed, I was reprimanded by a zone administrator when I called the area "depressed." The word did not sound "upbeat" enough; the image of the zone area had to be a positive one if the zone literature was to succeed.

Description of an Enterprise Zone

The enterprise zone I worked in was one of three in Philadelphia. The local Commerce Department and the Private Industry Council (PIC) offers businesses in the zone wage subsidies for employees during their training periods on the job for up to twenty weeks. The state offers tax abatements to firms that contribute to neighborhood organizations or improve land and buildings in the zone. The city may be reimbursed by the state for undertaking physical improvements in the zone and enhancing the employability of residents. The Commerce Department also provides a mortgage loan fund for construction and equipment through the local PIC. The state may reimburse businesses in the zone for up to $5,000 for security improvements to industrial properties in the zone. The state also foots the bill for the demolition of abandoned buildings to make way for new construction and provides zero-interest five-year loans for business expansion up to $50,000.

The zone is a narrow strip of land bordering the northern riverfront district, comprising about four hundred city blocks. The area is bisected by a narrow sidestreet, American Street, which in the zone widens inexplicably into a four-lane highway and abruptly disappears into a littered area of rowhouses reputed to be one of the most drug-infested neighborhoods in the city. The patriotic overtones of the street name are used in the development of zone literature, where themes of entrepreneurship, enterprise, and progress symbolically emerge.

Residents in the zone are ethnically diverse, but the four hundred-odd business owners who appear on the Department of Commerce's list as eligible for zone benefits and association membership are almost overwhelmingly white males. A handful of women appear, but only one runs her business (there is also a husband–wife partnership), and she has no employees. Two of the business owners are black. None of the business owners live in the zone; they all commute from more upscale areas of the city or the suburbs.

New or refurbished enterprises are located amid rowhouses and small Latino businesses in the enterprise zone. (Photo by Melissa M. Forbis)

Many of the entrepreneurs who form the core of the business organization, and the zone's most enthusiastic proponents, tend to be the kind of second- or third-generation immigrant entrepreneurs who settled in the area during the 1920s (see Chapter 10). They have retained their small to mid-sized businesses by diversifying into specialized product lines or services that are not easily affected by competition from more powerful conglomerate competitors. Like many of the small businesses that survived the takeovers of the 1980s, they are specialized companies that manufacture a very specific product: a certain type of hospital bed, a maker of wooden violin cases. Some companies distribute various kinds of industrial equipment, machinery, or auto parts.

Most of the industries in the zone are small, employing fewer than twenty people. The largest by far, a paper-box manufacturing company, employs 490 people. Some examples of the products and services the light-industrial manufacturing companies offer are warehousing and freight, ball bearings, metal moldings and parts, metal finishing, and scrap metals. There are several food-processing plants and a variety of textile manufacturers. There are several cabinetmakers and upholsterers.

Other businesses include a rather different sector of artists and craftsmen, attracted to the area by the low rents; they cater to a much more upscale market, featuring such goods as jewelry and gourmet foods. The artists tend to require highly skilled personnel, if they hire employees at all, and tend not to employ local residents. These businesses are newer and less well established than the typical family businesses, many of whom have been in the neighborhood for a generation or more. These business owners are not well represented in the business organization's membership.

Other businesses that share the zone with the industrial businesses include a variety of retail concerns. Especially noteworthy is a very large sector of auto parts shops, ranging from legitimate garages to "chop shops" where stolen and abandoned cars are harvested along the street for parts. In fact, one of the major eyesores in the area are streets lined with rusting cars in various states of decomposition. Car theft is a major source of concern to employers, who lose both customers and employees because of neighborhood decay and the damage done to parked cars by vandals and thieves.

The artists, the younger business owners, and those who cater to upscale markets such as business services, cellular phones, and antique restoration are much less interested in joining the business association unless they see it as the only way to obtain a particular financial incentive for which they may be eligible. By contrast, many of the older business owners, who may have inherited their businesses, join the association because they feel they "ought to belong to something." That is, they express respect for the tradition of business "giving back" something to the community, as one third-generation business owner expressed it. In this they are similar to the third-generation store owners on the Olney strip (see Chapter 12).

One important contrast between the enterprise zone business association and a more traditional business association is that the enterprise zone association is actually mandated by zone legislation. Unlike many traditional business and merchant associations, the organization is not a grass-roots organization. Membership in the zone association is restricted to nonretail businesses that fall within the boundaries of the designated zone. The geographical boundaries of the business "community" are not defined by the members but by administrative order. There is little sense of shared interest between the artists and the long-established businesses. The owners of the long-established businesses speak with bitterness and regret about the decline of the neighborhood and about vandalism and drugs. They express anger at both the city and the local residents for failing to maintain the area.

At times, the zone business association voluntarily engages in the same activities as a traditional business association, in the way of charitable donations to community organizations. For example, the association replaced a piano stolen from a local parish school. The business owners who are leaders are very concerned with establishing close relationships with the local police in order to enhance the security of their properties. To this end, they also take an active interest in the local police force and help fund a youth group founded by the officers. The rituals associated with charitable contributions such as the piano and the youth group tend to emphasize the separation between business owners and recipients. The business owners invite representatives from these groups to their monthly meetings and do not travel to the school or organization; the receipt of the contribution very much takes place on the business organization's turf.

Most important, unlike a more traditional business association, this one is provided with services and staff funded with public monies. Its existence is mandated by the administrative order that created the enterprise zone program, so it is not a grass-roots organization.

Association members also enjoy the privilege of a direct communication network with local, state, and national politicians. Most of the organization's activities involve lobbying efforts at local, state, and national levels. Political figures are regularly taken around and are photographed in front of new construction to show their support for the enterprise zone program. After the Los Angeles riots, even President Bush visited the enterprise zone.

Conflicting Agendas in the Enterprise Zone

Those who form the core of the politically active industrial business owners seem unaware of the program's origins and are rather selectively concerned with the very broad agenda that national politics has laid out for them to fulfill. Business leaders officially claim that unemployment is the root cause of the problems on their doorsteps: crime, vandalism, drug addiction, prostitution. Empowered with the staff and services provided by the government as part of the program, and allied with the highly visible zone program administrators in the municipal government, this small group of businessmen seem to have stumbled into an unlikely position of local influence and political limelight. Leaders of the business association are regularly called on by the media for commentary on almost every possible issue that directly affects Philadelphia's economic situation. In the confines of their offices, they are frank and aggressive about the ways in which they seek greater influence over a city government they see as mismanaged. This membership, which numbers about two hundred in a business community of 420 industries, sees its role in the community as a "pro-business voice," as their literature phrases it, in a city in which too much of the burden for social reform is placed on business. The business association leadership seeks to become the voice of the business community in the city.

The business association's board of directors consists of the zone administrators and a core of the most active business owners. They meet monthly, early in the morning, in a comfortable conference room in a community residence facility in the neighborhood. Coffee and pastries are provided; suits are worn. This would be an exclusively white male gathering if it were not for the inclusion of several women, well-dressed representatives of other local institutions, who are present at these monthly meetings. These representatives are not residents of the community but are employed in positions such as community liaisons from the public utility companies or the area hospitals. Attending these meetings is part of their professional duties, but they do not seem to participate in the activities of the organization. One of these representatives, for example, attended each monthly meeting armed with an expensive leather legal-pad holder and pen, which she opened faithfully each time, and closed again at the end of each meeting, having written not a single note. The pattern of silence among these members did not seem to upset the more active leaders of the association.

Everyone who attends these meetings is affiliated with some formal institution. Community leaders in the zone, such as religious leaders, block captains, or even local school board representatives, do not appear unless they are invited as recipients of some sort of charitable donation.

Other business is conducted at business luncheons, which are held between zone administrators and leaders of the association. These more informal meetings are cordial and relaxed, preceded by joke telling and banter. It is here that the activities of the group are discussed in more detail, rather than simply reported, as they tend to be in monthly board meetings. News about the activities of the association are disseminated to the general membership by means of a monthly newsletter and by an annual banquet to which all members are invited.

The leadership of the business association consists of a very small core of business owners. A position of leadership does not seem to have much to do with how prominent the business is or how wealthy the owner. The president, for example, drives a modest car and owns a very small business with no more than four or five employees. His prestige lies in the enormous amount of volunteer time he offers to the organization. His reputation is one of a civic leader, and he has received several awards, such as Businessman of the Year, from the city in recognition of his work. Association members speak with admiration of his considerable efforts on behalf of the organization and wonder how he can manage to run his business at the same time. They are afraid the organization will weaken when he retires because no one else seems likely to match his dedication.

Much of his activity involves maintaining the business association's relationship with the more "pro-business" factions of city government, such as the Department of Commerce. These activities involve a kind of lobbying effort. The business association president will receive announcements of legislation pending from the Commerce Department and will send the word out individually to members, asking them to contact their representative with the appropriate response. For example, a bill that would allow small business owners to test their employees randomly for drug abuse was lobbied for, even though none of the business owners in the zone had expressed any interest in drug testing and the cost was seen as prohibitive. In this way, the business owners active in the association function as a resource for political mobilization as well as some financial support for sympathetic officials at crucial moments. Although the association's political action committee (PAC) planned to support candidates from both parties, the association president believed that a conservative political agenda best served those who were "closely allied with" the Commerce Department. As he said, "If you are not a Republican, your heart wouldn't be in it," meaning the political organizing in which the association was involved.

Most of the approximately two hundred members who support the association with their dues are not closely involved in these political activities. Many businesses feel compelled to join because they "ought to belong to something." The association is able to advertise itself through its quarterly newsletter. The funds and staff for the newsletter are state monies provided through the Commerce Department. The Commerce Department has set up a Business Service Center for each of the city's three zones. These are set up expressly for the purpose of helping business owners make their needs known to city government and raising awareness in the business community about zone benefits.

The Exclusion of Retailers

Retail businesses are supposed to be excluded from the benefits package, but their owners may wind up on the Commerce Department's list as eligible for membership in the zone's business association, especially if they are seen as politically influential people. Unlike the industrial business owners, some minority retail business owners occasionally live within the neighborhood. Many minority owners who do not live in the zone still maintain kinship or friendship ties with the community. One might argue that this population, although excluded from the benefits, might have a higher stake in the long-term economic health of the area than the nonresiding business owners. But these retail business owners do not have the same resources that the industrial business owners have in terms of staff and funding.

Minority business leaders such as those active in the business association on the "Golden Block," a shopping strip serving Latino customers, are a case in point. Leaders of the zone's business association could establish some valuable political liaisons through the minority business leaders, and the Latino business owners would probably be welcome at its monthly board meetings. But the Latino business owners are not favorably disposed toward the zone association and its political activities, which they do not perceive as allied with their interests or that of the community.

While the industrial business owners in the zone have a publicly funded "business hotline" to city officials, the large number of Latino retailers in the Golden Block of the zone have met with more difficulty in getting public services. Because of a serious traffic bottleneck, the Golden Block is a very congested area. The Spanish merchants' association, however, has been unsuccessful in getting the city government to address this problem. In spite of efforts by zone administrators to publicize redevelopment in the industrial sector, this thriving shopping strip goes almost ignored in the hoopla over so many feet of industrial space constructed and so many jobs created. Part of an early effort in the 1970s to encourage minority enterprise, Latino businesses have undergone difficulties in staying afloat once programs were cut. Now, ironically, many of the incentives that used to go to minority business loans and benefits are available to the industrial sector.

Retail business owners in all parts of the zone also complain about the lack of city services, such as sanitation, transportation, parking, and law enforcement. Even when they have organized, however, their efforts are overshadowed by the political clout of enterprise zone leaders and administrators. There is also an element of ethnic division; the Korean retail businesses have a community network independent of the Latino retail businesses similar to the one that formerly existed on the Olney strip (see Chapter 12). Latino politicians in the City Council are thought to represent the interests of the Hispanic business owners as well as residents. By contrast, the enterprise zone business association, with its industrial owners, has city administrators who work exclusively for the association, as well as connections to various politicians for whom it lobbies and campaigns.

Conflicts between Residents and Industrial Business Owners

The residential and business communities in the enterprise zone are separate spheres with few formal or informal linkages. While zone leaders seem to assume that residents are indirectly benefiting from the program, the needs and desires of industry may be very different from those of local families. The best example of the way industrial subsidy programs like enterprise zones may divert resources from social programs and grass-roots community efforts, while claiming to serve them, is the zone's own Business Service Center at the Lighthouse Economic Development Project.

The Lighthouse once served as a settlement house for immigrants in the late nineteenth century. Now a community center, a large portion of the space and resources of the Lighthouse is channeled into the Business Service Center. The Center's Job Resource Network advertises itself to employers in the zone as a "screening" service for matching qualified applicants with potential employers. The purpose of an employment program is to place residents in the zone in jobs. According to the Center's own records, however, only about 10 percent of the applicants who use the Center are placed, and these applicants are not primarily zone residents. The Lighthouse is also meant to serve as a liaison between industry owners in the zone and the city government, in order to obtain better municipal services when needed and help business be aware of and take advantage of various financial incentive programs. These externally driven new activities have also drawn resources away from day-care and senior-center commitments and have created conflicts on the orgnization board.

The history and practice of U.S. enterprise zones point to an underlying flaw in the neoconservative ethic of business redevelopment: Economic growth is very ill-defined. Partly this reflects an overall assumption that any manufacturing base will foster the development of high-wage, high-skilled, high-tech industry. There is very little sense of precisely what kind of manufacturing sector enterprise zones ought to attract, or how a transformation from sweatshops to high-tech industry is supposed to take place. Since most economists are concerned about U.S. global competitiveness in high-tech industries, and since enterprise zones are a major part of current urban policy, the question of what kind of industry and what kinds of jobs would seem be a crucial one. But the intellectual debate in public policy literature, as well as the public discourse surrounding enterprise zones at the local level, does not address this question.

Perhaps the most salient problem with the enterprise zone program is the underlying assumption that residents are passive receivers of policy and that these neighborhoods must be saved by some outside force. Residents are seen as universally impoverished and helpless; they are a clientele to be served rather than viable and autonomous actors in their own communities. Hence, there is a lack of articulation between the political empowerment of industries that might wish to move to or remain in the zone and residents who are the presumed beneficiaries of higher employment and redevelopment. At business association board meetings, the paternalistic attitudes displayed seem to contradict the evidence on their own shopfloors and in the storefronts that there are many different classes of people at various income levels living, working, and participating in the community.

Voters in suburban neighborhoods construct pictures of inner-city problems from images on their television screens. The viewer or even the motorist through a "bad neighborhood" has no way of understanding the locally specific business and political networks that shape community boundaries. The political rhetoric associated with the enterprise zone creates an image of a lone entrepreneur riding into the ghost towns of the inner city to impose prosperity, law, and order. But in the zone where I worked, it was clear that the aspirations of the businessmen involved were more modest, more practical, and more personal. They were unabashedly interested in their profits, above everything else. If the more outspoken residents wanted to organize urban gardening projects, they would not receive much help from the tough industrialists, who had no time for planting flowers. Many of the businessmen believed that running a business left no time to devote to the political activities of the zone association, much less other civic activities. Perhaps granting rebates for barbed-wire fences around factories was an inadequate government response to gang violence, but even so, it was not a small businessman's responsibility to make up for the state's failures.

In the Philadelphia enterprise zone, only one representative of the residential community is included on the board, a Hispanic woman who runs a local social service agency. She is the board's last direct link with the residents. The history of the zone program reveals that initially attempts were made to undertake various projects in cooperation with area residents, such as a neighborhood cleanup and beautification campaign, as well as various attempts to attract more retail business to the area. These projects were eventually abandoned, however, because of differences of opinion between business owners, who saw the projects as impractical, and so-called militant residents.

Residents of the zone include several ethnic groups. Some of the more visible are long-established ethnic whites, African Americans, Puerto Ricans and other Latinos, Koreans and other Asians, and Palestinians. Resident empowerment organizations of ethnic whites, Latinos, and other groups are worried about the impact of gentrification on their neighborhood. They have created activist groups attempting to acquire and rehabilitate abandoned housing. For them, the enterprise zone and its business organization are not seen as potential allies but as competitors for space for housing their low-income families. The more "homegrown" business organizations, such as the Korean Businessmen's Association and the Spanish Merchants Association, are more closely allied with local interests. Nor do residents see enterprise zone businesses as a valued source of employment. The contradictory and inflated reports of job creation in the zone seem to indicate that there is little reason for residents to see the business owners as a source of improvement for the local community. Just as the rhetoric of the owners and administrators of the zone would indicate, the zone is aimed at the general Philadelphia business community, not the people who live within the zone.

Self-Reported Success in the Zone

However broadly the Reagan and Bush administrations defined the functions of enterprise zones, the business owners within the zone are mainly concerned with helping the small businessman. Other enterprise zones, both in the United States and in Europe, seem to lack this emphasis on the program as particularly directed toward the small entrepreneur. I suspect that although size is not an issue in the legislation, other small business owners have helped to invent and to utilize this notion of small enterprises, simply borrowing whatever other ideological components in the national package seemed appropriate to their interests. There is no contract between business and legislators about what industrialists ought to do (e.g., employ disadvantaged zone residents); the financial incentives are there for the taking. The association literature stresses the advantage of government financial incentives, which do not stipulate that certain disadvantaged employees be hired (Association newsletter 1988).

Zone administrators and business leaders also emphasize the way in which high city (not federal) taxes, particularly property taxes, gross receipt taxes, and the city's wage tax stifle "enterprise" in the city, preventing the establishment of new companies and driving older businesses to the suburbs. The business owners are correct in their assessment that high local taxes drive business away from the city. While business is growing in the suburbs outside Philadelphia, the number of light industrial businesses within the city has experienced a long decline. High taxes and security are universally cited by owners as the major concerns of businesses still residing within the zone. The enterprise zone program at the local level is touted as a way to ease the tax burden and stem the flow of businesses to the suburbs. But city taxes are very unlikely to decrease for business owners in Philadelphia, since the city relies on these taxes in order to continue providing basic services. Taxpayers outside Philadelphia are quite reluctant to assume the tax burden of maintaining city services and programs.

In assessing the long-term benefits of the enterprise zone program, we run into the problem of community boundaries. The charge of critics, that businesses are likely to leave the zones once benefits run out, needs further investigation. Will well-established businesses that existed in the community before the zone leave? Sometimes small family-run businesses die of "old age" when their founders retire and their children do not want to go into the business, which is a situation occasionally encountered in the enterprise zone in Philadelphia. Zone administration records show that some recipients of zone benefits have moved away from the zone and have left for the suburbs, indicating that incentives such as the zone offers are insufficient to court businesses to stay in the city. In general, zone benefits are unlikely to influence older, most established businesses. The newer, upscale, nonfamily concerns and the artists are not a source of much employment, if any, to local residents. It is likely that if the area did improve enough to influence rents, these businesses also would leave, and the cycle of decline would begin anew.

Who, then, is the "community"? If nonresidents are excluded, then only minority middlemen would seem to be a sensible public investment in terms of redevelopment. They have solid customer bases within the zone, many are also residents, and those who are not often maintain close kinship and friendship ties in the neighborhood. It seems likely that such businesses would have more of a long-term interest in the neighborhood than the subsidiary branches of major corporations and upscale goods manufacturers with little personal interest in the neighborhood. Minority (and female-owned) businesses are very rare overall, however, and are even less likely to be engaged in industry. This may be because of the large capital investment required to start up a business or because owning such a business involves highly specialized skills, with training that is available only through apprenticeship networks that have been traditionally closed to minorities and women.

Despite the uncertainty surrounding the zone's long-term impact on the area, the dynamics of the political relationships between business owners, political leaders, and large developers help sustain a conservative economic agenda even under the Democratic leadership of the city government. Both Democratic and Republican political leaders are under a great deal of pressure to cooperate with the enterprise zone program, since it presents jobs as a panacea for all sorts of social problems, and cooperation promises a certain amount of political influence and leverage in return.

Zone Administrators Measure Success

The self-reported success of the enterprise zone program does not bear objective scrutiny. The process first observed by Michael Harrington (1965) of sweatshop industries moving into areas abandoned by large manufacturers is echoed in the zone and depicted as "job creation" that gets the poor off welfare rolls. Progress is not assessed by the variable of how many square feet of construction have been built in the zone. Estimates of how many jobs the zone has created range from eight hundred in the press to over twenty-one hundred in zone records.

No study of the program's impact has been made by any outside evaluator. Instead, zone administrators are responsible for reporting the impact of the program to city officials, even though their jobs depend on their reporting success in the zone.

After the zone's establishment in 1981, the first report of its long-term success covered the period from 1983 to 1987. This report contained employment information on every business in the zone that had taken advantage of any of the program's well-publicized loan programs or security rebates over a five-year period. Every present and past employee of these companies was reported as a "job retained," and every new position as a "job created" (even those a company inadvertently added).

Yet many of these companies are not even very enthusiastic about the zone. For example, many of the companies that take advantage of the security rebate program refuse to join the business association because, in their view, it cannot help solve the area's problems. Many of the businesses whose employees are reported as jobs created or retained are simply businesses on the list of those waiting for a security rebate, not new businesses or businesses that would have moved if not for the zone program. Business owners complain bitterly that the process of waiting for the advertised rebate takes much too long, well over a year.

Is the program cost effective from the point of view of the taxpayer? Let us assume for a moment that if the enterprise zone had never been implemented, employment levels would have remained stagnant. Therefore, we accept the self-reported figure of 850 "created" new jobs in the zone. According to the zone administrator's reports, the total public investment in the enterprise zone I studied over the same five-year period, 1983 to 1987, was $8 million in public funds invested directly into area business by way of no-interest loans and wage subsidies, excluding an additional $84,167 in security rebates. This does not include staffing and funding the project and the costs of running the Business Service Center. Taxpayers, then, are paying $9,400 per "job created" to companies that may fail, move, or misrepresent the size of their payroll in exchange for political favors. Taxpayers are funding, in addition to this figure, up to $5,000 for security rebates and the salaries and costs associated with the staff of three at the Business Service Center as well as the two zone administrators who oversee the program. In addition, no distinction is made in the administrator's reports between seasonal and part-time work and full-time work, or whether the "jobs" in each company actually existed at the same time in the five-year period.

Job creation within the three zones for the city as a whole is low. For all enterprise zones in Philadelphia, the total public investment in individual businesses was $18,509,880, creating 2,173 jobs from 1983 to 1987. The overall figure per "job created" was $8,518 per job. (This figure excludes program costs as well as a total of

$163,585 in security rebates.) According to the job placement records of the Business Service Center, these jobs paid between $5 and $8 an hour and were full- or part-time jobs. Applicants did not have to reside in the zone; residency was not a requirement. One minority community leader complained that the job placement center in the zone had little impact on employment rates and merely duplicated other services existing in the neighborhood.

Of course, it might well be argued that creating jobs is good in itself, whether it serves zone residents directly or indirectly. But the argument cannot be made that the zone program removed the poor from welfare rolls if the evidence suggests that hires would have been made anyway. In addition, even if the jobs that the zone administrator claims to have been created were in fact created by the program, by their own accounts, this was accomplished at great public expense with no assurance of long-term stability.

Conclusions

Leaders of the association work hard to uphold their civic images with the city government, and the bureaucracy of the city government, as well as the media, is glad to have a "business" spokesperson for addressing some of the city's social problems. The optimism about the future of the neighborhood displayed by the leaders is good public relations, without the taint of overtly political linkages. Yet to present the industrialists in an entirely negative light would be unfair. The genuine concern for the neighborhood and for their employees displayed by a few of the most active leaders was unmistakable and completely sincere. It was also true that the way in which business owners talk about enterprise zones among themselves is not a discourse in which residents are seen as active participants in decisions affecting the business "community." Businessmen pride themselves on their concern with the "bottom line." While they may express disgust at the way "those people" (resident immigrants and minorities) fail to control their children in the neighborhood or condone drug trafficking and vandalism, they see the urban problems in the enterprise zone as a government problem, a family-values problem, or some combination. The average business owner who does not take an active role in zone politics does not see business as part of the problem or the solution.

The enterprise zone project was originally intended to foster economic growth in distressed urban areas. Researchers on the fiscal impact of enterprise have almost unanimously concluded that tax incentives and even regulatory relief do little to stimulate new capital investment (Bromley and Morgan 1985; Barnes and Preston 1985; Funkhouser and Lorenz 1987). The political impact of the enterprise zone program has had more far-reaching consequences. An aggressive core of business leaders has adopted the discourse of supply-side economics in order to further their own political interests in the Philadelphia neighborhood where their businesses are located. In turn, this political influence is paid for with media opportunities and lobbying efforts for local and state politicians. In this process, industrial business owners have been able to appropriate already existing community structures and programs targeted for retail minority businesses to further their own financial and political interests.

Despite the lack of formal oversight of the program and indications that the public investment made in the area has had little benefit in terms of eradicating long-term poverty in the zone, the political interests secured by its existence almost assure its continued funding and expansion.

In Philadelphia, the politics of enterprise zones is a fairly benign affair in comparison with some others in the country. In Baltimore, for example, a large industry won several tax concessions from an unwilling city government by threatening to relocate in an enterprise zone in another state. Even though Baltimore officials retained the plant by granting a generous package of tax incentives in a series of negotiations, they later questioned whether the firm had made serious relocation plans or whether they merely played Baltimore's enterprise zone program off against others to gain financial benefits that cost the city a great deal of needed tax revenues. In Chicago, another corporation was able to declare its own property boundaries an enterprise zone through political lobbying efforts (Guskind 1989).

If enterprise zones are adopted on an even larger scale, evidence from Philadelphia indicates that such programs will represent an enormous public subsidy of the kinds of insecure and low-wage jobs that would probably be created by economic conditions in many urban areas anyway. Though a small core of urban business owners may be empowered by organizing through the zones, the lives of residents will be little affected. Magazine photographs of newly renovated warehouse space in graffitti-spattered urban neighborhoods will not change crime and unemployment rates there, although billions of dollars of urban aid are being frittered away on the strength of such images. Much of the urban aid will continue to purchase lunches and stationery and rent conference space for interest groups. Much of the urban aid will buy equipment and burglar alarms for businesses that may or may not employ neighborhood people.

The net effect of enterprise zone programs, like other versions of industrial subsidies, is that they tend to cancel one another out. Legislators are pressured to gain for their districts the same kinds of financial incentives and regulatory relief available to another, until a "business friendly" atmosphere is created everywhere. This process is not necessarily seen as a disadvantage. As proponent Jack Kemp put it in May 1992, he envisions an enterprise zone "from sea to shining sea."

Bibliography

Barnes, Ian, and Jill Preston. 1985. "The Scunthorpe Enterprise Zone: An Example of Muddled Interventionalism." *Public Administration* 63:171–181.

Bothham, Ron, and Greg Lloyd. 1983. "The Political Economy of Enterprise Zones." *National Westminster Bank Quarterly Review*, pp. 24–32.

Bromley, Rosemary D., and Richard H. Morgan. 1985. "The Effects of Enterprise Zone Policy: Evidence from Swansea." *Regional Studies* 19:403–413.

Cobb, James C. 1982. *The Selling of the South: The Southern Crusade for Economic Development, 1936–1980*. Baton Rouge: Louisiana State University Press.

Funkhouser, Richard, and Edward Lorenz. 1987. "Fiscal and Employment Impacts for Enterprise Zones." *Atlanta Economic Journal* 15:62–76.

Goldsmith, William W. 1982. "Enterprise Zones: If They Work, We're in Trouble." *International Journal of Urban and Regional Research* 6:335–442.

Goode, Judith, and Jo Anne Schneider. 1992. *No Longer Black and White: The Complexity of Diversity in Contemporary Philadelphia*. Philadelphia: Temple University Press.

Gunther, William D., and Charles G. Leathers. 1987. "British Enterprise Zones: Implications for U.S. Urban Policy." *Journal of Economic Issues* 21:885–893.

Guskind, Robert. 1989. "Zeal for the Zones." *National Journal* 21:1358–1362.

Hall, Peter. 1982. "Response." *International Journal of Urban and Regional Research* 6:442–445.

Harrington, Michael. 1963. *The Other America: Poverty in the United States*. New York: Macmillan.

Keating, Michael, et al. 1984. "Enterprise Zones: Implementing the Unworkable." *Political Quarterly* 55:78–84.

Massey, Doreen. 1982. "Enterprise Zones: A Political Issue." *International Journal of Urban and Regional Research* 6:429–434.

O'Dowd, Liam, and Bill Rolston. 1985. "Bringing Hong Kong to Belfast? The Case of an Enterprise Zone." *International Journal of Urban and Regional Research* 9(2):218–232.

Witthans, Fred W. 1984. "Will Enterprise Zones Work?" *Journal of Small Business Management* 22:9–17.

Contributors' Notes

Janet E. Benson is associate professor of anthropology at Kansas State University, Manhattan, Kansas. She served as a Peace Corps volunteer in Kenya during the 1960s and since then has conducted fieldwork in India, Sri Lanka, the Caribbean, and the United States. From 1988 to 1990 she participated in the Ford Foundation Changing Relations Project. She is currently continuing research on immigration into southwest Kansas.

Michael Broadway is an associate professor of geography at the State University College, Geneseo, New York. He is the author of a number of articles on the beef-packing industry. Along with Donald Stull, he is currently editing a book on the role of the meat-processing industries in the transformation of rural America.

Carole Cohen has a master's degree in social work and is currently a Ph.D. candidate in urban anthropology at Temple University. Her research interests focus on immigration, ethnicity, and work, especially in regard to women.

Ken C. Erickson is a practicing anthropologist at present employed as a bilingual-education program specialist with the Kansas State Board of Education. His research interests include the study of the workplace in complex society, bilingual education, and Vietnamese American social organization.

Judith Goode, a professor of anthropology at Temple University, is past president of the Society for Urban Anthropology. She has conducted fieldwork in Colombia and Philadelphia and is co-author with E. Eames of *The Anthropology of the City* (1977).

303

Her most recent book, written with J. Schneider, is *Reshaping Ethnic and Racial Relations in Philadelphia* (1994).

Guillermo J. Grenier is the director of the Florida Center for Labor Research and Studies and chair of the sociology–anthropology department of Florida International University at Miami. He is the author of *Inhuman Relations: Quality Circles and Anti-unionism in American Industry* (1988) and co-author with Raymond L. Hogler of *Employee Participation and Labor Law in the American Workplace* (1992), and with Alex Stepick of *Miami Now: Immigration, Ethnicity, and Social Change* (1992)

Louise Lamphere, professor of anthropology at the University of New Mexico, was co-director of the Changing Relations Project funded by the Ford Foundation through SUNY Binghamton. She is the author of *From Working Daughters to Working Mothers: Immigrant Women in a New England Industrial Community* (1987). Her most recent book is *Sunbelt Working Mothers: Reconciling Family and Factory*, co-authored with Patricia Zavella, Felipe Gonzales, and Peter Evans (1993).

Cynthia Carter Ninivaggi is doing dissertation work on American adoptions in the anthropology department at Temple University. Her interests include anthropology of gender and kinship, the politics of reproduction, medical anthropology, and complex societies.

Alex Stepick is an associate professor of sociology and anthropology at Florida International University. He won the Margaret Mead Award in 1988 for his work with Haitian refugees. His book with Arthur Murphy, *Social Inequality in Oaxaca*, was published by Temple University Press. His two most recent books are *Miami Now: Immigration, Ethnicity, and Social Change*, with Guillermo Grenier (1992) and *City on the Edge: The Transformation of Miami*, with Alejandro Portes (1993).

Donald D. Stull is professor of anthropology and a research fellow in the Institute for Public Policy and Business Research, University of Kansas. His research, publications, and films have centered on applied anthropology, collaborative research, contemporary American Indian affairs and policy, and the consequences of economic development and rapid growth for communities on the High Plains.

Index

African Americans: from Caribbean islands, 131–132, 133; in Miami, 135–136, 138, 158–159, 184–186, 195n.1; in Philadelphia, 205–206, 211–213, 215, 222–223, 267

Alinsky, Saul, 221

Amalgamated Clothing and Textile Workers Union (ACTWU), 168–169

Apparel industry, 13; employment rates, 167; immigrants in, 164–179; impact of plant restructuring, 170–179; in Miami, 13, 164–179; in Philadelphia, 206, 208; restructuring of, 167–168; unionization of, 168–169

Applebaum, Herbert A., 151

Asian immigrants, 216, 225. *See also* Korean immigrants; Southeast Asian immigrants

Bahamian immigrants, 132

Barrett, James R., 52

Beef America, 97

Beefpacking. *See* Meatpacking industry

Bendix, Rhinehart, 179n.3

Benson, Janet, 12, 87, 91

Benson, Susan Porter, 11, 14

Blacks. *See* African Americans

Bluestone, Barry, 7, 112, 249n.2

Braverman, Harry, 9

Broadway, Michael, 8, 87, 96

Campa, Arthur, 87

Caribbean immigrants, 131–132. *See also* Haitian immigrants

Carpenters Union, 146–147, 148, 150

Chaffee, Sue, 182

Child care, 116–120

Cintron, José, 87

Clement, Elise W., 75n.4

Cohen, Carole, 15, 16, 207, 232

ConAgra, 32

Construction industry, 12–13; Cuban immigrants in, 146–149; language barriers in, 154–57; in Miami, 145–162; in Philadelphia, 211; safety issues in, 151–154; unions in, 146–149, 157–158, 159–160, 161–162; worker relationships with management, 150–157, 162

Contested Terrain (Edwards), 9

Cuban immigrants: in apparel industry, 164–179; in construction industry, 146–149; in Miami, 130–131, 132–133, 134, 136, 137, 138; in restaurant industry, 188

Cumulative trauma disorder, 74

Dade County, Fla. *See* Miami, Fla.

Deindustrialization, 7, 231, 232–233, 246–248

The Deindustrialization of America (Bluestone and Harrison), 7

305

Draznin, Debbie, 146, 182
Dunning, Bruce B., 106
Dupaco, 79; Hispanics at, 83, 95; management at, 94–96; Southeast Asians at, 85–86, 87, 88–89, 90–91, 92; study of, 87–97; turnover rate at, 87, 88, 89–90; unionization at, 90–92

Edwards, Richard, 6, 9
Enterprise zones, 17–18, 226, 281–282, 299–301; conflicting agendas in, 289–291; description of, 286–289; exclusion of retailers from, 292–293; historical origins of, 282–283; job creation within, 298–299; organization of, 285–286; resident/business conflict, 293–295; success of, 295–299; in the United States, 283–284
Equal Employment Opportunity Commission, 185
Erickson, Ken, 11

Finney County, Kans., 31–32; unemployment in, 32. See also Garden City, Kans.
Fund, Mary, 75n.4

Garden City, Kans., 8, 32–33; economic impact of meatpacking industry, 37–38; housing shortage in, 35–36, 114–116; immigrants in, 32, 33–34, 39–41; meatpacking industry in, 9–12; school enrollment in, 36–37, 101; social impact of meatpacking industry, 38–39
Garment industry. See Apparel industry
Garson, Barbara, 10
Gender roles, as shaped by workplace, 102–103, 121
Goode, Judith, 8, 16–17
Goode, Wilson, 223
Gordon, David, 6
Gottesman, Ronald, 73
Green, Hardy, 52
Grenier, Guillermo, 13, 146, 169
Grey, Mark, 87
Griffith, David, 112, 122

Hafidh, Hafidh A., 182, 184, 193, 194
Haitian immigrants, 1–2, 132, 139–140, 151, 181, 185–186, 187–188,

195–196n.2; language barriers faced by, 154–157
Hall, Peter, 282–283
Harrington, Michael, 297
Harrison, Bennett, 7, 112, 249n.2
Health care, 119, 209
Hispanic immigrants: at Dupaco, 83, 95; in Garden City, Kans, 33–34. See also Miami, Fla.; Puerto Rican immigrants
Hotel and restaurant industry, 13–15; impact of restructuring on, 194; labor-management relations, 189–194, 195; management strategies in, 186–194; unionization of, 183–184
Housing problems, 35–36, 114–116

IBP plant, 25–26, 29, 30, 31–32, 38, 39; interest in Asian workers, 89; job posting at, 47; safety at, 47–48; training at, 47; tour of, 44–49; unionization at, 89. See also Meatpacking industry
Immigrants: Anglo attitudes toward, 39–40; as affected by economic restructuring, 6–9, 18–19; in Miami, 129–135, 140–142, 145–150, 161–162; in Philadelphia, 203–204, 208, 209, 211, 214–218, 224–225; work ethic of, 187–188; workplace experience of, 4–6, 18–19. See also Apparel industry; Construction industry; Hotel and restaurant industry; Meatpacking industry
Immigration Reform Act of 1965, 214
Imperial Food Products, 74
International Brotherhood of Carpenters, 148
International Brotherhood of Electrical Workers, 232, 237

The Jungle (Sinclair), 63

Kansas, meatpacking industry in, 30–32. See also Garden City, Kans.; Meatpacking industry
Kansas Beef Processors, 32
Kemp, Jack, 284, 301
Kensington, Pa., 205, 225–226, 285
Koppel, Barbara, 10

Korean immigrants, 16, 17, 208; in
  Philadelphia, 216, 224–225
Korean merchants, 224–225, 251, 254–
  255, 267, 268–273, 275–276,
  279n.24

Labor and Monopoly Capital (Braverman)
  9
LaBorwit, Aline, 169, 171–173
Lamphere, Louise, 103
Laotian immigrants. *See* Southeast
  Asian immigrants
Latin Builders' Association, 148
LeMasters, E. E., 11, 151
Lexington, Neb., 30
Lighthouse Economic Development
  Project, 293
Longshore, Jay, 232

Meat Cutters Union, 29
Meat Inspection Act, 73
Meatpacking industry, 1, 9–12; absenteeism in, 97n.4; boning process, 78–
  87; child care issues, 116–120; cost-
  cutting strategies, 29–30; declines in
  employment, 27–28; disability among
  workers, 119–121; as affected by economic restructuring, 25–32; gender
  issues in, 101; head line, 60; gut table, 60–62; hierarchy in, 52–56; immigrants in, 10, 34–37, 64, 67, 83,
  84–87, 88, 90–91, 95; improvements
  in productivity, 28–29; interaction
  among workers, 66–67, 84; literature
  on, 51–52; as male employment, 111;
  management's view of workers, 92–
  93; probation period, 66; quality
  grade, 62, 75n.1; research methodologies for study of, 49–50, 97n.5;
  safety in, 47–48, 67–74, 80; skinning
  line, 57–59; slaughter process, 56–
  62; Southeast Asians in, 104; structural changes in, 27–30; time control
  in, 111–112; training in, 47, 64–65;
  trim line, 62; unionization of, 90–92;
  water use in, 75n.4; women in, 10,
  11, 101, 104, 105–111; yield grade,
  62, 75n.1
Mexican immigrants, 67, 83, 104. *See
  also* Hispanic immigrants

Miami, Fla., 8; African Americans in,
  135–136, 138, 158–159, 184–186,
  195n.1; apparel industry in, 13, 164–
  179; construction industry in, 12–13,
  145–162; Cubans in, 130–131, 132–
  133, 134, 136, 137, 138; economy in,
  134–135, 136–138; ethnic diversity
  in, 129–138, 149–150; ethnic tensions in, 158–161; Haitians in, 139–
  140; hotel and restaurant industry in,
  13–15; impact of immigrants on,
  129–135, 140–142, 145–150, 161–
  162; industrial profile, 134–135;
  Jewish population, 132–133;
  Nicaraguans in, 131, 138; as northern capital of Latin America, 129–
  135; segregation in, 135; Spanish as
  second language in, 139; tourist industry in, 182–186
Miami Beach Convention Center, 145
Montfort, 32, 38, 101
Morris, Steve, 12, 146, 150

Nader, Laura, 91
National Association for the Advance-
  ment of Colored People (NAACP),
  184
National Beef Packing, 73
Neighborhoods movement, 221–222
Nicaraguan immigrants, 131, 138, 149,
  157
Ninivaggi, Cynthia, 17
Norfolk, Neb. *See* Dupaco

Occupational Safety and Health Ad-
  ministration (OSHA), 29, 67, 74
Olney, Pa., 226–227; retail strip in,
  253–256
OSHA. *See* Occupational Safety and
  Health Administration

Palestinian immigrants, 225
Paternalism, 179n.3
Paules, Greta, 14
Philadelphia, Pa., 8; African Americans
  in, 205–206, 211–213, 215, 222–223;
  apparel industry in, 206, 208; decline
  of, 200–202; demographic trends,
  203–207; economy of, 200–202,
  218–225, 227–228; enterprise zones

Philadelphia, Pa. (*cont.*)
in, 17–18, 226, 281–301; fiscal problems, 201; as health-care center, 209; housing distribution in, 213–214, 218; immigrant workers in, 203, 208, 209, 211, 214–218, 224–225; immigration to, 204–206; impact of suburbanization on, 201; job loss in, 205 206–207; Korean immigrants in, 216 224–225; Latino community in, 224; leadership fragmentation in, 220–221; manufacturing sector in, 206, 207–208; neighborhood differences in, 225–227; neighborhoods movement in, 221–222; politics in, 202, 222–225; Puerto Ricans in, 215–216, 217, 218; racial issues in, 222–225; reform movement in, 219–220, 222; restructured economy in, 207–214; retail stores in, 251–279; segregation in, 211–214; service sector in, 209–211; social services in, 210–211; Summit Lighting plant in, 15–16, 19, 207, 227, 231–248; tourism in, 202; as viewed by residents, 199–200
Philadelphia Commercial Development Corporation (PCDC), 210
Philadelphia Standard Metropolitan Statistical Area (PSMSA), 200
Plumbers Union, 148
Polish Americans, 227, 239
Polish immigrants, 3, 15, 218
Port Richmond, Pa., 226–227
Puerto Rican immigrants, 2–3, 211, 215–216, 217, 218, 242–243, 258–259

Reich, Michael, 6
Remy, Dorothy, 10, 52, 238
Reproduction, Marxist concept of, 102–103
Restaurant industry. *See* Hotel and restaurant industry
Restructuring, economic, 6–9, 27–30, 140–144. *See also* Apparel industry; Hotel and restaurant industry; Meatpacking industry; Philadelphia, Pa.
Retail stores, 251–253; decline of local strips, 253–256; excluded from enterprise zones, 292–293; immigrant labor in, 266; Korean merchants, 251, 254–255, 267, 268–273, 275–

276, 279n.24; small, owner-operated stores, 263–273; social processes in, 273–276; supermarket, 256–263; white ethnic merchants, 263–265; women workers in, 260, 265
Rizzo, Frank, 223

Sawers, Larry, 10, 52, 238
Segmented Work, Divided Workers (Gordon, Edwards, and Reich), 6
Sinclair, Upton, 62, 73
Skaggs, Jimmy M., 51
Slayton, Robert A., 52
Southeast Asian immigrants: child-care arrangements, 116–120; at Dupaco, 85–86, 87, 88–89, 90–91, 92; in Garden City, Kans., 33, 34, 67, 99–101; gender issues among, 121; problems facing, 122–123; social network among, 113–114; women workers, 105–111
Stepick, Alex, 2, 8, 12, 14, 146, 169

Summit Lighting, 2–3, 15–16, 19, 207, 227; assembly workers at, 238–239; decline of, 231, 236–248; impact of deindustrialization on, 231, 232–233, 246–248; demographics of workforce, 234–236; ethnicity at, 241–243; labor-management relations at, 236–237; racial tensions at, 243–245; restructuring of, 232–234; socializing at, 245–246; union role at, 232, 237; worker solidarity at, 239–241; workplace relations at, 232–236
Supermarket, as workplace, 256–263; Latino workers at, 258–259; race relations at, 259–260; role of in community, 260–263; women at, 260

Thompson, William E., 52, 88
Tourism: in Miami, 182–186; in Philadelphia, 202

United Food and Commercial Workers Union (UFCW), 89–90, 92, 210
U.S. Department of Agriculture (USDA), 51, 60, 61–62

Val-Agri plant, 37
Vietnamese immigrants, 1, 11. *See also* Southeast Asian immigrants
Vogel, Lise, 102

Warner, Samuel Bass, 218
Weber, Max, 179n.3
Wilson Foods Corporation, 29
Women: in labor force, 102, 265; in meatpacking industry, 10, 11, 101, 103, 104, 105–111; as supermarket workers, 260
Wood, Charles L., 51
Workers' compensation hearings, 67–73

Workplace: analysis of, 9–18; changing nature of, 3–4; as affected by deindustrialization, 231, 232–233, 246–248; as affected by economic restructuring, 6–9, 25–32; relationships within, 9. *See also* Construction industry; Hotel and restaurant industry; Meatpacking industry; Summit Lighting